Become Ungove

"In *Become Ungovernable*, H.L.T. Quan offers us possibilities for rescuing the concept of democracy from its fatal entanglement with racial, heteropatriarchal capitalism. This phenomenal text urges us to seek radical democratic futures, not in more equitable modes of governance, but rather in revolutionary community-making practices—especially those emanating from anti-racist and abolition feminist traditions."

—Angela Y. Davis

"An unruly book. Leaping across broad swaths of time and space, H.L.T. Quan exposes the prison house of liberal antidemocracy and the accumulation of rebellions inside in order to construct a theory of democracy as radical praxis. 'Democratic living,' as she calls it, refuses the tyranny of order, embraces the unruliness of collective struggle, and recognizes freedom not as a destination but practice—an abolitionist, feminist, anti-capitalist, antiracist, radically inclusive practice. In other words, to preserve life and break liberalism's hold, we have to make a living. Quan shows us a way."

—Robin D. G. Kelley, author of *Freedom Dreams: The Black Radical Imagination*

"An elegantly written masterpiece that covers a breathtaking amount of intellectual, political, and geographic territory: from the pre-Civil War American South to rebellions in northern China to the Zapatista experiment in Chiapas, Mexico. Building on a vast body of feminist, Black radical, and abolitionist literature, H.L.T. Quan calls for a feminist ethic of care as a guiding principle for the future, rejecting state-centered solutions as non-solutions to our collective longing for freedom and free spaces."

—Barbara Ransby, historian, writer, longtime activist, author of *Making All Black Lives Matter*

"*Become Ungovernable* is a masterpiece expression of H.L.T. Quan's lifework. Reflecting analytical, theoretical, and creative insights cultivated through 25+ years as a documentary filmmaker and several decades as one of the most careful, uncompromising, thoughtful critical caretakers of the living Black radical archive conceptualized by the late, great Cedric Robinson, this book is a gift to all who are serious about the conjoined tasks of abolition and liberation."

—Dylan Rodríguez, University of California at Riverside, founding member of Critical Resistance and Cops Off Campus

"Quite simply a brilliant, original, and capacious work of political theory anchored in an erudite analysis of core concepts like representative democracy, democratic elitism, authoritarianism, white supremacy, heteropatriarchy, justice, and governance. A compelling and inspiring book that belongs in our movements and our classrooms."

—Chandra Talpade Mohanty, author of *Feminism Without Borders, Decolonizing Theory, Practicing Solidarity*

Black Critique

Series editors: Anthony Bogues and Bedour Alagraa

Throughout the twentieth century and until today, anti-racist, radical decolonization struggles have attempted to create new forms of thought. Figures from Ida B. Wells to W.E.B. Du Bois and Steve Biko, from Claudia Jones to Walter Rodney and Amílcar Cabral produced work which drew from the historical experiences of Africa and the African diaspora. They drew inspiration from the Haitian revolution, radical Black abolitionist thought and practice, and other currents that marked the contours of a Black radical intellectual and political tradition.

The Black Critique series operates squarely within this tradition of ideas and political struggles. It includes books which foreground this rich and complex history. At a time when there is a deep desire for change, Black radicalism is one of the most underexplored traditions that can drive emancipatory change today. This series highlights these critical ideas from anywhere in the Black world, creating a new history of radical thought for our times.

Also available:

Against Racial Capitalism:
Selected Writings
Neville Alexander
Edited by Salim Vally and Enver Motala

Ere Roosevelt Came:
The Adventures of the Man in the Cloak – A Pan-African Novel of the Global 1930s
Dusé Mohamed Ali
Edited by Marina Bilbija and Alex Lubin

Moving Against the System:
The 1968 Congress of Black Writers and the Making of Global Consciousness
Edited and with an Introduction by David Austin

Revolutionary Movements in Africa:
An Untold Story
Edited by Pascal Bianchini, Ndongo Samba Sylla and Leo Zeilig

Anarchism and the Black Revolution:
The Definitive Edition
Lorenzo Kom'boa Ervin

After the Postcolonial Caribbean:
Memory, Imagination, Hope
Brian Meeks

A Certain Amount of Madness:
The Life, Politics and Legacies of Thomas Sankara
Edited by Amber Murrey

Of Black Study
Joshua Myers

On Racial Capitalism, Black Internationalism, and Cultures of Resistance
Cedric J. Robinson
Edited by H.L.T. Quan

Black Minded:
The Political Philosophy of Malcolm X
Michael Sawyer

Red International and Black Caribbean Communists in New York City, Mexico and the West Indies, 1919–1939
Margaret Stevens

The Point is to Change the World:
Selected Writings of Andaiye
Edited by Alissa Trotz

Become Ungovernable

An Abolition Feminist Ethic for Democratic Living

H. L. T. Quan

First published 2024 by Pluto Press
New Wing, Somerset House, Strand, London WC2R 1LA
and Pluto Press, Inc.
1930 Village Center Circle, 3-834, Las Vegas, NV 89134

www.plutobooks.com

British Library Cataloguing in Publication Data
A catalogue record for this book is available from the British Library

ISBN 978 0 7453 4911 4 Paperback
ISBN 978 0 7453 4913 8 PDF
ISBN 978 0 7453 4912 1 EPUB

This book is printed on paper suitable for recycling and made from fully managed and sustained forest sources. Logging, pulping and manufacturing processes are expected to conform to the environmental standards of the country of origin.

Typeset by Stanford DTP Services, Northampton, England

Simultaneously printed in the United Kingdom and United States of America

Contents

PART II: LIFE BEYOND GOVERNING

for
crystal
and
all my sisters

Preface

This study recasts the many mystics and forgers of democracy and speculates on the meanings of living in democratic and just futures. Combining a careful exposition of White supremacy and its deleterious effects on democratic livability with a sustained examination of abolition feminism, I hope to flip the script on democratic thinkability. In my work as a documentary filmmaker for more than a quarter of century, I am frequently struck by how robust communities of people, both in and beyond the United States, meaningfully practice forms of democratic living, where sharing and loving, rather than accumulating and hoarding, dominate social relations. This is especially true among those who are frequently denied basic forms of justice—including the lack of recognition and representation—are excluded from social provisions, and are almost entirely shut out of policymaking apparatuses and arenas. In recent years, as Black Lives Matter! is sung on the streets across the globe, the halls of Congress and Parliament rarely prefigure Black lives as meaningful policy matters. Indeed, and at the same time that virulent right-wing populism is ascendant and on the move, the people who are marked as differently vulnerable (be they poor, people of Color, queer, migrant) are conjured and costumed as change makers, yet are rarely included in institutions and processes that matter. This work posits that democracy *as a form of governance* has limited use, conceptually or otherwise, for a people learning how to survive and thrive in solidarity, with dignity and justice for all. Reconceptualizing democracy *as a way of life*, however, enables it to be resourced for democratic living as a praxis. In *Become Ungovernable* I extend Cedric J. Robinson's work,[1] arguing that much of what has been taught about and thought of as democracy is hostile to democracy, democratic thought, and democratic living. I retool Robinson's term "antidemocracy" to expose this antidemocratic ideologeme.

If democracy can be conceived as a way of life, that is also true of antidemocracy. To properly assess the context from which practices of resistance emerge and how tools for democratic living are fashioned, I rely on historians, digging into not only the lifeworld of those living beyond the pale (that is, the ungovernable) but also the lifeworlds that spawn antidemocracy. In these times of climate catastrophes, pandemic, and White supremacy, it is tempting to leave borders and boundaries behind as we enter portals necessary for more just futures. It is nevertheless prudent to remember that while climate knows no bounds and diseases do not discriminate, spatialized differences accentuate vulnerabilities, especially within regimes of precarious labor. I also rely on feminist intersectional analytics to minimize simplistic renderings of life and living.

Part I of this book delineates the complicated metaphysics of governing, instantiating the ways in which people and communities are rendered governable, and how they persist in rule refusals, however momentarily. Who is marked as ungovernable frequently provides the reason for subjection and governing violence—the very conditions that render people and spaces vulnerable. How they refuse and resist governing and/or render themselves ungovernable bear lessons for democratic livability. Part II thus moves beyond governing to assess the many tools available—theoretical and practical, old and new—for democratic livability and just present/futures.

When I began this research, I had not imagined delving into the episteme or ideologeme of early American republicanism, especially that of Jeffersonian politics. Unpacking antidemocracy, however, cannot be done without a serious interrogation of Jeffersonian antidemocracy—an ideologeme whose architects explicitly embraced, if not outright extolled, the virtue of reducing the status of a people to that of chattel slavery—an antithesis of rule by the many. As the authors of the textbook *America: Past and Present* put it: "republicanism represented more than a particular form of government. It was a way of life, a core ideology."[2] If this is so, then to properly assess antidemocracy as a way of life, we must unearth the materiality that contributed to its alternatives.

This historical "detour" also took on greater urgency as ethnic studies, especially Black Studies, including critical race theory (CRT), became the targets of political attacks, legislative initiatives, and curricular backlash.[3] These attacks are anti-intellectual and antidemocratic, meant to be a misdirection and misinformation campaign against universities, public education, and, cogently, the general demands for equity and just policies. In the aftermath of George Floyd's and Breonna Taylor's deaths, when Black Lives Matter (BLM) and Movement for Black Lives (M4BL) organizers managed to galvanize over thirty million protestors during the 2020 protest season, right-wing forces sought to deflect and minimize the impact of these unprecedented mobilizations, including the irrefutable exposure of anti-Black violence, endemic racism, the absence of applicative justice for Black people, and the enduring presence of White supremacy. While these ideas and realities are not news to most people of Color, especially Black people living in the US, they have long eluded or sublimated in the collective consciousness of the White majority. This general awakening disrupted an unjust peace and summoned forth a well-financed and well-connected censorious mob, more at home in fascist regimes than so-called democracies.

Far from signifying nothing, the most recent attack on critical scholarship is a misdirection, aimed at not just a specialized field of academic studies but the very history of racial capitalism and gendered violence. After all, it was the wildly successful "1619 Project," spearheaded by Nikole Hannah-Jones of the *New York Times*, that caught the censors' initial crosshairs.[4] Hannah-Jones sought "to reframe the country's history by placing the consequences of slavery and the contribution of Black Americans at the very center of the United States narrative."[5] As Adam Serwer of *The Atlantic* and others have noted, "the fight over the 1619 Project is not about the facts" but about perceptions and investments in certain narratives.[6] More than five decades ago and within the context of another backlash against several decades of persistent mass protests for a more equitable and just life, James Baldwin anticipated such terror from basic historical learning when he observed that "we carry [history] within us," and "it is to history that we owe our frames of reference, our identities, and our aspirations."[7] That organizers of BLM, M4BL, and other Black feminist–led formations managed such a feat that had eluded previous generations of activists and organizers made them easy targets for the right-wing media machinery and further spawned a counterreaction minimizing their achievements.

As a matter of justice, then, intellectuals everywhere have a responsibility to mobilize with every tool possible, including intellectual resources, against authoritarianism, including this virulent manifestation. As such, it is instructive to revisit the lifeworlds of so-called revolutionary greats and the early thinkers and doers of American antidemocracy. Many of these "greats" pursued an elusive quest for perfect governing that nearly a quarter of a millennium later their descendants are still trying to keep alive by relying on a political sensibility partially grounded in historical amnesia.[8]

This book seeks to make two related arguments. First, ungovernability is an important theoretical space for thinking about resistance and mobilization. Second, resisting antidemocracy in these protofascist times requires a democratic toolkit that takes stock of ungovernable happenstance, wherever it might be. By bringing these into the same frame, I provide a gradual focus on democracy, not as a state formation or form of government, but as praxis, or a way of life, or "to get basic with each other," as the Black feminist Toni Cade Bambara put it.[9] To live democratically, we need life aids such as abolition feminism and alternative imaginaries of justice that engender democratic livability.

What are the governing projects? The most familiar ones confront highly visible structures of domination and oppression such as gender, nation, and class, as well as others that are more hybridized, fluid, and less visible. This work is a modest attempt at unlearning democratic elitism by exploring the speculative praxis of democratic living. To do so, part I digs into the politics of governability and the making of antidemocracy, especially early US history and the maintenance of White rule. Part II explores the spaces of ungovernability and speculates on various tools for democratic living, taking up diverse instances of rule refusals against tyranny, especially antiauthoritarian resistance, in the US and China.

This work foregrounds the big and small tyrannies of governing and the willful refusals against being governed. While the forms of state tyranny are innumerable and no doubt awesome, the tyranny of governing is even more saturated and permeable. As a form of absolutism or rule by a despotic government, tyranny is teleological and can take many forms by both state and nonstate entities. If total population control and management are the aims and ends of the modern state, as Michel Foucault argued, then absolutism is the metalogic that underwrites all modern projects, including state and nonstate governing endeavors.[10] This work locates and memorializes some of the ways in which ordinary, nonstate actors thwart state and nonstate governing projects. In electing ungovernable as an idea and a praxis, they take up refusal against state-building projects, but also against all forms of governing.

I argue that to build "a world where many worlds fit" as embodied by the Zapatistas' living ethos, a radical ethic of liberation and a praxis of radical inclusion are necessary.[11] It is a matter of record that, from the studies of race, gender, democracies and economies to sexuality and transhumanism, critical scholarship has unsettled foundational thought and broadened the parameters of thinkability. Guided by the principle that discovery logic is frequently a settler mentality,[12] instead of making claims of knowledge discoveries, this book resources and reclaims fugitive and subaltern knowledges that ground and nurture contemporary, democratic, anticolonial, and democratic thought and praxes. Logically, I draw from critical studies of race, gender, and sexuality, especially critical Black feminist scholarship, to furnish the necessary theoretical and methodological interventions to counter dominant discursive practices and incite narrative subversions.

Methodologically, this work does not reflexively label contemporary Republican politics, policies, or the court decisions advanced by Republicans as "conservative," because that term typically conveys an embrace of modest, piecemeal reforms that are aimed at maintaining the status quo. Ideologies and actions that seek to radically transform the status quo should not be misnamed or reflexively labeled as conservative. Such ideas and actions might advocate traditionalist, parochial, or elitist ontologies and epistemes, and the use of these terms would better reveal the ideological investments as well as their methods of achievement. Radical exclusion of the other, for instance, is not conservative but an extreme praxis and part of a fascist ideological toolkit.

As a signpost pointing toward unruly or ungovernable subjects, I read genderqueer or gender nonconforming as a gender-refusal praxis because historically countless trans and queer people have been marked for harm by association with counternormativity and deviancy, and they in turn marked themselves thus to signal the intentional reclaiming of their marginal, nonconforming subjectivities and lifeworlds.[13] This approach recognizes the radical potentials of "a politics where the nonnormative and marginal position" can be *a* basis for doing liberatory politics.[14]

As this work goes to press, the ongoing nightmare in Gaza intensifies, and censorious winds boomerang and ricochet, ensnaring antiauthoritarian thought and war criticism in their gust along with Palestinian lives that seem to matter so little—or not at all—to those who wield the mechanics of war and statecraft. I am reminded of Arundhati Roy's speech about confronting empire, delivered at the 2003 World Social Forum (WSF) in Porto Alegre, Brazil. Two decades ago, in the months before the invasion and occupation of Iraq, more than three hundred thousand people participated in the forum's opening march. Like the tens of millions across the globe, they were marching to preemptively protest what would be a preemptive war. While they did not succeed in stopping that war, this was an unprecedented show of people power against a war policy. Tens of thousands of forum attendees also went to the closing ceremony, featuring Roy along with scholar activist Noam Chomsky. Roy reminded the participants that confronting empire, including its war power, demands resourcing tools available to the many, and not just the few: "Our strategies should not only be to confront Empire, but to lay siege to it. To deprive it of oxygen. To shame it. To mock it. With our art, our music, our literature, our stubbornness, our joy, our brilliance, our sheer relentless—and our ability to tell our own stories. Stories that are different from the ones we're being brainwashed to believe."[15]

Become Ungovernable is a gathering of tools that includes the many scholarly works and movement endeavors that the imperial archive has long sought to evict. While many of the episodes of rule refusals showcased here are not new, they are different and differently peopled. These are stories about governing and the many attempts at ungoverning. They are also about the many shaming democracy of the few while forging democratic livability for the many, and about the quest to render justice as something more than whatever the powerful say it is. In confronting tyranny, therefore, it is also wise to remember that "we be many and they be few. They need us more than we need them."[16]

PART I

Antidemocracy in America

1

Against Tyranny: An Introduction

Philosophical intelligence is never so truthful, clean, and precise as when it starts from oppression and does not have to defend any privileges, because it has none.

Enrique Dussel[1]

Not all speed is movement. . . . If your house ain't in order, you ain't in order. It is so much easier to be out there than right here. The revolution ain't out there. Yet. But it is here. Should be. And arguing that instant-coffee-ten-minutes-to-midnight alibi to justify hasty-headed dealing with your mate is shit. Ain't no such animal as an instant guerrilla.

Toni Cade Bambara[2]

Imagine a great metropolis covering hundreds of square miles. Once a vital component in a national economy, this sprawling urban environment is now a vast collection of blighted buildings, an immense petri dish of both ancient and new diseases, a territory where the rule of law has long been replaced by near anarchy in which the only security available is that which is attained through brute power. . . . It would, in effect, be a feral city.

Richard J. Norton[3]

MANUFACTURED CONSENSUS

If governmentality is the grandest of modern obsessions, then being ungovernable constitutes its greatest threat. In *Philosophy of Liberation*, Enrique Dussel reminds us that "there is no philosophical practice without an academic 'apparatus' for instruction and learning."[4] In the west, one of the greatest noble lies—a manufactured consensus—is the idea that those who are being subjected to governing have authored their own subjection or their "consent to be governed." Justice theories foreground this malicious myth as a priori.[5] In *A Theory of Justice*, a work that dominates contemporary discourses on justice, John Rawls centralizes the "well-ordered society" as a "fundamental idea" for understanding justice as fairness.[6] The problem with this manufactured consensus on governing and desiring order is that it casts the absence of order, authority, government, and governing as alien, bad, chaotic, and inhuman.

Moreover, the ideologeme of settler colonialism, gendered racial capitalism, and heteropatriarchy justifies the very order of things that it conjures, and renders unthinkable those that it does not. As a paradigm, justice as a hegemonic academic apparatus necessarily fetishizes and services order and governing. This, then, is the metaphysics of ruling. Dussel, however, invites us to rebel against it by taking up a philosophy of liberation that prioritizes the wretched of the earth—"the oppressed as 'origin' and 'space'"—and their praxis of liberation as "a practical, ethical discourse."[7] Liberatory praxes are thus predicated on being in relations with the other, and acts of solidarity are relational.

To explore ungovernability and willful refusals, this book deviates from the manufactured consensus that fetishizes the state, order, authority, and power by the few over the many, while sublimating oppression and eviscerating the everyday dignity and struggles of the many. This work centers resistance against governing, real and imagined, frequently as work in progress, and rarely sanctioned by the state and its allies. Building on pathways laid out by Sara Ahmed, Cedric J. Robinson, Toni Cade Bambara, Dussel, and others, the following chapters explore the willful refusal by individuals and communities against the big and small tyrannies of rule and governing.[8] These willful communities and subjects take up refusal projects that more often than not wreak havoc on economic, political, sociocultural systems, as they inevitably lodge grievances against the metaphysics of ruling. In doing so, they also furnish tools for different praxes of being human, engendering alternative meanings for justice and ethics of living.

Such antisystemic and counterhegemonic labors frequently elude accountings of radical or revolutionary movements and mobilizations because they do not always directly confront state projects, though by definition they are rarely far afield. Moreover, as these ungovernable subjects and communities battle against governing, their fights are multifaceted and forge on multiple fronts. From struggles for land, reproductive autonomy, and gender nonconformity, to the freedom to preserve one's cultural heritage and create art, governing refusals—especially against normative regulations—take many forms.[9] If piracy, slave rebellions, and other acts against property predominated as threats to the nineteenth-century Atlantic imperial world order,[10] then flight, border crossing, anti-prison and police, and gender nonconformity constitute some of the most dominant acts of resistance against the neoliberal, White supremacist, heteropatriarchal, twenty-first-century world order. And yet they are mere ciphers of contemporary ungovernability, pointing to a broader and more capacious repertoire of resistance against order writ large—ranging from labor and peace protests to anti-apartheid, anti-violence, anti-moral policing, and extinction rebellions.

I take up ungovernability, and ungovernable subjects and communities, rather than anarchy and anarchist movements because anarchism in the west continues to worship at the altar of order.[11] While rejecting the fantasy of a "well-ordered society"—the façade that fronts modern paradigms of in/justices[12]—anarchists themselves are deluded in a desire for a fictive order predicated on the abstracted autonomous individual. Justice in a well-ordered society is a justice sheltered from compassion and solidarity for the weak, garrisoned within the cage of freedom as entitlement, all the while propped up by an empty throne of liberty.

Part I of this book thus interrogates the vagaries of liberty, in/justice, and antidemocracy. While extending this general interrogation of antidemocracy to account for contemporary currents of democratic thinkability, part II highlights tools that emerged from various spaces of ungovernability, including the everyday resistance of those who subsist on the margins and work within regimes of precarious labor. From migrant workers protesting in manufacturing plants in the People's Republic of China (PRC) to radical Black feminists furnishing abolition feminism, these contemporary rebels, like their peasant and slave predecessors, persist in refashioning tools for just futures and in the here and now.

THE MANY MEANINGS OF JUSTICE

Building on the work of Sara Ahmed, I take up Bambara's invitation to willfully resist submission to rule or governing, as part and parcel of making oneself "totally unavailable for servitude."[13] This is a "practical utopian standpoint"[14] that engenders active resistance against gendered racial capitalism and heteropatriarchy. Many of Bambara's stories are about communities *in* resistance, Black women organizers, and struggles for freedom *and* justice. In this "facto-fictive world,"[15] one finds an urgent recasting of freedom not as entitlement but as a revolutionary "process by which you become unavailable for servitude," and community or the collective as a space that nurtures "everyday practice of freedom" as well as "a second sight that gives us the knowledge that we have sovereignty, the authority to free ourselves on our own terms."[16] Here, Ahmed's use of "willful subject" and "willfulness" helpfully delineates the many ways in which oppressed people, especially women and people of Color, pervert domination and oppression, both as "a style of politics" and as "disobedience to the sovereign" because "to be judged willful is to become killjoy . . . one who gets in the ways of a happiness" or the unjust peace of the existing world order.[17] To make oneself unavailable for governing, to become ungovernable, is to style a politics that is willful and willfully antiauthoritarian.

In the west, an academic ideological apparatus, centering individual autonomy and liberty, evicts from justice the concerns and responsibilities for *substantive* justice, and replaces them with order. As Robinson argues, even its most radical interlocutor, anarchism, fails to dislodge this ideologeme because it remains faithful and obedient to the ontologies and lifeworlds that gave birth to it.[18] Part of this onto-epistemology centers on order as a life necessity and on the fictive autonomy of the individual. Where liberty is understood as an entitlement of the few, bodily autonomy, especially for the many, at best is considered an afterthought—worse, the denial of bodily autonomy becomes essential to perfecting governing and biopolitical management. The raging campaign against women's bodily autonomy in the US is a prime example. For feminists who persist on being willfully antiauthoritarian, bodily autonomy needs to be differentiated from the abstraction of "individual autonomy." Where antidemocracy is concerned, individual autonomy is an entitlement reserved for the few. In contrast, when bodily autonomy is *a starting point* of nominal freedom, it prefigures collective emancipatory projects for delving into the life, labor, and struggles of those who have been evicted from governing.

Many contemporary articulations of anarchism are fundamentally flawed because they merely constitute *an alternative order* not an opposition *to* order.[19] To understand this qualitative difference, we can think about how some practices of gender nonconforming, for instance, are informed by an alternative gender but not necessarily an alternative *to* gender.[20] Empirical accountings of withholding availability for governing—such as marronage, border crossing, prison abolition, and certain forms of gender transgressions—suggest that there exist not only alternative genealogies of anarchism but also alternatives to order and governing. There are also non-state-centric modes of refusal because not all popular resistance and acts of refusal are directed toward state projects. An over-valorization of state re/action has the effect of overshadowing or missing entirely alternative spaces, imaginaries, and life forms.[21]

James Baldwin long understood that the meanings of justice must be freed from the garrison imposed by the apparatuses of order and the state. To do so, we need to consider the source: "If one really wishes to know how justice is administered in a country, one does not question the policemen, the lawyers, the judges, the protected members of middle class. One goes to the unprotected—those precisely, who need the law's protection most!—and listen to their testimony."[22] Indeed, movements for justice are as much about the dethroning of liberty and freeing justice from forgeries as they are about bringing attention to social discontents and subjections. The struggles for reproductive justice by women of Color in the US, for instance, are not only about making demands on middle-class, White ciswomen and others to uncage their limited-choice framework, but also about unlearning freedom as an entitlement for the few. In so doing, these activists and scholars broaden reproductive freedom as they flesh out a more capacious justice framework, engendering bodily sovereignty, including reproductive autonomy, that previously was not available.[23] Beyond the skepticism of legal realism, the work by Loretta Ross, Dorothy Roberts, and Andrea Smith, among others, suggests that the struggles for reproductive justice are also about liberating freedom and justice from liberal notions of individual choice (à la the autonomous individual) that only a few entitled can afford, and from the elitist commitments to White supremacy and Black subordination that supersede all other concerns.[24]

IN THE LAND OF *SIBA*

Since being civilized has become synonymous with being governed, the threat of being and remaining ungoverned is perhaps the greatest threat to dominions. As James C. Scott points out, "on close inspection" of "Chinese and other civilizational discourses about the 'barbarian,' the 'raw,' the 'primitive' . . . those terms, practically, mean ungoverned, not-yet-incorporated."[25] Scott argues that "civilizational discourses *never* entertain the possibility of people voluntarily going over to the barbarian, hence such statuses are stigmatized and ethnicized."[26] In other words, those who are not legible to the state for the purpose of state management and administrative disciplining, or ungoverned, are ethnicized and tribalized—in a word, racialized. Racial projects are thus almost always governing projects.

Those racial, gendered, sexual others who are deemed "ungoverned" make up the "ungoverned periphery." This terrain, real or imagined, constitutes a "long-run" threat, embodying "a constant temptation, a constant alternative to life within the state" and beyond.[27] For this reason, those who willfully resist governing also must be deemed a remnant of the past and primitivized. But as Scott warns us, "once we entertained the possibility that the 'barbarians' are not just 'there' as a residue but may well have chosen their location, their subsistence practices, and their social structure to maintain their autonomy, the standard civilizational story of social evolution collapses utterly."[28]

The praxis of not being governed thus presupposes those prestate and counterstate entities—humans and communities—as willful subjects.[29] Ungovernability, as well as the art and will of not being governed, are therefore the material expressions of agents, those whom Ahmed calls willful subjects, making themselves unavailable for governing,[30] or the active refusal and the will to counter rule. Within the context of Moroccan history, for instance, *siba* (beyond the pale) sometimes is understood as anarchy. Scott maintains that siba is better understood as "institutional dissidence" or ungoverned terrain of "political autonomy and independence"—not being subordinated to the state. In this context, "political autonomy was . . . a choice, not a given."[31] In other words, those who chose the land of siba (ungoverned) instead of the land *mahkazen* (governed) "have self-consciously elected to move or to stay beyond the pale."[32]

According to the *Oxford English Dictionary*, "pale" in English denotes jurisdiction including colonial settlements. According to urban myths, there is an area in Ireland that used to be called "the Pale." There is also a region in the Russian Empire that was called "the Pale of Settlement." Pale is thus the figurative boundary or an actual area enclosed or fenced in by old wooden posts. The spaces within the wall or barriers, therefore, are deemed acceptable or restricted preserves. And not unlike the existence of maroon and free Black communities in the time of slavery or sovereign Indigenous tribes, beyond the pale lies the temptation and promise of deviance and transgression. Indeed, and since the Middle Ages, "beyond the pale" has taken on the connotation of being outside of acceptable behavior, or transgression understood as deviancy. In *The Audacity of Hope*, for instance, former president Barack Obama hinted at his support for the death penalty by referring to certain extraordinarily "heinous" crimes such as "mass murder" and "the rape and murder of a child" as "beyond the pale."[33] The land of siba, understood as "beyond the pale," hints at a contemptuous predisposition against transgressive subjects and spaces. The ungovernables and ungovernable spaces are thus beyond the pale—that is, beyond nominal jurisdiction and acceptability. In a word, counternormative.[34]

The archive of governing is replete with instances in which ordinary people and communities sought out the land of siba, though they may have called it differently depending on the contingencies of time and space. In our times, we have taken to calling them in descriptive, derogatory, and even aspirational terms such as "runaways," "fugitives," "FOBs,"[35] "wetbacks," "illegals," "deviants," "terrorists," and "queers." They are also whom Ahmed calls "willful subjects"—those who are, among other things, "unwilling to get along," "refuse to laugh along," or "identified as a problem" and are labeled disobedient simply for persisting.[36] If "some of us were never meant to survive,"[37] then to simply exist is to be willful and disobedient. Disobedience takes myriad forms—from the mundane to the fantastic, these willful subjects assert their wills and ways, all the while rendering themselves unavailable for governing and living beyond the pale.

With few exceptions, our collective quotidian life is governed by the big and small tyrannies of governments, capital, and cultural orthodoxies; therefore, living and dreaming beyond the pale are inherently impermanent. It would be a mistake, however, to interpret impermanence as lack of persistence. While the spatial and temporal dimensions of collective refusal to be governed shift, this does not imply that the will not to be governed is fleeting. Apparent obedience to rules and jurisdictions can also engender other forms of refusal.[38] Even a superficial review of the history of Black resistance against White supremacy, for instance—especially the epic debate between the accommodationist and integrationist strategies in the US that has spanned more than a century—affirms the notion that sometimes to *not* go along, you must at least perform getting along. By acceding to the Sultan's claim of spiritual authority, the Berbers persisted in the land of siba—remaining ungoverned, beyond mahkazen.[39]

This important distinction between the ungoverned and governed is captured in the ways we make judgments, design policies, and invest resources, among other things; it is based on the differentiation between "subject peoples" and "self-governing peoples"—or, more crudely, "'cooked' and 'raw,' 'tame' and 'wild,' 'valley people' and 'hill people,'"[40] or "nice people" and "trouble-makers." As Scott points out: "the linkage between being civilized and being a subject of the state is so taken for granted that the terms subject peoples on the one hand or *self-governing peoples* on the other capture the essential difference."[41] Indeed, who gets what, when, and where—the very questions underwriting the totality of modern distributive justice principles and informing policy design and implementation—are countersigned by the way we imagine, categorize, and differentiate those governed (deemed governable) from those who are ungoverned (or deemed ungovernable or deviants). Who lives, who receives low-interest loans, what activities get tagged as heinous and targeted for incarceration and premature death, or whose lives matter—these frequently depend on whether they are deemed "subject peoples" or "self-governing peoples," whether they are perceived as governable or ungovernable.

In the same way that Ahmed reads "feminism as an unhappy archive,"[42] I approach the willful resistance to governing as an "unhappy archive" of governing, filled with stories about women being unhappy. Specifically, it is full of stories "about women who are not made happy by what is supposed to make them happy."[43] So, the things that are supposed to make women happy, such as marriage and motherhood, actually make them unhappy. Similarly, the state, property, cultural normativity, marriage, and motherhood, which are supposed to make people and communities happy and fulfilled, have rendered them stateless, dispossessed, deviants. I dig into this "unhappy archive" of governing to sample a few stories about unhappy subjects and communities, their grievances about being governed, and their countering of rules.[44] These are stories about those willful subjects who frequently refuse to go along to get along, though sometimes they may get along *so as not to go along*. These are stories about communities that rebelliously build against being displaced, though sometimes they move along so that they do not get replaced along the way.

In this unhappy archive of governing, those deemed ungovernable subjects imagine themselves as self-governing peoples, though the "self" in this "self-governing" is not always autonomous or free from collective belonging. This "archive of the ordinary"[45] is peopled by individuals and collectives of peasants, slaves, women, queers, migrants, and other sociocultural misfits, in formations against tyranny. Unlike the subjects in Scott's *The Art of Not Being Governed*, this unhappy archive consists of more than a collection of subjects who turned away from state-building projects, though many of them are no friends or collaborators of the state. These are rule-breaking and rule-refusing subjects and communities who are unhappy with the state, as well as with capital and other sociocultural dominions. They refuse the dominant terms of order—be they political, economic, or cultural—and in the process get cast as ungovernable, with its attendant punitive and at times deadly consequences. Following Anthony Bogues's suggestion, by opening up this unhappy archive of the ordinary, I hope to not only supply "stories of resistance"[46] but to explore radical thought from perspectives of those who have made themselves unavailable for governing. As chapter 8 will show, for instance, among the many apolitical radical traditions, the idea of living unencumbered by politics and without government flourished in ancient China, and holds lessons for living beyond the pale and developing alternative ethics for sharing resources.

Centering on ungovernability diverges from anarchist studies that situate anarchy, anarchist movements, and anarchism as antitheses to the state (and sometimes capital). This divergence is not due to romantic nostalgia for a past where the modern state has not been conceived or is still in its infancy; nor is it a romantic longing for a future where the state withers away. Instead, I believe the state is *not* omnipresent. As Marx argued, history documents constant struggles by humans who find ways and wills to resist against tyrannies, including against the claimed sovereignty of class dominance. It is therefore neither controversial nor novel to note that humans and their communities have opposed misery, oppression, and unfreedom at every turn. They have coped with, struggled against, imagined, and built alternatives to tyrannies of all forms, for indeed, tyranny comes in many forms, and the state, modern or not, does not have a monopoly on tyrannies.[47]

This book, especially part I, therefore, devotes great attention to delineating antidemocracy and other forms of state-led tyrannies, centering the incompetence and immorality of the state and its allies, *along with other dominions*.

It divulges insights about living and dreaming beyond the pale—in the land of siba, however momentarily—ungoverned by state, capital and/or other forms of dominion. From everyday resistance by slaves to open rebellions by peasants, from workers protesting managerial despotism, to generalized mobilization against policing, from the language of *nüshu*, to abolition feminism as praxis—these stories bear witness to the assertion that willful refusal to be governed is essential to living.

SPACES OF UNGOVERNABILITY

Richard James Norton, a former US Navy commander with expertise in Africa and South America, coined the term "feral city" to characterize emergent spaces that are deemed "savage, toxic and ungovernable," and to convey the urgent and "latent threats to the United States."[48] Evoking T. S. Eliot's "The Waste Land," Norton paints a picture of a "rat's alley" for visualizing the danger accompanying the implied imminent fall of western civilization. Using Mogadishu as example, for Norton feral spaces are no works of fiction.[49] According to Anne L. Clunan, there has been "increased concern in policy circles over ungoverned spaces," which constitutes "a novel and inherently dangerous threat to the security of states and international system."[50]

As a framing device, "ungoverned spaces" underwrites national security directives, often prefiguring an antiterrorist narrative that governs the conduct of US foreign policy. It identifies huge swaths of the world and the people who reside in those spaces as problem areas, failed states, and troublesome subjects. In various National Security Strategy (NSSs) and Strategic Plan documents, especially reports on terrorism, this framing device appears frequently in association with "failing" or "failed" states to delineate the terms of US entanglements in global affairs, especially in the Global South, setting out the parameters of foreign aid and military presence.[51] The 2006 NSS employs this framing device to establish a causal linkage between terrorism and tyranny, and to provide a raison d'être for the preemptive, endless, and boundless global "war on terror."

Considering the recent official "conclusion" of the misadventures in Afghanistan by the US and its allies,[52] it might be helpful to revisit the blatantly absurd and tautological pronouncements of its strategic reasoning: "The terrorists' goal is to overthrow a rising democracy; claim a strategic country a haven for terror; destabilize the Middle East; and strike America and other free nations with ever-increasing violence. This we can never allow. This is why success in Afghanistan and Iraq is vital, and why we must prevent terrorists from exploiting ungoverned areas."[53] The conflation of Afghanistan and Iraq with "ungoverned" spaces supplies a ready-made justification for the

US invasion and occupation. George W. Bush's Secretary of Defense and an architect of US policy of preemptive and endless war, Donald Rumsfeld, foreshadowed this approach, casting a frightening and ominous possibility only a few months before what became a colossal failure in foreign policymaking, namely the invasion and occupation of Iraq: "When terrorists are driven out of countries—as they were in Afghanistan—they often find havens in *the world's many ungoverned regions* . . . [operating] *in the ungoverned areas*, using them as bases from which to destabilize democratic governments."[54] With Rumsfeld, we no longer must cope with only "ungoverned areas" but, ominously, "ungoverned regions"—an entire swath of nations that may or may not adhere to US terms of order. Yet the use of "ungoverned spaces," especially when weaponized for strategic aims, is not new. It echoes the ancient regime of colonial conquests and the idea of *terra nullius*—the brutal colonial principle, if fallacious, of empty land or "land belonging to no one." Just as *terra nullius* provided a moral and rhetorical basis for colonial conquest, settlement, and genocide, so today's "ungoverned spaces" is the Papal bull of Pax Americana (and others) for imperial rule in the forms of military presence and other regimes of governing.[55]

Similar to the use of *terra nullius* as a racial marker of "wild spaces" and the people who live there, so "ungoverned spaces" is a geopolitical simile for an area run by wild animals, and "ferality" is deployed to capture a sense of ruinous calamity in the absence of order and pending danger. In conjunction with urban spaces—as in "feral cities," ferality is almost always within the context of "failed states" or ungovernability.[56] Importantly, ungoverned spaces are also not about "the lack of governance per se, *but rather who governs these spaces.*"[57] It makes clear the logic of normative governing—only those who are deemed as befitting of rule are thus seen as legitimately sovereign, while those who are deemed as "rogue" or "deviant" are not only not fit to rule *but must be ruled.* Phil Williams's thesis in "Here Be Dragons" exemplifies this trend.[58] In this view, ungoverned spaces can be synonymous with "lawless areas"; what sets them apart has to do with having "different, alternative, and sometimes even hybrid forms of governance."[59] Danger lies not only in the completely "lawless areas" or the absence of state-centric governance, but also in multicentric governing, creating confrontations "between top-down control and bottom-up aspirations."[60] For Williams, "dangerous spaces" is a better fit for global insecurities,[61] capturing both characteristics that are intrinsic to ungovernability—implosion and contagion, where "a tipping point will push a state from weak to failing or a city *from stability into ferality.*"[62]

Not surprisingly, "preventive strategies are unworkable" and "the only alternative is mitigation,"[63] frequently in the forms of preventive, endless, and/or boundless war, given that "here be dragons!" in these othered, feral spaces. Unconcerned with the architects of those "feral spaces," the residents are targeted for surveillance, eviction, and annihilation. Their safety and security are an unthought. It is within this context that a modest proposal such as the Movement for Black Lives' Invest/Divest, which calls for a reallocation of social resources to prioritize the well-being of communities and the planet over that of the state and capital, has the effect of radically altering the presumed terms of order.

SPACES OF IN/JUSTICE

Critical scholarship on justice, especially by feminists, has taken up the Fanonian aspiration to decolonize epistemes in the form of theorizing with the oppressed. Like Dussel, they draw attention to the elimination or lessening of group oppression as a sine qua non for emancipatory theories.[64] Iris Marion Young's work on delineating the "five faces of oppression"[65] is especially instructive. Drawing on progressive social movements that emerged since the mid-twentieth century and her own experiential knowledge as an activist in the global movement against apartheid in South Africa, Young has proposed that we take up oppression's five facets (exploitation, marginalization, powerlessness, cultural imperialism, and violence) as the starting point of "enabling justice" theorizing to do more than merely maintaining the dominant paradigm, Rawls's justice as fairness framework. Given that "politics is partly a struggle over the language people use to describe social political experience,"[66] how we frame in/justice matters. Scholar and former civil rights attorney Lani Guinier goes further, proposing that instead of judicial supremacy, we should embrace "demosprudence," or looking to social justice movements and mobilization to learn the meanings of the law.[67]

Indeed, the usually sedated happenings at the US Supreme Court, where securing privilege for the few dominates, recently have undergone a quiet but noticeable shift as its crisis of legitimacy becomes increasingly more difficult to suppress.[68] Despite the exalted air of the Court, Justice Sonia Sotomayor frequently evinces misgivings about liberal jurisprudence and, more than once, employs demosprudence—a method of reading the laws imbued by the cries of mass movements for justice. Because this innovative tool emerged from neither political science nor philosophy but critical legal studies, it has fewer defects. Demosprudence is a portmanteau of democracy and jurisprudence; it denies the monopoly of elites (judges and legislators) by emphasizing the role of the many in lawmaking. Guinier introduced this concept as a heuristic tool, spotlighting "the relationship between the lawmaking power of formal legal authorities (whether judges or legislators) and the . . . often undervalued power of social movements or mobilized constituencies to make and interpret law."[69]

Democracy is at the core of judicial conflicts and, as such, demosprudence "is a democracy-enhancing jurisprudence" because it prioritizes "lawmaking or legal practices that inform and are informed by the wisdom of the people."[70] Oral dissent within the larger framework of demosprudence, without "the coercive power of the state," presupposes a broader audience for deliberation and, therefore, with greater democratic accountability.[71] Sotomayor is believed to frequently practice demosprudence through her dissents, seeking to speak directly to the people instead of her colleagues at the Supreme Court, on and off the bench.[72] For Guinier, Supreme Court Justices have a pedagogical function, not unlike social movements—they teach, and dissent is a "teaching moment."[73] Not all dissents engage demosprudence; nevertheless, through demosprudential dissent, even exalted Supreme Court judges engage in a praxis that opens up "an interactive and deliberative space between the people and the formal law makers," potentially producing new legal meanings.[74] This practice is "an antidote to judicial supremacy"[75] and a corrective intervention against democratic elitism.[76] Demosprudence, especially through dissent on the bench, therefore, suggests that unless and until the many are present in spaces of justice, justice itself remains cordoned off and illegitimate.[77] Approaching the law from perspectives of the people—who are more often than not victims of injustices—or framing injustice as oppression as Young did, or justice as compassion and in solidarity as I do, draws attention to the ways in which willful subjects and communities imagined and fought for justice in ways beyond the pale, and tills the fertile grounds of the radical imaginary domains of justice as praxis.[78]

AGAINST TYRANNY

Despite his fixity on western temporality, Foucault was correct about the modern obsessions with governmentality.[79] A general search for effective population-management (biopower) is intimately linked to the search for greater profitability and market dominance, and is akin to man mastering nature. Such mastery projects total domination under the jurisdiction in question, or within the pale. As a normalizing project, population-management norms governing and naturalizes the state—a foreign specie—as life imperatives.[80] The consent to be governed, a mythology scripted by European philosophers and sophists, underwrites creationist fictions to race and gender spaces and people into those who do and do not matter. These are exploitative contracts of domination, naturalizing group subordination and oppression.[81] They also categorize and mark the governed as human and the ungoverned as less than human, cauterizing justice with the worthy and severing it from the unworthy. The dominant discourse of in/justice in the west has thus been tyrannized by the very thing it seeks to supplant—a tautology that proclaims justice as raison d'être of state's existence while securing an orderly state becomes justice *causa formalis*. Within these spaces of in/justice, demosprudence is mere happenstance.

Remarkably, we more readily accept antiauthoritarian and antitotalitarian political ideologies than we are willing to reject forms of absolutism, such as White supremacy or heteropatriarchy. What does it mean to think of White supremacy or heteropatriarchy as tyranny?[82] It allows us to foreground absolutist rule, political, economic, cultural, even the affective, so that we may resist it. Thinking about White supremacy as a form of absolutism, for instance, requires us to attend to not only the state and structural dominance but also cultural practices, power relations, and subjectivities. In a critical analysis of Whiteness, Michael G. Lacy interrogates communicative strategies and uses "white absolutism" to refer to the rhetorical discourse that "offered ideal white racial identities and cultural norms to establish and justify white supremacy."[83] Here, "white absolutism centers white masculinity and justifies restoring white patriarchal heterosexual control by negating black, nonwhite and feminist archetypes that offer motives to conquer, control, and kill nonwhites" through the uses of "absolutist" appeals that "exists in coded and postmodern forms."[84] While this is a useful way to delineate its rhetorical practices, White supremacy as a form of absolutism moves beyond the rhetorical: it is highly strategic, even if its performance heavily relies on rhetoric. White supremacy is a regime of governing with its own apparatuses of disciplinary techniques, including ideologemes that may or may not deploy absolutist rhetorical tools. If White supremacy is defined as a belief in the inherent superiority of White people and therefore the right to dominate all others,[85] then, by definition, it is a form of absolutism and not merely a rhetorical method. Similarly, heteropatriarchy is absolutist when gender and sexual governance become the *causa prima* of social relations.

However reluctant we might be "to talk about 'tyrannical' as opposed to 'totalitarian' and 'authoritarian' forms of government,"[86] it is instructive to revisit this ancient notion because tyranny does not "merely identify but explain the persistence" of absolutist governing, including fantasies of autarchies.[87] As Catherine Zuckert argues, "tyranny is a persistent but complex human phenomenon," and because it is part of our life and world, we need to understand it in all its complexities and forms. Tyranny points to an absolutist predicament, a predisposition that incites discipline and ordering. To assert that tyranny has utility as a framework is not an appeal to ancient thought, but an entreaty to take up useful conceptual frames for delineating the many disciplinary regimes. For Newell, "tyranny is intrinsically connected to the relationship between human beings and nature."[88] In other words, human obsession with ordering nature drives the collective impulse to exploit and dominate nature. The tyrant is, therefore, someone who masters and seeks out absolute dominion, even if they only succeed in the dominion of one. Nietzsche understood as much when he suggested that self-enlightenment is a tyrannical form of disciplinary regime.[89] For Nietzsche, a tyrant is a lawgiver who sees lawgiving as a form of entitlement.[90] As the next chapter will show, White rule is tyrannical because White supremacists seek ruling as a form of racial entitlement.

Two related and mistakenly conflated concepts—autarky and autarchy—both have produced racial regimes that underwrite modern onto-epistemological projects. My investigation takes as a starting point the mythic ideas of White self-sufficiency (autarky) and its potent cousin, White absolute self-rule (autarchy). Reading White supremacy as tyrannical and a form of absolutist rule draws attention to the election of Whiteness as governing entitlement. White subjects electing themselves as lawgivers claim lawgiving for themselves as a form of entitlement. The absolutist will to White rule is the White supremacist tyrannical impulse to create a world in their own image—their *causa formalis.* As part I of this book reveals, within such a regime, freedom is indeed understood as entitlement, liberated from communal senses and collective mutuality, and emptied of virtues such as justice or equality that obligate the self to the other.

Nietzsche understood tyranny as "the taking as accomplished the world that one has defined and the forgetting that the world in which one lives is one that one has made."[91] To paraphrase: those who set the terms of order go about ordering the world accordingly, then "forget" that they invented a world in which the only way to escape is to completely disengage from those terms. The White supremacist is thus a tyrant who mechanizes racial regimes for governance then forgets that anti-racism and decolonialization are the only ways to move beyond racial absolutism.[92] Nietzsche also recognized a difference "whether it is 'Homer, or science (*Wissenschaft*) or the Bible that tyrannizes.'"[93] This difference is more than the substitution of one form of tyranny over another. The political ruler is different from the "tyrants of the Spirit" or moral discipline,[94] and White supremacists who tyrannize through the state governing apparatuses differ from those who tyrannize by normalizing Whiteness.

If governmentality is the art of governance,[95] then ungovernability and the crafting of rule breaking are intimately linked. Rule breaking is the means by which unhappy subjects and communities seek out to find themselves and do things that the tyrants refuse and end up in the unhappy archive. Historically, the ungoverned frequently seek to delegitimize and overthrow not only rulers but the rules themselves. Tyranny is a useful concept because it points to rulers and governors (as in lawgivers) and to how rules or lawgiving are entitled and sustained. Ironically, in his rush to concretize modernity, Foucault passed over Machiavelli for Nietzsche as a better guide for understanding modern governmentality, which is unfortunate because in the west no one is better than Machiavelli at understanding that the City of Man was only possible after humans invented then destroyed the City of God as a sacrifice *at the altar of political order.*[96] After all, Fortuna is even more unknowing than God, and she favors the bold.

Absolutism's appeal is expediency and, in gendered racial capitalism, it is about how to most effectively dispatch, however unhappily, the nonconformists and rule breakers who get in the way of securing order and wealth hoarding. If biohacking hacks bodily autonomy and undermines communal sovereignty—a frequent node for rule breakers—then data farming and hacking the body are essential to the twenty-first century's efficacious "surveillance capitalism,"[97] which affects, among other things, a labor regime that engenders death by work. Before the end of Man, many of us may end up being *robo sapiens* first, destined for a life on the margins or at the center, toiling away at every dictate of algorithmic controls. Authoritarians frequently make bold, if fantastic, claims that "I alone can solve this." The promise of a solution within grasp, especially in time of crises, renders the promiser attractive and creates the condition of possibility that, in the absence of other distractions (other pretenders), becomes more real. This is as true of the transhumanist claims that underwrite the new techno-autocracy as it is for the old populist authoritarianism. Populists who appeal to the expediency of absolutism frequently and opportunistically exploit this desire. The COVID-19 pandemic thus far, however, has revealed an unhappy truth buried in the avalanche of public lying: that tyrants make terrible governors, if the millions of deaths and hospitalizations are an indicator. Ready-made solutions, however bold, rarely are democratically efficacious.

Political theorists and observers frequently conflate the seduction of expediency with the efficacy of charismatic leadership. Weber, for instance, erroneously argued that modern politicians are likely those "who have no vocation and lack inner charismatic qualities that turn a man into a leader"; thus, lacking in greatness, they must depend on both coercive and bureaucratic apparatuses to maintain rule.[98] Charismatic rulers, Weber explained, possess extraordinary qualities and differ fundamentally from the rest of us. In this rendering of authoritarianism, for instance, the ruler merely is one who rules alone (or a *monarcho*)[99] not a tyrant (*tyrannos*). "Ruling alone" is considered a more neutral framing of an autocrat or an absolutist, instead of the implied despotism (*despoteia*) of the tyrant.[100] Plato (and later Aristotle) understood tyranny as a form of pathos, and famously argued that democracy is an inferior form of government compared to aristocracy and oligarchy because it is pathologically more vulnerable to mob rule and, therefore, on a slippery slope to tyranny—the most corrupt form of government. Tyranny is thus understood as "a general class of extremely bad regimes."[101] The problem with this classical reading is its inherent antidemocratic bias in the placement of democracy. Adjacent to tyranny, democracy cannot be trusted or valorized, and as such it embodied an internal threat to the ideal polis. The tyrant, costuming in populist appeal, is one who promises expediency and efficacy, dispatching all social problems with the magic of the state.[102] Democracy, on the other hand, is a prelude to tyranny, with an inherent antiaristocratic bias. As M. I. Finley explains, a society "in which discussion and debate are an essential technique, is a society full of risks."[103] Unhappiness thrives in a democracy as the *demos* are always wanting and, by the pure mathematical logic of power in numbers, the *hoi polloi* of the world insinuate their wills.

In these times of authoritarianism and lavish fascist desiring, a search for better tools for democratic livability must be intentional as a practical imperative. In this work, I explore several major concepts and ideas in western political thought—especially tyranny, democracy, and the ungovernable. I bring together two frameworks—democratic living, and justice as solidarity and compassion—to delineate these terms and question basic assumptions about relations of rulings, especially the so-called consent to be governed. An interrogation of these ideas and theories is neither a romantic attachment to "old ideas" nor a cynical attempt to rid such concepts of their resiliency. Instead, it is a recognition of the need for democratic ways of living and thinking in the times of antidemocracy. When even representational democracy is under frontal attack, substantive democratic politics serve as a reservoir for lessons in counterstrategies and alter realities. How have individuals and communities moved and continued to move, and to live ungoverned? What are the ways in which they imagine, build, and struggle to defend ungoverned life and living? These questions signal what substantive democratic politics and living could look like. A turn to this unhappy archive of governing is a necessary journey in the search for a democratic ethic of liberation.[104]

Unhappily, Black people, particularly Black women, are marked as angry, unruly, and dangerous by their mere presence within the system of White rule. As archetypes of "ungovernable" or troublesome subjects, they have been marked and frequently perceived as the cause and source of undoing the presumed well-ordered society. This work centers radical Black feminist methods, analytics, and ethos—especially abolition feminism—as tools for narrative subversion and as a radical ethic of liberation.

A number of radical Black feminist thinkers and cultural workers have built an infrastructure of resistance, supplying the frameworks for collective mobilization against settler colonialism, gendered racial capitalism, heteropatriarchy, and White supremacy, grounded in the faith and work of a community for just futures. Erica R. Edwards explains: "When Black women both served for target practice in the ongoing war against terror and were recruited to carry out that target practice, when Black books exploded in the US literary culture and in multicultural classrooms, and just as the Black literary text was up for conscription into the reign of US empire, Black women writers, in prose, poetry, drama, and invented genres like choreopoem, generated grammars of survival on the other side of terror."[105] And in so doing, Toni Cade Bambara and others like her crafted and are still crafting a Black feminist insurgency whose impact spans across both literary and "extraliterary" terrains.

Edwards and other Black feminist writers—including Toni Morrison, whose work Bambara showcased as an editor—attest that Bambara, more than many, understood the ways in which cultural work is essential to the larger struggles for justice and dignity, especially the role that the radical Black feminist imaginary plays in pushing the boundaries of thinkability and the unthought.[106] Bambara imagines Black feminist cultural workers as "paramilitaries" fighting in hostile cultural wars where their work as "image makers" and "image insurrectionists" were necessary for "a minute-to-minute battle over who will define/depict/disseminate"[107] their own work against, among other things, "the sociological production of Black pathology that lubricated the carceral build-up of the post-1968 decades and the attached narratives of Black deviance to the imagination of foreign threat . . . that justified increased policing domestically and abroad."[108] Commenting on Bambara's revolutionary thought and praxis, Eleanor W. Traylor notes that in *The Black Woman*, Bambara featured at the times deeply underappreciated Black woman writers whose voices "were (and remain) active participants in an ever-evolving movement whose impact at mid-twentieth century was perhaps *the most revolutionary cultural and intellectual re-imagining to have occurred in the United States since the birth of America in* The Declaration of Independence."[109] Building on the work of Wahneema Lubiano and others, Traylor maintains that however brilliant and significant the disruption incited by "the evolving civil rights, Black Power, Black nationalism, and black arts movement," these did not "fully" instigate a "radical reordering," nor have they produced a "critique . . . that would lead to the overthrow of global capitalism and/or homophobic patriarchy."[110] Bambara's showcasing of radical Black feminist work, textual and otherwise, is thus a project of insurgency and "recuperation of the self in a racist and sexist society [as] a political enterprise . . . that deprioritizes general difference in the interest of historical, activist continuity."[111] Rejecting an elitist essentializing of the "Black woman writer,"

Bambara instead elevated "an ongoing collective project of documentation that narrates the unspeakable and represents the failure of communication that results from surviving the incessant war."[112] Her visionary restaging of radical thought is the staging of revolutionary Black feminism as embodied by "the black women" who are

> involved in a struggle for liberation . . . our art, protest, dialogue no longer spring from the impulse to entertain, or to indulge or enlighten the conscience of the enemy. . . . Our energies now seem to be invested in and are in turn derived from a determination to touch and to unify. What typifies the current spirit is an embrace, an embrace of the community and a hard-headed attempt to get basic with each other.[113]

Seeded and fertilized by this radical tradition of Black feminist praxis, abolition feminism centers on justice, dignity, and livability by redefining safety and security as it retools the praxis of solidarity for mass mobilization. This framework and movement, largely nurtured by contemporary radical Black feminists such as Angela Y. Davis, Ruth Wilson Gilmore, and Beth Richie, to name a few, is a tool for democratic living and a concrete manifestation of the legacy of Black feminist radical imaginary for the just present/futures that Bambara incited. A democratic ethic of liberation would be inconceivable without such heritage. *Become Ungovernable* both relies on and extends that heritage for a robust interrogation of democratic thought and praxis as well as the many meanings of justice.

NOTES ON METHOD

The search for a democratic ethic of living demands not only a demystification of antidemocracy but also a deauthorization of gendered racial capitalism, patriarchy, white supremacy, ablism, heteronormativity, and other dominions.[114] To decolonize dominant ideologemes, including "democracy," therefore requires radical historiography; it involves deliberate remembering and exhaustive historical research, especially on mass resistance to delineate communities of women, men, and children, of their struggles, dreams, and desires as a people, not as a unitary self. Just as Indigenous communal sovereignty waged war against missionary claims, marronage and fugitivity frightened plantocracy, and peasant rebels threatened the mandate of kings, the very existence of the ungoverned belies the fantasies their enemies have created for them. Decolonizing orthodox anarchism entertains a possibility of a democratic anarchism that similarly holds out a promise that just beyond the official and fictive narratives lie the richness and rewards *of the real* and *its* possibility of alternative onto-epistemologies. I view democracy as fundamentally anarchic, full of risks, and potentially potent. In contradistinction to the western variety of anarchism, democratic anarchism is a social philosophy that as a starting point embodies the aspirations of the masses; rejects order as alien, irrational, and unnatural; and conspires in solidarity to bring about justice as compassion. While conventional understandings of anarchy (without rule) suggest a contradiction to or an absence of democracy (rule by the many), alternative genealogies of anarchism (including ancient Taoism) may show the way to a democratically grounded anarchism that relies on justice in solidarity and egalitarianism as precepts.

Emphasizing democratic praxis is the recognition that a just society needs to be imagined, built, and peopled from the ground up. The emphasis on solidarity and the "matrix of interconnectivity, mutuality, and accountability,"[115] in addition to the expansive recognition of power relations and histories, do not deny the need to nurture diverse individuals and relations; instead, they allow us to densely populate our imagination, adding to the toolkit formations and campaigns against injustices and unfreedoms. When anarchism is freed from its imperial and western heritage, and democracy is freed from antidemocrats, iterations of democratic anarchism are discoverable, can be known, and can engender the possibility of alternative epistemes, ontologies, and even ecologies.[116] Even as part II of this book takes up the governing regimes of labor, gender, and security, it pivots away from the metaphysics of ruling toward the intimacy of friendship, unruly politics of mutuality, and the ungovernable spaces and acts of refusal in between.

Throughout the book, I resource the philosophical works of Adrian Piper, Sylvia Wynter, Angela Y. Davis, and others, to explore compassion and solidarity as constitutive of a radical feminist ethic of liberation, especially as embodied by abolition feminism. Moreover, I seek out justice praxis as it appears in concrete reality, which at times bears little resemblance—and, worse, frequently is in direct opposition—to what is nominally understood as justice.

I argue that abolition feminist mobilizing in the contemporary United States is not so different from contemporary and past Chinese peasant rebellions in that they both place a claim on a very rich and complex terrain of emancipatory utopian longing and the practical and elusive quest for just futures. Decolonizing knowledges and praxes of modern epistemes, including anarchism and democracy, calls for threading such connections and reconnections—making it possible to demystify and withhold assurances of power and authority—and turning to the alternate spaces and moments wherein ordinary people and communities assert their own renderings of life and living, rather than those of the state and capital.

Radical histories from below, as illustrated in the ordinary archives of peasant, slaves, and urban rebellions, reveal that in the shadow of these real and fictive narrations about the state and capital are individuals and communities of people who render themselves unavailable for governing. They might have been the peasants of third-century BC in China; heretics of the twelfth-century anti-property movement in Europe; the Quilombos of the Palmares in seventeenth-century Brazil; the female slave rebels of Jamaica; the Apaches of Eastern Arizona; the Zapatistas of Chiapas; the Palestinians in the West Bank; the urban youths in West Phoenix; the Hmongs of Southeast Asia; the Liberian women who held sex strikes to forge peace and end a civil war; the border crossers, the dress crossers, the migrant workers in Michigan or China. They, their communities, and their yet unnamed progeny have been and are peopling the unhappy archives of governing. These are individuals and communities who show up. However briefly, however imperfectly, they show up, often unscripted and unimpressed by the awesome power of various dominions—the state, capital, heteropatriarchy, including the very force of history—even as their lives are under constant surveillance and suppression. For these subjects, no single violent abstraction can render them mute or incapacitated; their life goes on beyond the pale, sometimes encumbered by but not totally governed by the state, going against even when they appear to be going along, pushing and pulling the very technologies that seek to annihilate them. They refuse work, run away, lock up company presidents, kick out party functionaries, refuse to march, take on many lovers, kill their children, wage wars, create art, and cultivate lasting friendships. They do what they must to get and be free of the conditions that govern them, all the while busying themselves with friends, community and world-building, and dreaming of just futures.

In the face of coercion and tyrannical rule, these individuals and communities withhold both consent and legitimation; in the process, they render the state and its allies more transparently incompetent, brutal, and imperial. In these ways, they belie the state and its enablers' claims of intelligence, overwhelming force, and the power of exception, not to mention the various creationist fantasies, be they economic, political, racial, or sexual. These life forms are not subjectivities invented by the state; rather, they are the *ungovernable*, frequently intending to impede and negate "governmentality," or the organized practices that render subjects governable. If life is constantly patrolled by the state, to transport life from the state's dominion, it is necessary to disengage from the state, to break the theoretical and tactical addiction to the state, so that we may get to the other side of terror,[117] however momentarily, to find our collective ways toward freedom, justice, and livable life.

In situating abolition feminism as an analytic, method, and praxis, my task is similar to Dussel's in locating the radical ethics of care in the liberation of community from oppression and domination.[118] While *poiesis* has its place, praxis is acting with another such that, when in formations, we are in relationships.[119] Unlike hegemonic social or moral orders that presuppose rules, norms, and dictates of dominions, a radical feminist ethic of liberation creates the condition of possibility for being in relationship to actualize just present/futures. Whereas a moral order legitimizes oppression, especially against the poor, and is therefore a "praxis of domination," an ethic of liberation emerges from movements to liberate the oppressed from violence and subjection.[120] It is thus a practical and strategic liberation project that transcends the unjust present to be on the path toward just futures. The starting point is not biogenetic essentialism but rather a praxis of liberation.[121] For abolition feminism, it is acting to actualize visions of democratic living, radical inclusivity, and egalitarianism, grounded in horizontal relationships, dignity, solidarity, and an end to oppression and violence, of all forms.[122]

To unlearn antidemocracy, the following chapters delineate the political's promiscuous progeny and denaturalize the fictive autonomy of the individual—both have underwritten dominant principles of in/justice, including but not limited to freedom, liberty, and equality. This pivot incites radical democratic possibilities, foregrounding collective agency instead of the state, capital, or discourse, and compassion, solidarity, and dignity instead of appropriation, accumulation, and hoarding. An ethic of liberation peoples collective imagination with real voices and experiences of ordinary individuals and communities, fertilizing the terrains with fanatic scholarship and action in search of alternative ways of knowing, living, and dreaming. It privileges the idea that "men and women [are] divine agents" of history, instead of the "fractious and weaker allegiances of class" and other dead-end alliances.[123] In the process, and as Bambara suggests, making ourselves unavailable for governing includes making ourselves unavailable to the servitude of the material, epistemological, and metaphysical ordering. And therein lies the possibility of an alternative to order.

2
The Myth of White Autarky

The whites want slaves, and want us for their slaves, but some of them will curse the day they ever saw us.

David Walker[1]

The university space we want to build with you is a decolonial and abolitionist space. It works toward a world without the university. Because in that world, there will be no capitalist mode of production—no classes, no separate education, no avowed or unavowed colonial, racist epistemologies, no meritocracy, no need to select the more "talented," no need to assign human beings to a ruling, working, or middle class. This is our horizon. Through building collectively, we create a decolonial abolitionist university space from the margins to the center. There, we share our freedom imaginings, practices, and ways of being and knowing, in their difference, with their complexities. We build safety outside the system: safety that is not organized around violence, but around relations that need neither the state nor an inferiorized other.

Bacchetta et al.[2]

OUR REAL DISEASE

Today, in the era of the megahit musical *Hamilton*,[3] it might seem fashionable to be on the side of Alexander Hamilton in the larger debate about the size and strength of government. It would be a mistake, however, to overlook Hamilton's keen defense of property, elitism, and autocratic centralism. He might have opposed slavery, but he disdained democratic politics, as he insisted that "our real disease . . . is Democracy."[4] Unlike David Walker who understood that gradual freedom is no freedom at all, Hamilton, who grounded his political career on the idea of self-sufficiency and national economic independence, advocated for "gradual emancipation" and "consistently supported property rights over the slaves' natural rights to freedom."[5] Like many industrialist contemporaries who would later side with the Union, Hamilton opposed slavery as an institution on the ground that as a mode of production and accumulation, it was less efficient than a wage-based industrial economy. As the first secretary of treasury and (along with James Madison) one of two main writers of the *Federalist Papers*—the propaganda organ of the revolutionary class—Hamilton wanted to raise a nation-state aligned with moneyed interests, and "saw agrarian America as deplorably and even perilously underdeveloped."[6] He, like many of his progeny today, never really doubted his belief in the inherent superiority of White rule, deeming social inequalities as a natural fact that "would exist as long as liberty existed."[7] Sidestepping the dependencies on the appropriation of Indigenous land and Black labor, the contestations among White elites over the correct course of gendered racial capitalism and its efficacy of ruling would persist well beyond the Constitutional Convention, revealing the many mythologies of White autarky or self-sufficiency.

In November 1859, soon after John Brown's raid on Harpers Ferry in West Virginia, *Harper's New Monthly Magazine* ran a feature on "The Rice Land of the South." Noting that rice was "one of the great, universal sustainer of human life," lest *Harper's* educated readers overlook how central it was to the political economy, T. Addison Richards reminded them that

> in no part of the world, however, is the culture of rice more successful or the product so excellent as upon the Southern Atlantic and Gulf coasts of the United States. . . . Here are the rice fields of the South, *from whence came not only nineteen-twentieth of all the product of the Republic, but the chief portion of all which is distributed through the great channels of European commerce.*[8]

The source of such wonderous riches came from slaves. Indeed, after a lengthy and breathless account of rice cultivation, Richards shared that "the most novel and interesting study of the stranger here is that the aspect and the habits of the laborer employed."[9] He also observed that "to cultivate these lands by white labor, if practicable at all, would be unquestionably, at an immense sacrifice of life."[10] To Richards and his ilk, White lives matter, and it would be an "immense sacrifice" were there to be no more slave labor to furnish the political economy of the United States, laying bare the mythologies about an autonomous, self-sufficient "White" economy or autarky.

Three decades before John Brown and his compatriots seized the largest Federal Arsenal at Harpers Ferry in a bid to commence an end to a "slave country whose rights are disregarded by wicked, cruel and unjust enactments," a militant abolitionist and a tailor in Boston had recruited Black seamen and port workers to smuggle pages of his recent manuscript into their clothing to be distributed far and wide, calling upon the "Coloured Citizens of the World"—that is, the men, women, and children of Color—to stage a slave revolution. The pamphlet, *Walker's APPEAL*, and its circulation (predating by nearly two years both William Lloyd Garrison's famous *Liberator* and the most well-known of slave revolts in the US, Nat Turner's insurrection of 1831) would strike fear in slaveholding states—so much so that they sought Walker's capture for sedition and rushed through draconian laws requiring Black sailors to self-incarcerate during docking or outright banning port of entry to free Black people.[11] This response to evocation of rebellion is emblematic of apartheid or racial antidemocracy designed to protect and serve the rights and entitlements of a White slaveholding class.

Walker's APPEAL, as Cedric J. Robinson argued, embodies one of the earliest expressions of Pan-Africanism, Black internationalism, as well as Black nationalism, advancing both a Pan-African consciousness and an appeal to a Black cosmology.[12] These cultural and political expressions, especially their radical consciousness of racial Blackness, would find expressions later in the work of Black radicals, including Martin Delaney, Marcus Garvey, Malcolm X, and Angela Y. Davis. These expressions find echoes in radical political manifestos, including the *Combahee River Collective Statement*, that set out the terms for a radical Black feminist analytics and liberatory praxis.[13] Robinson insists that this incendiary work remains salient in scholarship and in justice movements, especially as Walker gave voice not only to the collective moral outrage against racial capitalism and White supremacy, but also for Black self-determination and group solidarity. As James Turner, Hasan Crockett, and others maintain, "the publication of *Walker's APPEAL* ushered in the second, militant, abolitionist movement" that ultimately brought an end to legal slavery in the US.[14] In our times of gendered racial capitalism and heteropatriarchy, Walker's critique of White antidemocracy promises another reckoning.

In the second half of 2020, when the world was awakened to the virality and potentially fatal consequences of SARS-CoV-2, tens of millions of people in the US and many global metropolises took to the street, marched, organized, and were gassed, beaten, and/or arrested for trying to draw attention to the epidemic of anti-Black violence, particularly police violence and homicide. They persistently made their presence known, and many have taken to the streets repeatedly since that summer. The 2020 mass mobilization, largely envisioned and organized by BLM, M4BL, and a loose network of affiliates, at a minimum suggests that while this may be a time of White supremacy, it is also a time of protests and rebellions that will likely persist until the time comes when as a society we have the political will to match our economic and rhetorical resources that would put an end to White supremacy and anti-Black violence.

In the meantime, and in the aftermath of more than six months of consecutive protests where millions by their presence and prescience forced this nation into a reckoning with White rule, the world witnessed the attempted siege of the US Capitol on January 6, 2021. Such a confluence of events evokes James Baldwin's instruction on White innocence and what it portends: "But it is not permissible that the authors of devastation should also be innocent. It is the innocence which constitutes the crime."[15] What might the next January 6 look like, and who will author that event? Equally important, how do we as "freedom-loving people" engage with such happenings? What are the democratic means for living in these trying times?

As an explanation for the January 6 insurrection, a manufactured consensus emerges in the political press suggesting a loose confederacy of "[illegible]" and opportunistic influencers who somehow miraculously achieved a feat that many acclaimed transnational terrorist networks failed to do in the two-decades-long US global war on terror: that is, they temporarily occupied the American Capitol, sending the vice president and members of the US Congress into hiding in fear for their lives.[16] In the immediate aftermath, many otherwise reasonable and respectable observers and analysts would have us believe that "misinformation and online radicalization led to the insurrection."[17] As this cutesy *Politico* headline "The Internet Is a Crime Scene" suggests, the internet is blamed as a culprit of radicalization and violence, spawned by wild conspiracies and alternative facts.[18] That would make QAnon the mastermind of what appears to be another chapter in an enduring process of what Dylan Rodríguez calls "white reconstruction."[19] It may be true that, aided by algorithms, internet disinformation fueled wild conspiracies,[20] but this ready-made causal explanation for the siege is dubious. Putting aside the near-unanimous outrage mainstream corporate media leveled at the January 6 mob, what has emerged is a narrative spectacularly silent on the corporate and political elite's role in this insurrection. Did the nominal head of one of two ruling parties have a consequential part in this attempted insurrection? The answer to this question is immaterial insofar as no single individual is ever fully responsible for an insurrection. However, every insurrection requires an infrastructure, not just ideology and spontaneous and planned actions, and this one was no exception. As the January 6 congressional hearings suggest, the infrastructure for the insurrection is more robust than critics have imagined. It involves the police, military, professionals, social media, foundations, women organizers, an heiress to a multibillion fortune, a private jet, and certainly the symbolic seat of American supreme political power, the White House.[21]

This siege and the rise of Trumpism warrant deep reflections about White supremacy and protofascist politics in the US.[22] Not quite in the shadow of the 2020 elections and the siege of the Capitol were the aforementioned nearly six months of consecutive protests, bringing an estimated 28–32 million people to the streets demanding an end to police violence, anti-Black violence, systemic racism, and White supremacy. By that time, "defund the police," the rallying cry of the 2020 protest campaign, had become less of an operationalized scheme to divest from policing and more of a declaration against authoritarianism, no less meaningful than *liberté, egalité, fraternité* (liberty, equality, fraternity)—the rallying cry of the French Revolution and the national motto of the anti-slavery Republic of Haiti.

These protests—largely led by young queer femmes of Color, particularly Black femmes—are part of the tapestry of the January 6 eruption, woven and cross-stitched by colonialism, gendered racial capitalism, and heteropatriarchy as well as a radical legacy of struggles against unfreedom and for just futures, secreted and announced over centuries in the making. Even before these latest waves of protests, the organizers and their formations have worked with discipline, imagination, and a certain rigor in analytics, ensuring what the historian Barbara Ransby calls "making *all Black Lives Matter*."[23] This involves extending the intersectional framework and praxes to interrogating difference, power, and privilege in the US and beyond. As Ransby has noted, the genealogy of BLM/M4BL has extraordinarily deep roots—dating back to the 1990s, and includes Black queer activism and Black AIDS mobilization (BAM); the Black Racial Congress (BRC); the community-building campaign responding to federal organized abandonment in the aftermath of Katrina; and the reemergence of the Black Left, including Pan Africanists and radical Black feminists, as well as the anti-prison network Critical Resistance and the women of Color formation against violence, INCITE!. Ransby also insists that the BLM/M4BL mobilization is akin to the BRC and its "sixteen-year precursor" because of its gender politics—situating "a Black feminist intersectional paradigm prominently within the larger framework of Black left and radical thought."[24] This is what contemporary radical Black feminist mobilization looks like—born of rich heritage and thriving in an ongoing effort to redefine what it means to be human, how to get free, and how to live with dignity.

As instantiated by Paolo Bacchetta and their coauthors, a radical abolition feminist vision is horizontal, in solidarity, and needs "neither the state nor an inferiorized other."[25] Echoing the language of what is now considered a classic manifesto of an ethic of liberation—the *Combahee River Collective Statement*—the authors insist on sharing both their methodology and ethic. Despite being considered "strangers within and without," their "experiences and how we make and share space together are indexes of power and viable categories" for an analytic of liberation.[26] Historically, radical feminists of Color, especially Black feminists, have consistently and vocally delineated an antiauthoritarian, antifascist praxis that is conscious of itself as antifascist; yet their contributions to a larger critique of democratic capitalism as a homegrown fascist formation had been largely ignored, particularly in the body of scholarship on fascism. This is so because fascism is usually understood as foreign. As suggested by recent scholarship, however, fascism is neither deviant nor alien to the US. As Oliver Cox explains, fascists are "the capitalists and their sympathizers who have achieved political class consciousness."[27] Fascism thus could happen anywhere capitalism thrives, and the US specie of fascism is imbricated in White supremacist consciousness of gendered racial capitalism and heteropatriarchy. As such, fascism is grounded on an admixture of a notion of self-rule and supremacy—*or the right to not be governed by the other.*

AMERICAN FASCISM AND THE BETRAYAL OF THE SELF

Fascism distinguishes itself by its singular insistence on self-rule. Absolute self-rule is fundamentally antidemocratic because, by definition, it is an assertion of autocracy. From the election of Man as the authority and master of the universe to the proclamation of White power over the other, absolutist self-rule is transparent both in its arrogance and its conceits. President Andrew Johnson and others, including Mississippi governor Benjamin Grubb Humphreys, insisting at the end of the Civil War that the US "is and it shall ever be, a government of white men," capture well the idea of White rule as the embodiment of fascist self-rule fantasy.[28] Historically, fascists refused to recognize anyone else's rule, including rule by the many, as legitimate. Self-rule accompanied by a politics of annihilation is fundamentally antidemocratic because it is an assertion of autocracy. What differentiates fascism from all other ideological formations is its virulent insistence on its right to rule or *the will to power*, even if it is delusional.[29] For American fascists, White supremacy and the inherent right to govern rarely are in dispute, even as the facticity of life irrefutably demonstrates White supremacy's inherent insecurity and unsustainability.[30] Insofar as Black feminist mobilizations have fought actively against White supremacy and White rule both in the US and in the African diaspora, they indeed have built an infrastructure of resistance against fascism here and abroad. The Black feminist poet Audre Lorde warned against a politics of silence when she admonished that "your silence will not protect you," and drew attention to the power of speaking out against injustices and unfreedoms, a practice long held by Black feminists throughout history.[31] Countering this conspiracy of silence around radical Black feminist contributions in the struggles against fascism, for instance, underlines contemporary abolition feminism as one of the most potent weapons against fascist politics and consciousness.

Living in a protofascist, authoritarian moment demands taking stock of antifascist tools.[32] The frequency with which the term "fascism" has been bandied about since the 2016 election (from the *New York Times* and the *Washington Post* to *Rolling Stone, Vogue, and Wire Magazine*) makes it difficult to ignore the relentless jingoism of American exceptionalism, hyper-militarist policing, and alternative facts that have come to characterize the hyperreality of American life in the last decade.

Specie Origin

As a specie, fascism emerged in the west. Whether it is an exclusive province of Europe, however, is not always apparent. Fascism typically is understood as an admixture of virulent nationalism, militarism, corporatism, and active campaigns of violence against perceived enemies.[33] Rarely successful in totality, fascism, as a cultural stratagem, seeks to annihilate the deviant other to achieve dominance in total. In other words, totalitarianism is fascism's singular preoccupation, even if it is not its achievement. Fascism, including the Nazi variety, generally is understood as not native to the US; as an ideology, it is largely believed to be an Italian and German product. According to dean of fascism studies, Robert O. Paxton: "conservatism, liberalism, socialism—all reached matured form between the late eighteenth century and the mid-nineteenth century."[34] Fascism, on the other hand, "was the major political innovation of the twentieth century."[35] It was, according to Paxton, "unimagined as late as the 1890s."[36] He even has an exact date and location for its birth: "officially, Fascism was born in Milan on Sunday, March 23, 1919."[37] Even within the context of the 1890s, Paxton clearly overlooked the Jim Crow counterrevolutionary ideography of the likes of *Plessy v. Ferguson*—the 1896 US Supreme Court decision that legalized racial segregation, the American version of racial apartheid. Fascism's specie origin is important not so much for claims of authenticity, but rather for revealing its mythic inventions, rules of engagement, and terms of order. According to those terms, fascism is not native to the US because something so awful must have come from outside of ourselves, could never have been part of our body of politics; for the means and intelligence to fight against it, we must therefore look elsewhere.

Closer to Home

That ninety Black Americans joined the more than forty thousand people from over fifty-three countries in solidarity with the Spanish Popular Front, fighting against fascism during the Spanish Civil War, points to not only the long struggle against fascism in the US, but also the ways in which African Americans presciently recast fascist developments in Europe as kin to White supremacy and racial apartheid in the US and elsewhere. Among the nearly three-thousand-strong US contingent of the Abraham Lincoln Brigade, were two Black women, one of whom was Salaria Kea. Kea, a nurse, sailed from

New York and was assigned to the American Hospital in Villa Paz, where she helped set up the first field hospital and found kinship with the Spanish peasants who were fighting against Franco's insurgency. Kea was captured by the fascists, escaped prison after seven weeks of captivity, found her way back to the hospital, and was later badly wounded—so injured that she could no longer work in the field and had to return to the US.[38] Back home in Harlem, Kea continued to fundraise for medical supplies and gave speeches raising awareness about fascism and the brigade's work. The fact that Kea and many Black Americans were against Franco's fascist insurgency in Spain or fascist Italy's 1935 invasion of Ethiopia is unremarkable, for there exists a record of African Americans being blacklisted during the McCarthy era for being "prematurely antifascist." What is more salient than this evidence of a legacy of active struggles against fascism, predating mainstream antifascist resistance, is the reason Kea and her comrades such as Langston Hughes and others gave for why they joined the brigade, and especially how they felt obligated to lead anti-fascist struggles. Kea pointed to Black people's long confrontation with racism and White supremacy for why she was fit to join, if not lead, the brigade, explaining that anti-Black violence and racism "are part of the picture of fascism."[39] Hughes, a queer Black man writing as a political correspondent, put it this way: "Fascists is Jim Crow . . . [In Spain], we shoot 'em down." He would later elaborate:

> We are the people who have long known in actual practice of the word fascism. . . . In many states Negroes are not permitted to vote or to hold office . . . freedom of movement is greatly hindered, especially if we happen to be sharecroppers . . . we know what it is to be refused admission to schools and colleges, to theatres and concert halls, to hotels and restaurants. In America, Negroes do not have to be told what fascism is in action. We know.[40]

In other words, Jim Crow apartheid is fascist. Hughes conveys a sense of familiarity and even intimacy with fascism that, with few exceptions, many scholars of fascism studiously ignored.[41] As Kea, Hughes, and other Black thinkers and activists understood, the architects of Nazism who came to the US in the 1930s traveled from the seat of Nazism to the heart of Jim Crow—namely California, among other places in the US—to learn about fascism from its source. Paxton might have pointed to Milan and 1919 as the birthplace and date of European fascism, but the 1920s revival of the Ku Klux Klan (KKK) in the US predated the rise of European fascism and Nazism's mass appeal by at least a decade, suggesting, at a minimum, a Eurocentric oversight on the part of Paxton and in the larger discourse on fascism.

Contrary to masculinist fictions about right-wing male leadership, in the 1920s when the KKK membership was greatest (4 million), it was under the tutelage of Elizabeth Tyler, a woman deemed as the KKK's most effective recruiter and mouthpiece.[42] Tyler was credited with expanding the KKK from strictly an anti-Black organization to also target Jews, Catholics, immigrants and communists. More recently, scholars such as Linda Gordon and James Q. Whitman explicitly note the kinship between US-bred White supremacists and early twentieth-century fascism and Nazism.[43] Whitman points to a 1934 meeting in Germany specifically convened to plan legislation for the Nazi race regime and its singular achievement in the form of the Nuremberg Laws. As it turned out, this "meeting involved detailed and lengthy discussions of law of the United States." Whitman reports that "the most radical Nazis present were the most ardent champions of the lessons that American approaches held for Germany."[44] He also noted that "in *Mein Kampf* Hitler praised America as nothing less than 'the one state' that had made progress toward the creation of a healthy racist order of the kind that the Nuremberg Laws were intended to establish."[45] In other words, for the Nazis to become Nazis as we now understand them, they had to learn to become American first.[46]

American nativism is thus a delusion masquerading as a political stratagem, even if White nativism is neither. Among its many conceits are that it is American, nationalist, and it is in defense of the homeland. In reality, its nativism appears imported; America is at best a fiction and a wrong address, and the USA as a collective body continues to deny the existence and legitimacy of its fascist ilk. In a word, self-denial. As the political, economic and cultural elites vociferously deny their kinship with the vulgarity of American nativism, (e.g., the likes of Trumpism, right-wing populism), the collective body sublimates its repressed White supremacist consciousness, even as many of its adherents live out a virulent and at times violent politics of "self-defense." "You shall not replace us" and "America First" are thus rallying cries of a grotesque projection and conflation of White identity and victimhood as embodiment of autarky (self-sufficiency)—a mythical but nevertheless morally bankrupt, historical fiction. This delusion has extended aid and comfort to many factions, and even political parties, with fatal consequences from torture and maiming to incarceration and deaths, including intentional destruction of family structures and the imprisonment of children. Such aggressive denial is more than a consequence of momentary national psychosis as exemplified by the Charlottesville demonstration of White nativist proclivities for Nazi fantasies and cosplay, or the more concerted display of White rule on January 6. These are sediments and accretion of centuries long policies of settler colonialism, White supremacy, heteropatriarchy, and gendered racial capitalism. However denied and deluded by the political establishment, the myth of White autarky is a potent mobilizing agent, extending aid and comfort to right-wing, authoritarian governments in the US and beyond.[47] Thus, White autarky transmogrified into White autarchy (absolute self-rule), presupposing freedom as White entitlement and liberty for the few who are fit to rule.

FREEDOM AS ENTITLEMENT

Notable flare-ups in the US, such as the public demonstrations of White supremacist fantasies in Charlottesville and later in the Capitol, are rehearsals for White autarchy. Even before January 6 and the rise of Trumpist idolatry, a fanatic movement with populist fixings gripped mainstream American politics and threatened to hijack establishment policymaking, namely the Tea Party movement (TPM). It materialized in a spectacular fashion—as public theater. In the midst of what would be known as the Great Recession with devastating effects on communities across the globe and less than a month after the historic inauguration of Barack Obama—the first African American to occupy the US presidency—former commodity trader and *CNBC* commentator Rick Santelli staged the infamous rant that publicly launched the Tea Party movement, on the floor of the Chicago Mercantile Exchange—one of the most active nodes of the global financial market that was then on the brink. In a five-minute soliloquy amplified by corporate media, especially *Fox News*, Santelli played the role of a fed-up protagonist reminiscent of the fictional reporter Howard Beale in the 1976 film *Network*. He blamed the catastrophic meltdown in the housing market and the foreclosure crisis on the financially entrapped victims of the predatory, hyperspeculative financial system, alleging a government bent on turning the country into socialist Cuba that enabled bad behavior by these "losers," even as he promised a "Chicago Tea Party in July."[48] The incident had all the flare of a well-financed and poorly acted high school drama, and Santelli delivered a denouement that was hard to miss. First he asked the traders on the floor—who were complicit if not likely more culpable than the victims of foreclosures for the collapsing financial system, if they were willing to "bail out" those who spent too much on their homes; the Greek chorus of traders shouted a unified "no!" Santelli then turned to the camera and called out then President Obama by name, asking "Are you listening?"[49] In an interview with the *Chicago Sun-Times* a year later, Santelli had this to say: "People ask me if I'm the father of the Tea Party movement. . . . I was the spark . . . that started it. If being the lighting rod that started the Tea Party is what's written on my tombstone, I'll be very happy."[50] He is certainly not "the father" of this movement. Comprehensive investigations into the event and making of TPM reveal that his performance was not spontaneous; it was a preplanned, carefully orchestrated media event by some of the most right-wing elements in the country, including the Sam Adams Project, Americans for Prosperity, the Cato Institute, *Reason Magazine*, FreedomWorks, and the Koch family.[51] According to Devin Burghart and Leonard Zeskind, immediately following Obama's victory, the Libertarian Party of Illinois sought to establish a "Boston Tea Party Chicago" through national libertarian and anti-tax groups. Dave Brady of the Illinois Libertarian Party chapter would later claim that they "gave Rick Santelli the idea for the Tax Day Tea Parties."[52] The rant as intended would be played and replayed, and *CNBC*, as a mouthpiece for the financial sector, a sector that was finally getting attention for the havoc it engenders in the global economy, was transformed overnight into a populous forum for elite grievances. The morning after, *Fox News* discussed ad nauseum a "Tea Party" that was technically nonexistent; by sundown, the Nationwide Tea Party Coalition was formed, and Americans for Prosperity and FreedomWorks created Facebook groups calling for protests throughout the country. Within forty-eight hours, an operative for FreedomWorks, Brendan Steinhauser compiled "ten quick easy steps to hold your own Tea Party," and sent it to right-wing commentator Michelle Malkin, who faithfully created a link on her blog for it.[53]

While media personalities and others might have exaggerated the impact of this media event, Santelli's contemptuous attack on the financially entrapped while shilling for the super wealthy is an important misdirection emblematic of the rise and impact of the TPM, revealing how right-wing populism has long been part and parcel of American antidemocracy. It portends a more robust enveloping of democratic elitism and a deepening of authoritarianism in the country.

TPM, by any measure, was not a grassroots movement nor did its interests advance the plight of the poor. Far from a spontaneous uprising of ordinary people, this astroturf operation was financed by the wealthiest of American elites and their foundations with the intended purpose of securing even more power in the hall of Congress and containing potentially progressive demands on the system. And like Santelli, many others also deny any affiliation with the public face of the TPM. David Koch, for instance, publicly told the *New York Magazine* that "I've never been to a Tea Party event. No one representing the Tea Party has ever even approached me," nonetheless privately took credit for their accomplishments.[54] The Santelli advert thus foreshadows what would become an increasingly more theatrical and public display of the so-called alt-right agenda embodied in the astroturfing mobilization of TPM and its later incarnation, the Trumpites—followers of a know nothing, morally bankrupt, billionaire megalomaniac.

Scholars have pointed to four cultural traits as the primary disposition and cultural expression of TPM supporters: authoritarianism, libertarianism, nativism and ontological insecurity or fear of change.[55] These also happen to be the dominant features of late twentieth-century and early twenty-first-century American "conservatism": the emphasis on deference to authority, the expressed belief that there should be no or limited regulations, the negative attitudes toward immigrants and immigration, and finally the general fear that things are moving too fast. These features are expressed in rhetoric and policy preferences, although they are inconsistently embraced by TPM acolytes and supporters. Not only are they inconsistently adhered to, but they are contradicted and even frequently *denied* by Tea Party activists themselves. For instance, despite the idealization of the US Constitution as a feature of the deference to authority and the law, and a professed belief in libertarianism, researchers have found that the support for the Constitution is not absolute.[56]

TPM is noteworthy because it brings to the fore politics of nativity, particularly White nativity, and is animated by a way of life that has become increasingly governed by extreme inequalities and an ideology of radical exclusion. Among other things, it reveals an increasingly tenuous alliance between White supremacy and gendered racial capitalism in contemporary US life. While in specific spaces, race remains a primary organizing principle for capital accumulation and maldistribution of resources (as in the case of the disproportionate impact of the Great Recession and the COVID-19 pandemic on various communities of Color, especially Black and Brown people), White supremacy, virulent nativism, and toxic masculinity occasionally get in the way of wealth hoarding.[57] Claims of White nativity and particularly the singling out of non-White immigrants as scapegoats for economic hardships, nevertheless, conceals the intensity of economic inequality.[58] TP politics hide the fact that, in today's corporate global economy, the extremely wealthy in this nation and their multinational corporations (run by predominately White CEOs and boards of directors) have little investment in the well-being of the poor and the working class as a whole. The alliance between White supremacy and wealth accumulation (which are dependent on a gendered racial hierarchy of labor) thus continues to serve up benefits for the few and detriments for the many, despite periodic public performances of explicitly rejecting vulgar nativist and masculinist politics, including Trumpism.

TPM membership reveals explicit ideological investments in the mythic autarky. Self-identified TPM members are predominantly White (79 percent) and male (61 percent), and profess a conservative, libertarian political outlook, although their stance on various policies is inconsistent and not entirely transparent. More than 80 percent are self-identified Republicans; and more than 87 percent are dissatisfied with the mainstream Republican leadership.[59] Belying enduring myths of an elective affinity between racial enlightenment and wealth, TP members are employed and likely to be wealthier with more education, and over 74 percent believe that it is not government's job to ensure civil and social equalities. Overwhelmingly, they were unsympathetic to immigrants and LGBTQ+ people; they opposed diplomacy with countries with a large Muslim population, and were especially resentful of racial equality. In short, they were "more likely to be protestant, evangelical Christians, Republicans, over age 64, college graduates, White, make over $100,000 per year, and male."[60] As summed up by Thomas and Jacqueline Keil, TP politics is "one of class, status, and racial resentment."[61] Given members' privileged social positionality, TP "racial resentment" appears to be less material based and more tactical, if not manufactured.

Fittingly, TPM infrastructure is set up by a few super wealthy people and their private foundations. Its organizational structures consist of the Tea Party Nation, Tea Party Patriots, ResNet, FreedomWorks Tea Party, and the Tea Party Express. These intimately connected groups form the infrastructure of the movement. In addition to the David Koch founded Americans for Prosperity, four other groups directly propel Tea Party politics through financial and/or logistic supports: The Competitive Enterprise Institute, FreedomWorks,[62] the Heartland Institute, and Americans for Tax Reform. *Fox News*, owned by News Corporation and Rupert Murdoch, is a powerful media arm of these tea party groups. These groups are supported by a larger "network of 33 right-wing, corporate foundations," including the Olin Foundation, three Scaife foundations, and three Koch family foundations. They in turn finance "an array of 75 right-wing foundations, think tanks, and policy organizations, most of which support part or all of the tea party agenda" and "organizations involved in actively mobilizing tea party activists."[63] In short, billionaires and major corporate foundations directly provided both the infrastructure and the financial support for the mobilization of Tea Party politics and activism, not to mention TPM's genesis and talking points. TPM's claim to grassroots authenticity, therefore, is not unlike Santelli's staged performance—it is theater, personal aggrandizement, and a political fiction.

Until recently TPM was thought to have gone the way of one of its chief protagonists, Sarah Palin—absorbed into the *Fox News* ecology until no longer salient; however, and like most political fictions, it has pedagogical functions with afterlives of its own. In particular, and in not altogether different costuming, Trumpites and their MAGA nation would deliver what TPM could not, a leading actor to weaponize identity politics and deploy a populism not seen in more than a century. As noted, news agencies and congressional investigations have independently found that many individuals who participated in the January 6 insurrection are also former TPM members and organizers.

The making of TPM was indebted to what Canada's current deputy prime minister and former financial reporter, Chrystia Freeland, calls "the rise of the new global superrich."[64] With their "dark money,"[65] these new plutocrats as a class are not that different from those Cox understood as capitalists who were conscious of their interests as a class—they are intentional about their class interests and are willing to invest enormous amount to effect change.[66] Indeed, Jane Mayer, Freeland, and others have documented the predilections of contemporary plutocrats as singularly self-serving and autocratic in their outlook, harboring an undeniably authoritarian impulse. Their weaponization of right-wing populism thus is not an anomaly but part of the capitalist toolkit for survival, and foundational to governing and achieving "a favorable situation for the exercise of free enterprise and not for the planning of a society that will make business a social service."[67] Freedom as entitlement is reassured by the undercurrents of White supremacy. Just as plantocracy secessionists asserted their entitlement to White autarchy in the early 1860s, today's plutocrats and their ciphers are ascendant, accompanied by the "fall of everyone else."[68]

White totalitarianism therefore is motivated in part by the need to annihilate non-White subjects as a matter of course, a precondition for sustaining the impossible—the mythic White autarchy, itself a delusion of autarky. If we were to read fascism, including Nazism, as White totalitarianism, then American White supremacists—including the nativists and neo-confederates—have been fascist before fascists were born. That so-called nativists must look to the Nazis for inspirations and aspirations speaks to the impoverishment of their own historical training. As suggested here, White totalitarianism inscribed itself onto the nation-state at the moment of conception, such that the very framework for US citizenship has been and continues to be predicated on the idea of White supremacist belonging with its uninterrupted history of nativist imaginaries and racist immigration laws.[69]

Antecedents

On March 23, 1861, less than sixteen years after it was annexed from Mexico and became part of the United States, Texas seceded from the Union and joined the Confederacy. By a vote of 166 to 8, the Texas delegates proclaimed the following:

> We hold as undeniable truths that the governments of the various States, and of the confederacy itself, were established exclusively by the White race, for themselves and their posterity; that the African race had no agency in their establishment. . . . That in this free government of all White men are and of right ought to be entitled to equal civil and political rights; that the

> servitude of the African race, as existing in these States, is mutually beneficial to both bond and free, and is abundantly authorized and justified . . . while the destruction of the existing relations between the two races, as advocated by our sectional enemies, would bring inevitable calamities upon both and desolation upon the fifteen slave-holding states.[70]

The assertions of presumed nativity, White superiority, and entitlement; the exhortation to defend White privilege; the denial of Black agency and Black people's right to have rights; the erasure of the Indigenous populations; and the exigency of Christianity, together serve as a basic framework of modern White supremacy and justification for White autarchy. As one of the most succinct and enduring expressions of White supremacy as a doctrine, its template copied with closely worded articulations appeared in literature of various White supremacist and nativist organizations throughout the US. Indeed, several questions contained in the KKK's original *Prescript* in the 1860s specifically sought to ascertain its prospective members' stance on these same set of issues and, according to Kathleen Blee, "the Klan explicitly [identified] itself as a fellowship, or clan, of besieged and enraged white men,"[71] defending their rights and entitlements.

From the plantocracy of pre–Civil War America and nineteenth-century Jim Crow economics to twenty-first-century neoliberalism, gendered racial capitalism deploys race, racialism, and racism as well as gender and misogyny to efficiently affect the processes of wealth creation, accumulation, and hoarding, all the while relying on racial and gendered violence for the enforcement of White autarchy.[72] What W. E. B. Du Bois referred to as "the discovery of personal Whiteness among the world's peoples," came into being alongside the reality that the only people who were, increasingly stigmatized by their color could be owned and sold as slaves.[73] It matured alongside the equally brutal notion that the land on which "nonwhite" peoples lived would be better managed by "White people," and the twinning of White autarchy with freedom as entitlement—or the "American Creed."

THE CONCEITS OF GOVERNABILITY

As historian Stephanie Camp noted in *Closer to Freedom*, amid revolutionary fervor and public discoursing on the inalienable rights of Man, the Virginia Assembly intensified its regime of governing over Black life, codifying policies that sanctioned dismembering, killing, and destroying recaptured fugitives.[74] Remarkably, these policies stipulated harsher punishments for routinized rebellious acts over the extraordinary ones. As she explains: "In 1748 Virginia's lawmakers distinguished between outlying runaways (short-term runaways, those historians now call 'truants') and outlawed escapees (now known as 'runaways' or 'fugitives'). Surprisingly, it was not the outlawed that most concerned the assembly, but the outlying. In that year, in response to the 'injuries' that lurking truants were said to cause, lawmakers went so far as to make outlying a capital offense."[75] That the routine rebelliousness of bonded people struck the greatest fear in the minds of slavocrats is not surprising as it belies many claims of governability, exposing the vain attempt of total domination. Governing, after all, especially population management, is about regulating not only what is structural and visible but also the relational and liminal. Labor management thus inherently is also biopolitical management. Camp points out that "the need for rules struck at the core of what it meant to be a master in the antebellum years. For slaves were more to their owners than just property, and more than just workers; they were the building blocks of planters' way of life, social mobility, and self-conceptions."[76] Like an autoimmune malfunction, this dependency warrants constant surveillance and suppression. Camp's brilliant retelling of Nancy Williams, who as a young slave woman attended "secret parties," draws attention to the role "the body played in the slave-holders' endeavors to control their labor force and black resistance to that control."[77] These outlaw slave parties are the "secret spaces in the woods" where only slaves knew and went for their own pleasure, including dance, laughter, and feasting away from the prying eyes of slaveholders.[78] As Camp explains: "Despite planters' tremendous effort, enslaved women and men routinely 'slip[ped] away' to attend illicit parties where such sensual pleasures as eating, dancing, drinking, and dressing were among the main amusements. . . . Slaves' illegal parties took place in the very woods and swamps with which many planters marked off illicit plantation space and declared off limits. Dense thickets of woods and murky swampland nonetheless proved irresistible to bondpeople who longed for places of independent socializing and activity."[79] These are the spaces beyond the pale, where "enslaved women and men ran . . . where they enjoyed music, dancing, the company of others, and a shared secret."[80] However furtive and momentary, communal living comes alive:

> "Night after night" women prepared dishes into the late hours. Then, "in the morning," they headed back to their cabins, carefully "destroying everything likely to detect them" on their way. At the same time, the "knowing ones" continued to plan the celebration, encouraging one another's high spirits "with many a wink and a nod."
>
> Finally the appointed night arrived. A little after 10:00 p.m. the music began when an "old fiddler" struck up . . . here at the party "every dusky face was lighted up, and every eye sparkled with joy. However ill fed they

> might have been, here, for once, there was plenty. Suffering and toil was forgotten, and they all seemed with one accord to give themselves up to the intoxication of pleasurable amusement."[81]

From outlaw parties and outlaw dances to reappropriation of food and clothing, Camp insists that these "small outlaw activities" are not unconnected to a people building and reinventing communal infrastructures and lifeworlds—lives and worlds that were so brutally and violently appropriated, for "it seemed that the freedom bonded people tasted at night compromised their willingness to be deferential and obedient during the day."[82] In one community, such pleasure taking so alarmed the White residents that they "predicted the end of slavery as they knew it" if such "subordination" persisted. Citing the *Preamble and Regulations of the Savannah River Anti-Slave Traffick Association*,[83] Camp reveals the paranoia and vain conceits of slaveholders insinuating their rules:

> Reappropriating the "fruits of their own labors," working only with "sullenness [and] discontent," and skeptical of the authority of their owners, bondpeople in their neighborhood were creating "such a state of things [that] must speedily put an end to agriculture or to negro slavery." Engaging in these small, outlawed activities, the association argued, the "negro ceases to be a moral being, holding a position in the framework of society, and becomes a serpent gnawing at its vitals or a demon ready with knife and torch to demolish its foundations."[84]

As the revolutionary theorist Amílcar Cabral insisted in the midst of an independent war against fascist imperial Portugal, domination and oppression inevitably encounter cultures of resistance, and while it might be conceivable to achieve total domination of material life, culturally it is much more difficult to do so.[85] By reclaiming their bodies and reappropriating their labor however momentarily, enslaved people no longer are performing the roles scripted by either the slaveholding society in general or the administrative functions scripted by this anti-slave association. As they "transgressed these borders and made spaces [and stealing time] for themselves" and their communities, they not only "acted on the assumption that their bodies are more than inherently and solely implements of agricultural production";[86] as Angela Davis explained half a century ago, they also sustained the infrastructures of resistance and mobilization, including the Black family—"the only life at all removed from the arena of exploitation" of gendered racial capitalism.[87] The biopolitics of gendered racial capitalism thus is predicated on the securing and perfecting the governing of Black bodies, especially Black women's bodies.

(As chapter 5 illustrates, the struggles for reproductive justice and redefining freedom to include bodily autonomy are central to the refusal to be governed.)

So it is that from slave patrols to convict leasing, from mandatory sentencing to stop and frisk, from passbooks and overseers to BBQ Beckys and Permit Pattys—the policing of Black bodies and the enforcement of White supremacy necessarily warranted an antifascist politics and movements for Black liberation. As White supremacy's singular preoccupation is achieving White dominance in total, even if in totality it rarely succeeds; dialectically Black formations, especially feminist ones, frequently have sought the expulsion and negation of White supremacist ideas and praxes. In this way, these formations are necessarily antiauthoritarian and anti-fascist, and contemporary Black abolitionist feminist formations are part of this larger anti-fascist tradition.

By happenstance and design, Black women and men have organized and fought against policing since the moment they became targets of White enforcement.[88] Resistance against White totalitarianism is thus neither new nor alien to the Black freedom struggles. What appears to be distinctive in these times is the irrefutable fact that young, queer Black feminists are at the helms of the most strategic campaigns against fascism, including abolition feminists waging campaigns against prisons and police, pivoting their mass mobilization squarely against the specter of mass surveillance and imprisonment—the singular and sustained achievement of White supremacy.[89]

This work contends that fascism as a specie cannot be separated from White supremacy and anti-Black racism; as such, studies of anti-fascist praxes that exclude or marginalize Black formations have not adequately explored the vagaries of fascism. As early as the 1940s, the Black sociologist Oliver Cox understood the US as a "capitalist democracy," where capitalism essentially relies on White supremacy and racial violence for accumulation. Thus, racial capitalism inbred fascist formations.[90] Before Cox, and like Kea and Hughes, W. E. B. Du Bois also understood that fascism is grounded in a politics of White ethnicity and the insistence of White rule.[91] Anti-Black violence and the extractive accumulative practices that rely on racialized police violence as enforcement are therefore fascist,[92] especially as fascism is imbricated in patriarchy, as Virginia Woolf understood it when she maintained that "the unequal distribution of power between the genders is a key element of producing fascism."[93]

Movements against capitalist antidemocracy, of which many are Black feminist mobilizations,[94] are thus necessarily formations against fascism. Their care and feeding of resistance against White supremacy is the social reproductive labor that engenders anti-fascist present/futures. If we extend Patricia Hill Collins's framework of a Black feminist ethics of care[95] as part of the democratic ethos of the larger Black radical tradition, radical Black feminist formations are understood as those that emphasize radical egalitarianism, and are explicitly anti-white supremacist, anti-imperialist, anti-militarist, and anti-prisons. Such formations rejigger anti-fascist politics to be explicitly anti-racist and anti-heteropatriarchy. Black feminist organizing for national and communal independence, including struggles against apartheid, indeed have positioned their struggles as mobilization against racial capitalism, militarization, and fascist governance as embodied in police and other national security apparatuses.[96]

Absolute White rule (autarchy) grounded in the mythic nativist convictions of autarky and White supremacy frequently have been accompanied by violence, including state and extrajudicial violence. The permissiveness on the part of political and economic establishments to condone, if not outright sponsor, vigilante violence is neither new nor alien to the republic; fascism, vigilante violence, and White populism create the political sensibility that allows for "a well-ordered society."[97] In the aftermath of the Civil War when the federal government made reparations to former slave owners, national politicians along with state and local government entities actively encouraged the rise of vigilante groups to achieve total domination over the recently freed Black population—something they clearly failed to achieve during the era of slavery.[98] The rise of the most notorious terrorist organization in the US, the KKK, is but one example of the mobilization of White civilian combatants in the war against people of Color, and especially against Black people.[99]

The right to White rule, as a form of entitlement and its fatal consequences, evinces a certain genocidal logic that conscripts both state and extrajudicial violence as normative enforcement. This epiphenomenon may explain the apparent confusion with the rise of Trumpism. To be clear, Trumpism is a symptom of White rule, not its cause. Just as "MAGA country" is an outgrowth of White victimhood and entitlement, Trumpist populism points to a robust enforcement mechanism of White totalitarianism, not unlike the "accidental" post–Civil War administration of Andrew Johnson.[100] Johnson was more popular in the 1920s than at any time during his political career,[101] and this popularity betrays the general consensus throughout much of the twentieth century that Johnson was the worst of all US presidents. This embrace also reveals a particular affinity between Johnson, a staunch adherence of White rule, and a decade in which US-led racial capitalism announced itself as a global contending force, accompanied by the towering height of Jim Crow. It was during this era that Jim Crow apartheid was characterized by the rebirth or maturation of White terrorism and anti-Black violence,[102] best embodied in the convict leasing system that lasted nearly a century.[103] Nevertheless, even with the KKK and other White supremacist organizations experiencing significant growth in the immediate aftermath of the Civil War, again at the turn of the century, and well into the first two decades of the twentieth century, they were merely spectacular samplings of the larger, less sensational totality.

RECONSTRUCTING BLACK RADICAL PRAXES

Indigenous and Black resistance against White rule, therefore, also have entailed struggles against White vigilante violence and terrorism. Radical Black feminist ideography and praxes—from anti-slavery to anti-prison mobilization, have redefined gendered violence to capture the capacious monstrosity of White rule even as radical Black feminist formations embrace and prioritize a radical egalitarianism and inclusiveness that are distinct from the virulent exclusionary and entitled politics of grievance and privilege of White supremacy. In sensibility and as an ideologeme, radical Black feminism's insistence on deploying the world as a stage and the necessity of fashioning a transnational critique of racial capitalism and imperialism—including in the campaigns against lynching at the height of the Jim Crow era and at the dawn of the American empire—points to their astute recognition of the nature of aggressive expansionism, geopolitical strategic alliances, and the spaces of struggles that would necessitate a complex, intersectional analytics befitting their lives and worlds. That they recognize capitalism is also racial and gendered, that white rule was political, economic, and cultural, and that to get free, one needed to overhaul not one but multiple, complex interlocking systems of oppressions, suggest that their arsenals would be capacious and fundamentally different from an absolutist singularity of the reigning antidemocracy.

Their enduring devotion to addressing violence, including police violence and mass incarceration, and their persistent vision for a critical humanist praxis of bodily sovereignty and community self-determination, points to their embrace of differential vulnerability, with an anti-masculinist and anti-militarist stance that is distinct from the fetishization of violence, youth, masculinity, and militarism characteristic of fascist idolatry. US-based radical Black feminist formations—including those in the radical anti-slavery faction of the abolitionist movement, the anti-lynching movement, the Black Arts Movement, the movement to abolish prison, the movement to defund the police, and the Movement for Black Lives—explicitly reject all forms of authoritarianism and totalitarianism, including but not limited to gender policing, ablism, heteropatriarchy, capitalism, and White supremacy.[104] In short, they are transnationalist, anti-capitalist, anti-racist, and radical egalitarians. These are also many of the characteristics that appear in the scholarship defining anti-fascist formations. Evidently, radical Black feminists are the archetype of an "antifa," even as antifascist political imaginaries continue to script antifa as masculinist and of European stock.

The writing of Anna Julia Cooper, an active participant in both the National Association of Colored Women (NACW) and the Pan-African Congress, especially *A Voice from the South* (1892), exemplifies and thus is foundational to critical feminist episteme. Her intersectional and transnational framing of Black womanhood points to Black feminist prescient and prefigurative anti-fascist politics. Cooper's work, in particular, casts bright lights on the kinship between Jim Crow and fascism. As Imaobong D. Umoren explains, "race women internationalists [like Cooper] were part of the wider movements of Africans, Afro-Caribbean's . . . and African Americans [. . . and] their sojourns enabled them to create and participate in the transnational black public sphere. . . a community beyond the imperial or nation state."[105]

Few from that era and in direct confrontation with Jim Crow fascism were more brilliant and tactical than Ida B. Wells. Wells was an architect of the Anti-Lynching Movement—a journalist and one of the most astute, thorough, and passionate students and reporters of White terrorism in the US. Her involvement in the opposition against the 1893 Great Chicago World's Fair includes seizing the fair as a world stage to expose violence and terrorism.[106] Her writing and efforts to publish the eighty-one-page pamphlet *The Reason Why the Colored American Is Not in the World's Columbian Exposition* would forever mark the Fair as not only the symbol of White supremacy but also how Black feminist political thought has prefigured a multifaceted analytics of contemporary anti-Black violence.[107] As Davis and colleagues have pointed out, "Black feminist intellectuals and community-based activists [like Wells] have relentlessly attempted to articulated gender violence with anti-Black racism" as part of "mutually connected systems."[108]

Largely written by Wells, though coauthored with Frederick Douglass, *The Reason Why* is a masterpiece and remains one of the most cogent analyses of race, gender, and terrorism. It is also one of the most factually comprehensive accounts of racial violence through lynching in the US. It is not insignificant that Wells initially planned to publish the study in English, French, German, and Spanish, and later resisted numerous attempts to encourage her to abandon the project. She traveled domestically and internationally ahead of the publication to raise funds for its printing. That she recognized the transnational character of solidarity is especially noteworthy. By insisting on the transnational dimensions of racial violence and White supremacy, Wells understood the need to link domestic racial policies with global, capitalist competition and extraction. The pamphlet became what historian Ann Massa calls a "militant Black symposium."[109] Even as many Black newspaper editors condemned it for its radical critique and exposition of "American skeletons" in public, Wells remained steadfast with its publication and her international campaign against what she called "19th century barbarism." She delineated an extractive racial capitalist system as manifested in the forms of the "convict lease system, the chain-gang, vagrant laws, election frauds, keeping back laborers' wages, paying for work in worthless script instead of lawful money, refusing to sell land to Negroes and the many political massacres where hundreds of Black men were murdered for the crime (?) of casting the ballot." She explains that anti-Black intimidation and terrorism were enforcements of White rule: *"the Solid South means that the South is a unit for white supremacy.*"[110]

The exchange between the social democrat Jane Addams and Wells over lynching is instructive. Addams had written an opinion piece in 1901, "Respect for Law," in which she condemned lynching.[111] Wells replied with her own, "Lynching and the Excuse for It," wherein she took Addams to task for assuming that Black men who were lynched had done something wrong.[112] In this way, and despite their prior collaborations on anti-racist work and Wells's admiration for Addams as "the greatest woman in the United States," Wells nevertheless deemed Addams's position no better than the prevailing patriarchal, White supremacist justifications for anti-Black violence. She explained: "Among many thousand editorial clippings I have received in the past five years, ninety-five per cent discuss the question upon the presumption that lynching are the desperate effort of the Southern people to protect their women from black monsters."[113] Whereas Addams saw racism as waste causing inefficiency or "loss of capacity," and lynching as a misguided use of violence stemming from faulty morality, Wells understood lynching as a completely different species.[114] For Wells, lynching was an instrument of terrorism and unchecked violence of a morally bankrupt and politically ambitious class.[115] It was an enforcement of gendered racial capitalism. So, despite the general progressive acceptance of Addams's argument about lynching as potent and thoughtful, Wells's reasoning exposes the tendentious thought in Addams's logic—the assumed lack of morality on the part of Black men and the limits of liberal feminism.[116]

Wells's astute analysis of the uses of sexual phobias and monsterization of Blackness as race and caste enforcement continues to have relevance today. M4BL, like its progenitor in the anti-lynching movement, understands that in the killing of Black people there is little correlation between crimes and punishment, but it almost always is intimately linked up with the morally bankrupt campaigns of law and order and the maintenance of a heteropatriarchal, White supremacist system that relies on racial gendered violence as its chief regulatory mechanism for governing. But as DoVeanna S. Fulton asserts, the bodies of Black women and men who have been conscripted into slavery dialectically reveal "an alternative version of the master narrative."[117] Fulton's work on the speech act of enslaved Black women as an exposé of slavery as an institution is instructive not only because it counters the fallacious myths of the Cult of True Womanhood,[118] but also because it verifies the inability of systems of domination, including slavery and White supremacy, to achieve perfect "soul murders."[119]

Take the case of Silvia Dubois, born in 1786 to a father who fought in the American Revolutionary War. Dubois had agreed to tell her story to the physician C. W. Larison, narrating a life story that spanned from the revolutionary era to the height of Jim Crow. She highlighted the fact that she won her own freedom by refusing to be further subjected to cruelty and violence—inflicted by "the very devil himself"—the mistress of the house, Mrs. Dubois. Silvia Dubois's biography, as recorded by Larison and "translated" into standardized English by historian and editor Jared C. Lobdell, represents an imposition and a separation between Dubois and her readers; it nevertheless instantiates the countless stories of Black resistance and resilience against White governing.[120] After taking her own freedom from a negotiated truce with the male head of the household, she returned with her daughter to her birthplace, Sourland Mountain, New Jersey.[121] Recorded three years before her death, her oral biography tells with wit a potent story about her mother buying her own freedom, finding herself in the Dubois household, how she "whipt her mistress and won her negotiated freedom," then journeyed with her child through the forest, how she relocated her long lost mother, and, finally, how she ended up in a settlement not far from her grandfather where she died.

Dubois's life exemplifies the many instances of willful refusals against both the terror and violence of slavery and White supremacy, as well as the feat of getting free and living beyond the pale. Painter argues that Black slaves resisted attempted soul murders through their own support system by employing various resources, including spirituality.[122] Scholarly works by Black feminists such as Painter and Fulton emerged from larger Black freedom struggles, including the movements for epistemic justice like the Black Arts Movement (BAM) and ethnic studies formations.[123] Indeed, it has been nearly half a century since Davis asserted in her pioneering study "The Black Woman's Role in the Community of Slaves" that if we really want to understand the system, we must examine not only its constitutive parts but also its most oppressed victims.[124] Demystifying the overreliance on the racial regime of the "black matriarch," Davis pivoted to Black women's quotidian life and took up Black female slave resistance as an attempt to remap the "historical matrix" of race, gender and class oppressions.[125] She began with the presupposition that "if resistance was an organic ingredient of slave life, it had to be directly nurtured by the social organizations which the slaves themselves improvise."[126] American racism and its "brand of slavery," she argues, targeted the Black family as an institution because homelife to slavery are the spaces beyond the pale, of ungovernability, where life, living, and rebellions are cultivated.[127] Cogently, she noted a fascist parallel, pointing out that the Nazi regime "made a conscious attempt to strip the family of virtually all social functions" in the hope of crushing the family so that "*it could not become a center from which oppositional activity might originate.*"[128] For Nazis and White supremacists, radical social reproduction has to be stopped where its care and feeding take roots—in the family. Hence, community (re)building, including the strengthening of the family as a social institution, is a site for theorization of social insurgencies, and in Davis's case, Black insurgency.

With the benefits of five decades of research and hindsight amounting to an undeniable historical verification of Black people resisting slavery at every turn, today we can say unequivocally that Davis's theoretical insight has proven to be both strategic and prescient. For Davis, community (re) generation beyond the pale is world-building that begins in the home.[129] She methodically reconstructed the scenes of living and resistance, placing her readers on the path to the slave quarter where she locates the sources of radical transformation. Thus, the dialectics of Black women's oppression is "far more complex" as it "was honed in the bestial realities of daily experience"; hence, "the slave system would have to deal with the black woman as the custodian of a house of resistance."[130] So it was that their "routine oppression had to assume an unconcealed dimension of outright counter-insurgency," and in the final analysis, their status was "a barometer" of "the overall potential for resistance":

> Attendant to the indiscriminate brutal pursuit of profit, the slave woman attained a correspondingly brutal status of equality. But in practice, she could work up a fresh content for this deformed equality by inspiring and participating in acts of resistance of every form and color. She could turn the weapon of equality in struggle against the avaricious slave system which had engendered the mere caricature of equality in oppression. The black woman's activities increased the total incidence of anti-slavery assaults. But most important, without consciously rebellious black women, the theme of resistance could not have become so thoroughly intertwined in the fabric of daily existence.[131]

Just as Robinson called for a disengagement from "the terms of order" a decade later, Davis anticipated the need for a more complex analytic to subvert the metaphysics of mastery—the metalogic underwriting the drives toward perfection and singularity.[132] As the next chapter reveals, just as we cannot rely on antidemocrats for democratic thinking, we need to move from the state houses to the slave communities in search of democratic livability. Pivoting away, as Davis has done, requires dethroning the mystics and forgers of antidemocracy and locating paths toward the ungovernable.

As the next chapter will further corroborate, Black feminist thought and activism have sought to do what justice and democracy as paradigms have failed to do—predicating democratic sensibilities with the many instead of the few, and privileging the well-being of the people instead of servicing capital and securing the state. The ability of BLM and M4BL to complicate state-sponsored violence against people of Color—not only in the form of police violence and prisons, but also economic, cultural, and environmental violence—hints at a profound understanding of our heteropatriarchal and White supremacist system as an authoritarian, protofascist system, and also of the nature of radical social change. It reveals the intentionality of a movement that is conscious of itself as a practical and pragmatic response to police violence, as well as a contending moral force of a nation. It should compel passion and conscience. For these combatants, freedom is not an entitlement but a fight against and flight from White supremacy, anti-democracy, and totalitarianism, toward a more inclusive and just world. If the most fundamental task of justice movements is to help us imagine our ways toward just futures, then perhaps we ought to pay attention and learn.

3
Democratic Thought and the Unthinkable

[illegible]

Aristophanes[1]

To say, as has sometimes been said, that Athens fostered democracies in the allied cities amounts to little since ... the word demokratia in the fifth century had emotive force but little empirical content.

Raphael Sealey[2]

In the early months of 411 BC, Athens had been at war with Sparta, and the disasters from the Athenian proxy war in Sicily were mounting, depleting the empire's resources and encouraging Sparta and its allies to exploit the occasion for a swift victory.[3] The Athenian Assembly had voted to expand its war machine, bureaucratized its war management in the hands of ten elderly men, and established contingencies for a state of emergency, including provisions to suspend consultation over military expenditures. For Aristophanes, there was "guarded optimism about Athenian chances."[4] Nevertheless, even after placing its primary governing apparatuses in the hands of the worthy, there was a real possibility for defeat, with "the empire ... in danger of unravelling."[5] As the fortunes of war were debated, the question for dramatist Aristophanes was how disputes can be resolved "without loss of face."[6] The solution, as *Lysistrata* intimates, is to have women resolve the conflict through their guile in the form of sexual deprivation or a sex strike, while funds were cut off by the Assembly's wise men. *Lysistrata*'s "fantastic and utopian features are a measure of the gravity with which the spectators viewed their actual situation," most of whom, if not all, were presumably male and presumed to care greatly about such matters. David Stuttard disagrees, noting the play's context: "by the time Lysistrata was first performed ... many of the poorer Athenian males were now manning the warships in the Eastern Mediterranean; Athens was hemorrhaging moneys, soldiers, and allies."[7] Within this context, the *aristoi* in the Assembly plotted to overthrow Athenian democracy and make peace with the enemy. By mid-411 BC, they staged an oligarchic revolution, with the effect of terrorizing the Athenian *demos* into *voting democracy out in favor of tyranny*.[8] Thus *demokratia*, as Raphael Sealey observed, conceptually "had only minimal value as a descriptive or empirical term; its force resided in its complex overtones of approval or disapproval, dissuasion or commendation, hate or love."[9]

A dramatist of a different sort, Walt Whitman, whom June Jordan remembered as a poet of democracy,[10] thought that in our time, "the great poems, Shakespeare included, are poisonous to the idea of the pride and dignity of the common people, the life-blood of Democracy" because "our literatures . . . have had their births in courts, and basked and grown in castle sunshine; all smells of princes' favors."[11] Whitman's prognosis of what ails democratic thinkability in the west as something born of aristocratic heritage lays bare an antidemocratic ideologeme that infects contemporary political theory as a whole.

Since the time of ancient Athens, what has been taught and thought of as democracy has in fact largely been hostile to democracy, democratic thought, and democratic living. By the twentieth century under the reign of Pax Americana, even with the collapse of the former Soviet Union and the Eastern Bloc—the Cold War alternative to liberal western regimes, democracy had gone through several transmogrifications, with a somewhat bad reputation, depending on which governing scripts were in play. Today, with mobs crashing at the gates everywhere, including the US, the façade of democratic governing is crumbling, if not reduced to a mere masquerade for something much more sinister.[12] As the previous chapter suggested, the insurrectionist attempt by White nativists and protofascists on January 6, 2021, is not the only example of "American democracy" at risk, although it may have furthered antidemocratic ambitions among political elites. In the last two decades, more than a dozen instances of right-wing authoritarian movements have made significant inroads in the US and beyond.[13] France's Marine Le Pen gained nearly 8 percent more votes in 2022 than in 2017.[14] As *Al Jazeera* noted, "Macron Wins Election but Le Pen's Far Right Goes Mainstream."[15] This rise of authoritarianism, including populist varieties, ranges from Europe's anti-immigrant national front parties (Austria, Italy, France, Germany, Russia, Spain, and Turkey) to administrative states in Asia (China, India, Myanmar, the Philippines, and Thailand) as well as in Africa and the Americas (Brazil, Nicaragua, Uganda, the United States, and Zimbabwe). Such immense spread of authoritarianism and protofascist politics in recent years raises a question about the conditions that give rise to antidemocracy, and the efficacy of democratic counterinsurgencies.

There is a symbiotic relationship between development and antidemocracy, and fascist politics is one logical outcome of savage developmentalism where expansionism, dispossession, and repression are prioritized.[16] While some of these order-obsessed regimes do incite instabilities at the very top, instigating governing declines, they must be helped along by "the many insurrections" from the bottom. The mounting attack on democratic forms of politics and life, frequently sponsored and aided by, if not instigated from, the very top, forestalls transgressive possibilities. These developments compel a reexamination of democratic thinkability and the unthought for finding our ways out of the authoritarian muck. In search of a feminist democratic ethos, in this chapter I extend Cedric Robinson's critique of political science in *The Terms of Order*,[17] and resource the ungovernable and willful refusal to be governed as a conceptual toolkit for thinking about democracy not as rule but as a way of life.

In *Terms*, Robinson advances three specific arguments that form a frontal attack against the dominant understanding of democracy, supplying the terms of disengagement against the discursive order of democratic thinkability. First, and like Whitman, Robinson insists that democracy in the west is born of an elitist, imperial tradition. Second, political science as a knowledge enterprise is wedded to mythmaking, particularly the myth of leadership, masquerading leaders as authority and leadership as governing, and concealing its elusive and vain quest for perfect governing—an impossibility. And third, he maintains that dominant theorization of democracy has been dismissive of the idea of "the people rule," and contemptuous of the "many" in favor of the few. Robinson's aim was much higher than a critique of democratic theorization, as it is merely an instantiation of a larger ailment plaguing political science as a field. Nonetheless, his deconstruction of democratic elitism as an episteme remains one of the most potent critiques against this theoretical enterprise and contemporary democratic thinkability.[18]

Robinson charged that so-called serious thinkers do not consider "all the people rule" as a possibility, let alone believe it viable. Thus, democratic theorization prefigures the eventual eviction of the *demos*. If the *demos* is evicted from democracy in favor of an elite few while "all the people rule" is an unthought, then that polity is no longer a democracy but an antidemocracy. And what if we were to seriously take up the idea of "all the people rule"? What if, instead of the absence of civil strife or the well-being of the polity, we prioritize the well-being of the people, of all the people, as the sin qua non for justice? I argue that democratic livability grounded in an ethos of radical inclusion demands just that—taking seriously the idea of "all the people rule." Democracy becoming praxis is thus inherently relational; instead of it being about rules and ruling, it is a way of life.

Democracy, rule by the many, presupposes the existence of communal relations and is therefore different from autarchy, or absolute self-rule. Adherents of democracy or democrats, tend to be suspicious of autocrats because they deem the many to be wiser and more just than the few. As such, democratic living presupposes not only the possibility of self-governance but also the necessity of communal relations, not absolutist rule. This relational dimension to rule by the many presupposes a precognition of mutuality and incites a praxis of solidarity.

Historically, being ungoverned is the most potent defense against tyranny and in defense of democratic livability. Being ungoverned is not (and should not be conflated with) chaos and/or the state of anarchy. While counterintuitive, the refusal to being available for governing or the withholding of consent to be governed by various dominions, especially autarchy, constitutes a powerful alternative to order. This refusal thus has pedagogical and emancipatory functions, especially for democratic living. Not surprisingly, democratic living often is an unthought in discourses on democracy; far from an oversight, this suppression functions as antidemocracy's political unconscious.[19]

This chapter digs into the complicated terrains of antidemocracy to make the case for democratic living as praxis. Here, I take up democratic living as antidote for living in these times of climate catastrophe, wealth hoarding, and white supremacy. In so doing and at the risk of not sounding "serious," I locate "all the people rule" as a starting point of democratic contemplation. Retooling some of the most potent critiques of dominant theorizations of democracy, including Robinson's, part I delineates the political undercurrents and ideological investments of the discourse on democracy in the west; part II charts the main currents of democratic thinkability, especially neoliberalism's deleterious effect on democracy; and part III grounds democratic living as a feminist ethic of liberation.

PART I. THE TYRANNY OF DEMOCRATIC THINKABILITY

Democracy has a complicated and contentious history. In in its most elemental form, democracy means rule by the people. "The people rule" assumes that juridical subjects are marked as those who belong. Some of the most widely read sources on democracy, including by self-declared democrats, are predisposed against democracy, distrustful of the *demos*, and frightful of their aspirations. Others, rather than getting bogged down by ambiguities and contingencies of democracy, take up citizenship instead—a facsimile of belonging and the art of exclusion. Yet others rehearse democratic chants only to conjure up specters of tyranny, pining for containment and curbing popular excesses. Perversely, the most influential are frequently those who claim to be revising or recalibrating for the purpose of saving democracy as we know it.

Democratic Elitism

Elitist theories of democracy typically point to the lack of self-control and unpredictability of the *demos* as grounds for mistrust and excluding the larger population from the political life of the community. These advocates, including some self-identified democrats, argued that size matters, and that the larger the community, the less viable it is for the people to be directly involved in the work of a democracy. Unfortunately, theories of direct democracy do no better than advocates of deliberative democracies in their defense of democracy as *rule by the people*. First, "direct democracy" is redundant, suggesting that forms of democracy other than the direct involvement of the *demos* are also rule by the many. Second, by presupposing nondirect democracy as viable, they undercut their own arguments about the need and feasibility for the *demos* to be involved in the work of the polity. As M. I. Finley astutely noted, "self-control is very different from apathy," and those who are apathetic are no use to the political life of a community.[20] While extolling the virtue of citizen subjects being directly involved in the polity beyond the narrow confines of elections as the essence of democracy, they do little to deflect the erroneous and elitist doctrine that effective popular deliberation is impossible on a larger scale (i.e., national level) because the populace's demands and deliberation are seen as extreme or lacking restraint.[21] This pathologizing of the *demos*—as extreme, ungovernable, and therefore unworthy—to justify exclusion and/or domination has proven extraordinarily effective by elites in various arenas. As the following chapters will show, the pathologizing of communities and people as ungovernable, troublemakers, or willful and therefore not trustworthy of political participation, has been extraordinarily violent, if not effective for radical exclusion and/or marginalization. After all, "American democracy" as apartheid is a historical verification of White belonging and the violent expulsion (with some strategic incorporation) of all non-White others.

Many critics of elitist theories of democracy, as Finley charged, did not succeed in their defense of democracy in part because they seek solutions to appease their detractors instead of defending the sine qua non of democracy—the *demos*' role as the deciders in chief.[22] Similar to Finley, Cedric Robinson exposed these onto-epistemological undercurrents of antidemocracy as products of western elitism and authoritarianism masquerading as modern science and rationality. He asked: "How is it that the celebration of democracy as the institutionalization of Just power . . . , is there never the slightest suggestion of the absurdity of identifying this construct with the reality of mass societies as they exist in North America, Western Europe and elsewhere?"[23] This, Robinson maintained, has to do with "democracy" being "disassembled, particularly by the invested, including political theorists for whom 'understanding' of democracy has become so expedient."[24] Joseph Schumpeter's delineation of the "democratic method," a pillar of elitist theorization of democracy, is a leap of faith that a political system would rule efficiently, primarily through containing the unruly passion of mass society.[25] Schumpeter's claim that "there exists no more democratic institution than a market" delivering "maximum satisfaction" reveals a deep utilitarian bias and breathtaking ahistoricity.[26] Given authoritarianism is ascendant, Schumpeter's enduring influence merits renewed scrutiny.

First, Schumpeter supplanted "the people" from "the people rule" then conflated "making decision" with "ruling," while dismissing "rule by the people" as "not sufficiently precise."[27] Materialized out of whole cloth, "democracy" is now reducible to "the democratic method"—understood as "that institutional arrangement for arriving at political decisions,"[28] with "competitive struggles for votes" synonymous with democracy.[29] It is not surprising that within this frame the people become a mere avatar of rule.

Such an eviction of the people from democracy is only possible when rule becomes the sine qua non for political association. The archive of western political thought can be understood as an enterprise devoted to governing and the naturalization of political authority. This democratic thinkability predefines the parameters of thought: "merely in terms of what is meant by the term 'the people,' one moves from democracy as the rule of the mob and of the rabble to its contrary, the rule of the functionally invisible and the invested. And yet there is a third meaning of the 'people' which seems to have had little practical value except to the unsophisticated, and that is, of course, the most obvious meaning: 'all the people.'"[30] "The people," evicted from substantive theorization, becomes merely "an ideograph," reducible to what is preferable—the selection of leaders as rulers.[31] While Schumpeter was not the first or only participant in this removal project, his pernicious influence endures because his work extends dominant thinkability on democracy, including neoliberalism's many creative and not so "creative destruction" of democratic ways of life.

Second, by employing unsubstantiated claims of market efficiency to justify a false analogy between democracy and the "market," Schumpeter followed a long line of "ideologues of a class and a civilization in formation, [who] subverted the fundamental ideas of which theirs was historically succeeding while laying the foundations for the political of a market society."[32] This theoretical restoration project was mostly preoccupied with producing an elitist logic and justification for a state that would be governed by the market, as Schumpeter inverted the idea of "the people rule" to that of "representative democracy." By the mid-twentieth century, however, "representative democracy . . . itself subverted by the behaviorists"; "democratic ethos . . . itself savaged by replacing concepts of process with system; the people with groups; representative with pressure group notables (or elites), with the effect of the people being further and further away from rule and from participation."[33] The virulent influence of Schumpeter's approach and democratic elitism would also infect other arenas of thought because justice too was gutted, eviscerating substance from form, as order and proceduralism became *causa formalis*.

The Fairness of Rules

Contemporary theories of in/justice suffer from a similar ailment as does democracy as a paradigm—a preoccupation with procedural instead of substantive justice. Like Schumpeter's *Capitalism*, John Rawls's *A Theory of Justice* is no less influential or pernicious. Dreamed up by "one of the most influential political and moral philosophers of the 20th century,"[34] Rawlsian justice is foundational, and as one scholar noted in an introductory justice theory textbook, everyone who comes after Rawls either refutes or extends Rawls's paradigm.[35] Contemporary conceptions of justice indebted to Rawls have not traveled far from his mid-twentieth-century liberal choice theorization of justice, disassembling and delimiting justice to procedural fairness in much the same way that Schumpeter delimited democracy to economistic proceduralism. Like the democratic method, Rawls's "justice as fairness" excludes material differences from theoretical consideration or explains them as excess or auxiliary. For Rawls, race, gender, and other important social cleavages are excluded from "the original position"—a mythical space central to his thought experiment[36]—generically dismissing race and gender stratifications as "particularly odious" and part of ancient regimes.[37] Since Rawls, theories of justice largely pivot on procedures, focusing on the "basic structure" of a "well-ordered society," while ignoring the very things that make justice an unreality for the many.[38]

The core assumption of Rawlsian in/justice, as Rawls restates, is "mainly concerned with ideal theory: *the account of the well-ordered society of justice as fairness*."[39] Charles Mills points out that on the question of race, Rawlsian thought, like liberal philosophy, suffers from "non-existent or at best problematic attempts to deal with race and justice."[40] This deracination is consequential: "Here is this huge body of work focused on questions of social justice—seemingly the natural place to look for guidance on normative issues related to race—which has nothing to say about racial injustice, the distinctive injustice of the modern world."[41] After examining all of Rawls's major books—works that sought to explain the meanings of justice, Mills found that "nowhere . . . does Rawls discuss the racial views of, for example, Locke, Hume, Kant, Hegel, Mill, or their relation to European colonialism."[42] Nor did Rawls take up race, racism, White supremacy, or colonialism for exploring in/justice as an episteme.[43] While his theorization remains foundational, in/justice is disembodied from the "hierarchies and accumulated advantages that are engendered by social differences such as gender, race, and class."[44] Thus, failing to successfully resolve the chronic tensions between two major principles—liberty and difference—Rawls either suppressed or naively ignored the material differences that exist within and among polities.[45] Having justice now disembodied and dispatched from the context in which it might be meaningful, Rawls proceeded to rely on ideational apparatuses like the "original position" and "veil of ignorance" to sever justice completely from reality, leaving the victims of injustices with only administrative violence with which to contend.[46] Like fish in water, Rawlsian justice thrives in antidemocracy, spawning absurd notions such as race neutrality and "reverse discrimination" in a white supremacist world order.

E Pluribus Unum

Rawlsian justice as fairness finds no quarter within the context of freedom and injustice of the antebellum US. The Confederate war was a defense of the plantocracy—an aristocracy of the plantation and the entitled autarchy of slave owners. "American democracy," as we know it and as de Tocqueville observed, was and is still an antidemocracy.[47] Part of antidemocracy's toolkit is a mythical pluralism inherited from the revolutionary elites—the idea that, like the marketplace, the American political system consists of multiple and competing ideas and factions. As a political ideologeme, pluralist conceptions of democracy come in several varieties and serve as a foundation of western liberal democratic theory. Its core assumptions posit that society consists of more than one group and these groups compete (with equal footing) to advance their own interests. The conflation of equality with equity is part of its mysticism, and "the people" is thus anemically reduced to equally competing social groups. As descendants from the likes of Plato and Schumpeter, pluralist adherents dismiss "all the people" out of hand.[48] Hewing close to Schumpeter's rational choice proceduralism, they insist that the basis of political legitimacy and therefore authority is the presumptive competition that determines winners and losers. Individuals representing groups compete, and the selection of winners are determined by various institutional arrangements. When leaders are elected, they therefore "won" a competitive struggle and are thus legitimate.

At the heart of this mythical pluralism is the conceit that democracy or the people rule cannot work in real life, and because it is so, its essence must be exorcised for the system to function. Pluralism is thus aspirational because the people do not rule, but groups of elites do, depending on the resources available to them, but always with elite governing.[49] Robert Dahl's seminal work on polyarchy, for instance, is a theory that confuses power with decision-making and conflates authority with governing, all the while defending and normalizing elitist rule. Purported to be the work of political science and empiricism, Dahl's theory, nevertheless, extrapolates gross generalizations from limited findings of small localities, and in one case, from only two small towns in the United States.[50] This antidemocratic episteme solidifies the notion that the people cannot be trusted with decision-making because they will likely opt for nondemocratic outcomes and, to prevent those very outcomes, institutional arrangements must be put in place to ensure that the political system will be protected from purely democratic elements. Dahl thus preposterously claims "polyarchy" as rule by the many. By the many, he meant the elites, and the institutional arrangements as the essence of democratization.

Pluralism thus takes on a peculiar quality, as it divides rather than multiplies the many into a few. Pluralism presupposes multiplicity; within the frame of dominant democratic theory, however, such multiplicity presupposes competing elites and, for Dahl, only well-heeled interest groups. By privileging stability and authority over all other considerations, pluralism betrays its name by presupposing that as a system it cannot accommodate democratic elements of the same said system. In short, its achievement is not a theory of democracy but a defense of antidemocracy, including democratic elitism—a bewildering, if more honest, label.[51]

In Fear of the Demos

In a more recent reappraisal of "democratic elitism," Heinrich Best and John Higley maintain that, while Schumpeter did not use this term to characterize his work, *Capitalism* constitutes "the most important effort to reconcile democracy with the existence of the elites."[52] They explain that democratic elitism "means only the elites play a major role in governance," and "holds that elites protect democratic order from the unsophisticated."[53] In short, this is a perversion of democracy, especially as "democratic elitism became synonymous with representative democracy."[54] Central to this attack on "participatory democracy" or "direct democracy" is, no doubt, the idea that apathy or "mass political quiescence is essential to the stability and health of democracy."[55]

Not surprisingly, if perversely, adherents of democratic elitism maintain that mass participation promotes inequality and contributes to the rise of illiberal regimes, such as totalitarianism, dictatorship, and/or fascism—in a word, tyranny. Both Plato and Aristotle laid the groundwork for this sensibility as they place democracy adjacent to tyranny, and their progenies identify the many as the source of that adjacency. It may be true that an unequal power relationship between the ruler and ruled can create conditions where the majority becomes disaffected and alienated, though no more vulnerable to antidemocratic forces than the elites themselves. As such, great attention must be paid to the "illiberal" or "antidemocratic" propensities of the elite, especially the ruling elite, as well as that of the mass. That a people can turn to White supremacy or become fascist is not evidence of ordinary people's inherent propensity to become racist; it does, however, point to the conditions of possibilities of fascism and White supremacy that need unmasking. By successfully subverting the meanings of democracy, theorists manage to produce a paradigm in which the very authority of the *demos* is transformed into a method of legitimizing elite rule.[56]

Schumpeter's thesis advancing democratic elitism serves as a metaphysics for the churning out of contemporary treatises on the virtues of western liberal democracies, as theorists of various political stripes casting doubt and blame against the *demos*, warning us against trusting the people to rule wisely and urging us to defend the authority of the state. Notably, and at the height of the war against fascism in Europe, a debate of sorts was ongoing in North America, centering on the nature of democratic living. As one contributor to the venerable *New York Times* breathlessly observed, "In the Legislature, over the radio, at the luncheon table, in the drawing rooms, at meetings of forums and in all kinds of groups of citizens everywhere, people are talking about the democratic way of life."[57] Charles A. Beard, the progressive historian revealed his own parochialisms as he predicted that democracy in the US would survive fascism if only because "there is in America, no Rome, no Berlin to march on."[58] In contrast, W. E. B. Du Bois vehemently disagreed: he understood the inherent contradictions of US antidemocracy when he insisted that fascism has White supremacist roots, explaining that American democracy would die "if it is going to use this power to force the world into color prejudice and race antagonism; if it is going to use it to manufacture millionaires, increase the rule of wealth, and break down democratic government everywhere; if it is going increasingly to stand for reaction, fascism, White supremacy and imperialism; if it is going to promote war and not peace; then America will go the way of the Roman Empire."[59] There were lectures on "the future of democracy," studies on the importance of education and civic culture, and theoretical tracts maligning too much dissent and the danger of having all the people rule.[60] Against this backdrop, the specter of an impending horde of right-wing populism yielded a must-seize opportunity for theorists to advance their antidemocracy in the form of rational pragmatism. These pragmatist elites, some calling themselves liberals and progressives, advocated social reforms to incentivize against the seduction of militancy. Others, even respectable reformers, advocated eugenics against the "unfit."[61] Democratic living as a notion thus emerged as a counterdistinction, not to elitism or racial stratification but an assessment of fascism. It is within this context that democratic elitism was offered up as an antidote to fascism (and presumably communism) and to ensure its success, theorists began to issue a series of prerequisites for the many to learn the art of living with democracy. With this metaphysics of authoritarianism intact, a civic culture could be taught, and rationalism could be learned, and the hordes of unlearned individuals eventually would graduate to the status of obedient citizen subjects.

PART II. THE TYRANNY OF THE POLITICAL

By the dawn of the twenty-first century, this citizenry has become unmoored if not entirely evicted from the apparatuses of ruling, not least in part due to relations of property. In her work *Undoing the Demos*, Wendy Brown raises a red alert on this "stealth revolution" against democratic societies, especially in the metropoles of the neoliberal world system.[62] She explains that a democratic transmogrification was brought about by neoliberalism, setting in motion "democracy's conceptual unmooring and substantive disembowelment."[63] In the span of three decades, "Western democracy" had gone "gaunt, ghostly, its future increasingly hedged an improbable."[64] Neoliberalism is thus more than a set of economic policies or an ideology; instead it is "a normative order" that has developed "into a widely and deeply governing rationality."[65] Placing partial blame on Foucault's hostility toward Marx's work for his failure (and presumably others') to anticipate the many formations of neoliberalism as it wages this revolution against the *demos*, Brown calls for the need to divest from Foucault's overvalorized *homo economicus* and instead embrace the political.

Undoing the Demos is emblematic of contemporary critiques of neoliberal governance and capitalism, thus instructive for cyphering contemporary democratic thought and thinkability. For Brown, Foucault's account of neoliberalism "differs significantly from conventional accounts"[66] at times resembling "an anti-Marxist rant," other times, reflecting "his own attraction" to neoliberalism.[67] So, despite providing a useful framing of neoliberalism, Foucault failed to capture its "stealth revolution" against democracy, missing out on neoliberalism as a normative order, as it devours democracy and devalues the political. In this neoliberal world order, the logic of economic being (*homo oeconomicus*) displaces all other logics of being, including, and especially, the political being (*homo politicus*).[68] Consequently, "the construal of *homo oeconomicus* as human capital leaves behind not only *homo politicus*, but humanism itself."[69] This vanquishing of homo politicus therefore is both the cause and effect of the undoing of democracy. Appropriating an Aristotelian metaphysics, Brown maintains that men, by definition, are political animals, and homo politicus is "the creature who rules itself and rules as part of the demos."[70]

At one level, *Undoing the Demos* is an epic documenting of human catastrophe in the making. At another level, Brown's remarkable text resembles an attempt to resolidify the currents of (neo)liberal political thought. The primary antagonist in Brown's tale is homo oeconomicus, and the magical creature that may save us all is homo politicus, as embodied (western) liberal political thought. In homo politicus, Brown's *demos* find their subjectivity, agency, sensibility, moral capacities, and sovereignty. The stealth revolution that neoliberalism has been waging against the *demos* is a frontal assault on homo politicus. It is also an exhaustive counterfigure of homo oeconomic as "the agent, the idiom, and the domains through which democracy—any variety of democracy—materializes;[71] and, "animated by and for the realization of popular sovereignty as well as its own individual sovereignty, the creature who made the French and the American Revolutions and whom the American Constitution bears forth, but also the creature we know as the sovereign individual who governs himself."[72]

Accordingly, homo politicus "withered in the seventeenth century" and "died in the eighteenth century" as capitalism matured and "Aristotle has been inverted, if not buried."[73] Some aspects of homo politicus, however, survived. Conjuring the political unconscious of social contract theory, Brown evokes the state of nature (à la Locke and Rousseau) to suggest a "primordial politicalness" that "never fades completely."[74] In these liberal political veins, then, homo politicus, however anemic, persisted, and "only toward the end of the twentieth century did *homo oeconomicus* (in its distinctly neoliberal iteration) finally gets the better of *homo politicus*."[75] Building on Foucault's characterization of homo oeconomicus as "eminently governable,"[76] Brown imbued the tragically vanquished creature homo politicus with qualities that may seem alien even to its progenitors.[77]

Brown's democratic imaginary of homo politicus finds little reflection in Aristotle's, even if she credits him for giving birth to such a fantastic creature, and ancient Athens for sheltering it. Aristotle's democratic imaginary is one that radically excludes and places democracy adjacent with tyranny, a source of our basic antidemocratic sensibility. Crediting him for the most progressive read of democracy, as "rule by the poor,"[78] she forgives Aristotle's "certain instrumentalism that could easily get out of hand."[79] Aristotle's argument about equality among male citizen subjects as homo politicus somehow holds no apparent contradiction with his explicit prescription for property relations that include women and slaves as incapable of the very same ethical-political sphere that Brown extols.[80] Aristotle's paternalistic proclamation that rules between citizens and noncitizens are "beneficial to both rulers and ruled," nonetheless, becomes a life raft for a resuscitation of the drowning homo politicus.

When Aristotle explains that "tyranny being the perversion of kingship; oligarchy of aristocracy; and democracy of polity [constitutional government]. . . . Democracy is directed to the interest of the poorer class,"[81] he meant that democracy was a degenerative perversion of a superior political form and implied that some concessions needed to be made to the poorer class because its presence promised permanent stasis or civil strife. Aristotle's chief concern was with maintaining social order, especially over the poor as its enemy,[82] while his aristocratic bias was also transparent: "Those constitutions which consider only personal interest of the rulers are all wrong constitutions, or perversions of the right forms. Such perverted forms are despotic; whereas the city is an association of freeman."[83] Aristotle conceded that democracy is the "least bad" compared with oligarchy and tyranny in descending order, it is nevertheless a perverted, inferior form of government, especially when compared to kingship and aristocracy. There is more than one form of democracy, but what differentiates them from an oligarchy primarily concerns relations to property.[84] Democratic passion has to be moderated because "tyranny grows out of the most immature type of democracy"[85] and "extreme democracy" where "all should meet to deliberate on all issues" is tyrannical.[86] Favoring moderation, Aristotle stipulates that democracy could be "more, or less, democratic,"[87] conveniently rendering democracy capacious enough to accommodate the subordinated social positions of women and slaves.[88] A political prescription of citizen subjects as equal and sovereign existing side by side with the unfreedom for women and slaves is more than instrumentalism getting out of hand. It is an antidemocratic ideologeme that is fundamentally hostile to difference. Aristotle evicted difference from his democracy so that equality and sovereignty could cohere even as he sought to naturalize the subordination and unfreedom of the other.[89] In short, an Aristotelian democracy is a place with distinction but without difference, and that distinction, he feared, is but the singular antagonism against the propertied class.

There is little doubt that neoliberalism's frontal attack on democratic living and the idea of rule by the people has been devastating, and with fatal consequences. This assault, however, is older than Brown purports. The homo politicus who might have been vanquished by the neoliberal stealth revolution (if Brown is right) was one that was not particularly interested in either radical egalitarianism or the type of substantive justice that is needed.

A resurrection of the political as embodied by homo politicus likely will not correct neoliberal's antidemocratic assault as much as it deflects contemporary antidemocracy. More than four decades ago, Robinson understood that emancipatory potentials of human communities lie not with homo politicus or any political order but in the absence of order. Robinson was clear about how we can be too reliant on the political, and this reliance is not incidental; he argued that what we need is to reject the political "as an ordering principle."[90] His critique of the political offers a robust counter-theorizing effort against neoliberalism and antidemocracy, including the political as order.[91] Theorists' reliance on the political as an episteme reveals their intellectual investments in establishing an alien concept—political order (i.e., the state) as a natural phenomenon. Worse, the state "in its highest form" is understood as the "most progressive manifestation that "had achieved political emancipation."[92] In this way, political liberty is the sine qua non of liberal ideology.[93] In trying to capture homo politicus in its most authentic form, Brown ended up excavating an entirely western genealogy, with nary a hint of registering a world that could exist outside of this peculiar occidental obsession. The problem with the political as a paradigm is that it "is always there" and always in the service of governing, setting down discursive terms for the naturalization of order.[94] The tyrant in the neoliberal world order might be homo economicus; tyranny, however, shows up in the form of homo politicus.

Searching for Unicorns

In the wonderful essay "From Marco Polo to Leibniz," Umberto Eco related a story about how medieval Europe convinced itself that unicorns existed and because it did not materialize in Europe, "tradition decided that unicorns were living in exotic countries, such as the kingdom of Prester John in Ethiopia."[95] Eco suggests that "when Marco Polo traveled to China, he was obviously looking for unicorns,"[96] and proceeded to report that he saw unicorns in Java when they were in fact rhinoceros. Eco explains that Marco Polo did not lie about seeing unicorns; instead, he suffered from a misperception resulting from his "background books" filled with "preconceived notions of the world."[97] And thus "we travel knowing in advance that we are on the verge of discovering, because past reading has told us what we are supposed to discover."[98] In other words, misperceptions or misunderstandings emerged as a result of seeing "the unknown in the light of the already known."[99] One could say that many contemporary critics of neoliberalism went looking for democracy and in the process found their unicorn in the homo politicus.[100]

Plato's *Republic* and Aristotle's *Politics* serve as background books or the political unconscious for contemporary democratic thinkability. To excavate a genealogy of democracy, Brown, for instance, invites us to reach back to ancient Greece and its lifeworld presumably because democracy was in its most authentic form. Grounded in these roots and relying exclusively on a few noted western thinkers to supply democracy's contemporary variants, Brown settles for a definition of democracy as that which "generates ambiguity and dispute."[101] She relies on Plato as a font of wisdom on the good life, including Plato's need for "remaking the soul," his concern over "the household becoming scenes of wealth accumulation,"[102] as well as his concession to include a few women into the upper echelon and his distaste for slavery.[103] Nevertheless, because he "dispatches *homo politicus* as he establishes the rule of the republic by philosophy,"[104] Plato must be dispatched to be replaced by Aristotle, even as Aristotle naturalizes the subordination of women and slaves while defending private acquisitions. After all, it was Aristotle who provided the life raft when he pronounced that "man is by nature a political animal" who cannot exist outside of the polis or political community.[105] So Aristotle supplied the artifact of the unicorn in the form of homo politicus.

Contemporary democratic thinkability dispels our mistaken need to rescue homo politicus or rehabilitate Aristotle; after all, Aristotle is still foundational and homo politicus remains paradigmatic, as it did more than four decades ago. Nonetheless, rehabilitation sometimes requires enlisting others for support. To fully rescue Aristotle from the ranks of parochial male classicists and prop up both Aristotle and homo politicus, Brown drafts Karl Marx and Hannah Arendt—two iconic thinkers who can supply the street cred needed to establish Aristotle's liberal ideologeme. In doing so, she astutely resuscitates Aristotelian economics, casting neoliberal's wealth hoarding as not only irrational but also detrimental to "the good life."[106] This rehabilitation also elevates Aristotle to the same class of modern liberal thinkers as Marx and Arendt.[107] Apparent contradictions notwithstanding, once this elevation is complete, wholesale appropriation of Aristotelian ethics can be extended not only to the critique of neoliberal economics but also to the justification of the exalted status of the political. The trouble with neoliberalism is not just that it replaces everything else with wealth acquisition, "if neoliberal rationality were to succeed" and the political vanquished, the *demos* may find themselves "discursively disintegrated" without the necessary language or sensibility to envision radical aspirations for democracy.[108] While neoliberal governmentality might have left homo politicus bereft of nothing other than memories of the state, this is in no small part due to the exalted status of political and state addiction, rendering the state's moral authority along with its memories as our own. It is the contention of this work that an abolition feminist ethic of care is far more superior and viable as alternative to existing dominant discourses on moral and ethics, especially one dictated by dominions such as the state, capital, and other cultural hegemons, including racialized logic or theocracy.[109] Writing amid a neoliberal insurrection, the poet June Jordan put it this way:

> Understandably we shrivel and retreat into stricken consequences of that catastrophe.

But we have choices, and capitulation is only one of them.

I am always hoping to do better than to collaborate with whatever or whomever it is that means me no good.[110]

Brown's sustained argument about homo politicus being more capacious than the inferior homo oeconomicus relies on her defense of Aristotle's politics and the polis as a metaphysics that has been sublimated but must be rematerialized. To the slave and female residents of Aristotle's polis, this characterization of the political community is, at best, an embellishment; worse, it is a specious hedge. Man is ordained to self-rule and be "deliberately governed," a means to perfectibility, and the political polis becomes an epiphenomenon, so capacious as a singular source of our senses and reasons, including our moral reflection and relations.[111] Here, our rootedness in the political being or politicalness is owed to moral reflection and association making. Other than "beasts and gods," Aristotelian dictates prefigure humans as destined to be ruled, for without the polis there is no justice, no spaces for an existence that "exceeds concerns of mere survival."[112] While there is little doubt that gendered racial capitalism, including its neoliberal varieties, has engendered violence, genocide, and antidemocracy, replacing homo oeconomicus with another subject of the same progeny, as Jordan warned, is potentially a costly hedge, not to mention leaving so much more to be desired. If our entire arsenal rests on the polis as a place where the human as political animal is at home and where human perfectibility can be achieved, it is resting on dubious grounds—grounds inherited from *an* Aristotelian epiphenomenon for householding (*Oikos*), where slaves and women as noncitizen subjects, teleologically existing to care and sustain the lifeworld of the polis and creating leisure for someone else; grounds where a philosophy of liberation of the many is profitably supplanted with an ethic of entitled freedom of the few.

The Mysticism of Ruling

The household or *Oikos*, the root of modern terminology for economics, is the basic unit in many Greek city-states, including Athens. Aristotle claimed that the household arrangement with its subordination of women and slaves under the patriarch is natural, thus ipso facto moral, and therefore morally acceptable to exclude women and slaves as citizen subjects.[113] As G. E. M. de St. Croix suggests, Aristotle, while acutely aware of class struggles in the ancient world, nevertheless studiously abandoned his otherwise extraordinary grasp of class analytic and the actual management of the household when he naturalized Athenian male superiority and defended class divisions and social hierarchies.[114] The slave economy, the dominant mode of exploitation in many

Greek city-states, was linked with the management of Greek households, and not unlike in Jeffersonian democracy, "the unspoken assumption [is] the men of property will own and use slaves."[115] The slave, Aristotle explained, is part of the household, and "the art of acquiring property" or wealth accumulation "is part of the household management."[116] Moreover, conflicts and struggles are among the differing classes of citizens, and not between citizens and noncitizen subjects.[117] With this, Aristotle supplied one of the west's first articulated defenses of slavery and the total exclusion of women and slaves from political life. Rationalizing the subordination of women and slaves, he proclaimed that "the slave is entirely without the faculty of deliberation; the female indeed possesses it, but in a form which lacks authority; and children possess it, but only in immature form."[118] This defense of slavery is possible not only by justifying a mystical superiority of the ruler and inferiority of the ruled, but also by suggesting a benevolent and paternalistic quality inherent in ruling. Unmoored from empiricism, Aristotle asserted an innate moral authority of the ruler over the ruled, ensuring the legitimacy of the ruler on grounds of absence and presence of virtue.[119] Like many subsequent slavery apologists, Aristotle settled the slavery debate by claiming that there are "benefits" that come with being ruled. As illustrated in the next chapter, where some erroneously imagined the rules of the polis to hold a certain promise of radical egalitarianism (the rules are beneficial for everyone), a slave might reason otherwise. Given that Aristotle scripted these subjects as deficient or lacking (of property, logos, temperance, and moral authority), he was quite clear about what he thought were the right relations of ruling—those who possess the faculty of the soul should rule those who do not, thus evicting women and slave, not only from political life but also barring them the status of ruler.[120]

In extolling the virtues of the polis, Aristotle was "speaking only of the *citizen* population."[121] In this self-serving paternalism and tautological rationalization, Aristotle was not alone in taking for granted "as did Greek thinkers generally, including Plato—that the class which achieves power, whether it be the rich or the poor, will rule with a view to its own advantage."[122] The stipulation to bar women and slaves from the polity notwithstanding, as he saw democracy as relations of ruling among citizens as equal and the citizenry as sovereign, Aristotle perceived individual political liberty as potentially dangerous to the collective whole.[123] Moreover, he was mostly preoccupied with "the freedom from the necessity of labour," or the leisure required to sustain a well-ordered society.[124] Such leisure or freedom is essential for production and the social reproduction of the polis. As de St. Croix explains: "the most significantly distinguishing feature of each social formation . . . is not so much *how the bulk of the labour production is done, as how the dominant propertied classes*, controlling the conditions of production, *ensure the extraction of the surplus* which makes their own leisured existence possible."[125] Aristotle considered leisure or *scholë* as a "concept of considerable importance,"[126] especially in the management of the polis.[127] This preoccupation with free time reflects that Aristotle's primary concerns were with the citizen population, not with the noncitizen subject. In this case, the ability to take part in the political life of the polis and the labor required for the social reproduction of the polis are paramount to citizens achieving the good life. For this leisure or free time to materialize, the children, women, slaves, or even an ox would suffice.[128] As Stalley explains: "Aristotle's conception of liberty is bound up with the status of a freeman as opposed to a slave."[129] While Aristotle might have recognized "the necessity for *the entire citizen body* to be sovereign" in the polis, he nevertheless saw the *demos* as an enemy within which they are deprived of even the basic capacity to elect their own representatives.[130] In sum, the Aristotelian metaphysics of ruling posits that the polis might be a vehicle to achieving the good life; it is the well-ordered polis and well-regulated social classes, however, that create the conditions of possibility for it, without which there is a slippery slope descent into tyranny.

Political theorists occasionally resurrect ancient thinkers, especially Aristotle, to provide cover for problematic retreading of old grounds. It is especially troubling when reactionary antidemocratic thought is refashioned to lend a sheen of postmodern sophistication in a time fraught with virulent White supremacy, the steady march of authoritarianism, and raging wealth inequalities. It may seem natural to begin a critique of neoliberalism and its destructive forces with Aristotle; after all, he furnished one of the most potent materialist critiques against wealth hoarding. It is troubling, however, to insist on an Aristotelian metaphysics of ruling as a salve for contemporary neoliberal ailments, given the fact that Aristotle did not offer a theory of democracy as much as filling our books with prejudice against the many, all the while "praising aristocracy, in teleological terms."[131] Critics of neoliberalism are not wrong in claiming that it is "quietly undoing basic elements of democracy," reconfiguring "principles of justice, political cultures, habits of citizenship, practices of rule, and above all, democratic imaginaries."[132] Plutocracy is indeed ascendant.[133] Liberal democracy has been hollowed out from its inception, imperiled by its own forgeries and metaphysics of ruling. In the pantheon of antidemocratic combatants, neoliberalism is but one among many, and the others—settler colonialism, heteropatriarchy, and White supremacy—are subjects that many a political theorist deems worthy of near silence. In the rush to resurrect homo politicus as a White knight in battles against neoliberalism's antidemocracy, they flatten out history, distract embattled combatants, and deform any hope of a radically and differently imagined democratic future.

Democracy is in mortal danger due to its still birth and a politics of disposability where humans are not only sacrificed[134] but maimed or treated as waste, and underwritten by a neoliberal logic that is also steeped in White supremacy, heteropatriarchy, and settler colonialism. Politicians frequently evoke the populace and demagogically seek to arouse passion and a sense of the common such that sacrifice by citizen is not a new phenomenon in political theater.[135] Meanwhile policies and social regimes that render people and their communities as either waste or to be maimed or debilitated, are rooted not in the idea of sacrifice but in the logics of displacement, replacement, and genocide.[136] In light of the recent elevations of right-wing governments and reactionary, protofascist populism, it is tempting to believe that antidemocracy and the unrelenting prosecution of democracy are recent phenomena. However, the critique of elitist theorizing of democracy—as exemplified by the work of Robinson and others—shows that from the moment the *demos* appear on the scene, be it in politics or in theory, they already were marked as troublesome subjects and difficult to be governed. By supposition, they are ruled by their passions as they cannot be ruled by reason, ipso facto the necessity of coercion. For the elite, then, the *demos* are by nature ungoverned, and since they are not likely to be persuaded by reason, force is the only alternative.

As Aristotle continues to adorn contemporary democratic thinkability, some settle for a definition of democracy to mean rule by the people, while stipulating that the *demos* may not be trusted to rule because "never did the demos really rule in liberal democracies, nor could it in large nation-states."[137] Such a position shortchanges the rich and complex history of mobilizations and struggles for justice by reducing democratic mobilizations to the phenomenon of campaigning for political recognition and incorporation.[138] As the next two chapters will show, this particular frame of freedom, unwilling to divest from liberal individualist preconceived ideas about liberties, readily avails itself to the savage logic of capitalist appropriation and exploitation and its computational logic of entitlement where freedom is reserved for the few and injustice for the many.[139]

PART III. DEMOCRATIC LIVING

National political deliberation in contemporary "democracies" largely consists of elections and, like those in the US, many are fraught with political shenanigans and mischief aimed at voter suppression, which are largely bankrolled by super wealthy individuals and groups.[140] The invention of the Tea Party movement, as shown in the previous chapter, underlines the rise of "the new global super rich" and their extraordinary grip on politics and everything else.[141] Emphasizing the deliberative dimension of democracy without addressing de-democratization does not get at the many troubles with today's politics. It is antidemocracy when the nominal democratic system's aim is to marginalize and/or exclude the role of the people from governance, especially in the arenas of policy design, formulation, and implementation. It is antidemocracy when the people are mere accessories of a procedure that preselects deciders and deliberators who will do the actual work of policymaking.

To normalize antidemocracy, antidemocrats need the *demos* to be both the source and cause of their own undoing. If the people themselves cannot be trusted, if the people themselves have no self-control nor the capacity for self-rule, then the polity cannot be trusted to them. If they are inherently ungovernable, the polity, even in their name, must exclude them for their own good, and this must be done because they cannot be governed. Devices must be invented and introduced—"safety" measures such as stringent requirements for periodic exercises in pseudodemocratic participation, namely elections—are implemented for the purpose of preselection and elitist prefigurative politics. Such measures are deemed as stop valves against corruption by extreme elements of the public. In such an arena, the substance of policies becomes less important than performative discourses, especially by self-declaring moderates who succeed by naming their opponents as extreme. Also in this arena, lying is not only a prerequisite of political discourse but must be elevated to a science. The marking of a people or community as ungovernable, as shown, is an old art, one born of aristocratic prejudices and antipathy toward democratic living. To turn antidemocracy into a virtue, over time this art has turned to a variety of discursive terrains and ideologemes, ranging from pseudoscientific knowledges to creationist fictions.

In *The Origins of Democratic Thinking*, Cynthia Farrar cautions against "the undercurrents in democratic thought."[142] She maintains that theorists hollow out and eviscerate the possibility of living democracy by convincing themselves that "democracy is fundamentally a matter of rules and procedures."[143] She casts contemporary political theorists in the same lot with their ancient progenitors in their shared fear and mistrust of mass "politics as dangerous."[144] In doing so, they ignore or deny an existence of a bottom-up democratic theory or "living democracy," thus preferring the "more manageable alternatives," such that "apathy and ignorance on the part of the mass of the population is regarded as a normal, predictable state of affairs, and indeed desirable."[145] As Robinson argued, both political order and political as order have long been a priori of western political theorization, ancient and modern.[146] Part of unlearning this antidemocratic heritage, Farrar insists, is a return to a normative political theory, centering not so much the desire for governance but "the dignity and moral worth of every human being."[147] The emphasis on dignity and moral worth assuredly has not been a preoccupation for dominant democratic theorizing. On the contrary, the discourse on democracy, then and now, is fundamentally elitist, while "our moral respect" for everyone equally "is generally expressed in purely procedural terms"—instead of "substantive respect" or according everyone with "genuine dignity."[148] Democratic theories are thus morally bankrupt because theorists are less interested in the "moral goals of society" and more in servicing the state. In prioritizing proceduralism, however benign, they "avoid ideal goals, concepts such as the good life."[149] Farrar's critique underlines how democracy without the many, without their way of life, is antidemocracy. To refashion democratic thinking as a tool for ethical living draws attention to how antidemocratic thought has informed our understanding of democracy and what democratic politics should look like. Regrettably, even as the works of Robinson, Farrar, and others have existed for more than half a century, contemporary democratic thought remains decidedly on the side of antidemocracy. Indeed, the degeneration of democracy into tyranny is part of the metaphysics of ruling.

Democracy's Untruths

One distinct antidemocratic tradition that has been taken as given is the adjacent placement of democracy with tyranny as exemplars of non-ideal governments. First Plato and later Aristotle insisted that in contrast to aristocracy and even oligarchy, democracy was an inferior or degenerative form of government.[150] In the *Republic*, Plato supplied this fiction with a typology of five regimes, ranging from Aristocracy to Tyranny, with Timocracy, Oligarchy, and Democracy in descending order—each degenerating from rule by the best or "*aristoi*" to the worst, "*tyrannos*," or rulers who are unrestrained. Democracy, characterized as mob rule, is adjacent to tyranny because Plato feared that the uncontrolled mob and their unruly passion jettisoning all constraints would inevitably morph into tyranny, or unrestrained power. Aristotle being much more concerned with empiricism than his teacher, collected data about political behavior, even though his political analysis fares no better than Plato's metaphysics and antidemocratic prejudice. Aristotle also relegated democracy (or mob rule) as a degenerative form of government.[151] For both, then, the free citizen subjects in a democracy are no different from tyrants because "they are enslaved by appetite."[152] Democratic passion is thus both the cause and source of tyranny. Plato, Aristotle, and their descendants thus not only dismissed democracy as an ideal form of government; they also dismissed ordinary people, and especially women and slaves, as ideal citizen subjects, never mind as rulers.

A major clue to Plato's own passion is his use of the term "noble lie" to explain that in ruling, the people require myths or untruths. These lies are necessary for the state to pursue goals that may or may not be in the best interests of the people.[153] In political theory, one of the most pernicious untruths about democratic rule is that democracy is adjacent to or on a slippery slope to tyranny. If tyranny is bad then the people must be saved from this disastrous inevitability, replaced by worthy elite. This and similar myths fortify and normalize antidemocratic biases into an ideological apparatus of ruling, underwriting elitist theories and elite theorization of democracy, such that antidemocracy shows up as democracy, and fascism as antifascist.[154] This subversion is rooted in an antidemocratic ideologeme that furnishes the necessary elements for a total interpretive system.[155] This enduring influence reflects a possessive investment in elite rule. As documented, political theory in the west owes a massive debt to classical thinkers for its antidemocratic dispositions, and as Robinson noted, "it has long been evident that the *Republic's* purpose was to mount a sustained attack on democracy."[156] The question is why this influence endures in political theorization in our time, a time where democracy is always aspirational. Robinson argues that contemporary elitist theory of democracy "did not so much appropriate Plato but rather mirrored its Platonic genealogy"—a genealogy of ideological prosecution of the *demos* and democracy.

So it is that we invented a series of untruths about democracy, mob rule, and the people, including the idea that, left to their own devices, the people are incapable of ruling themselves. If only "beasts and gods" exist outside of governing, then ruling is normed and reified through the device of the social contract, and naturalized by the fallacious idea that individuals and communities voluntarily submit to being governed, even by those who seek their total annihilation. The domination of the ungoverned becomes the first principle of government, and domination is thus self-mastery, oppression is bliss, and conquest is missionary.

Democracy on the road to modernity therefore submitted itself to enlightenment and graduated to the status of antidemocracy. Not entirely unexpected, however, and just as the many of previous eras announced their presence and disturbances, the *demos* of our time, with misgivings and mischiefs, stage their many insurrections to not only register their displeasure but also to provide historical verifications of alternative ontologies, different lifeworlds, worlds where they, not the *aristoi*, not the elite, supply their own ideologies, myths, imaginaries, and ways of doing democracy.

Tools for Democratic Living

A democratic way of life is not life without tyranny but life keeping tyranny in check. If the people are thought to be the bearers of tyranny, it is the people who must keep that tyranny in check. And since the people are incapable of self-rule, the antidemocrats reason, then the elite, the rational, and the pragmatists must step in to check the many and evict them from the right to rule in order to prevent tyranny. By tautology, given that it is unlikely that they will ever be ready to self-rule, the many will have to be educated in the art of democratic living even as they are being constrained from acting out their will or from ever ruling. As such, even the most thoughtful theoretical rehabilitation of representative democracy comes up short.[157]

The muck in which we find theories on democracy is not unrelated to the problem that Brown, Robinson, and others sought to expose—the inability and/or unwillingness of theorists, philosophers, and movement actors to cut off the king's head.[158] As discussed in chapter 2, "state addiction," or a preoccupation with the political order, places the sovereign or political authority at the discursive center. In treating order and governing as a priori, theorists traded a more substantive and robust, if more complicated, framing of "the people rule," and a much more radical possibility of "all the people rule" with rule, ruling, and nominal (institutional) arrangements for elections, so that even a few of the elite recognize elections as mere contestations among themselves.[159] Undoing this elitist thinkability is an imperative for considering democratic living and getting ourselves out of this theoretical cul-de-sac. Rather than obediently following "rules for radicals," it might be more instructive to subversively (re)stock tools for democratic living by looking to justice mobilizations and movements instead.

Like demosprudence, these tools are not likely found in the rarefied air of formal theory or philosophy, but on the streets and from many movements for justice. Considered one of the greatest community organizers in the mid-twentieth-century United States, Saul Alinsky wrote several books defending social movements and explaining what needs to be done on the ground. Unlike most writers of social movements and social change, Alinsky was not a traditional scholar, but an organizer who briefly spent time with the boss of Chicago's largest mob as a "nonparticipant observer," and achieved some successes on the ground as he jostled with industrial elites and civic leaders. His tactical principles, particularly ones featured in *Rules for Radicals*, have been studied and used in many grassroots organizations for over half a century.[160] Since tactics and strategies typically are understudied in social movement literatures because they are complex phenomena, *Rules* had a receptive audience.[161]

However, the work that put his tactical approach on the map was published more than two decades prior. In *Reveille for Radicals*, Alinsky laid out his thesis on organizing and social change, and sought to establish himself as an insider-philosopher of radical mobilization of the Gramscian variety.[162] He insisted that American democracy needed a radical rehabilitation that only "the People's Organization" could perform and only "Radicals" could appreciate "that *people are the stuff that makes up the dream of democracy*."[163] He explains that "democracy moves forward" when "the power of the people is transmitted through the gears of their own organizations."[164] Thus, organizing structures are essential for radicals to attain their goals. As if directly responding to Schumpeter's elitism, Alinsky insists that "[the people's] organizations are vital to the functioning of democracy, for without them, we lack all drive for the development of the democratic way of life. . . . Democracy is a way of life and not a formula to be 'preserved' like jelly. . . . There is no democracy unless it is a dynamic democracy."[165] To salvage and rehabilitate American democracy, radicals must work with the people, and "this can be done only through the democratic organization of our people."[166] Alinsky's formulation of "the People's Organization" is fraught with defects—not least are the overreliance on institution building, the hierarchical power relations within such institutions, and the framing of radicals as vanguards of the American reclamation project.[167] Nevertheless, more than many, he understood acutely the importance of local knowledges, and *Reveille* reveals a deep appreciation for local leadership. He warned that "even the best outside organizer, one who has democratic convictions and practices them, who has complete faith in the people and their leadership, cannot build a People's Organization to a complete structure . . . —*but only the people and their own leaders can build a People's Organization.*"[168] Outside elements forcing their way into the community "are doomed to failure simply because . . . they fail to grasp the simplest elements of democracy. . . . Their thinking and actions demonstrate the very antithesis of democracy."[169]

Despite the many contradictions in Alinsky's formulation of democracy, his idea that democracy is a way of life is more capacious than what has been offered up as careful political science. Using an example of organizers encountering obstacles thrown up by religious authorities, Alinsky suggests that organizers need to "recognize that the local organizations . . . are the most significant part of the democratic way of life," as they "represent the very skeleton of democracy." Democracy is thus "not a single, unqualified, primary loyalty to the state," but instead "provides the fulfillment of the hopes and loyalties of our people to all of the various institutions and groups of which they are a part."[170]

Unlike *Rules*, *Reveille* explicitly emphasizes that organizers need to commit to a democratic praxis and be in community with others as they seek to bring about meaningful change, and Alinsky militantly demands that popular participation be at the center of the democratic experience. Published only three years after Schumpeter's *Capitalism*, *Reveille* was a call to arms against apathy and elitist control of political life. In contrast to Schumpeter's "democratic method," Alinsky saw apathy as a tragic disease and asserted that "unless the American people are aroused to a higher degree of participation, democracy will die at its roots."[171]

For Alinsky, democracy is not a static or abstract concept, but a "dynamic expression of a living, participating, informed, active, and free people."[172] While the term "people's democracy" may seem redundant, it is in keeping with his delineation of democracy as "a way of life that belongs to the people."[173] Lamenting that "it is irony worthy of the gods that here in the greatest democracy on earth is found the least concern over the prime element of democracy"—its citizens,[174] he also notes, "democracy as a way of life has been intellectually accepted but emotionally rejected."[175] The source of this affect is fear: a democracy that is in fear of its people is likely to wither and die.[176]

Acknowledging that democracy can lead to tyranny, Alinsky asserted that it also possesses the capability to resist it: "fascism does not have a chance of establishing over a people who are active, interested, participating, co-operating, informed, democratically minded"; people are not fearful but confident in their fellow citizens.[177] The problem lies in thinking of "democracy only in terms of its forms and structure," but "real democracy" is like living: it "does not hold to a form; it grows, expands, and changes to meet the needs of the people."[178] While his proposition that "if democracy dies in America, it dies universally" is dubious, his recognition that "a democracy lacking in popular participation dies of paralysis" is consistent with both de Tocqueville's observation of "democracy" in the US as well as criticism of elite theory of democracy.[179]

Billed as "the original handbook for social change," *Reveille* devoted significant attention to the critique of the US as an unequal, unjust, and dying democracy. Published only two years after the revised edition of *Reveille*, *Rules for Radicals* takes on a greater authoritative, if less impassioned and profanity-laced, tone. *Rules*'s limitation, however, is not that it sounded less militant, and its tone certainly had little effect on its reach for it soon became one of the bestselling activist manuals. The problem with *Rules* is that it is about rules, and therefore did not work for many who did not fit into Alinsky's dominant frame of who and what constitutes a radical.

In contrast, Sara Ahmed furnishes a different approach to living democracy, explaining that living a feminist life "is about how we connect with and draw upon each other in our shared project of dismantling worlds,"[180] and it "does not mean adopting a set of ideals or norms of conduct, although it might mean asking ethical questions about how to live better in an unjust and unequal world."[181] By dismantling worlds, she clearly meant the "not-feminist and antifeminist world," or an unjust and unequal world. Because "feminism is about how to live, about a way of thinking how to live," it makes sense to question how to live in solidarity or in community, or how to think around and through gendered racial capitalism or heteropatriarchy. *Reveille* asks important questions about democratic livability while *Rules* sets downs rules for actualizing only one version of democratic life. Living democracy is an attempt to think through democracy, not as a norm (as in the democratic method) or a set of rules (as in *Rules for Radicals*), but as a way of life, and to raise questions that are grounded in the facticity of living in an unequal and unjust world.

One of Audre Lorde's most frequently cited essays and expressions, "the master's tools will never dismantle the master's house," is first and foremost a provocation—an admonishment against portending to advance liberation using the very same techniques that create conditions of oppression and domination.[182] Following Ahmed, it can also be read as a warning against the complacency of paradigmatic practices and "a call to arms: do not become the master's tool."[183] It might also be well-heeded advice about the importance of paying attention to tools. Therefore, at the risk of being overly instrumentalist where tools themselves become the end of living, it is necessary to ask the question: What indeed are the tools for radicals, feminists, democrats?

Unlike rules, where regimens and norms are preeminent, tools are flexible and contingent. Any given tools could create, solve, or not solve problems, especially if the problem is in/justice or inequality, and they could be retooled or casted out. Ahmed uses the term "tool" to connote "machinery of power" (such as a rod for disciplinary purposes).[184] She tells us that "words can be tools";[185] so are arms when they are used as "tools for the creation of wealth" or "when workers refuse to allow their arms to be the master's tool, they strike."[186] Tools that are introduced "to address a problem can be used as indicators that a problem has been addressed."[187] That is to say, tools can be used to not solve the problem as when a "program developed in response to a problem is assumed to resolve a problem"—so the solution itself becomes the problem.[188] *Rules for Radicals* could be a set of tools for actualizing democratic living and also rules for norming hierarchies and singularity.

A good example of a nominally participatory tool for widening popular input into policymaking ending up as a tool for elite malintent and mischief is the use of the local referendum and initiative mechanism to affect policy change. Popular referenda and initiatives are tools that were introduced to retain popular participation for a deliberative democracy. More than two dozen countries currently allow for such a process.[189] California's 1978 Proposition 13, the "People's Initiative to Limit Property Taxation," is a prime example.[190] It is known synonymously as the iconic "tax revolt" to be emulated nationwide. By putting California on a decidedly different track and ensuring the interests of property owners over public investments, it served as an exemplar for anti-tax forces elsewhere. It became a blueprint for elite policy workshops, hijacking one of the few instruments of "direct democracy."[191] Thus the growth of antidemocracy has been revved up not only by shifting norms but also by divestments and the reappropriation of institutional resources, including the refashioning of the *demos*'s tools against them.

The democratic toolkit assembled from the unhappy archive of governing and informed by a radical feminist ethic of liberation, therefore, would not have definable rules but would draw on memories of resistance and dreams of liberation. These tools may or may not have been "the master's tools," but would be willed to not become the master's tool. The toolkit for democratic living is analogous to Ahmed's feminist survival kit. She describes it as a "shared feminist project" and explains that it "contains my personal stuff, what I have accumulated over time; things I know I need to do and to have around me to keep going on," noting that the toolkit is more than what you put in it, but "it is the kit itself"[192]—as feminism itself is also a survival kit; it is a form of self-care or "feminist care."[193] This formulation of tools and toolkit is particularly instructive for rethinking anti/democracy in these times of big and small tyrannies. Democratic living in fascist times requires a particular toolkit that allows us to handle leaders, authorities, and tyrants claiming to rule on behalf of the people while silencing, imprisoning, and/or killing them. If fascism celebrates technology, masculinity, militarism, and a master race, then democratic living is undoing hierarchy, stopping wars and conquest, and privileging planetary justice and life over material acquisitions. Democratic living is thus itself an anti-fascist survival kit.

With few exceptions, mainstream contemporary theorists frequently exclude labor as an important dimension of a functioning democracy, and they especially exclude the critical function of reproductive labor. Given the long history of philosophers and theorists who excluded or marginalized women from major considerations such as justice and the good life, it is not at all surprising that theorists of democracy largely ignore reproductive labor in their theorization, especially on the leisure that underwrites doing democracy. In countering governing, reproductive labor necessarily involves the work that extends beyond the sexual economies of reproduction and its many violent geographies. Put differently, beyond the labor performed for childbearing and rearing typically associated with the maintenance of the private family, reproductive labor also necessarily entails the creative care labors that are linked intimately with family, community, and world crafting.[194] Reproductive labor is, as Ahmed puts it, "the labor of reproducing life, the labor of reproducing the conditions that enable others to live."[195] We know that labor includes reproductive labor, but as many feminist scholars have pointed out, when we systematically exclude reproductive labor from our theoretical consideration, especially from theories of social transformation and social reproduction, we systematically exclude women and all others who perform such labor.[196]

Democratic living needs radical feminist labor. In a prison nation[197] in times of mass incarceration and surveillance, abolition feminism furnishes tools engendering democratic livability. Abolition feminism performs feminist labor that cares and feeds an ethos of radical possibilities.[198] Democratic living is about recognizing that it takes more than a village to raise a child, for a child living on this planet in these times needs democratic living as a tool to survive and thrive. Similarly, if the Black freedom struggles in the US and in the African diaspora have fought in making "all Black Lives Matter," then the Black radical tradition furnishes tools for democratic living. If Black feminist formations have mobilized against authoritarian and militarist rules, then the antifascist toolkit contains democratic seedlings secreted by radical feminist rebellions and insurgencies.

Democratic living is thus aspirational living, living against tyranny, living while you were never meant to belong or survive.[199] Democratic living has been an unthought and was never meant to survive. As the next chapter documents, democracy in the US was not meant to survive; when it first appeared on the scene, it was designed to intentionally exclude 85 percent of the inhabitants of the land. The people on the land were not included in the settlers' land of democracy: ipso facto it is an antidemocracy. What labor went into sustaining antidemocracy, and what labor is needed to extend democratic livability? By focusing on democratic living instead of democracy, we can slow focus on reproductive labor—the labor that reproduces conditions that are conducive for democratic politics, that enable democracy to live, to overturn antidemocracy.

Democratic living is thus a shift away from the tyranny of antidemocracy and elitist theorization. Democracy, as Robinson understood, "is quite clearly a disciplinary matrix of Western political science,"[200] such that thinking about democracy tends to wed us to rules and governing instead of livability. It is therefore prudent to explore the imaginary domain of democracy's unthought and unthinkable. As shown, one such unthinkable has been the idea that "the people" actually means "all the people."[201] While not an unthought, lifeworlds and life forms have been abstracted violently into a void such that "the many" has been effectively conscripted to convey "a sameness, boundedness, citizenry, continuity, territorial and proximal identifications which are never fully empirical."[202] Delineating the unthinkable would compel us to take up all the people, along with democratic livability. Thinking about all the people and democratic living would give up the ghosts of democracy and instead point us to questions, road maps, and visions of justice, equality, solidarity, and friendship—all the things that thinking of lifeworlds and forms would enable us to do.

Democratic living is therefore a political disorientation, a praxis, that draws attention to the necessary tools that are life aids, but also the tools that have been deployed to take life and livelihood away. Indeed, the archive of antidemocracy as briefly delineated here suggests that democratic living will allow us not so much to set down rules we must follow, but raise questions about how we may live together as equals, being in community with each other, in solidarity, with justice and dignity for all. By mining the domain of the unthinkable we end up thinking about the ungovernable, those who have never consented to domination and oppression and how they have resisted against unfreedom, however momentarily. The political theorist Joel Olsen, for instance, insisted that to be oriented as a democrat, one must be fanatically against "White democracy" or White supremacist, apartheid democracy. His was a political disorientation and praxis that demand a revolutionary abolitionist ethic that predisposes one always be in a position looking for a fight.[203] Democratic living is therefore also an incitement of treasonous ungoverning, and the archive of antidemocracy and governing is therefore also an archive of the ungovernable, the archive of the unconsenting.

Had they been consulted, it is likely that the oppressed would not consent to be governed. As concluded by the 2021 Report "Struggle for Power" published by M4BL and CLEAR: "In the fight for Black self-determination, power, and freedom in the United States, one institution's relentless determination to destroy Black movement is unrivaled—*the United States federal government.*"[204] This is so because "Black resistance and power-building threaten the economic interests and White supremacist agenda that uphold the existing social order. . . . Over time, strategies for Black resistance have constantly adapted to counter the prevailing political social conditions of White supremacy, domination and exclusion. . . . No matter the strategy, the federal government has remained committed to undercutting radical organizers for racial justice and Black power whose insistence on exercising their inherent rights threatens White Americans' political and social dominance."[205] Antidemocracy's singular preoccupation has been the eviction of the *demos*, and in modern times few tools have been more deadly than anti-Black racism and White supremacy. Thus, if the role of the citizens is minimal in so-called representative democracy and that of mere claimants in deliberative democracy, then the people, preferably all the people, must be the starting point of any consideration of democratic livability. Rather than treating the many as a source of "the lethal poison of republics,"[206] democratic living draws attention to the ways in which people living together as equal and in solidarity have been fundamentally undermined by the republic itself. What follows, therefore, is a series of campaigns by the people who have been differentially marked as vulnerable and, momentarily or for an extended period of time, rendered themselves unavailable for governing. As beasts or gods, they are then marked as a troubled people and targeted for all manners of disciplinary regimes, including displacement, disappearance, and death, as they were never meant to survive, nor their consent acquired. And yet, they/we survive, doing democracy in ways that are beyond the pale, all the while beholding promises of *alternatives to order.*

4

Love of Freedom: Jeffersonian Anti-democracy and the Politics of Governing

By hard experience they had learnt that isolated efforts were doomed to failure, and in the early months of 1791 in and around Le Cap they were organizing for revolution. Voodoo was the medium of the conspiracy. In spite of all prohibitions, the slaves travelled miles to sing and dance and practise the rites and talk; and now, since the [French] revolution, to hear the political news and make their plans . . . by the end of July 1791 the blacks in and around Le Cap were ready and waiting.

C. L. R. James[1]

BLAMING THE VICTIMS

Less than nine years after the Santo Domingo masses sounded their collective drums, announcing the commencement of their revolution in 1791, some of their kin in Virginia, the slave capital of the United States, were fomenting an insurrection of their own.[2] Ironically, Gabriel's Rebellion of 1800, which until recently received scant attention, was frequently cited as the source of incitement for draconian laws against slaves in Virginia and elsewhere.[3] One record keeper, William Price Palmer—a retired doctor tasked by the Virginia General Assembly to "calendar and preserve the piles of disordered documents stashed in the state capital"—published the first account of this event nearly a decade later. Palmer's account is revealing not least because he had concluded that eventually the Black slave masses of Virginia would pose a threat to White people because they would have to consider "at some time or other shaking off the shackles of slavery . . . [and] of getting rid of their masters and possessing themselves of the country," but also because Palmer, perhaps in his own delusion, insisted that "the negro is by nature docile and affectionate."[4] Not insignificant is the fact that Palmer, as a mere document recorder, imposed an antidemocratic and racist filter, asserting, for instance, that Black people are "easily moved by passion . . . [their] dormant emotions once aroused, no restrain of reason or moral stands between [them] and the executing of [their] will," such that they would likely be vulnerable to demagoguery and end up betraying White people.[5] Consequently, Palmer placed the blame for the near insurrection at the foot of slaveholders—not because slavery is immoral and unjust, but because slaveholders were not vicious or brutal enough. Too much liberty and indulgence were the cause of rebellion, Palmer declared, for when slaves "wandered about without hinderance" they are likely freer "to concoct almost any evil designs without being even suspected by their indulgent owners."[6]

According to James Sidbury, Gabriel's Conspiracy took place during the spring and part of the summer of 1800 when Gabriel, a blacksmith who lived six miles outside of Richmond, Virginia, led a group of slaves in and near Richmond in a plan to take the city and abolish slavery.[7] They developed a military strategic plan to "divide into three columns, and enter Richmond after midnight on a Saturday . . . fortify the town, and demand the abolition of slavery."[8] Gabriel, his brother Solomon, and half a dozen others traveled to nearby counties recruiting members of the planned insurrection.[9] According to Douglas R. Egerton, this plot "was perhaps the most extensive slave conspiracy in southern history."[10] When the governor of Virginia and the future US president James Monroe sought out intelligence on the conspiracy, he reported that "there was 'good cause to believe that the knowledge' of the conspiracy 'pervaded other parts, if not the whole, of the state.'"[11] Gabriel's "contemporaries, white as well as black, believed that his plan stood a good chance of succeeding" and, had it been successful, "it might have changed not only the course of American race relations but also the course of American political history."[12] Even after the plot unraveled and no insurrection took place, Henrico County and nearby courts met and tried those caught for conspiracy and insurrection.[13]

Regimes of governing must necessarily imbricate in the displacement and disappearance of communities and peoples. Genocidal logic and policies are part of this toolkit, though frequently seen as governing's most extreme and final solutions. On the other hand, key to quotidian governance are more mundane practices of eviction and disappearance of undesirable subjects and their communities, so that incarceration, deportation, and dismembering communities are extensions of coercive governing regimes. As this chapter will show, central to slave governance is the idea that Black people needed to be rendered as docile, governable subjects. When this is not possible, the alternative is disappearance, which includes eviction from the US. David Walker was acutely aware of this logic when he saw past the rhetoric of resettlement schemes and understood them as removal projects. In contrast, historians typically frame support for colonization plans as a sign of progress, and even a form of atonement for profiting from slavery because they are almost always part of the stipulation for "gradual emancipation." The architects of Jeffersonian antidemocracy, namely Thomas Jefferson and James Madison, were among those who advanced such plans. As such, an assessment of Jeffersonian politics requires an interrogation of these proposals that sought to remove and evict Black people and their communities from their new homes.

Even though an insurrection did not materialize, Gabriel's plot is remarkable in part because it exemplifies how willful subjects perceive and seek to change their world.[14] As Sidbury points out, careful examination of court documents can produce a fruitful understanding of "the processes through which enslaved Virginians constructed a movement to end slavery."[15] Indeed, as information of the plot surfaced, a member of a prominent family in Virginia, George Tucker, called on the state's Assembly to take up his cousin St. George Tucker's plan for gradually ending slavery with "serious and candid consideration." Four years previously, St. George Tucker had penned a colonization proposal. In a letter to a member of the General Assembly of Virginia, he maintained that Gabriel's plot was verification of slaves possessing "the love of freedom": "The love of freedom, sir, is an inborn sentiment, which the God of nature has planted deep in the heart. . . . This celestial spark, which fires the breast of the savage, which glows in that of the philosopher, is not extinguished in the bosom of the slave. . . . Thus we find, sir, there never have been slaves in any country, who have not seized the first favorable opportunity to revolt."[16] The Tuckers, however, were not reflexive enough to recognize that Black people were their equals or could be fellow citizen subjects, and while St. George Tucker advocated an end to slavery, he also proposed that Virginia devise a plan to have Black people emancipated then settled "outside of the state, somewhere 'on the western side' of the Mississippi River."[17] Gabriel's conspiracy is thus particularly noteworthy because it was weaponized by slavocrats to intensify the governing regime of White autarchy. Palmer's portrayal of slavery in Virginia made it possible for him to overemphasize the importance of a charismatic leader and foreign influence and ignored "the possibility that enslaved black men in Virginia could have concocted and carried out the conspiracy themselves to obtain the freedom he recognized they desired."[18] His account contains many enduring tropes of slavery and thus governing, especially the idea that Black people are incapable of self-rule, and that enslaved people could desire freedom while still have "fidelity" and "utmost confidence" in slaveholders.[19] It is not surprising then that Palmer assumed "Gabriel and [the] rebels needed White instigators and planners" to carry out their plot.[20]

The privileging of individual charismatic leaders over community and movement collectives makes it easier to elide the scope of social grievances and discontents, while misrecognizing strategic methods of resistance emerging from communal mobilization. According to Egerton, of the many myths about the conspiracy, "the most durable is the erroneous idea that

Gabriel was a messianic figure, an early national Nat Turner who wore his hair long in imitation of his biblical hero, Samson."[21] Egerton's Gabriel is closer to a Black Jacobin who is "far from praying for the religious day of jubilee." Instead, he "labored to gather together 'the most redoubtable democrats in the state' to destroy the economic hegemony of the 'merchants,' the only Whites he ever identified as his enemies."[22] This historical Gabriel "engineered a complex conspiracy with branches in at least three Virginian cities was no apolitical servant but a literate artisan whose breadth of vision was truly international."[23]

There are at least three important considerations regarding the narration of Gabriel's Rebellion—namely, the plot, the plotters, and the ways in which this event impacted the disciplinary regime in the aftermath. The plot was both exaggerated and underestimated. On the one hand, its failure to materialize suggests insurgents were unable to seize whatever opportunities afforded them to stage an open insurrection, successful or not. On the other hand, if Monroe and others were to be believed, the plotters and their compatriots had in their sight not the taking of a single household or plantation, but the entire state of Virginia and an end to slavery itself. This points to the plotters' ambition and willingness to take on risk, also found in similar insurrectionist attempts. Monroe, for instance, was frightened by what the revolution of San Domingo's slaves may harbor, worrying out loud that Virginia's enslaved population too might be "infected with malady of insurrection."[24] White planters, especially Monroe, had good reasons to worry.

Of Gabriel, Egerton explains: "At the age of twenty-four, the huge blacksmith had decided that he, his wife, Nany, and his brothers would cease to live as slaves—or they would cease to live."[25] Gabriel's plot is ambitious: the conspirators strategized to seize the state, requiring no more than "1000 men strong," including the main column that would "move on Capital Square and seize the guns stored in the building," taking Monroe hostage, who presumably was sleeping nearby in the Governor's Mansion.[26] The plotters sought to build a broad coalition to include "poor White people," who Gabriel reasoned had no "more political power than the slaves did." Similarly, they planned not to harm the "Quakers, Methodists, and French people," allowing for solidarity with those who presumably harbored abolitionist sensibilities.[27] Hoping to use the banner "death or Liberty," Gabriel intended for the rebellion to have broad appeal and by "turning Patrick Henry's famous phrase on its head, it would also remind Whites that they too professed to believe in freedom."[28]

That the oppressed make use of, appropriate, and outright subvert certain narrative tools to push back against the systems that oppress them is not remarkable.[29] What is remarkable about the plotters' targeted message, "death or liberty," is that they had intended it as a hypertext. As court documents suggest, the insurgents fully intended to recruit from cross sectors of society, envisioning a radically different set of social relations than Virginian life offered at the time as they tactically made use of the most dominant master narrative in circulation—Republicanism and a professed love of freedom. By appropriating and subverting Henry's famous revolutionary slogan, "Give me freedom, or give me death," or perhaps Virginia's Culpeper Minutemen's flag of 1775, "Liberty or death,"[30] the insurgents clearly intended to expose the injustice and hypocrisy that existed side by side with the master narrative about freedom and equality. They understood that a nation that was intended to establish justice for all would not codify humans as parts. Nowhere is Walker's astute insight about American antidemocracy's dependency on slavery and the mythology of White autarky more evident than in Henry's revolutionary fervor. Despite his famously professed love of liberty, Henry "could not imagine freeing his bondmen" because of "'the general inconveniency of living without them.'"[31]

Henry, not unlike many of his peers, revolutionary or otherwise, thought that it was perfectly consistent to simultaneously love liberty and own slaves at the same time and to express this in the same constitution. Indeed, John Locke who was enormously influential with Jefferson and other drafters of the American Declaration of Independence and Constitution, had sought to codify White entitlement more than a century before when he drafted *The Fundamental Constitutions of Carolina* (1669).[32] As Locke's thesis on labor and private property continues to inform contemporary perspectives on governance and property relations, the somewhat understudied *Fundamental Constitutions*, considerably more impactful on quotidian life than Locke's other work, merits some scrutiny. If the entire purpose of a constitutional framework is to protect the interests of state and private investments and to contain emergent rule by the many, then it is logical for a scribbler to invent mythic devices such as "the state of nature" and "social contract" to normalize ideas about "the consent to be governed," or to reason that the tacit agreement for entering civil society was driven by a "natural" desire to protect one's body and property, as Locke later argued in *Two Treatises*.[33]

THE ENTITLEMENT OF RULE

First issued in 1669 at the behest of the Lords of Proprietor of the Province, and in effect for nearly three decades, Locke's constitutional framework sought to transplant European-style feudalism to the colony. There is little doubt that in the *Fundamental Constitutions*, Locke sought to serve the interests of his patrons, the Lords of Proprietor, and to institutionalize the entitlements and rule of the propertied class.[34] In the "Preamble," he stated that, "we must avoid erecting a numerous democracy" then proceeded to enumerate the eight Lords of Proprietor as hereditary nobility with absolute control over their serfs, ensuring no leet man or serfs "have liberty to go off from the land of their particular lord;" that "all children of leet man shall be leet-men" from generation to generation; and "*every freeman of Carolina shall have absolute power and authority over his negro slaves, of what opinion or religion soever.*"[35] It was not until a few years before the *Two Treatises* was published that Locke finally divested from the global slave trade as a government official and venture investor while setting down the rules for governing.[36]

If social contract theory essentializes the consent of free men to be governed, and the protection of private wealth serves as raison d'être for the emergence of modern states, then Locke's prescription for and justification of a stratified, slave-dependent Carolina colony reveals a materiality that was sublimated in his later writings. His world was in the midst of empire building, a world where desires for riches and settlements fueled expansionism and catapulted conquests, where slavery powered the global economy and drove national governments to transplant populations through decrees and genocide. Locke recorded and shared his patron Shaftsbury's conviction about the importance of trade for strengthening the emergent British Empire. Tasked with collecting trade and settlement data, he was fully aware of the importance of slave trading to the colonial economy and British empire. With intimate knowledge of slavery, the slave trade, and commercial enterprises associated with slavery, as well as the conditions in the colonies, and as author of one of the most draconian codifications of slave life in the colonies, it should not be surprising that his thesis on liberty resonated so well with slavocrats in revolutionary America, including the idea that the many consent to be governed by the few.[37] So while Locke might have believed that "no man, can, by agreement pass over to another that which he hath not in himself, a power over his own life,"[38] exactly whose life he was considering needs to be at the heart of Lockean hermeneutics. As an investor in the global slave trade, Locke was no stranger to the men and women who labored for his profits, and perhaps as a result, he felt a need to provide a theory, not unlike Aristotle's, that would sanitize the business of treating humans as property. Locke sutured up this cruel and dirty business with the idea of "legitimate slavery" that gave rise to the need to invent "legitimate" and "illegitimate" civil government. It could then be argued that illegitimate states must be those that enslave the *wrong* people, as Locke's later writings either explicitly sanction the enslavement of Black people or ignore them entirely.[39] He explicitly advanced the idea that property rights are natural, including in the state of nature, and that property in person is part and partial of such rights, "which in the Jeffersonian context included slaves."[40] Seeing themselves as rightful citizen subjects, slaveholders would absolutely object to their own enslavement and deprivation of political liberties on both political and moral grounds. They, however, did not perceive all others, even the women from their own class, as belonging to the same species.[41] Here the emergent bourgeoisie is seen as exceptional, and Man thus "had earned the right to be certain of security for which he contracted into civil society" where the state is controlled by those who "discovered in it an instrument for their own preservation."[42] The entitlements of such a state belong to Man, and only Man. As Carole Pateman argues, Locke was "far from being a democrat" and had little regard for the specific role of participation in a polity.[43] If democracy is a way of life as Saul Alinsky would have it, Locke and his philosophical progeny in Virginia and elsewhere were its enemies.

Not surprisingly, Locke's antidemocratic metaphysics inspired and underwrote relations of property, especially for the emergent propertied class of American revolutionary elites. James Oakes points out that "Locke's triad of 'life, liberty, and property' was the most widely invoked," with Jefferson replacing "property" with "the pursuit of happiness" and "Southerners uniformly presumed the primary of individual rights."[44] Lockean thesis on ruling is consistent with the Jeffersonian views that "society was a compact of solitary individuals" and the state's only function is to service "the need to preserve individual rights to life, liberty and property."[45] Secessionism and the Confederate's defense of slavery are therefore an outgrowth of this mindset, as without Jefferson's thesis on government, "secessionists in 1861 would have no clear justification for their action."[46]

SENTIMENTS OF LIBERTY

George Tucker was correct to recognize the inevitable impulse to revolt against slavery and the interests of his own planter class. In Dinwiddie, a town near Richmond where Black people were in the majority, former state senator Joseph Jones urged Governor Monroe to use execution and terrorism as appropriate responses to rebels and suspected rebels.[47] Almost immediately after the hangings took place and the few who escaped execution awaiting their expulsion, Virginian elites seized the opportunity to further consolidate their political and economic monopoly. When the legislature met that December, Monroe prepared a special message about the slaves' near insurrection in the midst of a "bewildered and vengeful" elite.[48] Virginian legislators would propose and pass two important resolutions to extend the arms of the state, seeking to render Black lives more governable. First, they expanded the state's coercive apparatus by centralizing control and strengthening the state militia.[49] Second, they heightened and systematized total surveillance of Black lives by broadening the already extensive slave patrol system.[50] They also sought, though failed, to repeal laws allowing for private manumissions.[51] Monroe, whose report to the legislature made such an impression that it achieved the desired effects of a flurry of proposals and counterproposals, argued that "the growing sentiment of liberty" and the "inadequacy of existing patrol laws" were the main causes of attempted insurrections. The problem, as he saw it, was not that slavery incites acts of rebellion, rather the failure of containment, especially the inability to govern, incites rebellion. Such opportunism for greater control of Black lives was not confined to Virginia. As historian Sally E. Hadden explains:

> After hearing about Gabriel's rebellion in Virginia, South Carolina governor Drayton swung into action, writing to his Virginia counterpart, James Monroe, for specifics about the event. At the same time Drayton sent out general orders to all parts of his state for the "patrol law of this state, to be enforced strictly, and steadily," and urged the general assembly to strengthen the laws governing slaves and freed slaves.[52]

Back in Virginia, one of the rebels who "had been on the periphery" of Gabriel's plot and escaped execution, ferry operator Sancho, was now seeking to reconstitute the rebellion and extend it to the Carolinas by using his knowledge about the river network. Sancho was familiar with the river system "that bound Virginia and the Carolinas to the Atlantic market," and "after the hangings of 1800," he took over the plot and recruited "black watermen."[53] And as "the last slave to be executed in 1800 . . . other slaves in and around Petersburg began to whisper that the dream of liberty and equality should not be given up."[54] Even as Sancho's plot unraveled in late 1801, and more rebels were executed, the Virginian elites were intent on achieving perfect governing for the total control of Black lives—from mobility to sexual desire and spirituality. The goal was "to better discipline a troublesome labor force and crush its rebellious spirit."[55] Real or imagined, the stories of the two Frenchmen[56] in league with Gabriel and his band of rebels, for instance, provided fuel for a campaign of fracturing solidarity among the urban working class. In 1803, White Virginians petitioned the legislature to prohibit interracial relationships and marriages, particularly between "White women taking Black Husbands."[57] Black Churches and their preachers would not be "allowed to retain their autonomy"; parishioners would be required to carry passes for patrol inspection while such passes were routinely not given out or not recognized, with the net effect of general decline in church membership or churches having to shutter entirely.[58] At the national level, the chief instrument for advancing this repressive ideology was a new president, Thomas Jefferson.

DESIRING PERFECTION

Candidate Jefferson was "not interested in petty piecemeal legislation designed to inhibit the growth of conspiracies."[59] What he sought was perfection in governability: "to eliminate the foremost model of black autonomy in the New World."[60] Jefferson, who thought "a little rebellion now and then" is a good thing in the midst of the new nation's revolutionary fervor, but with Toussaint L'Ouverture and the San Domingo's slaves waging their own revolution, now "would do anything necessary to isolate and or defeat that model of freedom."[61] Jefferson's revolutionary fear reached a level of paranoia and counterproductiveness: "Every barrel and crate imported to American shores, in the president's eyes, was contaminated with the disease of black liberty. 'Black crews, & supercargoes, & missionaries' from the island, he insisted, proved a very real danger to Virginia."[62] So it was that President Jefferson sought to enshrine his own brand of antidemocracy, where the many may rule could be good for me but not for thee.[63] Jefferson saw this as a matter of great urgency: "If something is not done, & soon done, we shall be the murderers of our own children [for] the revolutionary storm, now sweeping the globe, will be upon us."[64]

The historian Eric Foner suggests that Jefferson's writing "reflected a divided, even tortured mind."[65] For instance, as ambassador to France, Jefferson was worldly enough to understand that slavery as an institution was not sustainable; at the same time, he could not imagine Black people as his equals.[66] On the other hand, the specialist of "revolutionary greats," Douglass G. Adair maintained that Jefferson (along with James Madison) "considered themselves as political philosophers . . . And it was as *political* philosophers [that their] sociology . . . was conceived of in *political* terms. Their economic theory was *political* economy. The Jeffersonian system was a system of politics."[67] As a political paradigm, "Jeffersonian democracy" is understood as a politics that sought to establish an agrarian based society as a priori, framing manufacturing and city life as threats to the well-being of the political community.[68] Adair's frightening specter of rule by the many underlines a long lineage of antidemocracy, highlighting Jefferson's predilection against "unchecked urban life" as a "dark picture of the turbulent and lawless *demos* that dwelt in great cities corrupted by commerce":

> Where a city proletariat gains political power there can be no cure for its viciousness until sheer excess produces the inevitable tyrant. The despot's rigid absolutism will be a welcome relief from the spasmodic reign of democratic terror. And down through the years, from Machiavelli to Burke, from Florence to Philadelphia, quotations and paraphrases and quotations

> of paraphrases of Aristotle's original indictment were to be repeated interminably every time that hydra-headed monster, the mob, stirred restively and shook the ladder of degree.[69]

In contrast is "the common man to whom the legislator could safely trust the vote"—the farmer.[70] Jefferson and Madison's ideal polity therefore could not materialize without a labor-intensive agrarian society, thus an endemic dependency on appropriated Indigenous land and unfree slave labor. Not unlike their progenitor Aristotle, Jefferson and Madison viewed slaves and a slave-dependent economy as prerequisites for their ideal polity, relying on expansionism for "a stable, secure, and prosperous Empire of Liberty."[71] An interrogation into western democratic thought, therefore, is incomplete without a serious (re)consideration of Jeffersonian antidemocracy as concomitant of gendered racial capitalism.

Two years before Gabriel's Conspiracy, Jefferson coauthored with James Madison resolutions protesting the Alien and Sedition Acts as tyrannical.[72] Asserting states' rights, they claimed that these laws were unconstitutional "and that the necessary and proper measures will be taken by each [commonwealth] for cooperating with this state, in maintaining the authorities, rights, and liberties, reserved to the states respectively, or to the people."[73] In a word, nullification. Since then, nullification has been weaponized to withhold nominal rights and dignities to those who are excluded from White autarchy. In 1798, Jefferson did not extend the inherent right to dissent to noncitizen subjects, and as Egerton points out, "the egalitarian rhetoric that pledged to make good the promise of the Revolution was aimed only at White males; indeed, aristocrats like Jefferson could more safely preach equality in a slave society than in a free one."[74]

Today, children in the US are basically taught that "Jefferson believed in the *will of the people*" and that "Jefferson's most fundamental political belief was an "absolute acquiescence in the decisions of the *majority*."[75] "Jeffersonian democracy" thus underwrites the mysticism of the "American Creed." In its various incarnations and incantations, this ideologeme centers on an imaginary political system that at its core is a set of principles that include a series of political goods: free education, universal franchise, free press, and a "limited" government. "Jeffersonian democracy" also generally is understood as both a period of history—not unlike the habit of monarchies to date themselves such as "in the Elizabethan era" or "the Victorian Age"—and as an ideology or a set of principles that characterizes American "democracy" during Jefferson's era. These include a belief in republicanism, separation of church and state, and individual liberty, including the freedom of speech and a free press. Jeffersonian democracy is also understood as an agrarian, slave-dependent republic.

Some historians, especially historians of political ideas, claim that this era is marked with expanding democratization, namely a broader incorporation of the population into the political system, and a greater degree of deliberation on the part of the citizenry. This selected incorporation and greater degree of participation, however, involved a small fraction of the larger populace. Given that Jeffersonian politics assumes an explicit preference for a slave-dependent economy and a political system that radically excludes, such political enclosure better characterizes removal than inclusion, and antidemocracy, not democracy.[76]

One would be forgiven for having the impression that Jeffersonian democracy is in keeping with democratic principles of deliberative politics; after all, Jefferson himself was characteristically clear about what he envisioned for the nation. His inauguration address, for instance, explicitly promised the legal protection of minority rights.[77] Jefferson's ideals for an agrarian society, however, hued closer to Locke's feudal imaginary of the Carolina colony, and thus he harbored no illusion that "those who labor in the earth are the chosen people of God"[78] are the same bonded people who toiled the soil of Virginia and elsewhere as they made improvements on the land and enriched the coffers of the nation.[79] In keeping with the Lockean thesis on labor that those who made improvements on the land rightly possess the land, Jefferson deemed Native Americans as technologically and culturally inferior to Europeans, and as such, he did not consider European conquest and settlements oppressive, or the exclusion of Indigenous peoples from the political life of the nation injurious.[80]

As "the first sustained written assault upon slavery and racism to come from a Black man in the United States,"[81] David Walker's *APPEAL* is an indictment of Jeffersonian antidemocracy and thus a fitting response to Jefferson and his hagiologists. Walker, one of Jefferson's most astute interlocutors, noted that Jefferson had "declared to the world, that [Black people] are inferior to Whites, both in endowment of our bodies and of minds" and, as such, excluded them from any considerations of rights or liberties.[82] Walker laid bare the hypocrisy and consistencies of Jeffersonian slave-dependent economics and plantocratic liberal regime. Radically rejecting any notion of public good that could come from slavery and White supremacy, Walker would not concede to claims of altruism on the part of White planters and their practiced paternalism. As Peter Thompson explains: "Taking Jefferson at his word, Walker dismissed claims that a charitable paternalism infused the operation of slavery. Slaveholders were not and could never be respectable men. He went further, turning the tables on his *bête noire* by arguing that *Whites* had exhibited an aberrant historical development that placed them outside civilized familiar norms."[83]

As if Jefferson were his immediate interlocutor, Walker refuted racist tropes about Black people and strenuously objected to various resettlement schemes as a conspiracy among slavocrats to evict Black people. As Cedric Robinson maintained, Walker's "exposition on the Colonizing Plan as a stratagem to perfect slave control was rhetorically powerful and methodologically precise."[84] Walker understood that this was a scheme to separate slaves from the free Black population "from whom they might contaminate with forbidden knowledge and aspirations."[85] He insisted that Black people belonged on the land that they toiled without the benefit of acquisition or accumulation. Addressing the advocates of colonization, though he might as well have been responding to the whole of the plantocratic elite, Walker asked:

> Do the colonizationists think to send us off without first being reconciled to us? Do they think to bundle us up like brutes and send us off, as they did our brethren of the State of Ohio? Have they not to be reconciled to us, or reconcile us to them, for the cruelties with which they have afflicted our fathers and us? . . . Do they think to drive us from our country and homes, after having enriched it with our blood and tears, and keep back millions of our dear brethren, sunk in the most barbarous wretchedness, to dig up gold and silver for them and their children?[86]

Walker's revolutionary *APPEAL* is a call to arms—to refute racist slanders, to push back against genocidal schemes, and to assert dignity and selfhood against those who wish harm on Black people. In his attempt "to free his people and salvage America,"[87] Walker "merged Christianity, pan-Africanism, and national birth-right," envisioning an emancipatory politics that was entwined with liberatory knowledge as teleology.[88]

Written half a decade after the circulation of *Walker's APPEAL*, Alexis de Tocqueville's *Democracy in America* contains no such emancipatory fervor. Tocqueville claimed a particular exceptionalism for the US, where he believed aristocratic tendencies did not really take root.[89] He accepted slavery as abhorrent, but, as Jennifer Pitts acutely observed: "Tocqueville's statements in [*sic*] *Democracy* deploring the European settler's violence toward Amerindians and slaves never amounted to a critique of expansion and conquest."[90] What Tocqueville saw as two distinct systems—a political order that favored a form of radical egalitarianism as recounted earlier, and a social order that fostered and inbred inequality and prejudices—Walker saw as a singular system that was endemically violent, inhumane, unjust, and ungodly. Unlike Walker, Tocqueville could not reasonably conjure a solution to rid America of its peculiar institution precisely because he saw Jeffersonian antidemocracy and mistook it as a democratic revolution, thus having no need for another revolutionary alternative.

RADICAL EXCLUSION

The American planter class Tocqueville encountered in the early nineteenth century was much less interested in spreading equality or the pursuit of human perfectibility as they were in [illegible], in [illegible] and perfecting governability. Indeed, the conceit of Jeffersonian antidemocracy is the will to perfect governing—not merely to perfect slavery as a system, but also to achieve total governability. In contrast, Walker, like many Black radical abolitionists, advocated total and complete emancipation in contradistinction to proposals for gradual emancipation, which almost always were accompanied by schemes to remove a portion of the Black community from their homes.

There are at least three conceits inherent in these schemes to resettle Black people to the west of the Mississippi River or entirely off the continent. First, even the most brutal and inhumane system of chattel slavery cannot totally dominate a people.[91] As slavocrats such as Henry Clay and others conceded, free Black communities would necessarily serve as a reservoir of incitement for revolts and rebellions.[92] By their very presence, it was argued, the free Black population held promises of ungovernability; the community itself was a mobilizing resource for ungoverning, inciting and harboring treasonous intent. Second, "gradual emancipation" is a conceit of enlightenment. When forced to deal with the reality of mastering governing, slavocrats were compelled to make concessions, reflecting their intimate knowledge of the instabilities inherent in a way of life characterized by a permanent threat to a system that was neither moral nor humane. So much so that at the height of the Jeffersonian era, the more "enlightened" few, including Jefferson, opted for "gradual emancipation"—as a form of controlling their own dependency, a concession that they had to make. Black radicals who opposed slavery, however, had always understood the deceit of "gradual emancipation." Like his feminist progeny today who insist, for instance, that until Black women are free, no one is free,[93] Walker believed that so long as slavery is alive and only some Black people are free, no one is free. David Ruggles, the New York journalist and founder of the first Black magazine, *Mirror of Liberty*, echoed this in his 1848 letter to Fredrick Douglass and Martin R. Delaney urging that Douglass's paper *North Star* be published so that it could serve as an organ for radical antislavery messaging:[94] "Let the whole truth in regard to our real condition be so clearly shown, that our colored brethren, who believe themselves free, may understand, that in the United States of America, there are no 'free colored men'; and that there never can be, so long as there is not concert of action."[95]

The third conceit is the simple but profound knowledge that slaves will rebel if they have not already run away. In their delusion, slavocrats held on to a notion that slave revolts, when they did occur, were instigated and led by free Black people and their misguided White allies. However "intuitive" this perception might appear, it contains the dubious idea that slaves were not capable of tactical or strategic planning, or the desire to be free. As the Gabriel plot and others reveal, the self-serving trope of the happy slave is an erroneous supposition. Falsifying history, it presupposes a qualitative difference between free and enslaved humans, where those who are subjugated are without capacity or desire for self-rule.[96] However and as a matter of record, slave revolts and rebellions frequently were planned, carried out, and led by slaves. Just as maroon communities struck fear in the minds of many slave owners, so Black people becoming free make lies of White supremacist ideas about self-governance and their will to power.

Orlando Patterson asserts that the slaves were the first to understand freedom: they "get the unusual idea that being free was not only a value to be cherished but the most important thing that someone could possess."[97] Freedom is thus rooted in bondage and "has never been divorced from . . . its primordial, servile source."[98] Slaveholders' use of branding as a way of marking slaves as property is instructive. According to Patterson, its general use ceased by the mid-to-late eighteenth century; thereafter, it acquired a new function—as a form of torture, punishing and marking rebels and runaways. Remarkably, this particular form of torture did not change until slave owners discovered that recaptured fugitives wore their branded letters with pride.[99] If we think of marronage as spaces of freedom, or living beyond the pale, then the free Black population is an embodiment of the very promise that White planters fear—that there are limits to their infinite desire for governing, even when that fear is rooted in racist delusions. The fear, real or imagined, that plagued Jefferson and his fellow slaveholders, is the recognition that even acts of terror of their own making could be resourced and subverted by slaves as tools for undoing antidemocracy.

THE SPECTACLES OF TURBULENCE

Among Jefferson's compatriots, one who towered above all was James Madison, a lead architect of Jeffersonian antidemocracy. In one of the most celebrated writings by an American founder, *Federalist Paper No. 10*, Madison clearly identified the majority as an endemic threat to governing. Madison parroted the long-held antidemocratic prejudice that the many problems associated with governing are frequently due to the passion of a self-serving and "overbearing majority."[100] Such decisions, he insisted, are driven by self-interest instead of "rules of justice" or consideration of "the public good."[101] These governing problems are instigated by the many. Popular government is doomed and contradictory to the goal of establishing justice or achieving common welfare because "instability, injustice, and confusion introduced into the public councils, have, in truth, been the mortal diseases under which popular governments have everywhere perished."[102] If governing problems are sourced to either "conflicts among factions" or "the tyranny of the majority," and factions can never be eliminated, the only solution is to mollify the majority.[103] Madison thought that "faction consists of less than a majority" in the form of a republic as a stark relief from and contrast to the "spectacles of turbulence and contentions" of democracies, which are "incompatible with personal security, or the rights of property; and have, in general been as short in their lives, as they have been violent in their deaths."[104] Paradigmatically, "pure democracy" becomes "a society consisting of a small number of citizens" and has "no cure for the mischiefs of faction," and therefore is vulnerable to devolving into tyranny, if not anarchy. So similar to Alexander Hamilton, their primary interlocutor, Madison and Jefferson looked upon democratic politics as a source of ill will and bad omens and, in the end, only differed from Hamilton in their preferred mechanics for acquiring wealth. This mirage of difference, however, was enough for them to seize total advantage in their "remaking" of the elite revolution.[105]

Typically, the "Jeffersonian revolution" is understood as necessary for the preservation of "free government in America."[106] Madison apparently believed that what a Jefferson administration embodied was so dangerous that it could have invited a "military *coup de'etat*" as he expressed private relief when Jefferson saw no reason to deploy "a standing army."[107] Perhaps more than Jefferson, Madison believed that the elevation of Jefferson to the presidency signaled a radically different era. Historian Charles A. Beard concurred that the election of 1800 was "revolutionary"; however, he thought that Jefferson's victory should be interpreted as a consolidation of power by one group of economic elites over another, and, as slavocrats, Jefferson and Madison were merely tending to powerful "agricultural interests."[108]

Given their dependency on unfree, super-exploited labor, successfully consolidating plantocratic interests as a class required the state and its machinery to secure order, especially on the plantations. A lifeworld dependent on unfree labor inevitably must face the prospect of collapsing under its own weight from the combined effects of depletion of that source of labor, particularly in the forms of self-harm, runaways, and/or rebellions.[109] Madison, the author of the original "three-fifths compromise," must have understood well the signification of racialism and the ways in which race and White supremacy facilitated wealth accumulation and political dominion when he observed that "the mere distinction of colour made in the most enlightened period of time, a ground of the most oppressive dominion ever exercised by man over man."[110] Indeed, if the Jeffersonian revolution rests on the primacy of an agrarian economy, then plantations and other spaces of agrarian production and distribution become sites that must be surveilled and secured. Not surprisingly, it was in the shadow of this "revolution" that a renewed and intense interest in mastering governing emerged. Madison, whose grandfather allegedly was poisoned by several slaves, personally was always anxious and particularly fearful of slave rebelliousness. So much so that, despite claiming that he could ill afford to give up ownership of Billey—an enslaved man who Madison inherited from his maternal grandmother—he did exactly that, out of fear that Billey would infect other slaves in the Madison household. Biographer Noah Feldman makes it plain: "Madison was more concerned with the effects that Billey's experiences in antislavery Philadelphia would have on other slaves at Montpelier. His concerns were not for Billey, but for the preservation of the institution of slavery on the family plantation."[111]

And so, as the day is long, Billey wanted his freedom, and Madison wanted no risk embodied by Billey. Fully aware of the diabolical contradictions inherent in Jeffersonianism and again confiding in his father, Madison claimed that he could not do worse to Billey (other than selling him into a seven-year labor contract!) "for coveting liberty for which we have paid the price of so much blood, and have proclaimed so often to be the right, and worthy pursuit, of every human being."[112] Madison, Feldman explains, was a pragmatist who despite harboring "less" racial prejudice than Jefferson, nevertheless, shared with Jefferson the same fear of a freed Black people.[113] So, while "Madison cared deeply about principles,"[114] in his decision to sell Billey into indentured servitude, as in the "three-fifths compromise," pragmatism won.

FOR THE PRESERVATION OF THE FREE

A prime example of Madison's "pragmatism" and a major pillar of Jeffersonian antidemocracy is the three-fifths rule, stipulating that apportionment for representation and tax burden be based on counting "three fifths of all other Persons" as partial.[115] Feldman cites Madison's own admission that his initial proposed formula "derived from 'accident' rather than 'accurate calculation,'" yet, "Madison persisted his whole life in believing that his compromise had been 'very near the true ratio' with respect to the taxable wealth produced by slaves."[116] With this proposal, the "principle of representing slaves partially had been introduced into American political discourse, and had not been repudiated ever since."[117] While Feldman might be correct about Madison's three-fifths proposal as a calculus of political pragmatism of sort, it is far from a "principled" position and certainly not based on any recognizable democratic principle of representation for citizen subjects, partial or otherwise. What is clear though is the unprecedented codification of slaves as not fully human for the purpose of apportioning representation—a governing regime that was made possible only by reducing an entire social category of humans as partial. Like Madison, those who came to the 1787 Continental Convention and those who debated the "compromise" were not concerned about the representation of the interests of an enslaved population. In the face of restless and rebellious Indigenous and enslaved people, the consolidation of elite rule was on their minds, for it was much more promising for governing if there were to be little or no tension among the elite. Indeed, Benjamin Franklin gave away the game when he urged his fellow conventioneers that they were sent there "to *consult*, not to *contend*, with each other."[118] They were there to tend to the interests and dominion of their class, which could only be sustained if their apportionment was augmented by the odious three-fifths rule.[119]

Jeffersonian antidemocracy is grounded in three basic presuppositions. First, its authors explicitly rejected the idealized notion that indeed the many are "equal & independent,"[120] as the first draft of the Declaration of Independence stated.[121] Given that we cannot depend on the virtue of the electors, "but in the people who are to choose them," those who are deemed lacking of virtue, especially morals, are thus precluded or should be precluded from consideration, and are therefore, not part of "the people."[122] Here liberty is wedded to unaccountable virtue, those who have the moral authority to decide what constitutes virtue also get to decide who gets to be free. As Ronald Takaki explained: "Republicanism and virtue would reinforce each other: Moral character would enable republican man to govern himself."[123] And while Madison might have believed in the virtuous republican man, neither he nor his fellow *Federalist* authors placed their trust in the virtue of the many.[124]

Second, and at the heart of *Federalist No. 54*, is Madison's defense of apportionment, foregrounding the inconvenient truths of the three-fifths rule and republican elitism. Madison's reasoning for supporting it as "evidently the least objectionable" reveals not only the superficial difference among the framers but also the apparent callousness and moral bankruptcy that informed such a debate. Madison's "genius" was now on full display as he rejected the arguments that slaves "were either property or persons, not both."[125] He reasoned that by law, slaves were both—"in some respects, as persons, and in other respects, as property."[126] Madison's legal supremacist rationalization is startling:

> It is the character bestowed on them by the laws under which they live; and it will not be denied, that these are the proper criterion; *because it is only under the pretext that the laws have transformed the negroes into subjects of property*, that a place is disputed them in the computation of numbers; and it is admitted, *that if the laws were to restore the rights which have been taken away, the negroes could no longer be refused an equal share of representation with the other inhabitants.*[127]

Feldman interprets this reasoning as further evidence of Madison's pragmatism, especially because Madison did not have to acknowledge the fact that "his economic welfare depended on the labor of slaves."[128]

Federalist No. 54 as revelation reads like a defense of *the Law* and legal supremacy. If *the Law* can render a people as "persons," "property," or "mixed character," then it is an affirmation of the idea that if *the Law giveth, the Law can taketh away.*[129] And only those who are fit to rule can determine what the Law shall be. Moreover, and if we were to take seriously the intent behind *Federalist No. 54*, the main obstacle to the three-fifths rule might not have been the binary nomination of slaves as property or persons. To be sure there is ample evidence to support many historians' assertions, including Feldman's, that there were objections over how to nominally classify slaves in relation to apportionment. If, however, we were to take Franklin, Madison, Hamilton, and other conventioneers at their words, their chief concerns had to do with not whether slaves were property or persons, but how best to tax and represent wealth (as slaves were nominally understood). The objection to this rule would then have had more to do with a contestation among different factions of elites than with a philosophical debate about the humanity of the laboring classes. Had it been a debate about the humanity of the laboring class and of slaves and their political status, would not such debates and *Federalist No. 54* have focused on the franchise? White residents, many of whom could not vote, were nonetheless counted as whole and were included in the census. Why then was the issue of *their* apportionment not worthy of further debate? With this rule, however, the Constitution initiated its own process of nullifying justice for slaves, if not for the entire laboring class.[130] Despite this dubious accomplishment, Madison continues to be considered as more "enlightened" than his friend and collaborator Jefferson. Madison is credited with helping to end the international slave trade and later ending slavery itself. This revisionism is specious, considering Madison's massive contribution toward the nullification of applicable justice for African Americans in the US.[131]

Third, the metaphysics of Jeffersonian elitist rule can be sustained if and only if domestic order is ensured. Feldman intimates that Madison in his post-presidency "wanted visitors from around the world who would come to him [at Montpelier] as they had visited Washington and Jefferson, to see that his slaves were treated well."[132] If Montpelier, the Madison family plantation, "was supposed to stand in for a vision of republican tranquility—the one Madison had designed for the United States itself"—then it bears troubling reminders of "Madison's lifelong reliance on slave labor" and the nation's forever quest for domestic tranquility.[133] Within the larger frame of Jeffersonian antidemocracy, Madison's "principled pragmatism" therefore had less to do with virtue and more with the practical need for containing slave resistance and ensuring domestic tranquility—a neglected constitutional principle, yet likely one with utmost importance in the minds of framers, especially for Jefferson and Madison's own revolution.[134]

As Walker understood, those whose way of life was dependent on slaves lived in fear of slave revolts; thus, for the framers, "ensuring domestic Tranquility" was as essential as "providing for the common defense." Even with the frightful specters of a total slave revolution resembling the one that took place in Haiti, those who favored the end of the international slave trade, including Madison, nevertheless were in no mood to end domestic slave trading, which was considerably more profitable and beastly. Madison was not alone as many southerners supported the international ban, and with the largest slave population, Virginia stood to gain the most from the internal trade.[135] Men like Washington, Henry, and Jefferson took part in this lucrative business enterprise, with vested interests in quickening access to such pursuits.[136] Indeed, the date for which Madison received credit for terminating international slave trading actually marked a prohibition against congressional interference in its operations.[137] In supposing Madison's well intention and prescient contribution to this specific clause, not to mention, the three-fifths rule, historians like Feldman reveal less about their historical subject and more about their own investment in a rehabilitation project or a general apologia of the Founders' intimate dealings with slavery, including their fear of and paranoia toward slaves and slave resistance. If the plantations are indeed a stand-in for the Founders' visions for the nation, especially that of Madison's, then their embeddedness within slavery, as an institution and a way of life, must be the final arbiter of their conduct.

Accordingly, Madison's post-retirement turn toward gradual abolition should be understood as an attempt at atonement for a legacy complicated and troubled by slavery.[138] It is a peculiar form of atonement because Madison's proposal for slavery's gradual end consisted of a radical plan to evict Black people from the continent. For him, previous schemes by Jefferson and others had not gone far enough. Like Jefferson, Madison had privately confessed fear of violence of genocidal proportions should slavery end and Black people become free to live their lives alongside White people, and so he supported the general outlines of colonization schemes for deporting free Black people to Africa. Three decades later and now in retirement, Madison apparently had doubled down on his frightful projection.[139] Ever pragmatic, Madison, "believing that it was impractical to separate communities of free blacks from Whites," went further than all other mainstream schemes to proposed that not only free Black people but "the great mass of blacks" be evicted from the US and be sent to Africa.[140] In a letter written to Robert J. Evans, Madison proposed the following stipulation for any plan to end slavery in the US: "A general emancipation of slaves ought to be 1. gradual. 2. equitable & satisfactory to the individuals immediately concerned. 3. consistent with the existing & durable prejudices of the nation."[141] First, and betraying his own revolutionary inheritance, Madison insisted on a consensus that all solutions to "deep rooted and widespread evils" *must be gradual.* Second, this plan must secure "the consent of both the Master & the slave" to fulfill the second stipulation that it be "equitable & satisfactory." Slaveholders, therefore, should be compensated for "a loss of *what he has held as property guaranteed by the laws, and recognized by the constitution.*"[142] Contrary to his expressed claim in the *Federalist No. 54*, here Madison is quite clear about the actual status of Black people as property, especially since Madison did not make provisions to compensate the slaves. So, betraying his own claim of fairness, Madison envisioned equity for the Master, with only satisfaction for the slaves.[143] Finally, his coup de grâce came in the form of fulfilling the third requirement—to permanently evict Black people from American life: "To be consistent with existing and probably unalterable prejudices in the U. S. the freed blacks ought to be permanently removed beyond the region occupied by or allotted to a White population."[144] So fearful of imaginary Black vengeance and so absolute in his conceit, the usually fiscally conservative Madison contemplated an overall expenditure of upward $12 trillion in today's valuation.[145] He reasoned that such a great sum of money was completely worth it because the nation as a whole would "reap the benefit" from "planting one desert with a free & civilized people" and therefore it "ought to bear the burden." While Madison framed his proposal to raise part of the funds as a form of "atonement" for the displacement and dispossession of Indigenous people and their lands, it resembles a classic case of robbing Mary to pay Paul. This scheme would involve the "disposable territory belonging to the U. S."—namely Indigenous land—be sold off to finance reparations to compensate slaveholders.[146] Madison put it this way: "if in any instances, wrong has been done by our forefathers to people of one colour in dispossessing them of their soil, what better atonement is now in our power than that of making what is rightfully required a source of justice & of blessings to a people of another colour?"[147] Such self-aggrandizement and adornment notwithstanding, not unlike the delusions of color-blind, post-racial justice, Madison's atonement is thus one that requires no accountability of the self—only taxation of the other.

The influence of Jefferson's and Madison's reactionary thought in the making of racial antidemocracy in the US are enduring. This chapter sought out a particular past that sometimes gets lost in dominant hagiographies about the American Creed and liberal political philosophy. This oversight or willful forgetting persists into our current authoritarian attack on critical thought and the general attack on Black Studies. Thus, at the risk of treading old grounds, the life and work of Locke, Jefferson, and Madison are important and remain salient for deep reflection on contemporary politics and mass mobilization, and for finding ways toward just futures. Just as Locke supplied the language for Jefferson's vision of natural rights and the pursuit of property, Madison's lifelong view about the tyranny of the majority now furnished the grammatology for slavocrats, including John C. Calhoun's theory of the concurrent majority and advocacy of nullification, all the while embracing the empire of liberty.[148] These compacts are part of the larger liberal contract of domination meant to radically exclude, with the Madison-Jeffersonian framework being entirely consistent with, if not a more radical iteration of, the existing arrangement of White rule and the "Jacksonian democracy" that came later.[149] Indeed, while more vulgar, the Jacksonian iteration exposes Jeffersonian antidemocracy, and its tendentious presupposition of Whiteness as property and the entitled freedom of the few, as wholly consistent with their will to power.[150]

5
The Empty Sounds of Liberty

This party, with its every action, every word, every breath, and every heartbeat, has but a single resolve, and that is freedom—freedom made orderly for this Nation by our constitutional government. . . . We Republicans see in our constitutional form of government the great framework which assures the orderly but dynamic fulfillment of the whole man, and we see the whole man as the great reason for instituting orderly government in the first place.

Barry Goldwater[1]

One woman begged me to get a newspaper and read it over. She said her husband told her that the black people had sent word to the queen of 'Merica that they were all slaves; that she didn't believe it, and went to Washington city to see the president about it. They quarreled; she drew her sword upon him, and swore he should help her to make them all free. That poor, ignorant woman thought that America was governed by a Queen, to whom the President was subordinate. I wish the President was subordinate to Queen Justice.

Harriet Jacobs[2]

THE COSMETICS OF LIBERTY

Liberty is both a right and a privilege, depending on its context. Liberty represents free will as well as the absence of will, depending on one's religion. Liberty implies absence of constraints but also the presence of restraints, depending on whose liberty is in question. In its most authentic expression, liberty refers to the state or condition of being free—free from bondage, including spiritual servitude; free from incarceration, including mental manipulation; free from restraints, including self-harm; and free from tyranny, including despotism.[3] In western recorded history, liberty has been a perennial concern for rulers from Roman emperors and religious authorities to heads of modern states. Indeed, western philosophers have sought to illuminate the many meanings of liberty ever since the goddess Libertas personified the idea of freedom and was represented in coinage and usurpations.[4] In 1848 she showed up on the Great Seal of France, which was reproduced in the form of Frédéric Auguste Bartholdi's Statue of Liberty Enlightening the World, otherwise known as New York's green Statue of Liberty.

Around the thirteenth century, political connotations of liberty gradually displaced religious connotations, and once again its Latin roots resurfaced. By the mid-sixteenth century, the idea was mostly conflated with the status of a free man. Remarkably, in the modern world, the status of a free man is now reanimated in the symbol of a woman; so, Libertas the goddess of liberty—or lady liberty, for short—once again is synonymous with democracy, even the free world itself.

A perennial debate among political theorists and philosophers has been the metaphysical struggle between individualism and communitarianism. This is extrapolated to other areas of philosophical concern, including the contest between capitalism and communism, liberty and equality, or freedom and justice. Even debates about the state and economy writ large are frequently framed as one side favoring the community versus the other, the individual. What is germane, however, is the question: how has liberty been deployed as an instrument of governing?

Here too Aristotle's metaphysics is foundational, especially his privileging of the inherent virtue of the political community. His guidance is a misdirection, however, as he propped up order as virtuous: virtue is the mean between excess and deficiency, the disposition that is "equidistant from each of the extremes."[5] Aristotle also recognized that there are actions and passions that have neither a mean of excess nor deficiency, such as things that already imply badness or goodness. If liberty prefigures goodness, it cannot be either an excess or defect. If liberty is a mean between the state of unfreedom and total freedom, there exists the possibility of liberty's excess. It is worth contemplating what would have happened if the modern symbol of liberty was the pileus—the cap that marked a person as being free from bondage—instead of lady liberty, and was just as likely to appear on currencies. For the Greeks who lived in the time of a democracy existing side by side with slavery, to be free is to not be a slave.

Revealing a clear debt to Aristotelian metaphysics of ruling, despite its claims of moderation, contemporary radical Republicanism[6] owes part of its inheritance to Barry Goldwater. Accepting his presidential nomination at the 1964 Republican National Conventions, Goldwater famously voiced his speech writer's words: "extremism in the defense of liberty is no vice" and "moderation in the pursuit of justice is no virtue."[7] And despite his speech's many clues, few anticipated that liberty would become modern-day Republicanism's chief instrument of governing. In his political progeny's hands, liberty became so deformed that it is synonymous with the rule of law that Goldwater foreshadowed: "At this party, with its every action, every word, every breath, and every heartbeat has but a single resolve, and that is freedom—freedom made orderly for this nation by our constitutional government; . . . freedom balanced so that order lacking liberty [*sic*] will not become the slavery of the prison cell; balanced so that liberty lacking order will not become the license of the mob and of the jungle."[8] That today's Republican Party has moved so far to the right, with few exceptions, even its nominal leaders in Congress refuse to publicly acknowledge the validity and reliability of scientific findings on matters ranging from environmental to public health, suggests Goldwater's proclamation is more than rhetorical. What does it mean, for instance, to "make freedom orderly"? We do know that since 1964 Goldwater's acolytes put in place a permanent infrastructure for the prison industrial complex, that, among other things, has sought to evict various undesirable populations from the landscapes of the Empire of Liberty, especially if they were Black and Brown people.[9] Deemed as feral, these communities have been dismembered, social infrastructures divested, and the people targeted for organized neglect and to be warehoused in the larger prison nation, all to ensure freedom made orderly.[10]

At one level, Goldwater suggested what appears to be obvious—liberty and order are intimately linked—but what does freedom balanced mean? What is the virtue in order lacking liberty and liberty lacking order? If neoliberalism is any clue, then order lacking liberty is for the superrich, on the one hand, and, on the other, liberty is evacuated entirely from order for the poor and the meddlesome. Put differently, Goldwater's maxim anticipates or perhaps remembers a form of liberty's excess for the few, and order's excess for the many. On order's excess, Goldwater was quite clear—many point to Goldwater's "law and order" rhetoric that coincided with a new era of policing and mass incarceration, or the "war on crime."[11] While these observers are not wrong about the deleterious effects of the law-and-order rhetoric and the accompanying policies, they miss out on the thoroughness of this "crime agenda" and underestimate the comprehensiveness of the collusion between the state and capital in enacting that agenda. So while Goldwater got credit for framing the Republican modern electoral playbook, the Republicans do not have a monopoly on the war on crime and did not invent the idea of order's excess. Historian Elizabeth Hinton argues that post–World War II Republicans "did not engineer the War on Crime and the rise of the carceral state," and that crime control "dominated the government responses to American inequality and insecurity."[12] Indeed, "the roots of mass incarceration had been firmly established by a bipartisan consensus of national policymakers in the two decades prior to Reagan's War on Drugs in the 1980s."[13] As a response to demographics and mass mobilizations, vested elites sought to evict the masses of Black people, along with the urban poor. Hinton shows this crime business characteristically succeeded by failing and, government policies did not prevent crimes or increase public safety, let alone secure order; instead, its policies "escalated both violence and imprisonment."[14] Cogently, neither the "creative destruction" of environmental, financial, or labor regulations, nor market fundamentalism are legible as liberty's excess. Instead, it was order's excess—the fear of the imaginary mob and jungle—that won out in an all-out war on those who were perceived as troublesome and meddlesome.[15] Goldwater's "new" sensibility is a cipher for the larger campaign to reinforce an old order, pushing back against their democratic opponents' perceived gains. If the demographic transformation combined with a heightened phase of justice mobilization portended a possible curtailing of freedom for the few, then the deciding elite would need to close off access to political life—to "deactivate the mass."[16] This is a politics of deterrence and containment of domestic threats.[17] By deploying the term "forgotten civil right," Goldwater gave language to White supremacists, especially segregationists, to weaponize a politics of resentment and refusal, enabling a particular arm of the state and civil society to deter and contain democratic aspirations.[18] However, Goldwater was far from the first to articulate such a view.

SECURING FREEDOM MADE ORDERLY

The presupposition of order as ideal underwrites not only western liberal social theory's preposterous assumption that the consent to be governed is transcendent. It also supports the notion that those who are not fit to rule, and not fit to rule themselves, are always in need of order's excess. Of the innumerable groups designated as lacking the capacity to rule, especially to rule themselves, few have been singled out more than the people of African descent.[19]

In Trumpite lore, the close association between the 45th President and an earlier racist one, Andrew Jackson, is frequently evoked. Remarkably, those who draw this parallel tend to ignore the other Andrew—Andrew Johnson—as a likelier antecedence for Trumpites and neoconfederates.[20] Johnson's 1866 "swing around the circle" midterm campaign and the rallying cry, "you shall not replace us," could have been a template for the Trumpites' playbook.[21] In the aftermath of the Civil War, the anticipated radical transformation of southern life, particularly for Black people, did not occur. This failure partly had to do with reactionary forces seeking to sustain the old order, of which Johnson played an important role. Weaponizing real or imagined White fear and anxiety, Johnson helped advance the White-led counterrevolution against a more inclusive democratic life form, abolition democracy.[22]

Dylan Rodríguez proposes that we abandon the notion of Reconstruction as a federal government's failure to incorporate newly free Black people into the political life of the nation and permanently curtail the power of former slavocrats. Instead, he suggests we read this national project, especially the work of the Freedmen's Bureau—the agency nominally tasked with the work of Reconstruction—as the deliberate work of a counterrevolution.[23] Johnson's use of the political press and White supremacy partly explain his official acts intended to undermine radical change, including vetoing legislation that would support the Bureau's remedial work. Similar to Rodríguez, historian Hans L. Trefousse points out that Johnson was "determined to preserve the social order . . . with its insistence on White supremacy."[24] Johnson saw himself as a White supremacist and "conceived of an America ruled by whites . . . its benefits reserved for whites."[25] Citing Johnson's private secretary, Trefousse asserts that Johnson's conviction that White men are superior to Black people went beyond basic prejudice.[26] Beyond "morbid distress" and animosity, Johnson harbored contempt for Black people, especially Black people who were free. This "biased attitude" (or racism) "made it impossible for Johnson to sympathize in any way with policies furthering racial equality."[27] In short: "Johnson had no intention whatsoever reconsidering his policies of White Reconstruction."[28] His opposition against large-scale franchise for Black men and leniency toward Confederate traitors were thus consistent with his desire for a White Reconstruction.[29] The "Southerners were delighted" and reassured by Johnson's policies and, "in various areas of the former Confederacy, *they once more ruled supreme.*"[30] The "old" order of plantocratic dominion and Jeffersonian antidemocracy, once deemed a lost cause, is now resurrected in the form of Johnson's White Reconstruction.[31]

Critical to the extension of White supremacy in the aftermath of the Civil War was its fortification of the logic of gendered racial capitalism, with its constitutive coercive and bureaucratic enforcements in place. As Madison previously understood, the monopoly of White southern elites over land was central to the maintenance of Jeffersonian antidemocracy and, in the aftermath of the Civil War, Johnson as president would ensure it. In addition to protecting White suffrage, the means of production would also need to be secured and, in the agrarian dominated plantocratic South, the reappropriation of settler's land, or land reform, would also have to be prevented.[32] Johnson understood that if "he wanted to maintain the dominance of the White race, [he] could not permit the transfer of land to the freedmen."[33] Thus, the pardoning of treasonous confederates were not empty gestures; they were accompanied by reparation meant to restore "the landed property," with the belief that "blacks ought to labor for their former masters."[34]

Here, White supremacist ideology underwrites the governing logic of war reconstruction as a regime of development. Foreshadowing the Trump administration, Johnson's approach to the bureaucratic state allowed him to attack his own governing apparatuses as if he, the sovereign, transcended the state itself. Johnson aggressively attacked any serious proposals for structural reform as "unconstitutional, impolitic, and unwise."[35] For Johnson, "The South was either to be reconstructed according to his idea [as a White reconstruction], or it would not be reconstructed at all."[36] In this endeavor, Johnson did not effect change on his own and received much help from his confederates in the South and many compatriots in the North. That Johnson knew he must rely on patronage to secure compliance for his agenda suggests the limits to political leadership and leaders' abilities to make use of a ravenous state. Indeed, among White Reconstruction's many friends were those in the North who voted against anyone opposing the idea of permanent White rule and a restored white autarchy.[37] The regime of White reconstruction as development thus makes explicit a social contract as a contract of domination—a compact among White supremacists upholding White autarchy. The maintenance of white supremacy, however, requires a political economy that relies on the persistence of racial gendered capitalism. Like racism, this post–Civil War political economy, or Jim Crow economics, was not geographically tied to the South.[38] As W. E. B. Du Bois explains in *Black Reconstruction*:

> As slavery grew to a system and the Cotton Kingdom began to expand into imperial White domination, a free Negro was a contradiction, a threat and a menace. As a thief and a vagabond, he threatened society but as an educated property holder, a successful mechanic or even professional man, he more than threatened slavery. He contradicted and undermined it. He must not be. He must be suppressed, enslaved, colonized.[39]

In a word, negation. The idea of a (free) Black person threatens and negates the presupposition of White supremacy, and a free Black people embodies an implicit danger to absolute White rule.[40] Like Walker before him, Du Bois understood that the presumption that Black people had no capacity for self-rule was an essential element of the self-serving claim of segregationist policies and White rule. And like Ida B. Wells, Du Bois was acutely aware that Jim Crow economics was both violent and violently enforced. Cogently, he understood that Jim Crow economics, as an expression of racial capitalism—enforced by a host of Black codes and vigilante terror—is part and parcel of White rule.[41] Emancipation has deprived the slave barons of their primary engine of wealth—Black labor—"and with no method of earning a living, except by exploiting black labor on their only remaining capital—their land."[42] While a "veritable reign of terror prevailed in many parts of the South,"[43] Du Bois noted the ever-escalating and endemic violence and terrorism against the Black community as violence and terror became essential to governability.[44]

Du Bois thus saw through the transparent and self-serving propaganda against the Black vote, including the use of "brute force" to prevent it from happening.[45] More importantly, he understood that the attack on the idea of self-governance for Black people was deployed strategically against not only Black people but broadly applied to other non-White people as the White elite sought to establish its own "new form of imperialism."[46] First, the trope of incompetence for denying Black self-determination was effective because "the North had never been thoroughly converted to the idea of Negro equality . . . it was much easier to believe the accusation of the South" about Black inferiority.[47] Dubois was clear about how this self-serving imperialist logic extends to workers in Asia and Africa: "These inferiors were to be governed for their own good. They were to be raised out of sloth and laziness by being compelled to work. The whole attitude of Europe was reflected in America and it found in America support for its own attitude."[48] White laborers, rather than enjoining recently freed Black people as compatriots, "clung frantically to the planter and his ideals . . . [and] sought redress by demanding unity of White against black, and not unity of poor against rich, or of worker against exploiters."[49] Du Bois pointed to the use of violence and terror against Black workers by poor Whites as evidence of intraclass antagonism. When faced with economic precarity, especially if they had to compete directly with newly freed Black people, poor Whites turned "from service to guerrilla warfare" and "joined eagerly secret organizations, like the Ku Klux Klan."[50] Like its contemporary progeny, the vigilante White supremacist formation—the original Klan, was essential to White identity in the face of economic precarity.[51] Here Du Bois is among a few who thoroughly recognized that "the true significance of slavery [and its afterlife] to the whole social development of America lay in the ultimate relation of slaves to democracy."[52] What was obvious to him was the rhetorical power of the modern social contract, and how "the consent to be governed" as a principle was sacrosanct to modern ideas of governing. He was acutely aware that racial capitalism, accompanied by terror and violence, exposes its conceits for all to see because, after all, if liberal transcendence is to be believed, there would be no more discrimination based on race and color than there would be taxation without representation. Yet, having ample presence of both, American antidemocracy waged a revolution over one but not the other.

THE LIMITS OF REPRESENTATION

The Black male franchise, however limited, was a major indicator of Black political incorporation and democratization in the US.[53] Du Bois maintained that "votes for Negroes were in truth the final compromise between business and abolition and were forced on abolition by business as the only method of realizing the basic principles of abolition democracy."[54] At a minimum, democratic living and the principle of the consent to be governed require communities of people broadly incorporated into civil society, and for Du Bois "the abolition of slavery meant not simply abolition of legal ownership of slave," but also "the uplift of slaves and their eventual incorporation into the body civil, politic, and social, of the United States."[55] Thus, the totality of abolition democracy dictates the incorporation of Black people into the life of the nation, not only as *homo politicus* but also *homo economicus* and *homo socius*. For Dubois, it is an opportunity to build a foundation for "essential social equality . . . mutual respect," and social solidarity.

In delineating abolition democracy, Du Bois advanced basic parameters for authentic democratic living, one that democratic elitism failed to deliver. He argued that when faced with the prospect of a free Black population who fought for and demanded freedom, the US had one option: Black people "must have protection of the law; and backing of law must stand physical force. They must have land; they must have education."[56] In other words, conditions of possibility for democratic livability are predicated on a complex set of sociomaterial conditions, combined with a political infrastructure capable of radical inclusion. However, the history of violence and terror against Black people and the lack of substantive justice for all, as understood by Wells and others, confirmed what Du Bois thought—when faced with a possibility for democratic living, big business and slave barons chose autocracy in the form of White rule, with terrorism as its lieutenant.[57] In this epic battle between the autocracy of gendered racial capitalism versus democratic living, it appears that autocracy won out.

REPRODUCING AUTARCHY

The enslavement of Black people precludes any proclamations of universal liberty. As Harriet Jacobs, who lived in fugitivity for nearly seven years in a crawl space of her grandmother's house, understood: "Slave holders pride themselves upon being honorable men; but if you were to hear the enormous lies they tell their slaves, you would have small respect for their veracity."[58] For Jacobs and others like her, they either "reached freedom or the grave."[59] Thus, the trouble with tyranny, especially autarchy, is that maintaining permanent rule is a fool's errand. Put differently, government may reform, but the people revolt, and, in the face of tyranny, the will to resist, sometimes, overcomes the will to power. Totalitarianism, including racist regimes, relies on the perfectibility of dominion, and total acceptance of dominion without coercion, is rarely if ever possible.[60] This desire for total dominance is the vain attempt at absolute autonomy for the ruler and total governance over the ruled—body, mind, spirit, and emotions. Thus, those who profited from slaveholding, including many statesmen, were keenly aware of the profitability in depriving women and men of their reproductive autonomies. White dominion, especially in the time of slavery, relied on "the dehumanization of Africans on the basis of race, and the control of women's sexuality and reproduction."[61] As the legal scholar Dorothy Roberts argues, by extension laws were designed to enforce "this monstrous combination."[62] The "brutal denial" of Black women's reproductive autonomy is the verification of Jeffersonian conceits, and the pride of place of liberty in Jeffersonian politics is thus a deceit of governing. Given that slaveholders saw Black women as producers and reproducers, it was logical that they would also train their ideological arsenals against them, including the use of sexual terrorism.

As pointed out in the previous chapter, many southerners supported a ban against international slave trading, anticipating a comparative advantage from internal trades. The 1808 ban only "made enslaved women's childbearing even more valuable."[63] Controlling Black people, especially Black women's biological reproduction, was thus a national affair and central to the development of gendered racial capitalism. As Roberts explains: "Female slaves were commercially valuable to their masters not only for their labor, but also for their ability to produce more slaves. The law made slave women's children the property of the slaveowner. White masters therefore could increase their wealth by controlling their slave's reproductive capacity."[64] For instance, Jefferson was keen on monitoring women's menstrual cycles and regulating their work on that basis.[65] He was not alone. Historian Marie Jenkins Schwartz explains:

> Because no small part of a slaveholder's future earnings depended on the birth of children in bondage, slaveholders became concerned when a woman past puberty failed to produce a living child with regularity. They worried about her reproductive health generally and took action when they feared she would be unable to bear children. They offered inducements for marriage or threatened barren women with sale away from family and friends. They paid attention to sex ratios and purchased potential mates, or they allowed couples to court across property boundaries.[66]

In short, the reproduction of the plantocracy's source of labor and profit was regimented and governed. With coercive reproduction integral to household management, some even publicly encouraged other slaveholders to do everything to "render them prolific."[67] After all, "Black procreation not only benefited each slave's particular owner; it also more globally sustained the entire system of slavery."[68] Critical to wealth expansion, total management of Black reproduction along with the denial of Black bodily autonomy are essential to the maintenance of White supremacy and dominion. Crucially, Black women's resistance reveals how they "attacked the very assumption upon which the slave order was constructed and maintained."[69] Slavocrats had relied on Black reproduction for profit and power, even as they pronounced it a "degeneracy," and sought to micromanage their ways into Black women's wombs and minds. They vainly pronounced self-evident that their class interests were chosen because everyone else, especially Black people, are incapable of self-rule and in need of governing, thus electing themselves as rightful heirs of the state. But as Davis, Roberts, and others have argued, despite "the absolute power the law granted them" and the total monopoly of coercive apparatuses of the state, slavocrats "failed to crush slave women's sprit."[70] They also failed miserably in their attempt to perfect White male-only self-rule. Indeed, while slavocrats fought among themselves for the right to settle, plunder, and exploit, the many—especially the many Black men and women—fought them at every turn, and on occasion collectively conspired and coauthored small revolts and even open rebellions and mass insurrections, all the while imagining and dreaming of very different futures.

THE EMPTY THRONE OF LIBERTY

Within this context of coercive reproduction, Roberts insists that the meanings of liberty cannot be discerned without a serious interrogation of the ways White supremacist ideology has operated on the Black body.[71] The "killing of the Black body," she argues, is part and parcel of America's racist arsenals. From "the official denial of reproductive liberty" and the suppression of reproductive autonomy of Indigenous and Black women that seeded the roots of contemporary reproductive regulations, to the marshaling of pseudoscientific discourses marking Black bodies as inferior and degenerative (and Black mothers as unworthy and dangerous) and creating a biological underclass, this brutal suppression of autonomy makes lies out of claims of radical liberty. For Roberts, the denial of slave women's reproductive autonomy represents official denial of reproductive liberty, and Black women's resistance against the denial and suppression of their reproductive autonomy "demonstrates even more powerfully that reproductive liberty is vital to our human dignity . . . [and] a liberty worth struggling for—even dying for."[72]

Just as we need to ask the important question "Justice for whom?"—as Susan Okin did with respect to gender and the family[73]—we must also raise critical questions about whose freedom was in question when we interrogate the meanings of liberty. Here liberal conceptions of liberty are at issue. When "liberty is understood as a guarantee of government neutrality, as limited only to tangible harms and as a negative right," it presupposes the exclusion of social justice as ideal or normative.[74] As Roberts explains:

> While government neutrality protects citizens against imposition of state orthodoxy, it also means that the definition of liberty must take a colorblind stance in regard to reproductive policies. . . . Government neutrality conceals the racist origins of social practices that do not overtly discriminate on the basis of race. It ignores the way that the degrading mythology about Black mothers influences public policy as long as government officials do not explicitly act on the basis of race.

This self-serving claim of a "colorblind" post-racialism almost always functions as a stand-in for real accountability and reparation, while allowing ongoing wealth hoarding and political dominance, and conveniently foreclosing on any considerations for restorative and/or transformative justice.[75] Because the "dominant view of liberty reserves most of its protection only for the most privileged members of society," it "superimposes liberty on an already unjust social structure, which it seeks to preserve against unwarranted government interference."[76] Just as democracy has degenerated from rule by the many to elite decision-making, liberty now morphs into unimpeded freedom to exploit and plunder.

Not unlike the western anarchism that cannot break free of the autonomous individual, the entire edifice of self-styled libertarianism relies on an idea of personal autonomy that conscripts individual liberty as a public good. Today among right-wingers and neo-confederates, including libertarians, no single idea captures their imagination more than the exalted status of liberty. Without any sense of irony, these American "libertarians" openly and persistently demand the curtailing of women's reproductive autonomy and the systematic exclusion of LGBTQ+ people from the polity, not to mention the censorship of critical public discourse on race and racism. Today's libertarians are not the first Americans to privilege liberty over social justice. They are merely the latest descendants of those who professed love for freedom on the one hand while holding the whip with the other. The privileging of individual autonomy diminishes social obligation and other values like justice, solidarity and dignity. As Roberts explains, "the primacy of liberty, which shifts the burden of persuasion to those seeking to limit individual choice, does not allow for the possibility that other concerns might have equal constitutional or moral importance."[77]

As Robinson observed in *Black Movements in America*, "America had been and is still a nation of freedom *and injustice*."[78] The decoupling of liberty from social justice makes it possible for freedom and injustice to harmonize.

This twining is integral to liberty's excess and antidemocracy's conceit. The dethroning of liberty, exposing it as mere façade of antidemocracy, is instructive for unlearning democratic elitism. As delineated in chapter 3, democratic elitism presupposes a functionary state wherein public goods like civil rights and civil liberties are not universally extended. Those who are marked as different and are differently vulnerable are then variously co-opted and/or cooperated with, depending on their worth to the system, with their lack of worth weighted in proximation to violence and harm. Not unlike the few elite women of Plato's *Republic*[19]—some are co-opted, others are discarded, and yet others are barricaded behind walls as threats and ungovernables. This is a calculus of governing, not a principle of democratic existence. The deforming of liberty is thus a logical extension of democratic elitism. If the elite decide, then they will decide what is reasonable to them and beneficial for themselves. Just as they have consistently denied reproductive autonomy to the many, especially women of Color, and have gone to great length to enforce that unfreedom, they have raised armies and empires for the freedom to wage war, colonize, and exclude. Liberty's excess therefore makes it possible for democracy to degenerate into democratic elitism by curtailing the freedom of everyone who is not part of the elite. As such, contestations over the right to rule and the refusal to be governed rage from the womb to the statehouses and imperial palaces.

As suggests here, when resistance to tyranny begins and ends with liberty, transformative justice projects are abandoned along with used up dreams of freedom. Indeed, when we excavate the archives of resistance to governing, the most powerful and compelling mass mobilizations have been those who also fought for something *more* than liberty. For instance, the Black radical tradition has been decidedly about more than a struggle for individual autonomy, even as it foregrounds liberatory subjectivities. Radical traditions that foreground liberatory subjects while centering on communities instead of individuals have tended to be more capacious. The search for ontological wholeness, as Robinson asserts, is thus not one that deals out individual liberties, but engenders communal emancipation and alternative lifeworlds.

Antidemocracy relies on authoritarian excesses, and a deformed liberty is one that reserves all for the few and nothing for the many. Goldwater's turn of phrase, "freedom made orderly" exposes modern Republicanism's pejoratives, and reveals how antidemocracy relies on both liberty's and order's excesses. On the one hand, it preordains order as a priori such that order is the requirement that begets freedom or personal liberty; this is order's excess. On the other hand, it conveys a particular sensibility that assumes a special group of deciders who are also preordained to render freedom orderly; this is liberty's excess. Antidemocracy presupposes that freedom is made orderly and can only be made orderly through curbing democratic excesses. The state, far from a limited framework, is the leviathan that secures freedom for Man. If Man is the stand-in for the many and, given that only some men are Man while others are not, with liberty now personified in the feminine form of freedom, liberty is therefore always at risk of being accessorized.

Securing order renders it vulnerable to a state of being in excess and predisposes the possibility of permanent insecurity. In security related industries, excess procurement contributes to redundancy and waste. When not properly regulated, excess can lead to insecurity. The state in search of order establishes antidemocracy for the purpose of freedom made orderly. Within the context of American antidemocracy, including its neoliberal phase, a few elite deciders largely have elected themselves to hoard liberty's excess while imposing an excess of order on the many who already are excluded from deliberation. But an excess of order implies that there exists an ideal amount of order. Given that order is prefiguratively a virtue, a deficiency in order thus raises the possibility of bad outcomes—a bogeyman in the form of anarchy and chaos. Our historical detour thus far, however, suggests that while order's excess is real, the presupposition that there is an ideal order, or an ideal amount of order, seems entirely dubious.

PART II

Life Beyond Governing

6
From *Homo Politicus* to *Robo Sapiens*: An Interlude

Where are we? In the middle, at the beginning, the end?
Who is we, is it you plus me, or something else expandable, explosive,
the salt and pepper of our thoughts,
the something that may outlast our divinities?
. . .
What are the links between the space and me?
Where do questions on the infinity of time and space lead to?
Civilization built on revenge shall disappear.
So would others. Could we then go on thinking?

Etel Adnan[1]

DISORIENTATION

"You bum, why did you hit me?" Xiao Zhen Xie asked in Chinese to her assailant, a man much younger than she who was handcuffed, laying on a stretcher after being pummeled. According to eyewitnesses, Xie "then turned to the crowd of people who gathered and exclaimed, 'this bum, he hit me,' as she raised the stick she was holding and sobbed, 'he hit me, this bum,' she repeated."[2] News reports later recounted how a thirty-nine-year-old man attacked two elderly Asian Americans that morning in San Francisco—the mecca for Asian Pacific American Islanders (AAPIs) living in the US. To himself, the White man must have appeared bold as brass. He first assaulted eighty-three-year-old Ngoc Pham, leaving him at the scene with head and neck injuries, then went on looking for the next victim. A few minutes later, he found the seventy-five-year-old Xie, punched her in the face, while she was waiting on a traffic light. Later, still unable to see out of her right eye, she recounted how even as her eye was bleeding and she was "very traumatized, very scared . . . her instincts kicked in to defend herself." Through her daughter Dong-Mei Li, Xie shared that she "found the stick around the area and fought back."[3] Video footage shows Xie taking a wooden board from her shopping trolley and fashioning it as a defensive weapon. Afterward, even as she was experiencing post-traumatic stress and afraid to leave her home, Xie refused to keep the nearly one million dollars that had been raised on her behalf, insisting that "this issue is bigger than her."[4] Indeed, the day before her assault, another White man had shot and killed eight people, six of whom were Asian/Asian American women, in the Atlanta metropolitan area.[5]

In a tone-deaf statement meant to convey her concern for the attack on both Pham and Xie, San Francisco Mayor London Breed declared that "we need to understand, not only what is going on, but why these attacks occur . . . because in some cases they didn't include any robbery and theft"[6]—revealing Breed's absolute cluelessness about the surge of hate-motivated attacks against Asian American Pacific Islanders living in the US, especially on elderly women. In March 2020, Stop AAPI Hate began collecting data as a response to the escalating hate incidents against the community. Xie is right that her assault was not isolated, but part of a larger epidemic of rising and permissible racial hatred against AAPI people. At the time of the Atlanta killings and Xie's attack, Stop AAPI reported nearly 3,800 hate incidents in less than a year—a 150 percent increase, with 1,600 incidents in the golden state alone.[7]

However, by the onset of the COVID-19 pandemic, the US was already well on its way to achieving an unprecedented increase in racist and xenophobic incidents. White supremacy was ascendant and on the move. Indeed, one of its loudest mouthpieces was occupying the presidency, affirming policies that separated children from their families, and in the case of China—crucifying a people, even as he openly voiced desires mimicking that nation's tyrant while coveting its riches. That China and by implication the Chinese people were already a target of the Trump administration's xenophobic rhetorical war is not surprising given that Trump and his acolytes were following a long line of US politicians reaching for one of their oldest political tools—finding a model scapegoat to use as their punching bag.[8] If the making of US antidemocracy is dependent on the praxis of radical exclusion, than the people of Asian descent (or "orientals") are the archetype of the permanent, alien other—fit for exclusion and eviction.[9] That China was a contending force in the geopolitical economy made it and Chinese people easy primary targets. What might be unprecedented is the proliferation and permissiveness with which the spate of "anti-Asian hate" incidents occur. This amassing of racist enmity, especially physical assaults against AAPI women and girls, rivals or dwarfs previous racist campaigns.[10] It is thus especially noteworthy that Xie, an elderly Asian woman—an archetype of the ableist, agist, orientalist trope of a pliable, weak, and submissive woman—fought back and, nominally, won. Her refusal to go along as a compliant object in a moment of extraordinary violence is the antithesis of racist scripting of what governable oriental bodies look like and how they should behave. Even as corporate media fed a steady diet legitimizing the Atlanta killer's defense for his repressed corporeal desires, the image of Xie beating up a thirty-nine-year-old White male defies the bad-faith gendered racial regime of a docile, compliant, oriental effeminate body, ever ready to be served up for sexual fantasies, consumption, and conquest, or, at best, as mere human machine only fit for laboring.[11] Like Xie, the many who do not easily fit into the historically anemic Black/White binary of racialist schemas, occupy a liminal space between subjection and liberation, neither here nor there, or in between, beginning and end, triangulating and [illegible] entanglements—forever negotiating the many paths, forward and backward, toward alter realities that hold promises of a less miserable life.

In the early decades of the third millennium, then, even as we contemplate futures of planetary justice, we continue to live in a world where capital is free, property is privately owned, and humans increasingly are marked as either data, disposable or deportable. Katherine McKittrick puts it this way: "We presently live in a moment where the human is understood as a purely biological mechanism that is subordinated to a teleological economic script that governs our global well-being/ill-being; . . . capital is thus projected as the indispensable, empirical, and metaphysical source of all human life, thus semantically activating the neurochemistry of our brain's opiate reward/punishment system to act accordingly!"[12] Within the context of surveillance capitalism and benign acceptance of virulent authoritarianism, the (re)acquaintance with Sylvia Wynter's work, particularly her assertions and reflections on western epistemology and probing questions about being human, could not have come at a better time. For more than half a century, Wynter has exposed the limits of and impositions by liberal humanism—inadequacies that have become themselves reified and potentially catastrophic. A Wynterian mode of reading in these times equips us with a radical reorientation, perhaps a disorientation, from our current predicaments—one that would, if not undo, at least unsettle the status quo and facilitate rethinking the human and entertaining the unthought. This reorientation is a warrant for rewriting knowledge and reclaiming a mode of being for a new ethic of liberation and democratic livability[13]—one outside of "the purely secular, biocentric and homo *oeconomicus* form"[14] or its alternative—the punctured life raft held out by *homo politicus*.

The quest for transformative, especially planetary, justice could do worse than starting with Wynter's philosophical corrective intervention. Extending the work of Fanon and Foucault, Wynter insists that our current predicament is bereft of just possibilities, not least because we are indebted to Man. As a particular genre of humans, Man is narcissistic, self-serving, overemployed, and overrepresented in the story of humans and corresponding epistemes, limiting our thinkability about the many ways of being human. Wynter thus calls on us to look beyond Man toward other genres of humans and other modes of being human.[15] Locating the archive of the ungovernable puts us on the path of humans as beyond a "biomutationally evolved, hybrid species—*storytellers who now storytelling invent themselves as being purely biological*."[16] The invention of Man is thus one that reifies a specific genre of human and superimposes it to the totality of human life. In this way, history "is always already coded, already *history*-for, always already an ethnohistory."[17] Unlike the people's history of the variety that Baldwin incites with its promise of critical reflexivity, this History sublimates the ontological other and imperializes one specific mode of being, forever fixed in a Black/White Manichean world.[18]

Wynter points toward a profound need for tools to cope with ongoing and emergent catastrophes. However represented and overemployed, Man, as archetype of the totality of human life forms and worlds, is inadequate, and humanity when reducible to Man is morally bankrupt and culturally a dead end.[19] Nevertheless, this has been the order of knowledge, one that governs and imposes a singularity of its own terms of dominion as an imperium, precluding and foreclosing other modes of being.[20] If we are not yet capable of telling richer stories of humans, what hope do we have for telling the stories of a multispecies planet, let alone saving it? How deprived are our conceptions of justice when justice is the province of only Man? If "there has been no history of the human," except the "universal histories" that are conceived in "monotheistic religious terms," how is solidarity possible?[21] A narrative subversion demands a decolonization of western thought and historiography, and as Wynter insists, "the lived experience" of actual humans calls into question the viability of Man and the biogenic obsession of western thought. The end of Man thus necessitates not the end of history but only an end to certain historiography.

When stories of humans and ecologies are shared and learned as multilayered, multimodal, polysemantic, and in hypertext, possibilities exist for alter realities, multiverses, and messy temporalities. Clearly there are alternative modes of being, in worlds where life may be ungovernable—where individuals and communities assert a democratic praxis as a way of life, with possibilities of life and living beyond the terms of capital and the state, and beyond governing. In and among these alter spaces are the spaces of otherness—spaces of ungovernability, geographies of undesirable bodies and praxes, and of alter onto-epistemologies. Appropriating a term from architecture, Foucault helpfully characterizes these spaces as heterotopias.[22] He explains that heterotopias are counter-sites or "a kind of effectively enacted utopia," and exist "in every culture, in every civilization" as "real places—places that do exist and that are formed in the very founding of society" but are "simultaneously represented, contested, and inverted."[23] Here/there, with no discerning spatiality or temporality, we find not grand schemes and overbearing rules but fleeting encounters with an approximation of something just imagined and willed into reality. Heterotopias are thus practical and, unlike utopias, do not present themselves as perfect or unreal.[24] Such heterotopic spaces and happenings are also the main fixtures of prison nations, occupied territories, runaway slave encampments, and other not-yet-named dominions. A Wynterian intervention presupposes "a world where many worlds fit"; to imagine it needs the [illegible] "simultaneously mythic and real contestations" in those alter spaces and temporalities of deviancy and ungovernability. These counter-[illegible] can be resourced for learning about subversion and living beyond the pale. They can also be tricked up as utopian, scheming on a grander scale for perfect governing. For instance, transhumanism, with its promise of radical inclusion through perfectability is instead a facsimile of human transcendence based on fantasies of techno-utopias and progressive singularities. Within the context of a geopolitical ecology, where communal displacement and community dismemberment are routine, today's used up dreams of belonging are the emptied rhetoric of tomorrow's nightmares.

More than four decades ago, Vincent Chin was beaten to death in a racist-fueled violence executed by two unemployed White men. The men who beat Chin to death mistook him for Japanese—a stand-in for the global forces that had rendered them redundant. Reacting to the absence of justice for her son, Lily Chin reportedly said, "Vincent's soul will never rest."[25] She left the US after living here for five decades, even as her son's death galvanized the mass mobilization of the larger AAPI community. Until recently, Chin's killing was considered "the archetype of anti-Asian violence"[26]—racial assaults fueled by xenophobia and ignorance as embodied politics of grievance and resentments. As the recent data on anti-AAPI violence suggests, Asians and Asian Pacific Americans remain illegible where it matters. Given the frequent inability of the larger population to "distinguish among Asian subgroups, all Asians face the same real and dangerous threats of anti-Asianism."[27] AAPI are thus rarely seen as legitimate citizen subject—less *Homo sapiens* and more *Robo sapiens*. More often than not, they are scripted as the alien other, the perfect and perfectly obedient robotic workers—neither capable of independent thought nor self-rule. Within this frame, a reverse instrumentalism is at work; while not fit for belonging, their labor is essential for powering the new techno-autocracy.

Far from being settled, the question of belonging is thus especially salient in these times of violent borders and heightened nativism, as demands for migrant justice also expose how settlements and coloniality persist.[28] Especially confounding is the fate beholding those who have been marked as a permanent alien, targeted for expulsion, and never meant to belong. A shift away from anthropocentric notions of justice thus demands more encompassing justice paradigms. Critical humanist discourses, including the work of Wynter, have propelled our understanding of humans as praxis and the need to pivot away from Man toward a more encompassing and comprehensive framework for understanding human ecologies—from settlement and coloniality, to sustainability and decoloniality. Critical planetary justice, for instance, embodies a deliberate attempt to disrupt if not resolve this dilemma, imbuing justice with substantive meanings, applicative procedures, and ecological concerns. Within the context of precarious planetary life with many species being at risk of extinction, it seems prudent to ask questions that place in/justice, including planetary justice, at the center of critical social inquiries. This engagement demands robust and comprehensive analytics generally found in intersectional, multimodal feminist approaches such as abolition feminism, Indigenous ecofeminism, or a materialist multispecies framing similar to Donna Haraway's proposed tentacular thinking—to name a few.[29]

THE ARITHMETIC OF PERFECTABILITY

In the shadows of today's techno-autocracy, with its many fantastic promises of perfectability, including immortality, are the many lives in the balance, governed by an increasingly brutal labor regime. Living in a time of data farms and social grading, human lives are becoming multifractal as our data are being extracted and compiled largely for the purpose of governing—both in and out of the marketplace.[30] A sampling of life, our data clones are becoming ever more complete and stabilized in the metaverse, even as human lives, for many, are becoming ever more precarious and fractured. Humans are living fragmented lives, largely governed by an invisible algorithm of a neoliberal metalogic where times are computed in fractions of seconds, and our ever increasingly large data files migrate in nanoseconds and are processed in hyper fiber optic cables, in terabits and fractal dimensions. Biometric data, the human footprints and signatures, can be gathered by MEMS (microelectromechanical systems) or motes.[31] Motes, sometimes known as smart dust, are nanotech in the form of wireless devices and can be as small as a grain of salt, fully fitted with sensors, cameras, and communication capabilities to transmit data back for processing in, perhaps not yet a quantum computer, but a super powerful computing base. As Bernard Marr of *Forbes* magazine puts it, "With such a small size, these devices can stay suspended in an environment just like a particle of dust."[32] So small that they cannot be detected with untrained eyes, and so sophisticated they can be made to be stepped on by unexpecting targets, to collect and process data, wirelessly communicating and transmitting data to the cloud, a base computer or other MEMS.[33] And the data generated could have a life of their own, including incriminating people or being extracted for profit.[34] Contrary to liberal conceptions of Man, today's humans are not entirely self-possessing—they do not necessarily own their data or memories, but are mere sources for data mining.

The humans, whose data are collected through various devices and mechanisms and fed into computing algorithms to be measured and monetized, mostly are unable to take possession of such data as personal property, while the very instruments of their governing are fetishized as the solutions that will bring affluence, especially comfort, security, and even affection.[35] We and our lifeworlds are transformed, frequently without our consent, all the while becoming more financially entrapped and tyrannized by the calculus of wealth hoarding.

In addition to border security and warding off external threats as if they were apparitions that could be waved off by magic wands, the work regime, aided by "smart" technologies, is constant misery for the many and, within this new regime of labor precarity, "being on the clock" has become more like a prison sentence than practicing one's craft, let alone fulfilling one's passion. What makes work life so miserable, especially for low-wage workers, is the "big advance" in algorithmic scheduling combined with a computer-aided monitoring regime. As Emily Guendelsberger explains:

> Work schedules that used to be drawn up by managers now rely heavily on algorithms that analyze historical data to predict exactly how much business a store can expect in the upcoming weeks. As it's most accurate with the most recent data, this means many workers' schedules vary wildly week to week and are made and posted the day before they start—making it impossible to plan anything more than a week in advance. Business also saves a ton of money by scheduling the absolute minimum number of workers to handle the predicted business.[36]

Indeed, work, aided by algorithms, has changed life a great deal. In low-wage sectors a worker's life is almost entirely governed by other forces beyond their control, where "insane technology advances of the past decades have *time to lean* and *time to clean* from subjective things determined by a human manager to objective quantities determined by computer that calculate, monitor, and min-max every second of worker's time on the clock."[37] Contemporary work regimes, like other regimes of governing, seek total governance or perfect governing. It can now track and enforce specific guidelines, with "monitoring equipment integrated into tools workers use to do their jobs can clock and track nearly any task a worker does in real time. . . . [Such] systems can be set to harass, nag, startle, or otherwise trigger a worker's stress response every time she lags behind."[38]

In *On the Clock*, Guendelsberger brilliantly recreates Barbara Ehrenreich's famous low-wage investigative report in the aftermath of the 1996 welfare reform law, with her own experience working in three of the most iconic low-wage workspaces—Amazon, Convergys, and McDonald's. She provides illustration after illustration of how work itself does not lift anyone out of poverty, and exposes the cult of work as a conceit of a system that makes mincemeat out of laborers through algorithm and total surveillance.[39] Many analysts, politicians, and media personalities—"real, respected people with real, respected jobs"—are largely out of touch with the reality of the contemporary work regime, and are thus "incredibly insulated from how miserable and dehumanizing the daily experience of work has gotten over the past decade or two."[40] Offered up as a reality check, she raised questions about quotidian life, that salaried and higher wage workers take for granted, as a cipher into the wretched conditions of this work regime.[41]

Rather than trying to prove inequality and exploitation in low-wage sectors as Ehrenreich did, Guendelsberger takes them as a given, and instead reveals what jobs in low-wage sectors are doing to those who work them, spotlighting the most iconic of corporations and the most brutal work sectors. Based on investigative research and experiential knowledge from working these jobs, she concludes that the working class in the US are being subjected to what is best understood as an automated neo-Taylorism—the new algorithm aided by techno-science. Their work life is governed by algorithms, tasks are timed automatically, and performance and work presence are surveilled constantly and digitally. Such governing technologies have mortal consequences on the workers, such that they are always "in the weeds"—their workplaces are "terribly toxic place for human beings."[42] Alluding to the rise of protofascist politics, she rhetorically and poignantly asks: "If the data says everything's great, why is America *freaking the fuck out*?" Her findings point to one possibility—"because the systems we use to compile and analyze data don't consider America freaking the fuck out to be relevant information."[43] This suggests there is a different calculus at work, one that counts humans as excess and waste to be fixed and deployed as laboring machines, and/or collaterals when in need of a redirection.

Across the ocean, their counterparts working at Foxconn assembling plants toiling over shiny new gadgets, especially those inside the People's Republic of China, fare no better than those assembling boxes at an Amazon warehouse or flipping burgers at a McDonald's in the US. Noting that in the 1970s the Japanese came up with the term *Karoshi* (death by overwork) to draw attention to the phenomenon that emerged in the aftermath of the 1973 energy crisis, which served as a catalyst for widespread workplace restructuring and led to fatalities from work exhaustion, Guendelsberger calls for a similar concept in

English to draw attention to the cruel and unsustainable work regime and its deadly consequences.[44] As the next chapter reveals, during the same decade that US headquartered high-tech corporations sought to reassert Pax Americana in the form of saturating the global market with highly sophisticated gadgets like smartphones and tablets, global workers saw "Foxconn Jumpers" emerge as a phenomenon, and death by overwork became a global issue. Indeed, *karoshi* no longer is limited to Japan as there are now similar terms in various Asian languages, like Mandarin and Korean.[45] As it turns out, the racial regime of orientalism, however unstable, never quite faded away, and continuously conscripts Asian bodies as perfectly docile laboring machines, regimented and predestined for death by work.

Just as those whose land and labor were appropriated to make it possible for the development of capitalism in Europe and North America, the people who labor in the world of techno-science, building and assembling the devices that create the conditions of possibility for technologically enabled aspirations, including cyborgs and super AI, are today's wretched of the earth: caught in the web of global value chains of high-tech manufacturing that relies on outsourced, precarious, and totally regimented labor, with a work regime governed sometimes by the very technologies that they assembled and paid for with their lives. As the next chapter will show, far from freeing humans from our wretched conditions, data mining and hoarding—extracted and appropriated, hidden and known—predict, anticipate, and govern every human impulse and desire. The neoliberal work regime that gave rise to transnational production processes involves chains of many suppliers and subcontractors, making it possible for corporations to maximize productivity and profit. Minimizing costs and accountability means that those who work to produce shiny new toys—so desired that affluent consumers consider staying up all night to stand in line for an opportunity to spend money on yet another sleek, cool, sexy gadget—are forced to bear the brunt of the violence imbued in the process as they are forced to keep up with the corporate demands of speed, precision, and the min-max of every second on the clock. In this brave new/old world of surveillance capitalism and technological fantasies, their lifeworlds and memories are extracted as a matter of course to be filed, processed, and vaulted in governing algorithms in the elusive quest for singularity. Unlike the hyped-up AIs that continue to misrecognize human others,[46] however, these wretched of the earth are sentient beings who have ideas and wills of their own, and who are willing their own dreams of transformation into the present-future existence.

7

iLife and Death: The New/Old Capitalist Algorithm

Life is meaningless.
Every day, I repeat the same thing I did yesterday.
We get yelled at all the time.
It's very tough around here.

Ah Wei[1]

If you don't want to be loudly awakened at night from deep sleep,
If you don't want to constantly rush about again by airplane,
If you don't want to be investigated again by the Fair Labor Association,
If you don't want your company to be called a sweatshop,
Please treat us with a little humanity.

Yu Zhonghong[2]

SURVEILLANCE CAPITALISM

In the midst of a global pandemic that counts five million deaths among its casualties[3] and a week before its annual signature event, the Apple Worldwide Developers Conference (WWDC), its products launching pad, Apple released its fifteenth annual supplier report.[4] Befitting of a company that has more wealth than 96 percent of country GDP's in the world,[5] the 113-page glossy report bears the Orwellian branding—"People and Environment in Our Supply Chain"—and features Apple's senior vice president Sabir Khan who opens the report with his best imitation of an aspirational TED-talk tidbit, declaring that "Apple is a technology company, but we never forget that the devices we make are imagined by human minds, built by human hands, and are meant to improve human lives."[6] While its products might have acquired the status of a fetish, there is little mystery in how people and environments are consummated within Apple's supply chains. Kahn's corporate message is in keeping with Apple's claim that the more than two million people "covered" by its "health and safety standards" in 2020 is evidence of Apple prioritizing "health and safety," putting "people first," and "protecting the planet."[7] Far from hyperbole, Apple spent billions on marketing its claims of corporate responsibility, especially its privacy policy.

Couched in the language of human freedom and autonomy, Apple famously declares that "privacy is a fundamental human right," and that "you control what you share."[8] While Apple claims to be different from Google, Facebook, Amazon, and other companies, Apple, like them, is hoarding billions of users' information. In 2018 Apple CEO Tim Cook, while not mentioning Facebook and Google by name, directly attacked the "the data industrial complex." Handpicked by Apple's founder and previous CEO Steve Jobs who was famous for his paranoia and secretive, tyrannical managerial style, Cook, matching his predecessor's enthusiasm for secrecy and lack of corporate transparency, pounced on Apple's competitors for hoarding and monetizing data. While privacy advocates accuse Apple of doing the same, Cook's keynote address was a "scathing attack" on data farming, as if Apple's massive hoarding of cash and data were unrelated to its cutthroat labor practices and obscene profit margins. With nary a sense of irony or humility, he characterizes competitors' "stockpiling of personal data" as entirely destructive:

> These threads of data, each one harmless enough on its own, are carefully assembled, synthesized, traded, and sold. Taken to its extreme this process creates an enduring digital profile and lets companies know you better than you may know yourself. We shouldn't sugarcoat the consequences.[9]

Cook points to what is increasingly difficult to miss and a key mechanic of surveillance capitalism—the hoarding of data, especially personal data, for monetization and accumulation.[10] Not unlike the surveillance of labor by management in previous eras, this compulsive mining and hoarding of personal data is meant to anticipate, predict, and govern consumer behaviors in a hyper-consumerist ecology. More than a decade ago, Google's former CEO and chairman Eric Schmidt called attention to Google's ability to augment humanity:

> Ultimately, search is . . . literally all of your information. . . . We can suggest what you should do next, what you care about. Imagine: We know where you are, we know what you like. . . . A near-term future in which you don't forget anything, because the computer remembers. You're never lost.[11]

Unlike Google, Facebook, Amazon, and others, however, Apple makes it a point to advertise its products as synonymous with individual privacy. The 2019 "Privacy—That's iPhone" ad campaign focusing on Apple's approach to privacy on mobile devices, for instance, draws attention to how we "over-share" personal data online in mundane ways that, should such sharing occur in the real world, would be utterly absurd and appalling.[12] The Identifier for Advertisers (IDFA) is a device ID that app makers use for targeted advertisements—a primary mechanism for monetization in the app economy. It is also how Apple "protects" user identity, by creating a default off mode where users could opt in, instead of the usual default on mode. But as John Koetsier at *Forbes* asks, is Apple policy a "Privacy Power Move or Cash Grab?"[13] This is an entirely appropriate question given that the worldwide app economy is a multitrillion-dollar industry, with Apple exercising unprecedented sector control.[14] As Koetsier notes, apps make money through advertising, providing "63% of the revenue for gaming apps, and 66% of the revenue for non-gaming apps," and "when an app generates ad revenue, Apple doesn't get any of it."[15] Apple would get a massive cut if app makers play by Apple's rules when opting for either subscription (15 percent after the first transaction) or in-app purchase (30 percent of all transactions). Apple, like its competitors, also hoards data and is intimately involved with the data industrial complex. Reed Albergotti at the *Washington Post* (owned by Jeff Bezos of Amazon) explains: Apple has "access to a trove of data that nobody else has" through its App Store, where it "could be used to make strategic decisions on product development."[16] Thus, Apple exercises the kind of territorial governance and planetary influence over its ever-expanding ecology that, perhaps, only few nation-states enjoy.[17] Tech monopolies such as Apple and others "aren't just powerful because they are big or profitable. They are also the omniscient rulers of their platforms."[18] As the previous chapter suggests, this is what a techno-autocracy looks like. With the aid of its hidden and not so hidden algorithms and labor regime of precarity, its corporate tentacles slither and elongate into the deep reaches of human entanglements, fractalizing biohumans to mere data. Cook is thus correct when he observed that this situation is entirely unsettling; Apple, however, is an active engine of growth against personal and communal privacy, not to mention the brutal neoliberal regime of living in the twenty-first century. If the worker suicides at Foxconn factories, one of Apple's main supply chain partners, are an indication, then "dying for an iPhone" is a literal expression of Apple's money-making magic that no multibillion-dollar ad campaign can cover up.[19]

Death by Labor

If the first decade of the twenty-first century was marked by mass suicides of farmers in the Global South, accompanied by evictions and foreclosures in the Global North due to financial liberalization and debt entrapment,[20] then the following decade's rash of suicides by Chinese tech workers at Foxconn—the world's largest electronic manufacturer and an important partner of the Apple empire—marks the disconnect between the brutality and seediness of labor and the fetishization of the new techno-aristocracy and its fantasy of augmented humanity. The exuberant anticipation of and enthusiasm for Apple's next shiny object is emblematic of this troubling development. Regardless of whatever the next fetish object might be, more than likely it will bewitch both the financial and techno press, ensuring Apple's ever-escalating stock prices to continue.

Prior to 2010, there were two known suicides of low-wage workers reported at Foxconn industrial park in Shenzhen, China. In 2010 alone, there were fifteen suicide attempts by mostly young workers, ages ranging from seventeen to twenty-eight, of both genders (four female and thirteen male), and almost all were successful. Those who survived live with lifelong debilitating injuries. In the last ten years, no single year accounted for as many suicide attempts or deaths at Foxconn factories as 2010, though suicides by workers have continued.[21] Remarkably, these suicides and suicide attempts have been resourced as workers' "weapons of the weak."[22] In January 2012, for instance, a hundred and fifty Chinese workers staged a two-day protest on the roof of a Foxconn factory in Wuhan, China, threatening to kill themselves as they drew attention to the tyranny of work and the inhumane labor conditions.[23]

At the end of 2010, China's economy surpassed Japan's for the first time as the second-largest economy in the world, only after the US.[24] During that same year, "Foxconn jumpers" trended online, capturing the visceral phenomenon of workers committing suicide, though jumping was far from the only method of killing oneself or drawing attention to the neoliberal regime of precarious living. Headquartered in Taiwan, Foxconn Technology Group (Foxconn) is the world's largest electronic manufacturer, and Apple's largest assembler of the iPhone—one of the world's most popular smartphones. It is also an assembly subcontractor for the world's largest tech companies, including the US's most valuable companies—including Amazon, Apple, Alphabet (Google's parent company), Hewlett-Packard, Microsoft, and Vizio. Foxconn's operations are massive—accounting for an estimated 40 percent of world consumer electronic manufacturing, with assembly plants in North and South America, Europe, and Asia, including twelve factories in China that employ more than a million Chinese workers.[25] "Foxconn Jumpers"—shorthand for the waves of worker suicides—are thus undeniable evidence of something amiss in the world of iPhones, Kindles, and Xboxes. Perhaps not all is shiny and new or smart with the global supply chains for Apple and other high-flying stock tech giants. As the satirical column "Media Suicide Watch" in *The Secret Diary of Steve Jobs* accurately captures:

> members of the media have been killing off their own credibility at an alarming rate in an effort to help a powerful corporation downplay a string of suicides at a labor ~~camp~~ manufacturing facility in China. All of these media outlets are promoting the ridiculous notion that Foxconn's suicide epidemic is not an epidemic at all, because it's way below national average suicide in China.[26]

Thung-hong Lin, Yi-ling Lin, and Wei-lin Tseng argue that the suicides on the shop floor are linked to the authoritarian labor regime at Foxconn—a major node in the global value chains (GVCs).[27] Ironically, in death, the ghosts of workers manage to make visible the not so mysterious and obscene profit margins of high-tech companies, an awareness that the workers may not have achieved while alive.

iREFUSE

2012 had just started. With less than two weeks before the start of the Lunar New Year and nearly a decade before most people in the world would learn the name of the city Wuhan, a hundred and fifty workers congregated on the rooftop of a three-floor, $1 billion Foxconn manufacturing plant. Similar to its operations in other cities within China, the Wuhan facility employs more than thirty-two thousand workers. The workers were protesting the horrific work life at Foxconn, although the immediate source of discontent was the recent forced transfer from Shenzhen where they had relatively better working conditions, and with better pay.[28] The roof was very cold that day, causing some workers "who couldn't stand the freezing temperature" to faint.[29] Workers were posting news in real time with their mobile devices, though likely not the same brands they were assembling. Given that "Foxconn jumpers" were trending, "government mediators quickly arrived at the scene, and took pains not to add fuel to the fire."[30] Workers had threatened mass suicide, but after two days they were "coaxed down by Foxconn managers and local Chinese Communist Party officials."[31]

Not unlike the wave of farmer suicides in India in the previous decade pointing to unlivable life on the margins of subsistence, the wave of Foxconn worker suicides in China since 2010 caught global media attention, notably prompting an investigative series by the *New York Times* and *ProPublica*.[32] As Lin et al. point out, the public were shocked by these "jumping suicide incidents" by Chinese migrant workers, and criticism of labor practice was widespread. Critically, expanded coverage of suicides "triggered more workers' suicides," and by the end of 2010 "there were at least twenty-five suicides cases committed in Foxconn factories."[33] Global value chains have created a situation where Foxconn plants are "shaped by the global fragmented despotism" that subjects workers, "especially migrant workers, to . . . arbitrary [managerial] power, and rule enforcement of managers and forepersons, who also face harsh top-down pressure from their own superiors and clients."[34] They argue that the tragedies of workers who are confronted with desperate and perilous work conditions are "deeply rooted in the fragmented and chaotic structure" of the GVC system. Specifically, "to satisfy the demand from global customers, the factory regime ignored the workers' physical and psychological conditions. By means of arbitrary capricious managerial power, the factory regime shaped the 'despotism' on the shop floor."[35] This coercive work environment leaves workers feeling abused, isolated, and alienated. The suicides among workers, especially migrant workers, are a form of resistance "to the despotism on the shop floor."[36] So, instead of singling out "Foxconn as a sweatshop that wields military-style management," we need to look to "the intervention from the global brand owners, together with Foxconn's fragmented governance, [as] an important institutional factor that causes suicides."[37] Dialectically and with limited means, these same workers tool the "Foxconn jumper" phenomenon as a mobilization resource to demonstrate their refusal for total work compliance.

That January in 2012, a wave of strikes and mass labor protests took place throughout China, some involving tens of thousands of workers, and the Wuhan mass suicide threat was part of this trend. These reported worker suicides and threats of mass suicide (or "jumping incidents") are "the tip of the iceberg of the increasing number of labor protests throughout China," where there is a "growing labor movement and civic engagement."[38] Like the protest at the Wuhan facility where workers were assembling Microsoft computers and game consoles, the public threat of mass suicide by workers is a performative act, staged for the purpose of securing public empathy and persuasion, particularly to force managerial hands for better negotiated outcomes. Chan, Selden, and Ngai explain that "the specter of suicide, which had taken so heavy a toll earlier at Foxconn facilities in Shenzhen, now haunted central China."[39] On April 25, 2012, less than three months after the threat of mass suicide, another two hundred workers "walked off the factory floor over the loss of overtime payments," and chanted angrily on the rooftop, demanding "Wo yao jiaxin!" (I want a raise!). This time, to avert "possibility of a prolonged walkout or worker suicide," officials conceded to increasing wages, including weekend overtime wages. Chan et al. argue that such concessions are part of the "wide repertoire of 'protest absorption' techniques" to cope with the increasing ungovernability of workers as they "learned to bargain collectively."[40] Given that labor discontent consists of a long list of grievances beyond wages and benefits, especially draconian managerial measures governing break time, scheduling and promotion, the potential for labor unrest could be massive, as it takes on an antiauthoritarian character.[41] When confronted with a managerial regime that rivals tyrants of old and befitting of characterization by Lin et al. as managerial despotism,[42] workers do not always hang their heads in resignation; they also walk off the floor, get on the roof threatening to jump, and riot. Sometimes the riots are so massive that the company is forced to shut down its operation as news of the unrest reverberates across oceans.

WORK UNGOVERNED

On September 23, 2012, a week after the release of the new iPhone 5,[43] several thousand workers took part in a riot at the nearly eighty-thousand-worker Foxconn plant in Taiyuan, a northern city less than six hundred miles from Wuhan, and three hundred miles from Beijing. Contrary to media coverage based on management's characterization of the event as "a fight among factory employees," the riot broke out after a factory security guard assaulted a worker for not having his identification when entering a Foxconn residence hall. Worker riots as a form of labor protest are as old as governing itself, and this particular fuse was lit by staff brutality against workers, emblematic of mass worker discontent. In previous months and perhaps in anticipation of the release of the latest iteration of the world's most desirable smartphone, these "workers had clocked as many as 130 hours [compulsory] overtime"—three times the maximum allowed, with 13:1 or even 30:1 work to rest schedule.[44] While the iPhone 5 later would be "hailed as a thinner, faster, and brighter model" and became the second-bestselling iPhone ever, workers' days off were canceled, including sick leaves.[45]

On that September night, thousands joined the midnight riot in which they destroyed the things that were destroying them—"security offices, production facilities, shuttle buses, motorbikes, cars, shops, and canteens in the factory complex." They did not stop there: "Some broke windows, demolished company fences, pillaged factory supermarkets, and overturned police cars" before setting them ablaze. By the early hours of the morning, five thousand riot police officers had converged on the site, eventually taking control of the entire complex, walling off workers inside, and arresting some while holding others in place. Befitting of an Orwellian Big Brother, Foxconn announced "a special day off" for everyone at the plant, with the iPhone division promptly reopened after that special day off.[46] These protests and acts of refusal at Foxconn are far from unique inside the People's Republic of China (PRC)—where the second-largest economy engines the growth of millionaires and billionaires while proliferating workers' misery and premature deaths. If anything, they are endemic to a system that hoards wealth for the few and spreads pain and misery to the many, and are therefore part of the larger movement against tyranny in the workplace and beyond. Protests by peasants and workers are typically perceived as protests over "grievances." Implying that their unhappiness is petty, they are thus seen as less important because analysts erroneously perceive their "grievances" to be less general or systemic in objectives, and/or less desirable, let alone bring about structural changes. While they might be less sensational than the large-scale "democratization" anti-state or religious-based protests that are more legible to western analysts and observers (who at times also are biased by their anti-communism), these "local" everyday protests by workers and farmers inside China are also part of the larger praxis of refusal against authoritarian governing, as they point to sociomaterial as well as affective concerns that extend beyond the state.[47]

THE NEW, OLD ALGORITHM OF APARTHEID

On an early, cold day in January 2013, while affluent residents may have been creatively killing time, more than a thousand migrant Chinese workers took over a Japanese-owned electronics factory in Shanghai and held eighteen Japanese and Chinese managers hostage for almost two days.[48] According to the *South China Morning Post* and the *Asahi Shimbun*, the workers first held a strike then seized the factory, taking management hostage, including the company's president, a Japanese national. It would take more than four hundred Chinese anti-riot police to break the siege and relieve the hostages. The police raid inflicted injuries on some workers; the managers, while temporarily locked up by the workers, were left relatively unharmed.

The strike and siege at the Shanghai Shinmei Electric factory might have been spontaneous or planned, depending on the narrative of the event. What we do know is that they were immediate responses to an announcement about the factory's new labor disciplinary policy. The new policy, among other things, included "heavy fines, demerits and immediate termination" against workers who made mistakes. According to the workers, there were as many as "49 unequal clauses," ranging from two-minute bathroom break limits, being heavily fined for lateness, and being fired for repeated offenses. One account on a microblog points out that workers "earn less than 2,000 yuan [$321USD] a month . . . [yet] could be subjected to fines of 40 to 100 yuan for arriving late or spending more than two minutes in the toilet."[49] The worker-management resolution came in the form of a company-issued apology and a revised disciplinary policy, along with a promise of salary increases.

Revealing the nonsensical myths of a "national economy," this siege was peopled by Chinese migrant workers in a Japanese-owned factory in Shanghai to protest, among other things, the pending acquisition by a Chinese company. The protestors besieged both Japanese *and* Chinese managers, and the siege was broken up by the enforcement of the Chinese state and its police apparatus.[50] That the protestors were migrant workers is also not insignificant. Migrant workers in urban China are mostly internally displaced Chinese from rural areas, whose livelihood have been effectively destroyed by neoliberal economic reforms, land theft, and forced removals.

According to government data, China has been experiencing the largest internal migration and displacement in its long history—perhaps the largest peacetime migration in human history, dwarfing both the Irish and Italian migrations to the US, and even the total number of forced removals of Africans in the Atlantic slave trade or the total number of Indigenous people in North America displaced by settler colonialism in the heyday of the Age of Empire. Less than a decade ago, there were officially more than 140 million migrant workers inside China, approximately 10 percent of the total population.[51] Today and in the manufacturing services and construction sectors alone, there are approximately 288 million migrant workers—a population larger than Indonesia, the fourth most populous nation on earth, and 20 percent of China's total population.[52] This migrant worker population, largely from rural areas, constitutes more than one-third of the entire working population inside China. Yet, while serving as "the engine of China's spectacular economic growth," they are marginalized, discriminated against, and their "children have limited access to education and healthcare," and are frequently separated from parents for extended periods of time.[53]

Nearly three decades ago, some observers referred to this mass internal displacement as China's apartheid. So, it is not an exaggeration to characterize the status of today's migrant population as living dead, ghosting and haunting the ever-expanding Chinese economy. As Chen Guidi and Wu Chuntao capture in their now famously banned book *Will the Boat Sink the Water?* (2006), "Sometimes the unmistakable life and death is blurred: a person may be dead and gone and yet remain among the living."[54] With the liberalization of the economy, an unprecedented mass migration sped up nearly four decades ago, and there are approximately a quarter of a billion people who are internally displaced at any given time. Forced to migrate to various cities from poor, rural areas in order to make room for capitalist development and in search of livelihoods, they (if they are lucky) find work in the factories of the big cities such as Beijing, Shenzhen, and Shanghai.[55] In Beijing, for instance, depending on the year in question, migrant workers could be as much as 40 percent of the total population, and as high as 86 percent of the working population in Shenzhen are migrant laborers.[56] Not incidentally, these migrants also are frequently seen as the cause of the countless mass protests and social upheavals inside China. So too are the communities they left behind in search of livelihood. As it turns out, their rural kin—facing poverty, eviction, land theft, and other indignities of life on the subsistence margins—would launch one of the most iconic protests in contemporary China.

THE MAKING OF "CHINA'S PARIS COMMUNE"

The revolt and subsequent siege of Wukan began in late September 2011, and it would take nearly twelve weeks and more than a thousand police officers laying siege to this small village of thirteen thousand residents before a truce was declared.[57] Given the existing data on mass protests against land and labor disputes,[58] this particular revolt is not unusual. As Rachel Beitarie of *Foreign Policy* points out, Wukan "embodies social changes brought about by more than thirty years of economic reforms"—that have left upward of several hundred millions displaced and bereft of resources or opportunities for a livable life.[59] The villagers' grievances are ordinary and typical of millions of farmers in China, namely government corruption, confiscation of lands, forcible evictions, and fraudulent sale of land to developers. The scale of malfeasance rivals some of the biggest heists in history, and so brazen is the fraud that sometimes unsuspecting residents would not realize their land was stolen until construction work commenced on it, frequently by the multibillion-dollar real estate company Country Garden.[60] Local officials, Wukan residents alleged, embezzled more than $110 million through the sales of more than 80 percent of their arable land.[61]

The 2011 Wukan rebellion thus began as an ordinary, peaceful sit-in protest by villagers demanding a return of their land and the right to farm.[62] As their ranks grew, protestors acted similarly to their Foxconn counterparts—they destroyed the things that were destroying them. They targeted buildings and industrial equipment, and blocked roads. Characteristically, the police intervened, arrests were made, and *protests escalated*. Many protestors suffered injuries, a few very serious ones; the next day, armed villagers took over a police station. Provincial riot police showed up and, in concert with private security, acted like "mad dogs, beating everyone they saw"; at which point, the assault became indiscriminate as more protestors were beaten, including children and the elderly. Predictably, protests further escalated, and fittingly, the *South China Morning Post* later declared: "20 Years of Anger Unleashed."[63] By December 11, a few days shy of twelve weeks since the uprising began, local officials and police were forced to flee Wukan. The local police offices were locked up and wealthy residents fled their homes, while the villagers held daily protests, took over their own village, and established their own independent governing structure—a temporary, independent, popular committee. During the next ten days, one western reporter compared Wukan to the Paris Commune, while a Hong Kong journalist compared the situation to the spring of 1989 in Tiananmen Square prior to the massive crackdown.[64]

By conventional measures, the protests were a triumph. No looting occurred during the ten days when villagers *were ungoverned* by the police and Communist Party functionaries. The protests were nonviolent, and the police stations remained locked and intact, "as were the houses of local elites and families of officials, most of whom have left the village." Beyond these corporate media self-imposed limit tests, Wukan was even more telling. The critical care labor needed in any given community remained intact if not enhanced, as protestors cooked and fed each other while building a movement from the inside out. They even provided nourishment to encamped reporters while coordinating mass rallies, making protest signs, holding press conferences, and recording audio and videos for YouTube and other social media platforms.[65] One journalist described Wukan this way: "[The] intoxicating atmosphere of unity and generosity where cab drivers drove protestors for free, and thieves vowed to switch professions, [buoyed] by a feeling that all was good and possible."[66] During this entire time, riot police and paramilitary troops surrounded the village, cutting off the villagers from the rest of China, all the while Wukan was peacefully regenerating itself.

After eleven days of standoff, the Wukan villagers secured the release of one of the three detainees.[67] Most surprisingly, they also received news that all their demands would be met. The resolution was materially consequential: authorities apologized and acquiesced to independent village elections with secret ballots and independent observers and, most significantly, some of the confiscated land would be redistributed. The popular committee structure remained intact for nearly five years, with as many as 107 representatives overseeing the working of the village. In the first election, they were voted to their positions by 85 percent of the villagers, with "all seven protest leaders elected into public office."[68] One won the position of the village party chief, ousting an incumbent who held the seat for forty-two years. Throughout this entire protest campaign, the villagers made it very clear that they were not against communism; instead, they were against the small and large tyrannies that were oppressing Wukan. Sally Wang of *South China Morning Post* sums up the situation thus:

> Year after year, the people of Wukan saw their collective farmland being lost to developers. Little by little it also became clear to them that the Guangdong Village's leaders had cheated them out of their rightful compensation. One day, they could take no more.[69]

While "Rural standoffs usually end with the arrest of the ringleaders and increased security presence for the remaining residents,"[70] somehow these Wukan villagers managed to beat the odds, however temporarily.[71]

In the span of a little more than three months, Wukan captured the imagination of social activists worldwide and a small segment of the global media. Its immediate achievements dwarfed any single Occupy Wall Street (OWS) campaign in North America, and served as inspiration for other Wukan-like protests inside China.[72] However ephemeral, its success has been compared to the Arab Spring, and the Wukan uprising was thought of as the beginning of a new era of Chinese peasant rebellions. Tellingly and in an unguarded moment, mid-ranking official Zheng Yanxiong lamented: "As villagers get smarter, they become harder to manage."[73] So it seems that the party officials and Wukan police have discovered an uncomfortable fact that peasants, migrant workers, and others can indeed be very difficult to manage, especially so when they have long memories. After all, even the Confucian court scholars of old frequently had to remind themselves that naturally governments reform while the people revolt.

THE MANY ITERATIONS OF UNGOVERNABILITY

These peasant and migrant worker rebellions are *iterations of ungovernability*, postmodern stories of modern resistance. Some are deeply situated in a practical utopian standpoint, both ancient and contemporary. Physically located far from the financial nodes of the global economy and begun only a few days after Occupy Wall Street, the 2011 Wukan village uprising captured global attention, anticipated the coming decade of labor-based democratic, mass mobilization inside China and in Hong Kong, and suggests a well-rehearsed practice of ungoverning.[74] The Wukan rebellion, the riot at Foxconn facilities, and countless other contemporary mass protests inside China (as well as pro-democracy protests in Hong Kong) are grounded in antiauthoritarianism and/or anti-capitalist, democratic imaginaries. While not always aided by new shiny gadgets and techno-science, these protests and mobilizations nevertheless strike back against the very ecosystem that put in place the emergent techno-aristocracy, stripping bare the fetishized algorithms of savage developmentalism and its attendant expansionism, violence, and antidemocracy. These acts of refusal are not unmoored from the larger radical traditions of resistance and rebellions against violence, cruelty, and illegitimate or dubious claims of governing. In their individual and collective refusals to submit to workplace management, despotic wealth hoarding and other big and small tyrannies, the workers and peasants took ownership of their lives and land, however momentarily and, in the process, affected a different (multi)modal praxis of living. While not always arriving at happy endings, their stories stir memories of resistance and incite dreams of liberation. In the words of the great anti-colonialist, anti-fascist, militant labor organizer and historian Ngo Van Xuyet: "In China, as in the West, utopia, so deeply rooted among the dispossessed, proceeds from a popular understanding of emancipation whose memory must be preserved, before it disappears in the tortuous and brutal adaptations to economic modernity that perpetuate the burden of the coercions of the past."[75] In Ngo's last work from 2005 that captures so well his utopian spirit, he reminds his readers that Chinese peasant rebellions are a prologue to and nourishment for contemporary mass protests. Thinking about peasant rebellions makes it possible to think about alternatives *to order* and the need to make ourselves unavailable for governing, however momentarily. For those whose lives subsist on the margins, pushing back against tyranny, however big or small, is a way of living, for to live there is to fight and dream of another possible world.

8
Governments Reform, People Revolt

The people are the most important element of a nation: the spirits of the land and grain are the next; the sovereign is the lightest.

Mencius[1]

Capital has no misgivings about its own divinity.

Enrique Dussel[2]

NEITHER KING NOR SUBJECTS

Raised by a single mother and second only to Confucius in influence among Chinese thinkers, Mencius is perhaps most notable for reminding rulers of the Warring States era (475 BC–221 BC) not to get above their stations.[3] Imbuing the people with an inherent right to revolt and court ministers with a moral obligation to dethrone the unworthy, Mencius, a contemporary of Aristotle, taught that heaven sees with the people's eyes and hears with the people's ears, and when the people are unhappy, the mandate for ruling no longer exists.[4] Notably, as scholars, Mencius and his peers saw themselves as worthy, and being governed as virtuous. And yet, as minions of kings, *even they* conceded that while government may reform, the people will revolt, and when reformation fails to achieve its intended purpose of pacification and deterrence, it threatens deinstitutionalization and even total collapse of the state. For Mencius, not unlike Dussel, acts of refusal and collective defiance are rooted in injustice and the general neglect of common welfare, and therefore ripples can turn into tidal waves, leading to the overthrow of rules and ruling. The court scholars-ministers of ancient China, especially Mencius, understood that unless and until the government serves the welfare of the people, it deserves no less than the people's contempt—and that they will eventually rebel and bring forth the wrath of heaven.[5] Thus the ideological convulsion that declared, "Like the sun rising in the east, the unprecedented Great Proletarian Cultural Revolution is illuminating the land with its brilliant rays" reveals the frightening prospect—perhaps not so much of the influence of western imperial decadence, but rather this sage warning about rules and governing, not to mention the memories of homegrown resistance against imperial dominions by formerly revolutionary but now Great Leaders.[6]

Indeed, in the rich archive of Chinese peasant rebellions, there are ancient utopian thoughts, practical strategies of military insurgency, and tragic tales of personal aggrandizement and collective failures, all embedded in the complex terrain of Chinese radical apolitical thought and praxes. The idea of living unencumbered by the political and without government, and the necessity of overthrowing oppressive cultural praxes, is not foreign but has accreted over several millennia. It predated the emergence of Qin Shi Huang, the First Emperor (Shǐ Huángdì, 221 BC) of a unified China, and persisted well after the collapse of his dynasty. The unhappy archive of governing contains the stories of the Five Pecks of Rice Rebellion, the Red Scarf Rebellion, the Taiping Rebellion, and the all too familiar May Fourth Movement and subsequent peasant revolution of 1949—to name a handful. However, as an intelligentsia, the Confucian court scholar-ministers were much less invested in the people's way than were their Taoist counterparts; after all, they had few desires surpassing their ultimate aim of serving a worthy sovereign.

In *Ancient Utopia and Peasant Revolts*, Ngo Van Xuyet[7] maintains that utopian thought, including narratives of utopias—generally understood as a western phenomenon—can be found in Taoist thought and in archaic peasant communities in China, predating western anarchistic thought by a millennia.[8] Contrary to western mythologies and fetishism about Taoist thought and practice, Chinese utopian longings, Ngo explains, were "distinguished by both mysticism and the supersession of mysticism in the practice of life and earthly combat."[9] Utopia thus is understood as "the dream that has not been realized" *but not unreal*, and shares with its western counterpart "the same dreams and aspirations . . . [with] the same uprisings full of the poetic fervor to reach heaven. It is as if all these revolts, without ever meeting, spread throughout space and time, feeding the flames of subversion and hope for the whole planet."[10]

Among its many aspirations, the Taoist dream of having "neither king nor subjects" is a departure from both traditionalist Confucianism and democratic elitism. As delineated in part I, democratic elitism relies on the supposition of the "mob mentality" or the many as pathos—that is, the many are pathologically incapable of rule, self-rule especially, as they lack impulse control that might prevent them from doing bad things. Classical and modern "democratic thought" largely has been furnished by antidemocrats who harbored antidemocratic biases. The Confucian school of thought, on the other hand, has served as "the ideological foundation of the ruling feudal classes," as it teaches "the rules of proper living" consisting of hierarchies of king and subject, father and son, husband and wife, and brother and sister, grounded in the five cardinal virtues—"filial loyalty and piety, equity, courtesy, common sense and reliability, [and] the strict separation between the sexes" to one's social locations. In contrast, Taoist teaching emphasizes a return to nature, simplicity, and life "stripped of all conventions, without law or morality," and in "small autonomous community."[11]

Retelling the story of the legendary king of Xia as told by Master Taoist Lieh Tzu, born more than two decades before Plato, Ngo insists that Taoism most "reflected the thought of peasant plebeians."[12] Lieh Tzu's story is one that "expresses the common dream of the oppressed peasant serfs: the absolute absence of any power above their heads, the desire to be liberated from labor, the aspirations for a long and happy life, the desire for free union between men and women, and finally, their desire to escape the perpetual threat of massacre under the authority of the feudal warlords of the era."[13] Taoist teaching "rooted in the peasant soil" is thus fundamentally "anti-feudal and anti-traditionalist," and "unlike those Confucian philosophers who abandoned themselves to the destiny dictated by Heaven (*Tien Ming*), the Taoists led their lives by following the motto, 'My destiny depends on me and not on Heaven' ('*Wo ming tsai wop u tsai t'ien*', Pao p'u-tzu).'"[14] Predating liberation theology by two millennia and the anti-property movement in Europe by at least one, peasant movements in ancient China, included those that led to generalized peasant insurrections that "put an end to the First Empire" (209–207 BC), and later the collapse of the Second Han dynasty (220 AD).[15] These revolts were infused with Taoist teachings, emphasizing the right to land and livelihood—the same motto that has incited rebellions and rebellious thought from Africa, Latin America, and Southeast Asia, to the Vatican and the American South.[16] Citing the *Taiping Jing* (*The Canon of the Great Peace*)—a critique of "social inequality, the parasitism of the powerful and discrimination against women," Ngo maintains that these "ideas stoke the fires of the millenarian dream of the peasants to establish humanity without rich or poor, without nobles or serfs, under heaven."[17]

One Taoist sect, the Five Pecks of Rice, collected rice as a form of payment for being taught the way, including how to be responsible for "the material wellbeing of the people."[18] Adherents were responsible for redistributing the rice at public food stations or "Inns of Equity," where rice and meat were stored and given to travelers. Drawing from the *Three Kingdoms*, Ngo renarrates a utopian community where

> wayfarers could eat [at the Inns of Equity] until they had their fill. If they abused this privilege, the Spirits of the Tao caused them to become ill. There were no prisons; those who had committed minor crimes were made to reflect upon their misdeeds while walking the one hundred steps and their crime thus absolved. Those who had committed serious crimes, after their third such offense, were executed. There were no government officials.[19]

Another Taoist, Pao Ching Yen (circa third-century AD), is believed to be the "first libertarian anarchist" who taught "methods of struggle against despotic absolutism," and the idea that the world was a better place when there was no king. Pao's anarchism is without the usual specter of chaos: "during the time when there was neither oppression nor violence. . . . Neither power nor profit germinated, and disorder and calamities did not occur."[20] However fantastical their imaginary domains, these Taoist thinkers taught and showed how to be defiant as they openly questioned inequities and injustices "under heaven." Within the context of agrarian crises and calamities, they seeded fertile ground for ongoing peasant revolts and rebellions. In this Manichean materialist world and within the imperial archive of the grand historians, it was the peasants aided by ghosts who would bring down unjust order. Taoist followers, especially those who belonged to powerful cults that openly challenged social inequalities and hierarchies, including opposing slavery, were thus labeled by the establishment as followers of "demon religions" (*gueiao*), and were suppressed, sometimes with disastrous outcomes.[21]

The Yellow Turban Rebellion,[22] perhaps the most iconic peasant rebellion in China and an inspiration for countless ancient and modern peasant insurgencies, began as a response to the torture and execution of more than one thousand Taoist fighters.[23] Occurring at the end of the Han dynasty, this religiously inspired insurrection confronted an imperium that had reigned for nearly four centuries. Insurgents wore yellow scarves, signifying the color of heaven, to mark their membership in the Taoist cult, and known as the ant-rebels because there were so many in their ranks.[24]

Faced with poverty, famines, starvation, corrupt warlords, and an incompetent and corrupt central government, poor settlers of the South (who were forced to migrate by the agrarian crises in the north) rose up in 184 AD, and revolted against high taxes, high rents, religious prosecutions, slavery, and general tyranny. Howard S. Levy credits the rebels' food distribution system as an effective recruitment strategy, documenting how one rebel leader of the western factions gained popularity and notoriety after setting up public stations along the roads, "stocked with provisions of rice and meat [where] passers-by could freely enter and take enough food to satisfy their hunger."[25] The peasants were especially attracted to Taoist teaching against economic injuries and call for equal distribution of land and other social rights.[26] Especially in a time of widespread sickness and ill health, peasants and other commoners were impatient with imperial medicine and actively sought out Taoist healing arts.[27] Along with food distribution, the rebels' healing praxis was an effective recruiting and mobilizing tool.[28] During the insurrection, rebels seized cities, important urban centers, and military outposts, and occupied mountainous regions and open plains.[29] Despite the deaths of their leaders, rebel militancy persisted. Ultimately, it would take more than two decades of combined forces of local warlords and the Imperial Court to render the yellow-turban-wearing rebels no longer a military threat.[30] Ngo credited the Yellow Turban Rebellion with the collapse of the Han Empire—considered one of the greatest and most enduring dynasties in China.[31] If the proliferation of contemporary rebelliousness in China is any indication, memories of resistance and dreams of neither king nor subjects are difficult to suppress, even with the brutal Cultural Revolution that sought to deflect and misdirect the sources and causes of ungoverning, as it sought to conceal its own vain attempt at perfect governing. This too is what antiauthoritarianism looks like, even if scholars frequently mistake communal, anarchic resistance centering on mutuality as trivial complaint or mere expression of quotidian grievances.

LAND, LABOR, AND LIVING

A few years after the Chinese Revolution, Vincent Y. C. Shih conducted a brief survey of "rebel ideologies in Chinese history" and concluded that not only did rebellions occur with "disconcerting regularity," the rebels also "had a surprising uniform mental outlook and view of things."[32] Shih discovered that "the recurring circumstances" included predictable social discontents such as "government oppression, land concentration, heavy taxation, corrupt officialdom, and deterioration of conditions in general," with land and taxes as their primary preoccupations.[33] Even when the demand for equal distribution of land was not explicit, "the concentration of land in the hands of a few has always been one of the main factors in China's revolts, uprisings, and rebellions."[34]

Life on the margins of subsistence also defines conditions of contemporary agrarian precarity, as one bad season can spell catastrophic outcomes. Nearly a billion people go to bed hungry every night, and the COVID-19 pandemic has driven hunger to unprecedented levels.[35] Indeed, as food insecurity and other basic subsistence issues such as clean water and shelter plague an increasingly larger swath of humanity, movements for land sovereignty and food justice demand greater attention from activists, scholars, and policymakers alike.

In the aftermath of the Chinese (1949) and Cuban (1959) Revolutions, the world was alight with attention on peasant mobilizations, and the elusive quest for radical transformations to bring about another world. Yet, by the end of the twentieth century and apart from the Zapatista uprising, interest in nonurban forms of protest waned and disillusionment with previous utopian longings for peasant revolutionary transformation largely calcified, especially with disturbing and unjust developments in previously heralded spaces of revolutions.[36] Not incidentally, there exists a distinct bias in the coverage of peasant revolts and rebellions as narratives rarely center voices from below instead of the elite, as "historians and journalists, for the most part, write history from the larger urban centers and from the perspective literate elites."[37]

This epistemic injustice where ordinary people, especially people who work the land, are deemed unideal revolutionary subjects and therefore unworthy of scholarly attention, contributes to the general lack of interest in life on the subsistence margins. With few exceptions, the peasant population and rurality typically are seen as backward, and "treated as the more-or-less passive recipient of projects hatched and implemented from above."[38] Worse, peasant ways of life, including moral and ethical outlooks, are deemed as backward, traditional, primitive, and/or reactionary. And yet, understanding subsistence ethics is critical not only for decoding contemporary agrarian resistance but also for learning an ethic that is part and parcel of the claim for dignity and respect from below, which, more often than not, embodies the persistent refusal to be governed.[39] Beyond the "moral economy of the peasant" is a praxis of mutuality that underwrites alternative rendering of justice, especially one that is relational and grounded on compassion. Even when they may very well reflect the political economy of the community, human actions and values cannot be reducible entirely to rational economic calculus, such that in life—both in urban and rural settings—there are social values, even dominant forms, that "lie beyond immediate relations of production and serve both to create and to signify the existence of a community—one that is more than just an aggregation of producers."[40] Without romanticizing the super-exploitative and appropriative feudal system of past years, precisely because the precarious life on the margin of subsistent living that exists in our era of rampant wealth hoarding and its accompanied amoral political economy, that an ethos grounded in a sense of communal obligation and compassion is needed to speculate on an applicative justice framework for the many.

Rather than relying on elite theorizing or an antidemocratic philosophy, subsistence living and life on the margins provide a wealth of resources for learning about living with dignity and compassion, and how to meaningfully render solidarity as relational. Within the larger frame of accountability and communal relations, compassion is a social praxis that centers the regards for the other, especially the circumstances and needs of others, so that harm calculus reflects collective well-being instead of privatized accumulation.[41] To be sure, "rituals of compassion" can indeed function as disciplinary techniques for social control; nevertheless, assistance in the form of mutual aid has long existed as a tried-and-true practice of solidarity for those who live on the margins—be they queer and trans people living with HIV, displaced workers during the COVID-19 pandemic, Black people in the Jim Crow US, villagers in agrarian Southeast Asia, or displaced migrants since time immemorial. The practice of helping or being there is also a form of a social compact and a tool of conviviality, wherein which action and entanglements define the terms of mutuality.[42] Mutual aid makes justice as compassion viable, and as Pierre-Joseph Proudhon and Peter Kropotkin understood, mutualism and mutual aid are some of the most potent weapons of the weak against capitalist appropriation.[43]

Western contemporary thought on mutuality, however, tends to conflate cooperatism and mutual assistance with anarchism, while ignoring robust traditions of similar practices in Asia, Africa, and Latin America that emerged independent of western anarchist trajectories. For instance, Cooperativa Agricola de Cotia (COTIA)—the agricultural cooperative that went on to serve as a model for early agrarian cooperatives in Brazil—was founded by Japanese migrant contract workers in the late nineteenth and early twentieth centuries, who were more likely influenced by religious teaching such as Shintoism and Zen Buddhism than western anarchism. These Japanese migrants, recruited to Brazil with false promises of land, soon learned that they were in fact part of the larger elite strategy to Whiten Brazil's labor force in fear of a newly emancipated Black population.[44] Transplanting cooperative praxes from their home country, COTIA members cultivated and traded fresh fruits, produce, flowers and poultry. In the 1930s, with a population of more than six hundred thousand, Japanese migrant farmers left the harsh life of the coffee plantations, and instead "routinely formed agricultural cooperatives" as a matter of course.[45] By 1937, only ten years after being established, COTIA grew into the largest agricultural cooperative in Brazil. By the 1970s, based on its operations, COTIA set precedents for laws governing cooperatives throughout Brazil and other regions in Latin America.[46]

As Joana Laura Noguiera and João Nicédio Alves Noguiera point out, when early cooperatives in Brazil emerged, there was no "legislation that had institutionalized collective action and given it a formal identity."[47] Thus while not indebted to the Rochdale principles inspired by the "father of the cooperatism," Robert Owen,[48] COTIA nevertheless had "a culture of community action and collective problem-solving," embodying "essential elements of the Rochdale philosophy: free and voluntary association, democratic management, economic participation of the membership, autonomy and independence, training and skill building, collective action, and community well-being."[49] As evidence of COTIA's enduring influence, today cooperatives, ranging from agriculture and credit to housing and labor, exist in one-third of municipalities in Brazil, revealing a robust legacy of countering capitalist logic and a viable praxis of mutuality and solidarity.

COTIA is emblematic of the larger movement for food and land justice, including the social solidarity economy, that has captured global imagination and mobilizing energies, relying on the principles of dignity, solidarity, and mutuality. Indeed, mutual aid and cooperatism have proven resilient as life aids, especially in these times of pandemic and wealth hoarding.[50] When even the chronically insular Vatican must attend to planetary concerns, especially with the trinity of livability—land, lodging, and labor—it is difficult to deny this movement's appeal.[51]

A more concerted mobilization of global Indigenous and farm workers is discernible and has drawn greater attention to the demands of food and territorial sovereignty movements, especially following the Zapatista uprising in the late twentieth and early twenty-first centuries. In contrast to the tendency toward the singularity of the autonomous individual, the Zapatistas' praxis of radical inclusion, emphasizing "a world where many worlds fit" (*un mundo donde quepan muchos mundos*), capaciously hacks back against appropriative and exploitative living and embodies a radically alternative ethic of liberation.[52] Emphasizing Indigenous, communal autonomy, instead of entitled liberty, participants who were peasants, fishers, and food producers from more than thirty countries at the Forum on Food Sovereignty in 2017 in Bueno Aires drafted the "Declaration of the Forum on Food Sovereignty, Territories of Peace for a Dignified Life."[53] They demanded an end to violence, broadly defined, and committed themselves to the defense of territories "against the violence of the capital, the commodification of life and the destruction of consequence of megaprojects in the name of so-called 'progress.'"[54] As it turns out, living on the margins during the time of disposability—where neoliberal governance affects ways and means that render some people as plutocrats and others as data or waste and not meant to survive, also dialectically incites living with mutual aid and in solidarity.[55] As this chapter shows, that these communities as counter-sites have always existed suggests a discernable and viable praxis of the commons,[56] with meaningful lessons on justice as compassion and in solidarity—be it a subsistent Taoist society where the notion of living is wedded to the idea of an apolitical communal existence without government, or a transplanted Japanese diaspora in post-emancipation Brazil, or the free Black communities in Jim Crow apartheid—where the repertoire of living included social practices that are organized around the principle that people create wealth not for accumulation but for sustaining life, or wealth creation *contra* accumulation.[57] Echoing the Zapatistas' rallying cries for mutuality and dignity, the participants who gathered in Buenos Aires insisted that livability is predicated not on the freedom to impose unjust laws and policies or "the will of the powerful," but on a social solidarity economy that is free from violence, and a community existence based on the idea of a dignified life in peace:

> ENOUGH VIOLENCE! . . . We recognized ourselves as anti-capitalist, anti-patriarchy, internationalist and anti-colonialist and we take on the commitment they imply as challenges for our everyday life, within our organizations and in the search of ways to bring about a new society, a challenge we deem both possible and necessary to achieve.[58]

In expressing "solidarity with all the people of the world in resistance," they committed themselves to transforming "all of our territories into TERRITORIES OF PEACE FOR FOOD SOVEREIGNTY, POLITICAL SOVEREIGNTY AND A DIGNIFIED LIFE!"[59] Thus, not unlike their progenitors of the previous eras of peasant and slave rebels or their contemporary counterparts in urban communities, they are redefining safety and security. And in doing so, they invite a different justice praxis, one that centers on community, solidarity, and mutuality.

JUSTICE AS COMPASSION AND IN SOLIDARITY

Just as freedom should not be the will of the powerful to impose, so should justice not be whatever the powerful say it should be.[60] Moreover, justice must be freed from the tyranny of the fictitious idea of the autonomous individual. Indeed, the exalted status of individualism that privileges individual autonomy over all other virtues or public goods, is not a Left-versus-Right problem, but a problem of classical liberalism—the dominant philosophy in the modern west. Individuals are as atomized, supra-ego pathologically transcending all entities, and the presupposition of individual liberty as a public good informing sociomaterial values, and by implication, public policies.[61] It is within this garrison that the empty throne of liberty sits, reigning over the dominion of a few. Among right-wingers and neo-confederates, for instance, no single concept captures their imagination more than the exalted status of liberty, except perhaps the delusional sense of White superiority. Democratic elitism, especially in the form of Jeffersonian antidemocracy and its progeny, attests to liberty loving groups and individuals, especially politicians, exercising little restraint in the curtailing of the freedoms of others, especially women's reproductive autonomy and gender expressions. This seeming contradiction is not a contradiction, but a long practice of privileging liberty as an idea while countering justice as praxis. The nullification of equal justice (or what Naomi Zack calls the absence of applicative justice) for Black people in the US, for instance, is intimately linked with the contestation between freedom and justice, wherein liberty reigns, gifting freedom to the few and injustice to the many.[62] The privileging of individual autonomy, as pointed out in chapter 5, diminishes social obligation and the worth of other human values, including justice, solidarity, and dignity—thus severing social justice from liberty. Justice subordinated to exalted liberty does not merely delimit justice to only distributive matters as exemplified by the justice as fairness paradigm. In reality, it is a shell game—a cipher for ensuring injustice operating in an orderly fashion, especially in the maintenance of the status quo, even as extreme wealth hoarding, an epidemic of police homicide, and the mass incarceration of poor people—especially Black and Brown people in the US and beyond—threaten the very existence of the polity.

Political theorist Asma Abbas insists that "suffering ought to be liberated from the question of death if a democratic politics is to remain loyal to whom it is at least nominally serving," suggesting that suffering is "the core of transformative politics."[63] A justice praxis that is grounded on not only responsibility and accountability,[64] but also solidarity, especially out of an acute recognition of the suffering in the lives of others, is one that centers compassion, mutuality, and friendship. A more practical and transformative approach to justice—one grounded on an ethic of democratic living—is thus a life aid for countering the intensifying administrative violence in everyday life, especially life on the subsistence margins. From demosprudence to movements for liberation, if the proliferation of big and small rule refusals is any indication, even the staid business at the US Supreme Court cannot entirely be sheltered from the rousing cries of solidarity and the (multi)modal imagination of the many pedagogies of the oppressed.

9

Speculative Justice and the Politics of Mutuality

Kindness eases Change.
Love quiets fear.
And a sweet and powerful
Positive obsession
Blunts pain,
Diverts rage,
And engages each of us
In the greatest,
The most intense of our chosen struggles.

Octavia Butler[1]

We will not cancel us.

Adrienne Maree Brown[2]

Abolition is not absence, it is presence. What the world will become already exists in fragments and pieces, experiments and possibilities. . . . Abolition is building the future from the present, in all of the ways we can.

Ruth Wilson Gilmore[3]

TRANS SPECTACLES AND QUEER LIVES

Despite living in the wealthiest and nominally most trans- and queer-friendly country in the world, trans and genderqueer people in the US experience greater stress, discrimination, and violence; with shorter life expectancy; and are at higher risk of being unhoused, under and unemployed, in poor health, incarcerated, and experiencing premature death than any other demographic group. These accountings are before factoring in race and class differentials.[4] It is noteworthy that trans people are more racially and ethnically diverse than the general population; less likely to own a home (32 percent compared to 67 percent of the general population), and more likely to live in extreme poverty. During the COVID-19 pandemic, for instance, the LGBTQ population experienced significantly higher rates of food and housing insecurity, and disproportionately ranked higher among those who owe back rents.[5] The following is a data snapshot on the trans population, collated from various surveys of LGBTQ people in the US:

- 48 percent had experience of being fired or denied a job at least once.
- 43 percent had been denied a promotion or received a negative evaluation.
- 42 percent had attempted suicide.[6]
- 39 percent reported having symptoms consistent with mental health.[7]
- 54 percent experience some form of intimate partner violence.[8]
- 71 percent of trans students of Color reported being harassed at school (compared to 59 percent White transgender students).[9]
- Trans women of Color experienced four times the average unemployment rate. The overwhelming majority experience being racially and sexually profiled as sex workers.

The Human Rights Campaign periodically draws attention to the epidemic of violence against trans people, noting that many "transgender and gender non-conforming individuals have been killed" for being trans.[10] In sum, trans people living in the US face a myriad of challenges—from extreme poverty, lack of health care, to stigma, harassment, discrimination, and premature death, including extraordinarily violent deaths. In their most comprehensive study, the National Transgender Discrimination Survey concludes: "It is part of social and legal convention in the United States to discriminate, ridicule, and abuse transgender people and gender non-conforming people."[11]

It is not an exaggeration then to say that trans and genderqueer people face extraordinary precarity and cope with tremendous harms. Remarkably, in the last five decades or so, trans and queer community activists have modeled a form of democratic living so compelling that feminists and radicals have taken up their visions and praxes integral to freedom struggles. Perhaps because trans people challenge so many fundamental assumptions about identity, body, and desire, and undermining gender as governance, the mobilization for trans justice holds out a certain promise for a radically transgressive feminism and transformative justice on the margins.

The terribly difficult work of movement and world-building is made more complicated by many gender troubles—not least is the idea that gender as a social construct *with* material consequences continues to elude analysts and activists alike. The imaginary feminist communities, wherever they might be, are not immune from episodic internal strife, even epic ones. The contentious debate about the meanings of gender, for instance, is emblematic of the complex and confounding praxis of solidarity, especially feminist solidarity, including coalition politics and its facsimile, "allyship." Like most divergences and acts of nonconformity, those who rebel or find themselves astray, while not always ideologically nomadic, nevertheless, could face the wrath of orthodoxies and may end up with expulsion.[12] However, beyond the titillation of corporate media and right-wing truthiness machines[13] seeking to manufacture and capitalize on internal disagreements among the Left, public disagreement among feminists presents an opportunity to take up difficult dialogues about solidarity and friendship that demands serious consideration.

Too frequently, bad faith[14] underwrites public debates over the meanings of gender, further obfuscating the sociomateriality of trans and queer lives. The fact of the matter is that transgender lives remain in the quotidian shadow, with many under siege, as a limited few reaps the benefits of temporary relief through notoriety and momentary fame. After all, the seduction of affluence and proximity to rule are partially about cooptation and assimilation. As the statistical accounting reveals, however, trans and gender nonconforming people continue to be targets for harassment, intimidation, discrimination, incarceration, and premature death, especially at the hand of vigilante and state violence. This deathly accounting portends a politics of accountability that an ethics of radical egalitarianism demands. Feminism's claims of radical egalitarianism and ethical ways of life must contend with the well-being and livability of those lives that are in the balance. The question thus is not about who are the "real women" or even the "real feminists," but about how capacious feminisms and feminist praxes need to be so that trans lives are livable and thriving. If we need to move beyond the tyranny of immediate experiential knowledge, then perhaps, and as the philosopher and artist Adrian Piper insists, we need modal imagination as an approach so we can live beyond debilitative lack of imagination, bad-faith disagreements, and dead-end relationships.[15] As Kara Keeling concludes in *Queer Times, Black Futures*, "within this here and now exist yearnings and openings, experiments, errant wanderings, radical refusals, and creative projects; here and now are echoes from hopeful past . . . unpredictable alliances, theories, knowledges, and connections that might operate on a register that is incommensurate with the calculated risks speculative capital already assumes through its investments in existing relations, even as, perhaps, such unpredictable and random connections have been anticipated, domesticated, dominated and conquered in advance."[16] Gender as governance warrants disruptions and revolts, if not outright rebellions. As shown in previous chapters, the quest for perfect governability has been at best a delusion, even if the effects of its murderous mechanics are always menacing. Rule refusal, including gender nonconforming and revolt, has a way of disrupting even the most spectacularly dreamed up plans for total dominion. Herein lies the tools for a speculative praxis that beholds the promise of radically reimagined worlds and multimodal living. As sites of contestations, such tools can be resourced for transformative reckoning.

SPECULATIVE PRAXIS

In a remarkable study of deviance as resistance written nearly two decades ago, Cathy J. Cohen helpfully delineates a rich terrain for exploring emancipatory praxes.[17] By way of destabilizing the exalted politics of respectability, Cohen maneuvers around stigmas and deviance and, in the process, resourcing queer of Color critiques and intersectional feminist analytics, to delineate the shortcomings of queer theory and masculinist African American studies in their shared pathologies, and to broaden feminist frames to reveal new spaces of possibility.[18] Mining works in Black queer studies, she explains that centering on deviance can "generate new theories and models of power, agency, and resistance in the lives of marginal people."[19] Focusing on those who are marked as deviant and stigmatized, including poor, trans, and queer Black people, Cohen calls for scholars to "take up the charge to highlight and detail the agency of those on the outside, those who through their acts of nonconformity choose outsider status."[20] This chosen outsider status is instructive for insurgent politics toward transformative justice. Given the precarious lives of these subjects, their deviance is both a reflection of circumstances or "constrained choices" and intentional, especially for "the creation of spaces or counter publics, where not only oppositional ideas and discourse happens, but lived opposition, or at least autonomy, is chosen daily."[21] Cohen suggests that counterpublics in the form of community building give rise to spaces "where seemingly deviant, unconnected behavior might evolve into conscious acts of resistance that serve as the basis for a mobilized politics of deviance."[22] Retooling her prior commitment to resourcing deviance as resistance, Cohen fleshes out community building as relational and communal.[23] Enacting deviancy is the embodiment of the refusal to be governed, and for trans and queers of Color, it is the bringing together the many practices of pushing back against the intersecting and simultaneous forms of domination.

Indeed and in the midst of a prior backlash against economically struggling queers of Color, Cohen, in the now classic 1997 essay "Punks, Bulldaggers, and Welfare Queens," helpfully suggests that queer of Color critiques bring an epistemological advantage to the theorizing of queer lives subversively transforming the existing status quo, particularly those not sanctioned by the state, capital and/or heteropatriarchy.[24] For Cohen, the radical potential of queer politics, if any, would likely "be located in its ability to create a space in opposition to dominant norms, a space where transformational political work can begin."[25] A transgressive politics of queer solidarity is thus not a biogenetic embodiment but is fleshed out in communal entanglements of insurgent formations, in insurgent praxes.

While commenting on contemporary feminist activism and the BLM movement, Cohen revisits the theme of feminist trans and queer leadership, noting that today BLM activists are queering the community with their presence in the movement as well as queering movement leadership structure and ways of doing things.[26] She reminds her readers of the strategic feminist analytic that holds emancipatory promises embodied in BLM-led [illegible] activism. Their "lens allows for and promotes different types of allegiances, not only racialized allegiances but also allegiances based on the positionality of people relative to the state, which queers us all or produces a bond of unity needed for the type of mobilization that we're beginning to see."[27] She again cautions against a form of politics that idolizes spectacularity and performativity over substantive liberatory praxes, and insists that "a radical trans analysis makes clear that our struggle is not so that everyone can find their essentialist selves, but instead this movement is about breaking down systems of oppression based on gender and class and race and sexuality that limit the ability of people to have full and happy lives."[28] In short, a trans feminist politics is radical and transformative, not because it is essentialist but because it is broadly inclusive and intersectional.[29] A radical feminist trans praxis is thus intentional and capacious in the work of transforming institutions and power relations, and creative enough to dream up imaginary domains for the not yet known.

Extending Cohen's intentional deviancy to the larger body of work on outlaws and unruly subjects, it is possible to frame queer community-building as a collective praxis of deviance and counter-norming, of making oneself unavailable for governing. Ahmed puts it thusly: "the "queer subject within straight culture hence deviates and is made socially present as a deviant."[30] Indeed and within the larger body of feminist scholarship, especially work on genders and sexualities, the repositioning of deviance and transgressive, speculative praxis has been retooled as a corrective intervention for queering and reimagining liberatory politics by taking up various unruly subjects. Angela Y. Davis's work on the blues women is a prime example, anticipating Cohen's argument about unruly subjects and speculative justice. In *Blues Legacies*, Davis retools her intersectional analytics employed in earlier works on women, race, class and resistance, and insists that the blues women such as Ma Rainey, Bessie Smith, and Billie Holiday, "played a decisive roles in shaping the history of popular music culture in the United States,"[31] and through their body of work, including performances, left behind a legacy of feminist praxis that pushes against moral certitudes, normative desires and various forms of social oppressions, including and especially, violence against women.[32] As its genre implies, the blues are meant to narrate "the social and psychic afflictions and aspirations of African Americans." In this way, "menacing problems are [thus] ferreted out from the isolated individual experience and restructured as a problem shared by the community"; and "can be met and addressed within a public and collective context."[33] Take Davis's characterization of Bessie Smith's "Hateful Blues" for instance: "This rough-and-tumble, sexually aware woman is capable of issuing intimidating threats to men who have mistreated her, and she is more than willing to follow through on them; she is spiritual descendant of Harriet Tubman, who, it is said, always warned her passengers on the Underground Railroad that no one would be permitted to turn back, that they would all forge onward or die at her hands."[34] This portrait "served as a reminder of African-American women's tradition of womanhood, a tradition that directly challenged prevailing notions of femininity."[35]

By giving voice to collective threats and affirming Black people, and especially Black women's "absolute and irreducible humanity," they cannot be reduced to "rowdy and hardened women," so that the portraits they shared of themselves "offer psychic defenses and interrupts and discredits the routine internalization of male dominance" and other forms of oppressions.[36] In so doing, they left behind a legacy of those who have been stigmatized and perceived as nominally deviants, who lived and built counter publics that held new spaces of radical possibilities, constituting a queer legacy of deviancy and ungovernability.[37] Che Gossett points out that transgender liberationist history in the US is largely peopled by poor urban queer and gender nonconforming people of Color, who fought back against police violence and repression—the same subjectivities that Cohen insists we must not leave behind in our rush toward the liberal fictions of opportunism and race neutrality.[38] Such legacy can also be appropriated and sanitized. Gossett explains: "as sites of queer and transgender resistance are folded into the state through inclusion and tolerance as technologies of governance, the desires of the communities from which those sites emerged are actively censored, denied, stifled and extinguished through state and police violence."[39]

Nevertheless, Kai M. Green asserts that trans "as identity, trope and analytic" is generative for "troubling the water" for lesbian feminism and queer studies, particularly as a register for "decolonial demand," an episteme, and a reading praxis.[40] This multidimensional approach is encompassing, with "ontological, ideological, and epistemological ramifications.[41] With an eye on the "moments of fissure, contradiction, and coherence," Green suggests that transformation is fraught, thus requiring "tracing and understanding" the process that may be "already present, yet unnamed."[42] Echoing Lorde's insistence that difference can be generative instead of destructive and Marlon Riggs's poetic rendering of Black queer subjectivity, Green maintains that "a Trans* method demands being more attuned to difference rather than sameness, and the need to understand "that our sameness will not protect us."[43]

A NEW ANALYTIC FOR DEMOCRATIC LIVING

Similar to Cohen's retooling of deviance as resistance, Green's Trans* analytic probes the spaces of liberatory politics, and in so doing, presupposes a disoriented futurity of trans queer becoming. Such an analytic sees orientation as "something we *do*, not have."[44] As Ahmed explains, thinking about orientation points "to the future, to what we are moving toward," and "keep[s] open the possibility of changing directions and of finding other paths."[45] If democracy is a way of life, then democratic living is an orientation that allows us to take up residence as inhabitants of the realm of the many's rule, but also a turning away, a disorientation from antidemocratic praxis and values—a disorientation that necessitates the destabilizing of normative citizenship and governing ideations, including gender ideations.[46]

As shown throughout this work, the most potent critiques of democratic elitism, including queer of Color critiques and Trans* analytics, draw from the spaces where the polity excludes certain bodies, communities and praxes, marking them different or as out of place. Queering democracy is, however, more than the inclusion of out of place bodies. Instead, making democracy queer means unsettling the terms of order—a disorientation from elitism and the consent to be governed, including governing analytics and the grammatology of gender.[47] Indigenous peoples who have refused colonialism's settler terms of governance—be it in the Pacific, Asia, Africa, the Americas, or Palestine—have indeed embodied various praxes in dis/orientation with radical legacies to impart. As Angela Davis, Gina Dent, Erica Meiners, and Beth Richie have pointed out, useful tools for responding to endemic violence, gendered and otherwise, demand an entire ecology—a world-building effort that includes "essential tools, practices, languages, analyses, and mutual aid networks out of anger, love, and necessity."[48] To coexist in mutuality, decolonizing gender and queering democracy therefore necessitate rescripting a usable justice for insurgencies. For a world where many worlds fit—from subsistence to mutual aid and love, a new ethic for democratic living demands profound shifts away from the hostile terrains of gendering as governing, toward a radically different ecology and other ways of doing justice.

SCRIPTING GENDER JUSTICE

The only form of writing that got the attention of the militarist Japanese occupying force in China was *nüshu*—the secretive, little known, phonetic script, dreamed up by peasant women, and used almost entirely by women in Hunan, China, as early as the Song Dynasty (960–1279), or even earlier.[49] So fearful were the Japanese occupiers of rebellions by local Chinese that they suppressed nüshu for more than two decades. In postrevolutionary China and like its former enemies, the Mao Tse Tung government during the Cultural Revolution (1966–1976) feared it as a "witch's script" and followed an even older script of governing—censorship, attempting total suppression of nüshu.[50] The rest of the world was not introduced to this script until 1982, when scholar Gong Zhebing reportedly heard a story from a local official about a deceased maternal aunt who had learned and used it. With the help of the locals, Gong would eventually find a blue cloth that contains nüshu inscriptions, belonging to the peasant woman, He Xijing of Baishui Village.[51] It turns out that the script itself was written by another woman, Hu Cizhu of Getan Village—she was born in the early twentieth century and had been dead for more than five years at the time of "discovery." Fortunately for Gong, Cizhu's daughter, Gong Zhebing, was able to assist in locating another informant, Gao Yinxian of Puwei Village, where nüshu is believed to have been originated. Soon and through Gao, Gong met the fourth critical informant and practitioner, Yi Nianhua of Tongkou Village. Collectively they and the script attracted national and international attention, with scholars, artists, entrepreneurs, politicians, and tourists of all things exotic, hot on their heels.[52] And nüshu would take on a life of its own, its praxis and legibility entreating both aspirations and warnings.

It is believed that only women used nüshu to communicate with one another, without male detection or ability to decipher.[53] Contemporary observers expressed bewilderment that women in a remote region of China, of different ethnic backgrounds and with varying dialects, invented a common language widely used and flourished. But use it they did, for at least a millennium, until the last original speaker died at the at age of ninety-eight in 2004. As Cathy Silber explains in her dissertation on nüshu, the idea of a hidden language invented by women was compelling because it holds "a utopian appeal for many women engaged in their own struggles against gender oppression."[54] This same supposition would end up extending the use of another script—an orientalist governing script that relies on long-held suppositions about Confucianist and feudal China, and their accompanying tropes of "oriental women," especially women in feudal China.[55]

Colonial discovery logic superimposes itself on everyday life, including on the ways this knowledge is encountered and represented.[56] As one of the researchers who went to Jiangyong in the 1980s to study the only known language invented by peasant women and was becoming endangered, Cathy Silber, even as a doctoral candidate, was seen then as an authority in this emergent field. She also encountered pressures to frame nüshu in a particular way to render itself more palatable for western, liberal consumption. An editor at *Ms.* magazine pressured Silber to characterize the script as heroic, emphasizing its exclusive female practitioners in way that was consistent with *Ms.* mainstream feminist readers' expectations of nüshu as "a brave and secret practice." In this vein, Silber was told explicitly that *she could not give even the appearance* of an absence of coercive penalties for its use:

> I had written, "Like most men in Shangjiangxu, Yi's grandfather didn't object to *nüshu*—it was just something women and girls did, like embroidery. He did forbid her to write that letter, though." In the page proofs, the first clause of the first sentence had been deleted and the second sentence had been changed to "He did forbid her to write that letter, though; for other women *nüshu* was an act of resistance for which they faced threats of violence and outright battering."[57]

This rescripting makes clear that the orientalist prefiguration operates and endures through acts of nominal allyship, a facsimile of solidarity. When Silber retorted that she had "no evidence of women facing threats of violence for writing in *nüshu*, but that in fact all evidence insist that *nüshu* was an accepted part of local culture," she again was discouraged from framing it as an accepted gendered activity, and was urged to "imply that *nüshu* writers risked bodily harm" so it would not be seen as "just another girl thing."[58] Ironically, while Silber was encouraged to extend the tired women warrior trope to the nüshu practitioners by emphasizing "the strength and ingenuity of Chinese women," she clearly was dissuaded from sharing the fact that *it was* the larger local culture that nurtured nüshu as "an accepted part of [itself]."[59]

Silber's instructive encounter with *Ms.* is emblematic of the sensationalism and knee-jerk reception when nüshu became legible to the broader world. That reception was both simplistic and dichotomous in its treatment of China and Chinese women as *objects* of social inquiries. It demonstrates the nature of epistemic injustices and injuries that emerge out of seemingly friendly terrains, resembling the many missed opportunities in justice mobilization wherein "allies" are misaligned while doing solidarity. It also reflects a troubling interplay between the orientalist trope of foot binding in Confucian feudal China, on the one hand, and the hyperinflated woman warrior trope, on the other, where observers and students of the "newly discovered" script salaciously reconstructed the horrors and miseries of androcentric feudal China and the mysteriously exotic *laotong* relations of sworn sisters. In so doing, they miss out on a critical opportunity to resource friendship as a life aid and a mobilizing tool.[60]

The term *laotong*, meaning "old-same," refers to nonbiological sibling relationships between female friends. Depending on local customs, not all laotong are formalized by contract, and they generally are considered some of the most important social bonds women have, sometimes even stronger than their biological and/or marital relations.[61] As a style of friendship and resource sharing, it is one of the most enduring bonds one can cultivate and remains a source of strength for the participants. It is also fodder for erotic speculation and exoticization.

Lisa See's acclaimed 2005 novel *Snow Flower and the Secret Fan*, published not long after the death of the last original practitioner of nüshu, sensationalizes both nüshu and laotong relations in the best orientalist fashion.[62] *Snow Flower* is told in the voice of Lily, the "one who has not yet died," referencing the other half of the laotong relation with Snow Flower, her sworn sister.[63] Lily is also See's avatar for the transformative power of nüshu. Succinctly, the novel is a story about how Lily finds her subjectivity through Snow Flower sharing of the secret fan containing the mysterious women's script. Within this historicization, Lily functions as an interloper from one domestic episode to the next, temporarily disrupted by one historical event—the Taiping Rebellion (1851–64) seeking to overthrow an imperial court (the Qing dynasty)—that shows up as the "rebels causing trouble somewhere," forcing Lily to move away from her family. Unsurprisingly, the novel devotes significant attention to foot binding, arranged marriages, submissive wives, worthless daughters, and mysterious female relations with the attendant titillation over implied homoeroticism. While See's intent was to "expose" the heteropatriarchal lifeworld in premodern China and celebrate the strong resilience of sisterhood and Chinese women's strength of character, the novel flattens out any historical complexities and cultural nuances, and presents the most familiar of orientalist tropes and bitesize liberal feminist euphemisms ready-made for consumption by a largely western readership. There is little doubt that See performs a yeoman's labor in fleshing out the androcentric world of nineteenth-century China, drawing attention to Chinese female oppressions and subjection. Nevertheless, and from the very first sentence, her story about nüshu and women's resistance is historically confused, and, at best, unreliable. Even Lily's nüshu inspired laments about how she came in the possession of the secret fan is decidedly anachronistic.[64]

Despite its gratuitous restaging of familiar orientalist tropes, *Snow Flower* mostly succeeds at drawing from the well of sisterhood and female friendship. Through the exposition of nüshu, See suggests that only through this script that binds women—in the form of Lily's correspondence with Snow Flower (and not through her official biography) do we get to know the real Lily. Indeed, nüshu as a praxis is relational, and friendship, especially female friendship, has long been a tool for writers to reveal gendered lifeworlds, and to problematize political alliances and lines of solidarity. Nüshu and the social bonds mediated through its praxis point to gendered social reproduction and creative care labor, functioning as a hidden transcript or public secret, and a survival kit.[65] After all, nüshu was used widely by women, through calligraphy on papers and fans, in embroideries on headscarves, handkerchiefs, and even pillowcases. They can be exchanged as gifts and correspondences, and at end of life, to be offered up to the ghost, burned, or buried. For at least a millennium, women used nüshu widely to communicate with each other about domestic and communal life, express longing and commiserate, and share in the delights of the limits and failures of those more powerful than they. Indeed, using this coded communication, not unlike many hidden transcripts of slaves and prisoners,[66] women intimated with each other and openly critiqued the male imperial gaze and positionality. Whether there was violence behind the suppression of such praxis is thus immaterial so far as these women were concerned, because their affective labor was devoted to caring and feeding *the social bonds between them*, not the terms of the patriarchal order in question.

Fei-wen Liu explores nüshu as an experiential phenomenon, likening it to the women's blues in the US. Liu insists that nüshu and its spoken iteration, *nüge*—as songs sung by women—should be understood as a form of reflexivity or self-aware reflections, inherently dialogic with transformational effects. Not unlike the women's blues or yellow music,[67] many nüshu scripts contain laments about misfortunes, poverty, the miseries of marriages, overbearing mothers-in-law, domestic violence, as well as longing, friendship, and pleasure. The potency of nüshu is in the sharing both as gifts and as performance—singing out loud to oneself and to an audience, including mixed gender audiences. In these ways, nüshu and nüge as expressions are forms of venting, naming sufferings and powerlessness, and giving voice to the act of surviving—in short, living out loud.

Similar to Silber, Liu maintains that it is a fundamental misunderstanding to interpret nüshu as a "weapon of empowerment" or form of resistance, pointing out that it was neither a secret nor suppressed as men simply accepted both nüshu the script and nüge its orality in songs, as female activities. She points out that nüshu was visible *and* audible in Jiangyong—"its sung aspect opened *nüshu* to those who were unversed in the women's script, including men."[68] Because "men paid scant attention" and "made no effort either to hold back the circulation of *nüshu* texts or to become literate in the script," nüshu "stands as evidence of women's failure to gain recognition from men"; thus, it remained unknown outside of Jiangyong.[69] Liu attributes nüshu's illegibility to its historical and cultural context—a male centric and moralistic society, and "the marginalization of sung performance."[70] It was therefore generally ignored rather than suppressed, suggesting an absence of intentional coercion. Instead, nüshu was "dismissed by Chinese scholar officials as trivial and vulgar," and any "'feminist messages' . . . encoded in centuries-old *nüshu* remained concealed and obscured."[71] That nüshu is not legible itself does not render it less significant to students of radical (oral) traditions, nor is its trivialization and marginalization by Chinese literary canon evidence of its lack of profound insights. Not unlike the blues, nüshu/nüge "as social text embody and nurture women's collective consciousness, individual identities multi-positioned perspectives, moral pursuits, and hopes and fantasies."[72] As nüshu is most potent when shared and performed in nüge, it is particularly seductive as a speech act because it embodies all three primary modes of persuasion—*logos*, *pathos*, and *ethos*.[73] Their inventors had deformed the official language (i.e., *hanzi*)—that was either forbidden or inaccessible to them—to create an entirely new linguistic structure built on the spoken words of not one but several ethnic groups,[74] suggesting that these peasant women, like the blues women of another era and context, powerfully performed unruly subjectivity beyond the impoverished imagination of bourgeois feminist ideography. Indeed as "writing subjects and singing protagonists," nüshu/nüge practitioners embodied lifeworlds "that engage their collective consciousness, individual subjectivities, life decisions, and coping strategies,"[75] instantiating a powerful mode of living, even if it inconveniently eludes easy gender analytics.

A World Where Many Worlds Fit

Within this particular unhappy archive of gender governance, we find a world where many worlds fit, with space for women born of rules and restrictions as well as songs, laughter, and many scripts for friendship and mutuality. If justice is nonideal, substantive, and embodied in everyday praxes, then compassion, solidarity and even love and friendship are important dimensions of it. Justice as compassion and in solidarity signals that as much as solidarity is praxis, a strategic coming together, justice is necessarily about living in mutuality. Here, justice itself is praxis and relational; being just is thus an orientation toward just futures, even if the extant lifeworld is far from just. Justice in solidarity thus implies that it is in the praxis of mutuality where we locate meanings and spaces of justice. Justice then is not a dictate of a state, whatever the powerful say it is, nor the Law. Instead, it is relational, with others, in real life, living out loud, in solidarity or mutuality, and hopefully, with respect and dignity. Unlike jurisprudent supremacy that excludes the *demos* with the injurious effect of demeaning the laws, fronting movements for justice as pedagogy and radical freedom struggles as primary spaces for learning the meanings of justice and freedom allows us to democratize knowledges about justice and unfreedom.[76] Justice in solidarity thus also signals the importance of strategic formations—the coming together for the purpose of mobilization and countering injustices and indignities. The coming together or formation of alliances of communities, peoples, even nations, are evidence of recognition and consciousness of some perceived mutuality and reciprocation of shared experiences and common futures, and positing them as *a* basis for fomenting just action. Indeed, while oppressions alone do not necessarily bring people or communities together, shared conceptions of justice historically have built unaligned communities, nations, and even worlds. Third World consciousness and the historical struggles against colonialism, for instance, are verification of peoples coming together based on the recognition of shared experiences of vulnerabilities, coloniality and racial capitalism, where race-class consciousness formed the basis for strategic mobilization countering western hegemony and birthing dreams independent from western epistemes.[77] If gender justice must necessarily be about mutuality and friendship, then justice as compassion and in solidarity detours away from ideal-theorizing of justice and bad-faith dealings, as a disorientation toward mobilization and dreaming for another lifeworld as just imperatives.

10
Toward a Democratic Ethic of Living

Who can use the term "gone viral" now without shuddering a little? Who can look at anything anymore—a door handle, a cardboard carton, a bag of vegetables—without imagining it swarming with those unseeable, undead, unliving blobs dotted with suction pads waiting to fasten themselves on to our lungs?

Arundhati Roy[1]

Liberation ethics . . . takes its point of departure in an affirmation of the real, existent, historical other.

Enrique Dussel[2]

We are all part of one another.

Yuri Kochiyama[3]

ALIVE AND NOT ALIVE

The new coronavirus, 2019-nCoV, which causes COVID-19, has wreaked havoc on the social body as much as it has on its human hosts. While the pandemic raged, the virus itself is not considered to be alive. Some specialists in the biological sciences described it as being only "pseudo-alive."[4] Without a living host, viruses are not viable organisms, this state of pseudo-living persists until they find available bodies to accommodate them. Yet even in such a state of pseudo-life, 2019-nCoV has proven that it harbors real potential for highly (re)productive capacities, threatening to bring about an end of life to humans and communities around the globe. It also has proven repeatedly during its short pseudo-life that to persist as a destructive form, humans must do our part—serving as hosts to its virulent destructive capacities as authors of our own demise. And yet, therein also lies hope, as "it is entirely possible that the outbreak could be controlled and even eradicated . . . [with] the joint efforts of the whole society."[5] Like most contemporary catastrophes, then, we as humans have in us the ways and means, however difficult and elusive, to counter this ongoing challenge, as mutuality and solidarity hold out the promise of a less tragic ending.

Nevertheless and despite the miraculously efficient discovery and development of COVID-19 vaccines and other counter measures, the pseudo-life of the coronavirus remains more resilient than scientists anticipated. In this time of neoliberalism, with its hyper-mobile and speculative financialization and privatization, the woeful absence of a coherent public health infrastructure and social safety nets foreclosed the possibility of an effective social lockdown needed for viral containment. In the wealthiest of nations, not only are we bowling alone (as Robert Putnam might have put it),[6] we are often not even bowling at all. And all the while the precarious life of not having enough dangerously fuels the pseudo-life of the virus, even as the wealthiest individuals and families hoarding all the gains of the financial "recovery" from the temporary market tantrums of spring 2020, evidenced by how the "1,000 richest people on the planet [recouped] their COVID-19 losses within just nine months, [even as] it could take more than a decade for the world's poorest to recover," with women among the hardest hit.[7]

In late spring 2020 at the early stage of the COVID-19 pandemic, even the nonscientific press had intensified their coverage. Three years in, many virologists have had to retract or correct earlier, more optimistic pronouncements.[8] In those early months, though, essayist and novelist Arundhati Roy adroitly framed the pandemic as "a portal" that portended promises and possibilities as she laid out what should have been intuitive when countering this maddening pandemic that was fast becoming an endemic. Roy makes it clear in the pages of the *Financial Times* that "historically, pandemics have forced humans to break with the past and imagine their world anew. This one is no different."[9] As she explains: "We can choose to walk through it, dragging the carcasses of our prejudice and hatred, our avarice, our data banks and dead ideas, our dead rivers and smoky skies behind us. Or we can walk through lightly, with little luggage, ready to imagine another world. And ready to fight for it."[10] While not a biologist, Roy demonstrates a remarkable ability to capture the pathogenicity and transmission of the virus with an acute insight into our neoliberal condition, while presciently anticipating the virulence of both—the COVID-19 virus and our extant social conditions.[11] Insisting that this epic tragedy is not new, she noted some countermeasures, especially lockdowns "worked like a chemical experiment that suddenly illuminated hidden things," revealing the sickness and pathologies for the whole world to see.[12] In the US as in India, the policies implemented largely benefited the most privileged and powerful. Just as the economic recovery from the Great Recession largely left behind the poor and people of Color,[13] the COVID-19 pandemic disproportionately harmed poor people, especially Native Americans and African Americans.[14] The same pandemic that left tens of millions out of work, especially women,[15] also enriched the world's billionaires to the tune of more than $2.5 trillion, so that 2,189 billionaires now have more than $10.2 trillion in private wealth, while millions more are pushed into extreme poverty.[16] Perhaps when the pandemic ends, if it ends, its brief will be thicker and more extensive; for now, there is still much we do not know other than that it is an amoral virus. Nevertheless, Roy insists that "in the midst of this terrible despair, it offers us a chance to rethink the doomsday we have built for ourselves."[17] Framing any crisis, including the pandemic, as an opportunity, is fraught with the risk of opportunism and neoliberal quick fixes; and yet, Roy's capacious framing holds out utopian promises and demands refusals.

MYTHIC BEINGS

Justice theorizing is both normative and futurist. Thinking about justice and working toward just futures are also moral acts. There is therefore no theory of justice without moral consideration. It is not difficult to extrapolate from Roy's suggestions for how to live in the time of COVID-19 and come to larger lessons for democratic living. What she demands, however, is nothing less than an appeal to democratic living as an ethical stance, including the appeal for solidarity as friendship and mutuality. As if responding to Roy's general call, youths, many femmes of Color, stepped up and stepped onto the streets in 2020, in their millions, demanding not only an end to police violence and homicide, but to think anew of safety, security, and solidarity. Among other things, "Black Lives Matter!" signifies self-affirmation and consciousness of mutuality. It is troubling that we rarely frame mass mobilization as desire for friendship, or foreground love as a motivation for movement formations. While their enemies rarely attributed these dimensions to protestors and those who willfully resisted the dominant orders, a love for justice, freedom and community is one of the oldest reasons behind people organizing themselves into collectives and working for just futures. Andrew J. Jolivétte, for instance, suggests that centering "love as a radical act that defies boundaries" is generative for a pedagogy of liberation.[18] He explains that because "we cannot presume to know what is best for our communities . . . only these communities can inform the moral ethical questions that need to be addressed."[19] Radical love engenders a "revolutionary space where justice, new racial representation, and political contestation are central to dismantling ongoing colonialism in the United States and globally."[20] For him, radical love is a viable "strategy for social transformation," because it creates space for "being vulnerable."[21] Within the context of vulnerability, radical love is a means of being accountable to communal well-being and just futures. If solidarity is about being in community with, especially as co-conspirators of liberatory formations, then radical love may salve the endemic harms and violence that are difficult to avoid. And if democratic livability necessarily involves radical inclusivity and egalitarianism, presupposing recognition of beings and entities that are not yet known, then love, friends, and friending are life aids for expanding justice praxis as relational.

The discourse on friendship is likely as old as philosophy itself, even if it has been decidedly less fruitful and illuminating compared to the myriad ways that friends show up in our life. In the west and among "serious thinkers," with few exceptions, friends are mostly interlopers and friendships transactional; although, to be sure, from Aristotle and Durkheim to Foucault and Piper, "true" friendship, while rare, holds certain promise of an enduring mutuality and even passion.[22] Aristotle, for instance, while insisting that "it is a thing most necessary for life,"[23] defines friendship in functional terms: pleasure, usefulness, and the pursuit of common good.[24] Not surprisingly, he suggests that the bond of friendship may itself be stronger than justice.[25] It is Aristotle's third attribution of friendship—the pursuit of common good—that prioritizes the relational, as it points to association and the larger community. It is also where Aristotle is most unhelpful but instructive, pointing to the ways that Aristotle and his progeny have had many difficulties encountering difference. As suggested throughout this book, Aristotle's aristocratic prejudice precludes him from countenancing the unruly mob and relegates democracy as a degenerate form of governing. This inability to countenance both the mob and democracy stems from his ideas about distinction and difference. The difference between master and slave, man and woman, and the aristoi and the hoi polloi, are in the content of their characters and fundamentally irreconcilable. For Aristotle, natural differences render equal sociopolitical associations or equal treatment dubious, at best, giving rise to degeneration at worst.[26] Within this frame, friendship is a nonstarter, except for the few who share all things in common. He thus poisoned the chalice of friendship with his elitism and, however useful his emphasis on the necessity for mutual association, we need a better guide to learning about friendship and an ethic for democratic livability. Given that democratic living without radical inclusion and egalitarianism would be a dead end, the denial and suppression of difference prefigure elite rule. The need to draw upon and "get basic with" friends, friendship, and friending are thus important pedagogies of living.

What's Love Got to Do with It?

Well before Anna Deavere Smith was credited for having invented a new form of theater, Adrian Piper's art and meta-criticism, described as "often humorous and, frequently disturbing," broke ground and created spectacles for a new generation of artists to explore alternative perspectives and personae.[27] Piper's "My Calling Card #1" and "My Calling Card #2" were a series of performances in the late 1980s initiated through the titular calling cards, where she interpolates and imbricates her identity as a Black woman. These two-inch by three-and-a-half-inch cards are brown and white, addressing unknown individuals as "Dear Friend," with messages that call attention to the fact that the recipients are being racist or sexist without realizing that they were violating her personal space or privacy. These cards are meant to invite reflections on action concerning individual perceptions of race and gender, as Piper enacts her performance through text as well as handing out the cards at cocktail parties, dinners, bars, and dance parties to those who make racist remarks (Calling Card #1), or presuming that unaccompanied women invite advances from total strangers (Calling Card #2). The address of "dear friend," implies discourse is possible and even welcomed, as the reader/recipient is placed in a position of accepting responsibility for their perceptions and behaviors. Like the larger body of her work, these calling cards draw from Piper's experience as a light-skinned Black woman. As Larissa Pham recently explains, they address "the material reality of race, sex and class in America while engaging with social dynamics through performance, asking her audience to consider positionality within the world."[28] As a Kantian reader, Piper understands well that sometimes we do know better and should do better because "reasons may have objective validity without our being moved to act on them . . . [and] our *recognition* of their objective rational validity may compel or necessitate us to act on them despite our resistance" to do so.[29] If her performance art is embodied philosophy, then Piper is suggesting that the basis for our ethical behavior is linked with our recognition and "when our actions fail to accord with what reason requires, it is because 'certain drives interfere.'"[30] Here, art itself is a form of philosophical counter-interference, and Piper's art is not only consistent with but also extends her moral philosophy of just action.[31]

Piper instructively points out that we need "modal imagination in order to extend our conception of reality—and, in particular, of human beings—beyond our immediate experience in the indexical present."[32] She insists that modal imagination—the ability to imagine ourselves in different lifeworlds that could or might happen—is necessary for "the significance of human interaction," namely compassion. This speculative envisioning presupposes the idea that not only can we imagine what actually exists but also "what might exist in the present or past, or someday exist in the future."[33] The ability to experience compassion for the other requires our ability "to achieve not only insight but also an impartial perspective on our own and others' inner states"—a habit of modal imagination.[34] Without this facility, we would not be able to relate to the self or the other: "So not only would others' inner states be imaginatively inaccessible to us but our insight into our own would be almost non-existent, or at least extremely primitive. We would experience our inner states as we do subtle changes in the weather for which we have no words."[35] Our capacity to reason and comprehend the world would thus be extremely limited, if not entirely debilitated, resulting in a "primitively self-centered and narrowly concrete conception of human beings," our "social relations would be correspondingly bereft," and life entirely unsatisfactory with dead-end relationships.[36]

Genuine friendship "is governed by substantive moral principles of conduct and emotion," while compassion requires "an empathetic imaginative involvement with the other's inner states" to adhere to substantive moral principles.[37] Compassion is thus contingent, and friendship is full of risks.[38] But our ability to relate, to empathize, especially to suffering, makes compassion possible, engendering moral justification for solidarity action.[39] For Piper, moral theory is "genuine theory," and can both constitute and regulate "our empathic imaginative responses to another's conditions in a morally appropriate way." Whether moral theory is "genuine" is less material than whether it offers up ways to affect just futures. If moral theory as imaginative responses and multimodal cognition engenders substantive just notions,[40] then a moral theory that centers on solidarity as compassion and friendship with accountability and an eye toward just futures is usable. It can be (re)tooled to affectively mobilize outrage and respond to the conditions of savage developmentalism, where humans are marked and treated as disposable or as waste.[41] Thus while differing from Dussel's delineation of a liberation ethic, what Piper offers as a moral theory is entirely different from what is nominally understood as a moral order, typically associated with prevailing social orders and normative regulations.[42]

Elsewhere, I have argued that within the context of White supremacy and an unconscious authoritarianism, there exists an epistemic injustice wherein the moral authority of a police officer who kills is a given, while the Black victims, survivors, and/or witnesses of police violence are denied the right to be believed. This is partly because their moral agency is denied, and that denial creates the conditions of possibility for injustice and injury.[43] Piper explains that we "discount a victim's perception of wrongdoing because we devalue her status as a victim, or her social relations to the transgressor, or to the system of social practices that may bestow legitimacy on that transgressor."[44] These two dimensions are related, because "part of what constitutes that position of power surely must be *em*powerment, in the form of the presumption of moral rectitude, by the same community that confers legitimacy and status on that agent in the first place."[45] When this occurs, there is therefore a need to assert an alternative moral universe and/or an ethic of liberation.

In sum, moral theory can help us "make sense of our moral experiences: to identify another's conditions as one of suffering . . . or our own behavior as that of rendering [mutual] aid."[46] In this way, solidarity is prefiguratively relational, not strictly as doing charity for the unfortunate, but an extension of the self being in formations with others. When justice is at issue, moral theory not only has a place, but serves to account for un/just actions, as in/justices demand outrage and counteraction that ideally should be informed by compassion, solidarity and even friendship.

IN FRIENDSHIP AND SOLIDARITY

As part of a larger project to extend "the meaning of culture," and convinced that "authority must reside in the community . . . and it must be tied to, once and for all, the persons who not only do care, but will go on caring,"[47] the Community Documentation Workshop (CDW) starting in 1976 conducted a series of oral histories with "ordinary people" who "have worked and lived in the area." Its purpose was to reconstruct the history of the lower East Side of Manhattan, New York. The CDW was persuaded by the idea that while the majority is not always right, "everyone always has some right" and, therefore, the meaning of culture, especially a democratic culture, cannot be learned without "ordinary people" grounded in communities where they live and work. Among CDW's gathered oral histories is the extraordinary narrative of Yuri Kochiyama—a fish merchant's daughter.[48]

Although known mostly for being a confidante of Malcolm X, however meaningful and consequential that friendship might have been,[49] Kochiyama is exemplary in the ways she resourced friends and friendship as life aid.[50] When this legendary community organizer died in 2014, she passed on a legacy of over six decades of doing justice work, especially how she resourced friending as one of the most important tools for community and world-building. Historian Diane C. Fujino calls this legacy a "heartbeat of struggle," and states that her life "will forever be synonymous with creating a better world for the 'togetherness of all people.'"[51]

The more theoretically sophisticated may dismiss the values that Kochiyama's life and work bring to the table of learning and in the pursuit of justice. However, the ways she gathered people and communities together and on the move embody an enduring praxis of generations of women of Color cultural workers and bridge leaders who have built and sustained communities, big and small. Kochiyama would say that friends are the only few you should put on a pedestal because "what you put on [it] will be your main influence in your life."[52] These love subjects are "family, friends, and humanity; service to community, concern for human rights, justice, and human dignity."[53] For her, the freedom struggle is inherently communal, as "life is not what you *alone* make it."[54]

Throughout Kochiyama's adult life, she consistently prioritized community work and communal well-being instead of self-interest. Her granddaughter, Akemi Kochiyama-Sardinha, for instance, recalls fondly her grandmother's "passionate commitment to community service" and her belief that the needs of community are transcendent in comparison to "the everyday situations that concern the rest of us mere mortals."[55] As Kochiyama-Sardinha shares in the foreword to her grandmother's memoir, "While my grandmother's memoir is undoubtedly full of paradoxes, contradictions, and odd silences, her commitment to humanity and social justice is and has always been unambiguous and unconditional."[56]

At the time of her first oral history interview in 1981, Kochiyama recalled vividly and viscerally the impact of the "Little Rock Nine" and the "Hiroshima maidens" on her political awakening.[57] Later she would recall that "it was after meeting Daisy Bates that [she] began to take a serious interest in the civil rights movement,"[58] and that her family volunteered to host one of the survivors of the atomic bomb attack on Hiroshima (the *hibakusha*)—Tomoko Nakabayashi—for one weekend in their crowded apartment. As Kochiyama tells it: "Tragically, [Tomoko-san] died several months later on the operating table. She was the only one to die during their eighteen-month stay in the U.S. . . . We still have a picture of Tomoko-san with our children. We did not want them to forget her. We also wanted our children to make the connection with the atomic bombing of Hiroshima and to remember that an American Jewish Hospital gave service gratis for eighteen months of plastic surgery to the young Hibakusha women."[59] If it were just these fleeting encounters, perhaps Kochiyama's life narrative would not be so instructive for learning about solidarity as praxis in friendship. However, she and the Kochiyama children later would participate in other events that placed them in formations with the survivors of Hiroshima, Nagasaki, as well as the Nanjing massacre,[60] and, ultimately, they would also become enmeshed in not only the Black and Puerto Rican freedom struggles, and the struggles to free political prisoners, end discrimination and prejudice against Asian Americans, support reparations for the sex slave survivors of the Japanese occupation in South Korea and the Philippines, advocate for trans and queer justice, champion stopping war and Islamophobia, and advancing prison abolition—to name a few of Kochiyama's many entanglements with friends and freedom struggles.[61]

As her granddaughter attests, Kochiyama devoted "practically every waking moment of her life to the struggle," and, also, to friendship. When she was eighteen, Kochiyama wrote down her basic life philosophy, "My Creed," that includes "to never break one link of friendship, regardless of the time or distance that separates me from that friend, even if that friendship is only a memory stored away in my heart and mind."[62] While in adulthood she moved on somewhat from some of her promises to herself, she remained faithful to her personal "creed" on friendship. Her granddaughter captures well the labor and love Kochiyama put in to rendering that creed a reality:

> Anyone who knows Yuri knows that she has a lot of friends. . . . A good listener and avid letter writer, Yuri has an amazing capacity to offer support to and keep in touch with countless friends across distance and time. From high school acquaintances to political comrades and prisoners, to the numerous students she has met throughout her many years on the college-speaker circuit, Yuri manages to stay in contact with almost everyone she has ever met. Sending postcards, letters, holiday greetings, flyers, announcements, and petitions to all of these folks as well as to anyone and everyone who writes to her is one of the primary reasons why she gets so little sleep.[63]

Well before the coming of the internet and social media, Kochiyama understood the power of friends, friending and social networking. Fujino characterizes Kochiyama's labor as akin to "pumping life and energy into the Movement and sustaining the struggle, especially at times when it seemed to be dying." For Kochiyma, it was a near obsession. On the struggle to free political prisoners in the US, for instance:

> As she had done with the Nisei soldiers a quarter century earlier, Yuri felt the internal pressure, almost an obsession, to stay up until the wee hours of the night writing letters to prisoners, writing articles for Movement Publications, and organizing events to defend political prisoners. She maintained detailed, up-to-date records such that she became a major source of information on political prisoners. She also became situated as one of the first persons prisoners called when released. And with her large political and social networks, she created a wide support base for political prisoners.[64]

While her friendship with Malcom X has been credited with Malcolm's turn toward Afro-Asian internationalism, historical friendships and alliances also animated and incited Kochiyama's solidarity praxis, such as the friendship between labor leader Sen Katayama and Black poet Claude McKay, who together established the Communist Party of New York, or the collaboration between US Black soldiers and Filipino guerrillas fighting against Spanish and American imperial designs, or the Venceremos Brigade organized by the Students for a Democratic Society (SDS) in the 1960s in solidarity with the people of Cuba.[65] Cogently, her style of friending is not unique but in keeping with solidarity praxis, if solidarity is understood as "mutuality, accountability, and the recognition of common interests as the basis for relationships among diverse communities."[66]

Chandra Talpade Mohanty explains that feminist solidarity "foregrounds communities of people who have chosen to work and fight together,"[67] such that "relations of mutuality, co-responsibilities, and common interests" are the sediments for mobilization against domination and oppressions.[68] Indeed, historically, friends and friendship associations have been intimately linked with mutual aid societies and cross-border organizing.[69] For instance, during the nationalist struggle for independence in Viet Nam, the Vietnam-America Friendship Association, founded in 1945, morphed into "the Vietnamese Committee for Solidarity with American People" and was instrumental in "citizen diplomacy" as a counterpoint to US geopolitical maneuverings. Judy Tzu Chun Wu explains that, as vehicles for hosting delegates of radicals, these friendship associations were crucial in the larger multifront approach to mobilizing against imperialism and for peace, involving "one united front against the U.S. in Viet Nam; one united front of Indochinese nations against the U.S.; and one front formed by the people in the world against U.S. imperialism."[70] Wu points to the Anti-Imperialist Delegation, which included Black and Asian American radicals like Eldridge Cleaver, Alex Hing, and Pat Sumi, as instrumental in shifting public opinion against war and for peace as well as deepening international political networks.[71] Like these "traveling radicals," Kochiyama's twinning of her struggles for justice with friending suggests an intentionality and pragmatism of astute community organizers who understand and appreciate the power of social networking and the affective dimensions of praxis as relational. Indeed, late in life and adored by younger generations of activists and cultural workers, Kochiyama would again and again urge them to persist in "crossing borders" to make justice a reality.[72]

Ironically, even as cis White male identity is frequently deployed and weaponized for political gains, and social theorizing becomes increasingly more sophisticated, there is a general turn away from social identities as a basis for understanding social formations and mobilizations. Judith Butler, for instance, argues in a recent article that "vulnerability cannot be the basis of a politics, if by 'basis' we mean a human disposition or condition that gives rise, logically or temporally, to a political framework."[73] She maintains that vulnerability must be called into question, not because "systemic destruction or abandonment" are not material or devastating, but because there is a danger in ontologizing vulnerability as a positionality for political mobilization.[74] Butler suggests that this problem has to do with the ways in which being "named as vulnerable" the subjects could be "deprived of their power."[75] She is right to note that those who are vulnerable are not powerless and have developed infrastructures and networks of their own. However, social movement scholars, including Mohanty and Wu, have long understood that one's social identities, including being marked as differently vulnerable, may or may not explain movement membership or give rise to movement formation.[76] Moreover, the assumed "elevation of paternalism" is not a precondition of addressing vulnerability and group harm, but reflects a limited imaginary domain of what is possible, in policy and otherwise. The pernicious assumption that the state or an equally powerful entity (e.g., the citizenry of the Global North) monopolizes solutions (while being a source of the problem itself) does not reflect the contending and confounding forces that collectively contribute to the plight of the vulnerable. Instead, such paternalism, if it exists, more likely reflects a form of addiction to the state, and not the actual preference of the many involved. Empirically, solidarity networks, including loose affinity groups, frequently embody a praxis that extends beyond the state and even outside the terms of order or beyond the pale. In other words, their ontological totality precludes accepting oppressions and vulnerabilities as the *only conditions* of their complex lives.[77]

For Kochiyama and many who are intent on being in mobilizing formations, while the repertoire of their solidarity praxis is not entirely grounded in shared vulnerabilities, their common experiences and critiques of domination serve as viable nodes in various networks of mutuality. Mohanty, for instance, suggests that the very process of identity and consciousness formation are entangled in acts of mutuality and relationship building. She notes that "the home, community, and identity all fit somewhere between the histories and experiences we inherit and the political choices we make through alliances, solidarities, and friendships."[78] Be they the underground railroad, agrarian cooperatives, friendship societies, or Kochiyama's friending, networks of mutuality long have functioned as critical infrastructures of resistance and mobilization. Moreover, and as Kochiyama's life and work illustrate, a people's conditions and dispositions are not the same, although they may serve as a resource for movement identity, formation, and mobilization. Her experience as a survivor of federal incarceration may have attuned her to injustices in the lives of others who were situated similarly as victims of racial and other forms of oppression, but it was also living in Harlem and organizing against anti-Black racism that put her on the path of abolition feminism. So, while vulnerability itself may not serve as the *only* basis of a politics, especially a politics that would give rise to radically transgressive acts against this unjust world order, it seems imprudent to dismiss or homogenize the many who have been marked as differently vulnerable as a viable node of political alliances and solidarity in a rush to move beyond the fixities of social identity.[79]

Abolition feminism, as an ethic for democratic living, shows how networks of solidarity—grounded in radical egalitarianism and inclusivity—are sediments built up from experiences, consciousness, and modal imaginations of those who are differently vulnerable. Their vulnerabilities are neither liabilities nor disabilities as their enemies frequently make them out to be, but are merely manifestations of existing power relations and the sociomaterial conditions that are frequently beyond their control.[80] Such vulnerabilities are the comorbidities of life on the margins, and while they may not be the determinants of mobilization, their realities are consequential. As Cohen's work elucidates, one's positionality and relations to harm do not automatically confer a radical, transgressive politics.[81] As the exploration of abolition feminism praxis confirms, this transgressive politics is akin to a "radical trans feminist politics that is thinking about and rooted in the transformation of institutions that would oppress and limit people's understanding and performance of gender."[82] It is this communal form of intentional politics that presupposes the collective. It does not rely on or settle for essentialist identification. Instead, it is "tied to a transformative liberatory agenda"[83] that seeds mutuality and communal well-being as praxis.

THE UNGOVERNED PERIPHERY

If colonial spaces are harbingers of what is to come in the metropoles, then Puerto Rico, not New York or California, beholds the futures of the US, bearing grave warnings. Almost a decade before millions of people in the States took to the street to protest violent policing and police killings, tens of thousands of Puerto Ricans from every walk of life sought to draw attention to what the American Civil Liberty Union (ACLU) calls "an outlaw police force." Like their counterparts in the States, they have been marching and protesting police violence. In its damning and comprehensive 2012 report *Island of Impunity*, the ACLU concludes that this second-largest police department in the US is "dysfunctional and recalcitrant," where the "use of excessive or lethal force is routine, and civil and human rights violation are rampant."[84] Similar to what community organizers in the states would discover a few years later, it finds that the Puerto Rico Police Department (PRPD) utterly failed at their job at "policing crimes," especially domestic violence and sexual assault, while excelling at deploying force against protestors attempting to suppress political expressions and mobilizations. The US Department of Justice's own 2011 comprehensive investigation reveals that it was the police that was the source of many crimes, with nearly 10 percent of the entire police force arrested for engaging in criminal activities.[85]

As the primary law enforcement agency on the island, the PRPD is instrumental for colonial enforcement. Its habitual use of force was "designed to suppress protected First Amendment rights."[86] This is what normative policing in anti-colonial spaces looks like, designed especially to suppress and deter decolonization. Remarkably, even the DOJ could not ignore this normal policing practice as its report advises the reader: "It would be *an enormous mistake*" to read this as the work of a few bad apples.[87] The island's governing regime has been equally uninterested in transforming policing, such that these "failures" are features, and not bugs, of law enforcement. Reports such as the DOJ's *Investigation of the Ferguson Police Department, Freedom to Thrive* (2015), and others verify what normal racialized policing looks like beyond Puerto Rico.[88] It should come as no surprise then that "defund the police" resonates so strongly with so many on the island. It is fitting that in the midst of mass protests in the states, Puerto Rican activists in Harlem, as part of a larger loose network of solidarity, were well-placed to transform their Puerto Rican Day Parade into a rally and march to defund the police.[89]

While some have lamented the lack of concrete reforms in the aftermath of an unprecedented consecutive mass protests campaign in 2020, there are immeasurable shifts in conviction about the need to eradicate anti-Black violence and the desire to work toward an anti-racist society, especially among communities of Color. To that end, activists and movement organizers are emboldened by the outgrowth of public demonstrations of anger and impatience toward rhetorical, performative expressions of solidarity. Instead, they want substantive, demonstratively consequential actions.

Their impact, both small and big, is seeding change in ways that are not always highly visible but are discernible. During the nadir of another protest era, the historian Robin D. G. Kelley noted that measuring movement impact is not easy, especially when the political environment is severely circumscribed.[90] For Kelley, one of the primary functions of radical movements for justice is to help us think the unthought, imagine the impossible, and dream freedom that is not yet known. It is thus unwise to mistake silences for absences, especially given that the largely corporate controlled media is unlikely to amplify social justice movement gains or those movements' most ambitious aspirations. Moreover, the impact and achievements of BLM/M4BL mobilizations both before and after the 2020 protest season are deep, however intangible. As Barbara Ransby points out in her definitive study of contemporary Black freedom struggles, *Making All Black Lives Matter*, "this is the first time in the history of US social movements that Black feminist politics have defined the frame for a multi-issue, Black-led mass struggle that did not primarily or exclusively focus on women."[91] Ransby maintains that BLM/M4BL, embodying the most potent dimension of networks of organizing in contemporary struggles for liberation, enacting "a Black feminist intersectional praxis in the campaigns, documents, and visions" that "championed a grassroots, group-centered approach to leadership" inherited from a legacy of

Black feminist organizers like Ella Baker, and as such, they "patently rejected the hierarchical hetero-patriarchal politics of respectability."[92] In these ways, "Black feminist politics and sensibilities have been the intellectual lifeblood of this movement and its practices."[93]

Contrary to White supremacist propaganda and corporate media manufactured frames, BLM/M4BL organizers are committed to the practice of radical inclusivity and anti-violence consistent with an abolition feminist praxis. As they understood violence to be broadly defined and sourced, democratic living is only viable when prisons are obsolete and police redundant.[94] Constitutive of the hard work of thinking and dreaming in the direction of these campaigns of protest, their mobilization's immediate genealogy dates back to the Michael Brown-Ferguson protests in 2015, and the Oscar Grant-Oakland-Bay Area protests in 2009, with the Trayvon Martin 2012 protests sandwiched in between. It is this extended campaign, spanning more than a decade of feminist protests, that rivals the nineteenth-century antilynching campaign in endurance, and surpasses its audacity in reach and ambition.

What BLM/M4BL organizers also accomplished is a general awakening. Perhaps for this first time, the US as a country is compelled to reflect *en masse* on its anti-Black racism and White supremacist past *on Black feminist terms*. As it is an ongoing process, a more usable past is being (re)remembered every day. Racialized epistemes, especially White innocence, are shaken out of their complacency, as the epistemology of ignorance is denied its claims of legitimacy and moral certainty.[95] Even as the Republican-led and corporate-sponsored censorship campaigns against critical race and ethnic studies rage on, grassroots journalism and alternative media continue to provide extensive coverage of ongoing struggles for a more inclusive and equitable civil society.

Far from the harsh spotlight directed at the *New York Times*'s infamous "1619 Project," and inspired by DeNeen's Brown's reporting on the Tulsa Race Massacre (recently brought to public consciousness by HBO's *Watchmen*), the University of Maryland–based Howard Center for Investigative Journalism, for instance, recruited students from historically Black colleges and universities (HBCUs) as part of its campaign to diversify journalism (both journalist corps and perspectives), and to develop a body of work about newspapers "that published headlines, cartoons, stories, and editorials that aided and abetted racial massacres and lynchings."[96] On October 18, 2021, this collective endeavor bore fruit in the form of *Printing Hate*: reproducing more than thirty stories culled from more than five thousand newspapers with a century's worth of coverage (1865–1965), including ones about how the Black press sought to subvert the dominant narrative and provided counter-coverage to raise awareness about lynching in the US.[97] In the process they also compiled an accessible database, comprised of nearly a hundred newspapers that are still in existence. As the student-journalists explain:

> For scores of years, newspapers printed hate, leading to racist terror lynchings and massacres of Black Americans. Hundreds of White-owned newspapers across the country incited the racist terror lynchings and massacres of thousands of Black Americans. In their headlines, these newspapers often promoted the brutality of White lynch mobs and chronicled the gruesome details of the lynchings. Many White reporters stood on the sidelines of Jim Crown lynching as Black men, women, teenagers and children were hanged from trees and burned alive.[98]

Printing Hate thus "examines the scope, depth and breadth of newspapers coverage of hundreds of those public-spectacle lynchings and massacres." On the same day that this project went live, *Axios*—considered a must-read news site for leaders in business, finance and government—explicitly embraced the project's objectives, citing Brown to emphasize its key takeaway.[99] So, even as the US Supreme Court persists in its recalcitrant stance on unconditional "qualified" immunity doctrine as a shield to protect and preserve violent policing,[100] and as a campaign to censor critical thought continues in state legislatures, school boards, and classrooms throughout the nation,[101] these students, in Brown's telling, represent the aspirations of tomorrow. This is what critical resistance in the era of abolition feminism-led movement building looks like.

The infrastructure for rebelling against such existing dominant journalistic practices and academic ideological apparatuses have been built and secreted for more than a century, most recently laid down by grassroots networks and organizations, including the more than two-decade old prison abolitionist network, Critical Resistance, and the abolition feminist network, INCITE! Women of Color against Violence. Intent on destroying the things that are killing them, these networks and their affiliates explicitly reject White supremacist and democratic elitism, pining for another world.

FREEDOM TO THRIVE

Writing in the midst of an earlier social, or, more accurately, racial, awakening in the US and at the height of a global movement to materially and discursively decolonize, historian Louis Ruchames compiled an indispensable sourcebook of *Racial Thought in America*, noting that "racial thought is as old as civilized man."[102] Citing economic historian Friedrich (Otto) Hertz, Ruchames insists that "modern racial theories were sketched in outline" in

Aristotle's episteme.[103] Racism and racialism as we know them, he argues, are new insofar as "ethnocentrism and slavery were additional elements of the cultural heritage which the early colonists brought to the American continent."[104] Racial (apartheid) democracy as a framework, however, persisted, with few exceptions.

The slave revolution in Santo Domingo represents one of the most radical attacks on the very idea of western civilization, liberalism, and their many self serving conceits, including burgeoning democratic elitism. As C. L. R. James insisted, "the old colonial system and democracy are incompatible"[105] For James, "democracy" was no match for political independence, without which, "the men, women and children who drove out the French . . . could not maintain their liberty."[106] Racial "democracy" thus flourished side by side with colonial systems, such as those in South Africa, the US, and Brazil. For James and other anticolonial thinkers, there is a fundamental incompatibility between democracy and coloniality. That they existed side by side for centuries and were both defended with great passion by western thinkers, suggests either collective disingenuity or a forgery of one or the other. And since the human remains and ecological disfigurement left behind by colonialism are irrefutable, and it is farcical to contemplate collective self-deception in total, it must be that racial democracy is cooked up by mystics and forgers who were more invested in conquest and colonization than the lofty claims of their progenitors. As delineated in part I, iterations of democratic elitism endure in the form of racial democracies because of elite insistence on a White autarchy. As chapter 4 demonstrates, abolitionist conceptions of democracy fundamentally undermine racial epistemology and challenge the very idea of elite rule.

A pioneer in critical prison studies, Angela Davis maintains that our contemporary prison-dependent and security-obsessed society's carceral trajectory represents a collective failure to enact abolition democracy—a term resourced from W. E. B. Du Bois.[107] Extending Du Bois's work, Davis proposes that we undo our dependency on prisons and the larger carceral logic. Abolition democracy, she insists, poses a major threat to White supremacist democratic elitism as embodied by Jeffersonian antidemocracy and its various facsimiles. She points out that prisons "have thrived over the last century precisely because of the absence of [a host of democratic institutions] and the persistence of some of the deep structures of slavery."[108] As delineated by Du Bois, abolition democracy is thus a living praxis that prefigures a polity favoring a social welfare ethos along with principles of inclusivity.[109] Both before and after the Civil War, a new democratic thinking emerged out of movements to end slavery and to open up the previously closed political system. Such envisioning was championed by the most radical elements of the anti-slavery movements, especially Black abolitionists such as David

Walker and feminists like Sojourner Truth and Frederick Douglass.[110] So, while Du Bois is credited with framing abolition democracy as an alternative to the burgeoning development of Jim Crow or apartheid democracy, Truth and Douglass understood the necessity of an intersectional approach to the franchise and the importance of radical inclusivity when thinking about transformative politics.[111] It was Walker who, like James more than a century later, recognized that White supremacy is (or colonialism and racial capitalism for James are) fundamentally incompatible with democracy. Thus, what Du Bois sought to explain in *Black Reconstruction* was not only the disappointment of the missed opportunities, but also the visions that the most radical elements of the anti-slavery movement aspired to and demanded of the polity for which they had labored and agitated without enjoying its benefits.[112] Du Bois explained that in the aftermath of the Civil War, there were "two quite distinct but persistently undifferentiated visions of the future"—one envisioned a "universal democracy," and the other "was entirely different and is confused with democratic ideal" as embodied by the "new industrial philosophy" or industrial capitalism.[113]

Du Bois, the sociologist, would conclude that racial capitalism and elitism "murdered democracy in the United States so completely that the world does not recognize its corpse."[114] As a counter distinction, abolition democracy presupposes the moral obligation to not only end slavery as an economic system, but also the color caste system that underwrites White supremacy. Du Bois acutely understood that to be free is greater than nominal freedom. There would have to be "a minimum capital in addition to political rights," as well as labor attaining power over capital and industry.[115] Du Bois thus shared his enthusiasm with many leaders of the anti-slavery movement, and saw the possibility of a political community that prioritizes social welfare and livability of its people as an antidote to what he diagnosed as a common ailment among all democracies—the great mass of people who may be "ignorant and poor," who inspire the inevitable question "Can Ignorance and Poverty rule?"[116] For Du Bois, the principles of abolition democracy—the institutional framework that creates the conditions for a successful transformation of an enslaved population to fully incorporated citizens—are the minimal requirements of a "universal democracy," for anything less is a conceit.

Instead of its elitist forgery—"White democracy" or apartheid democracy—abolition democracy and its principles were dismissed summarily with a level of paranoia and convoluted logic that rivals the Jeffersonian era's anxiety over slave rebellions. As one observer noted, "the Southern people would prefer their total annihilation" to seeing people of Color fully incorporated as citizens.[117] As it turned out, any optimism grounded in the idea that "the Republican party, united with abolition-democracy and using their tremendous moral power and popularity, their appeal to freedom, democracy and the uplift of mankind" was no match for "the threatened fortress of the new industry."[118] The Republican party of that time, however sympathetic to the cause of abolition, was so committed to democratic elitism and White supremacy that when Johnson took the helm of the presidency, there was no great shift in policy except in rhetorical form.[119] Abolition democracy lost out, as Du Bois saw it, because the industrial form of capitalist development lost to its agrarian counterpart, as northern White laborers were seduced by the promise of the social wages that accompanied racial capitalism.[120] Worse, the North also "was not disposed . . . to defend universal suffrage or even democracy."[121] In the final analysis of the era in which the slaves and their allies forged a self-resurrected democratic possibility, Du Bois characterized the attempt at abolition democracy as a "splendid failure." He summed up the heroic struggle to incorporate Black men into the polity as "Athanasius contra mundum, with back to the wall, outnumbered ten to one, with all the wealth and all the opportunity, and all the world against [them] . . . fighting the battle of all oppressed and despised humanity of every race and color, against the massed hirelings of Religion, Science, Education, Law, and brute force."[122] It would take nearly another century before a critical mass again paid attention. This time, the frontal attack against racial democracy takes the form of abolition feminism—a refreshingly creative re-rendering of abolition democracy.[123]

Recognizing that abolition democracy was born out of mass struggles by the poor against capital, contemporary movements to end prisons and violence as regimes of living are deliberate in their theoretical and practical concerns about being transgenerational, including reaching back to the antebellum era to learn the lessons of slavery and its afterlife. Abolition democracy 2.0, seeded by critical Black feminist analytics, is similar to the process that Du Bois characterized as "self-resurrection of democracy." It brings into question basic assumptions about democratic livability precisely because it aspires to radically include *all the people.* Following the Black and feminist radical traditions of prefigurative politics, BLM/M4BL, BYP100, and other abolition-feminist-led formations painstakingly set out to model democratic practices. They insist on radically substantive articulations of justice, ranging from migrant and trans justice to reproductive and planetary justice, and are willing to put in the labor to render life and association anew. Prison scholar activist Ruth Wilson Gilmore best characterizes this capacious frame in a recent conversation with *The Intercept*:

> abolition has to be "green." It has to take seriously the problem of environmental harm, environmental racism, and environmental degradation.

> To be "green" it has to be "red." It has to figure out ways to generalize the resources needed for well-being for the most vulnerable people in our community, which then will extend to all people. And to do that, to be "green" and "red," it has to be international. It has to stretch across borders so that we can consolidate our strength, our experience, and our vision for a better world.[124]

In many ways, then, the contemporary confrontation to bring about abolition democracy 2.0 is not unlike previous confrontations—when encountering the limits imposed on democratic living by gendered racial capitalism, heteropatriarchy, and settler colonialism, the many refuse to acquiesce to the terms of order. However momentarily, they do the work of living democracy, including destroying to build anew, all the while envisioning just futures.

In recent years, abolition feminism has pushed free the parameters of thought on prison and police, and critically rescripted the meanings of safety, security, and livability, all of which have serious implications for the meanings of and mobilizations for justice. Thus, abolition feminism is the feminist analytic and philosophy that are rooted in the struggles for freedom, and the insistence that freedom is contingent on securing safety and livability for everyone. This framework and praxis necessarily entail radically rethinking prison, police, and other regimes of violence and governing.[125] Building on the legacies of radical, queer, Black, socialist, feminist principles and the praxis of radical inclusivity, contemporary abolition feminists insist that until all of us are free, none of us are free.

Angela Y. Davis and Gina Dent furnish a startling comprehensive vision of abolition feminism and why we need it, reasoning that it is the "best response to endemic forms of state and interpersonal gender and sexual violence."[126] This response hews closely to "the everyday practice, collective experiments driven by necessity, practice, and reflection" akin to an ecology of "sinewy networks that crisscross time and space."[127] By resourcing abolition feminism as praxis, justice has the potential to be embodied, capacious, and substantive. As Allegra M. Mcleod points out, "abolitionist conceptions of justice present a formidable challenge to existing ideas of legal justice."[128] Within this frame, justice is inherently relational, a "holistic engagement with the structural conditions that give rise to suffering, as well as the interpersonal dynamics involved in violence."[129] Demosprudence, while appearing to be a radical intervention for correcting jurisprudential supremacy and democratic elitism, pales in comparison. Dwarfing demosprudence in ambition and scope, abolition feminism casts a shadow on the entirety of liberal jurisprudence as its practitioners seek to undo the juridical infrastructure of White supremacy and heteropatriarchy in total.

If at the dawn of modernity Hobbes had fashioned fears of physical death to justify brutal regimes of governing, staking their claims on the ground of well-being, contemporary abolition feminists refute the claims of legitimacy made by authoritarians and leviathans everywhere. One of the most important contributions by abolition feminism is how it reframes safety and security, and in so doing, induces a series of legitimacy crises for the state and its allies. Like feminists in Asia, especially those in Okinawa, South Korea, and the Philippines, abolition feminists in the US, led by radical Black feminists, have trained their attention on rejiggering the idea of law and order, drawing attention to anti-Black violence and violence against women through various regimes of surveillance, mass incarceration and policing.[130] The *Freedom to Thrive* report, for instance, explicitly challenges the efficacy and legitimacy of prison and police regimes as credible sources for "the freedom to thrive." This report is a collaboration of three entities: namely, the Center for Popular Democracy (CPD), Law for Black Lives, and Black Youth Project 100 (BYP100), that are themselves networks of numerous grassroots organizations, constituting the larger abolition democratization movement.[131] Turning away from the habitual reliance on prisons, and on the police as moral authorities and experts on all things concerning safety, the Report instead calls on readers to reimagine "safety & security in our communities."[132] It correctly asserts that budgets "reflect the spending priorities and types of investments the institution deems to be sensible, practical and effective" and, as its "Executive Summary" succinctly puts: "The choice to resource *punitive* systems instead of stabilizing and nourishing ones does not make communities safer."[133] *Freedom to Thrive* points out that "study after study shows that a living wage, access to holistic health services and treatment, educational opportunity, and stable housing are far more successful in reducing crime than police or prisons."[134] Fully three years before "defund the police" finally got a public airing during the 2020 season of protests, it furnishes a comprehensively documented "current and prospective campaigns that seek to divest resources away from police and prisons toward communities and development."[135] As part of the "reimagining safety & security," *Freedom to Thrive* calls for, among other things, participatory budgeting and the use of "the invest/divest" framework for resource sharing, challenging core assumptions of the neoliberal regime of governing. Invest/divest is a modest practical proposal for reallocating social resources to center the community and planetary well-being, encompassing both policing matters and sustainable energy use.[136] Not unlike demosprudence that seeks to embed lessons from movements for justice in the reading of the law, the invest/divest framework emerged from M4BL and abolition feminist insights, embodying a democratic ethic of community and world-building. Invest/divest is thus a praxis of the here and now, conveying the spirit of abolition not as absence but presence—an emphatic response that belies the propaganda against abolition feminism as the thing that only destroys instead of (re)building worlds.

The emergence of abolition feminism owes in no small part to the work of Davis and a group of scholar activists associated with Critical Resistance and INCITE!—two formations that have been pivotal to the most significant shifts in prison studies and abolition consciousness. BYP100, BLM, as well as M4BL are only several formations that have benefited directly from and continue to build upon the larger framework of radical, Black, queer, abolition feminism.[137] This loose network of feminist community organizers and scholars both powerfully critique American antidemocracy, and supply compelling logic and visions of alternative realities where abolition democracy is viable. In *Unapologetic*, Charlene A. Carruthers maintains that "democracy and the promise of perfecting it in this country is one of the biggest lies ever told," and that "true democracy" has never existed in this country.[138] They instead insists that we explore spaces of mobilization for experimenting and implementing "practices that match the type of world we want to create":

> I don't know what democracy looks like outside of the practices and cultures we've built within various movement spaces. Many times it feels like we're playing governance, just like we played house as children. Some people can borrow from and incorporate Indigenous governing practices, but many of us have no clue our ancestors made decisions before colonialism and the transatlantic slave trade. And of what we do know, not all of it is what we want today. . . . We can build from what's come before us and innovate at the same time.[139]

Carruthers is pragmatic, tasking community organizers to "change the terrain and conditions" of collective struggles, centering on the idea of self-determination.[140] Here, self-determination is counter distinct from individualism, involving "a body of communities—and those who make up communities—determining how they will thrive and how their lives are lived." As they explain, "making collective decisions about how our lives are lived is governance," and it is there where "we can live out the project of collective liberation."[141]

Thus, democracy as an idea is discarded and replaced by a democratic praxis grounded in a communal ethos for deciding "how they will thrive and how their lives are lived." This is what democratic living looks like because it is within these spaces of mobilization where we get glimpses of how people struggle, protest, get basic with each other, and make possible "rights and the power to govern and not just to be governed."[142] As an abolition feminist, Carruthers is clear that "we don't have to wait until every prison is emptied to deal with conflict and harm," and as the *Freedom to Thrive* report attests, communities and organizations around the world, aided by the deep knowledge that "police and jails do not make communities safe, and in many cases actually undermine safety," are demanding and contesting for the critical resources that actually make communities safer, all the while modeling what democratic living looks like IRL.[143]

Grounded in a utopian impulse accreted over generations, abolition feminism, therefore, capaciously envisions doing democracy that embodies aspirations of "the many rule," for a world where many worlds fit. As a method, it has shown itself to be as practical in specificity as it is ambitious in its imagined terrains, especially in the forms of sociocultural formations and projects, including prison moratorium and the invest/divest framework.[144] Davis, for instance, while arguing for the need to engage in "difficult dialogues"—on subjects ranging from transphobia, the occupation of Palestine and the boycott of the state of Israel, to the ever-expanding carceral state and the epidemic of police violence—also urges organizers and groups to not conflate "movements with mobilization" or mistake silences for absences of radical struggles, protests, and change.[145] Abolition feminism, she insists, is the defining framework for the twenty-first century.[146]

For Davis, feminism is more than the question of gender equality, and certainly more complicated than the question of gender, though the concept of gender itself must be so thoroughly broadened to be as encompassing as possible because "feminist methodologies impel us to explore connections that are not always apparent."[147] At the heart of this feminist ethos is the desire to approach "theoretical explorations and movement activism in ways that enlarge and expand and complicate and deepen our theories of practices of freedom."[148] When abolition feminism is defined as "feminism within an abolitionist frame," and "abolition within a feminist frame," feminist theoretical and organizational terrains are thus broadened to include the "deep relationality that links struggles against institutions and struggles to reinvent our personal lives, and recraft ourselves."[149] Building on many feminisms, the abolition feminist approach is thus intersectional, multimodal, and multigenerational. Davis understands "feminism not as something that adheres to bodies, not as something grounded in gendered bodies, but as an approach—as a way to conceptualizing, as a methodology, as a guide to strategies for struggle."[150] The spaces of struggles and imaginary domains of abolition feminism are thus broad and vast—including, but not limited to, struggles to end criminalization and captivity, violence against women, anticolonial and anti-racial capitalism, and to promote freedom and justice, including planetary justice.[151]

As a method of struggle and getting free, abolition feminism thus has in its sights gendered racial capitalism, heteropatriarchy, White supremacy, and settler colonialism, positioning itself against violence of all forms. As an ethical approach, however, it is even more ambitious in its multimodality, recognizing and drawing connections among and between discourses, institutions, identities, and ideologies.[152] Its emphasis on radical inclusivity, solidarity, and self-determination echoes many of the most radical and ambitious movements for justice from previous generations. Abolition feminism is also futurist, not only because it seeks to transport us to more just futures, but also by refusing to fix concepts and ideas such as gender, woman, or even freedom, it makes spaces for future generations to enjoin their own contexts and priorities. By emphasizing deep relationality and a multigenerational approach to building spaces of struggles and reframing concepts such as gender, abolition feminists consistently place themselves at the forefront of some of the most important radical and transgressive social movements of our time.

RECRAFTING SELF, COMMUNITY, AND WORLD

In a speech four decades after Assata Shakur's arrest by the New Jersey state police became a symbol of the US government's domestic campaigns to police and annihilate the Black freedom struggle in the US, Davis adroitly reframed the debate on safety and security.[153] She points out that even forty years after being shot then convicted of murder and later broken out of prison, Shakur, who is still exiled in Cuba, was placed on the FBI's Most Wanted Terrorists list and continues to be perceived as a threat today.[154] Davis thus calls attention to the way in which the state creates insecurity in the name of national security.[155] By "incorporating the logic of the very terrorism with which they have falsely charged [Assata]," this strategy is a deterrence against the larger movement for freedom and justice, and to stop radical mass mobilization in its tracks. Shakur, now as a stand-in for radical Black feminist struggles, allows Davis to springboard into a more capacious frame for feminist analytics, activism and mobilization, incorporating prison abolition and gender transgression as intersections that produce "some of the most interesting theories . . . ideas and approaches to activism."[156]

Davis, whose life and work are deeply entangled in countless campaigns to render prison and police redundant, insists that trans activists are doing some of the most insightful work on prison abolition. Drawing from the example of the San Francisco–based Transgender, Gender-Variant & Intersex Justice Project (TGIJP), founded by Miss Major and led by trans women of Color, Davis calls for a more robust (re)imagination of intersectional feminism and feminist praxis grounded in their experiences and analytics. TGIJP's work, she explains, is "deeply feminist" and "at the intersection of race, class, sexuality, and gender" given that "they have to fight to be included," and with members "who constitute the individuals who are *most* harassed by law enforcement, *most* arrested and incarcerated," their work "moves from addressing the individual predicaments of the members . . . to larger questions" about prison.[157] Davis thus concludes that "they have worked out . . . a deeply feminist approach, [that] we would do well to understand and emulate."[158] Because "prisons and police are constituted as normal," the particular struggles of trans prisoners, especially trans women prisoners, help feminists better understand normative gender and gender training, in and outside of prison, and "to learn how to think and act and struggle against that which is ideologically constituted as 'normal.'"[159] In other words, by queering gender and moving outside of the biocentric male/female binary, this praxis "radically undermines the normative assumption of the very concept of gender," and in so doing it disrupts the status quo, including the carceral society.[160]

By centering abolition on the one hand and the required provisions necessary for rendering prison redundant, if not obsolete, on the other, abolition feminists like Davis strategically pivot on well-being and social relations, instead of governing. By framing freedom as "a constant struggle," Davis, for instance, disrupts fixity, opening up feminist frameworks toward possibilities that are still unthought. Because "Black feminism emerged as a theoretical framework and practical effort demonstrating that race, gender and class are inseparable in the social world we inhabit," the insistence on understanding "the intersections and interconnections" of various movements for freedom is inherently part of the "feminist process."[161] Carruthers points out that terms such as "double jeopardy," "triple oppressions," "interlocking oppressions," and intersectionality" are theoretical concepts and frameworks that Black feminists use to delineate their lifeworld as well as epistemological advantages.[162] Thus their definition of radical Black feminism hues closely to that of Davis,[163] while relying on Critical Resistance's delineation of abolition as "a long-term political vision with the goal of eliminating imprisonment, policing and surveillance, and creating lasting alternatives to punishment and imprisonment."[164]

For Carruthers, the Black queer feminist lens as praxis is grounded "in Black feminist and LGBTQ traditions and knowledge, through which people and groups bring their full selves into the process of dismantling all systems of oppressions," including the carceral regime.[165] Strategically centering on "alternatives of self-governance and self-determination," like Cohen, Carruthers calls attention to the "Black queer feminist framework" as a critical intervention that "holds out the radical potential for liberation for all."[166] By emphasizing radical inclusivity and deep relationality, abolition feminist formations such as BYP100 explicitly embrace solidarity campaigns as part of their "method" to end interlocking systems of oppressions of people, wherever they are and whatever their vulnerabilities.[167] These solidarity campaigns are possible because they imply reciprocation, mutuality, and interconnections. As Davis suggests, because the abolition feminist framework is intersectional, it foregrounds deep connections, allowing it to map linkages between the technologies that are used to police borders in North America, occupied Palestine and the old alliances of apartheid South Africa, or the authoritarianism that undergirds Apple's supply chain.[168]

A FEMINIST ETHIC OF LIBERATION

If movements for justice are insurgent social pedagogy, then abolition feminist formations and mobilizations have much to teach us about democracy as a way of life. To imagine a society without racism requires us to want a society without prisons, along with a radical reimagination of security. In their call for a restorative justice framework, abolition feminists ask us to imagine "a society that is secure" without "the kind of security that is based on policing and incarceration"; and a transformative justice framework that enables us to "imagine a very different kind of security in the future."[169] For abolition feminists, as the *Freedom to Thrive* report suggests, the security in the national security state, as manifested in the forms of the police and carceral society, is not security for the many, but the securing of order for the state, capital and other dominions. Reimagining security, therefore, involves "the abolition of policing and imprisonment as we know them."[170]

Centering on the well-being of people, community and ecology instead of the state, capital and dominion, abolition feminists like Davis and others delineate a life-affirming praxis, urgently needed in these violent times. Carruthers, for instance, points to the lessons of the Alabama Committee for Equal Justice for Recy Taylor, survivor of a 1944 gang rape, to forge a difficult dialogue not only about the need "to craft effective liberatory strategies for all," but also how the security and well-being of people, especially the well-being of victims and survivors of violence, must be at the center of movement strategies.[171] This struggle, Carruthers reminds us, was amid a larger, global struggle against fascism. Critically, the human rights campaign on behalf of Taylor ironically "went beyond her" and took on a new life with little regard for her well-being or security. Here, Carruthers is consistent about the collective need to address "the safety of young Black women leaders who live with daily threats of violence and harassment for daring to uplift ourselves."[172] Elsewhere, they draw attention to the fact that Black queer and trans feminists face persistent threats and acts of violence for speaking out, writing about, and working to end oppressions and engender justice.[173] This pattern is consistent with the long history of the US government and its allies directing violence and terror against communities and groups that they deem as threats to the status quo. As shown in this book, containment campaigns of repression are rarely incidental as they tend to aim the most deadly arsenals against vulnerable communities, particularly against Black freedom fighters. Assata Shakur's persecution, for instance, is emblematic of this practice, though her case is far from being isolated, as Carruthers, Davis, Kochiyama, and countless others have written and spoken out about the enduring campaign to suppress and deter democratic resistance, including nonviolent, legal protest actions. Carruthers and other M4BL activists have pointed to the case of Josh Williams and the FBI's recently established "Black Identity Extremist" (BIE) section as part of its counterterrorism division as contemporary examples of the persistent use of national security threat—a carceral trajectory of the war on terrorism and crime—to entrap activists and organizers who actively engage the Black freedom struggle.[174]

Josh Williams was first arrested in 2014 while protesting against the police killing of Antonio Martin, only a few miles from Ferguson where the police killed Michael Brown. He had been actively protesting the Ferguson killing for months and emerged as a recognizable activist in the community. Having no prior record and being eighteen, Williams was charged with among other things, second-degree burglary and first-degree arson, for taking a bag of chips and setting fire to a trash can at a convenience store. He was given an eight-year sentence in a plea deal. Joining the Ferguson protests the day after Brown's death in August, Williams had stayed on the street every day through the day he got arrested protesting the Martin killing in December. Insisting that mass protests will continue so long as there are police killings, Williams pointed to lack of applicable justice, and was convinced that the police were making "an example" out of him[175] when he became a target of the FBI's Black Identity Extremists (BIE) program.[176] Operated from 2017 to 2019, this counterterrorism program targets Black people whom the FBI deemed ideologically inclined to "likely" take up violent actions against the police and other policing authorities.[177] As if to signal its own ideological predispositions and promising to counter the threat of "black extremists," the FBI organized an operation named "IRON FIST" to gather intelligence and conduct assessments of so-called BIEs. Operated from 2018 to 2020, IRON FIST used advanced surveillance intelligence and facial recognition algorithms, and sought to use felony status, if any existed, against people who were allegedly BIEs subjects.[178] While White supremacist formations are specifically targeted, BIE is a broader and more encompassing frame. Indeed, leaked FBI documents revealed that the agency targets BIEs (along with "anti-authority extremists" and "animal rights/environmental extremists") with higher priority than White supremacists, who are much more likely to carry out acts of violence, especially mass shootings.[179] Remarkably, at a March 2018 congressional briefing, high-level FBI officials could not explain how the FBI came up with the BIE designation in the first place.[180] Similar to the counterintelligence campaigns that sought to annihilate the freedom struggles in the mid-twentieth century and the legislative agendas of slave-holding states of the nineteenth century, the state's and its allies' intentions are clear—to secure order and antidemocracy by containing and annihilating individuals, communities, and formations that are deemed as ungovernable.

Dialectically, abolition feminists set out to reimagine safety and security to end all forms of violence, which necessarily entails overhauling liberal feminist understanding of violence against women and violence in general. Practiced in mapping interlocking systems of violence, Davis, Beth Richie, Andrea Ritchie, and other feminists of Color have reformed our understanding of violence by broadening the spaces of violence against women from the private quarters of the home to the larger regimes of violence, including but not limited to poverty, police, and prisons as well as governing systems, such as settler colonialism, racial capitalism, White supremacy, and heteropatriarchy as well as gender.[181] Extending Beth Richie's work, Carruthers defines violence as "a constant, systemic killer of possibility," mapping out the roots and routes of violence that include poverty, criminalization and incarceration, lack of bodily autonomy, physical, sexual, and environmental harms as well as political and cultural repressions.[182]

Indeed, Ritchie, cofounder of INCITE!—a women of Color formation dedicated to end violence against women in all forms—helpfully extends a capacious intersectional analytic to recast what she calls the "violence matrix," revealing the gendered violence that Black women experience is co-constitutive of "a tangled web of concentrated structural disadvantages that are profoundly intense and forceful," including institutionalized racism, gender and class oppressions, heteropatriarchy and generalized administrative violence.[183] Violence against Black women and women of Color, thus, does not exist in a vacuum, and must be "understood as part of a larger pattern of social neglect based on their race, gender, and other socially stigmatized identities that are marginalized in contemporary society."[184] Extending the work of Kimberlé Crenshaw, Richie insists that critical to Black feminist theorizing is the delineation of intersectionality as "relational, structural, political, and ideological."[185] By broadening the frame of gendered violence against Black women to extend beyond "domestic" or intimate partner violence to include "America's prison nation" and its carceral regime, Ritchie and other abolition feminists provide a multilevel analysis of violence and its sociomaterial conditions, ranging from public policies that perpetuate the marginalization and precarities in Black life, to heteropatriarchal gender and sexual regulatory controls, to police tactical responses to pregnant women and trans people. By taking up not only the household but also community and state as spaces of harm and violence against women and girls, they point the way toward a more fluid and expansive anti-violence formations, as instantiated by the politics and tactics of BYP100 and Say Her Name![186]

The violence that women experience within the "violence matrix," as Ritchie and INCITE! acutely understood, shows vulnerabilities and harms "in ways that are specific to their positions as racialized subjects and bodies," and by insisting on a simultaneous trimodal level of analysis using all three contexts where abuse takes place—the household, community, and the state—to reframe violence, they provide feminists with tools to reimagine what it means for women, particularly Black woman, to be safe and free from such harm.[187] Critically, by locating additional spaces of violence, especially outside of the home, abolition feminist analytics move us away from "the hegemonic notions of intimacy in the relationship" and the family as the only spaces where abuses occur. In this way, feminist analytics of abuse and power can move beyond the private/public dichotomy that scripts violence against women as a private matter, thus foreclosing additional possibilities for collective interventions.[188] By taking prison and violence in tandem, therefore, abolition feminists are able to reveal the interlocking system of oppressions that manifests in carceral regimes or the "prison nation," and the mechanisms, including cultural praxis, that sustain the gendered violence matrix that forecloses radical possibilities for transformation.[189]

TOOLS FOR DEMOCRATIC LIVING

In *Growth Against Democracy*, I argue that the ubiquitous national security state *predates* the 9/11 phenomenon; instead, it is a feature of neoliberal regime of governing, and a logical consequence of the savage developmentalist logic that conscripts order and antidemocracy, along with aiding and abetting the accumulation and hoarding of wealth, as primary functions of the modern state.[190] In the age of hyper-speculative financialism and surveillance capitalism where automated algorithms govern hyperinflated returns on investments, financial expansionism and wealth hoarding necessitate repression and premature deaths, including death by work. To sustain and hoard ever higher levels of wealth as normal, the system securitizes itself in the form of a prison nation, as carceral society increasingly relies on the suppression of 99.8 percent of the population, especially populations residing in locations dispersed among its transnational nodes of accumulation in the global economy. Even as it does so, it instigates instability and disorder from the very top, all the while relying on a loosely defined, multifaceted police force endowed with unconditional "qualified immunity."[191]

Authoritarianism and hyper-securitization, therefore, are not bugs but features of (neo)liberal governing.[192] Violence is endemic to (neo)liberal living. What makes abolition feminist analytics and praxis especially helpful is how abolition feminists take the fight to end violence from the living room and the dark alleys all the way through the well-lit halls of the state, seizing the very ground upon which the (national security) state claims its legitimacy for its specious existence. By exposing the capacious apparatuses of violence inherent in gendered racial capitalism and its constitutive national security state and precarious labor regime, abolition feminism exposes the conceits of the state's moral claims for its existence and capabilities. The state, these feminists argue, does not protect and serve the many; instead, it harbors ill intents and endeavors all sorts of violence and insecurities. As sampled throughout this book, the data they furnish are murderous and brain numbing, aided by innumerable eyewitness accounts and testimonies, both in real life and virtual, of victims and survivors of said violence and subjections.[193]

Precisely because abolition feminism, as framed by radical Black queer analytics, insists on a comprehensive, multimodal, and intergenerational approach to contest, improvise, and transform the very meanings of what it means to have safety and security, it is futurist, constituting one of the biggest threats to the state and its allies. It needs to be reiterated, however, that abolition feminism, like its intersectional analytics, was seeded and remains grounded in movements and mobilizations for justice, including just futures. Thus, unlike liberal progressivism endemic to modern discourses of transformation, abolition feminism's transgressive commitment to just futures is steadfastly tied up in today's past and present injustices.[194] Their fights against injustices are here and now. Entangled in collective action and scholarship, they assuredly expose nominal political common sensibilities as fraudulent and deadly. As we have learned, assumed features of a democratic society such as freedoms of speech, association and protest are not inalienable rights but reserved entitlements for friends of the state and capital, or the few who can afford to litigate after the fact. The prison nation, with which neoliberal governing sought to systematically erode the "rights, privileges, and opportunities afforded disadvantaged groups,"[195] emerges not as a sociomaterial consequence of ad hoc politics or politicking; instead, it is the logical consequence of a system that treats domestic and international stability as a prima facie of national achievement, while democratic living becomes the public enemy of economic expansion and a theoretical unthinkable.[196] The quest for state security and capitalist expansion, at the expense of freedom and safety of everyone, has always meant that the other (as frequently constituted as racial, gender, sexual, poor and/or with disability) bears the repression and suppression. As a number of feminist scholars sampled in this work, including Edwards, Richie, Hinton, Williams, Quan and Willoughby-Herard, to name a few, have pointed out, their very presence in urban spaces sometimes is enough for many, especially Black people, to be marked as dangerous and a threat, warranting countless war arsenals seeking to remove them and deracinate their communities from the landscape.[197]

The threat to "national security" has served well the goal to contain and deter mass mobilization and to deactivate or annihilate those communities and people who are thriving, as the case against the Black freedom struggles in the US and the African Diaspora has shown. Threats from below or democratic uprisings, including movements for economic and planetary justice, whether fictitious or legitimate, almost always incur the greatest wrath and bear the brunt of state ferocity and repression.[198] In this regard, abolition feminism—as embodied in formations that are led by radical Black queer feminists like BYP100, BLM, and M4BL—poses a direct threat to the state, capital, and their enabling governing ideologemes. As Fanon understood many decades ago, imperial regimes of governing expose their moral bankruptcy by their own murderous violence and utter lack of ethical standards. In contrast, abolition feminists envision an entirely different mode of living.[199] Rather than defining security as the terms of order—namely, cultural hegemony, stability of the state, police control, stable markets, gender fixity, absence of protest, and so on—abolition feminists define security as well-being, freedom from harm, community integrity, bodily autonomy, and so on.[200] In short, by pivoting away from the terms of order, abolition feminism centers human values instead of dictates of the market, the collective instead of the individual, and the many instead of the few. Within these utopian frames, justice is neither blind nor an entitlement but embodied and substantive—such that economic, gender, racial, and even interspecies and/or planetary justice are concrete demands that compel the collective to broaden not only the meanings of justice but also democratic praxis as a way of life.

Perhaps, as Davis, Dent, Meiners, and Ritchie insist, just futures depend on "Abolition. Feminism. Now."[201] As concrete demands, ideas about community safety and security are grounded in the praxis of land sovereignty and, by extension, bodily autonomy and self-determination. This is what decolonizing democracy looks like. While not always free from fraught histories of their own—especially ones marred in hyper-individualism, materialism, narrow nationalism, and liberal humanism—these conceptual frames, however imperfect, undergird the ways in which organizers and movements navigate, improvise, and negotiate their terms of engagement as they struggle, imagine, build, and transform communities and lifeworlds. As the report *Freedom to Thrive* reveals, well before the protests against the killings of George Floyd and Breonna Taylor made "defund the police" legible in public discourse, communities throughout the US and in Puerto Rico have already proposed and carried out ways and means for securing well-being for community members, despite official and unofficial policies of organized abandonment.

Moreover, from the Quilombos of dos Palmares in Brazil to the Zonas people in Southeast Asia to Palestine, from Tahir Square in Cairo to Old San Juan in Puerto Rico and Wukan, China, the history of movements for justice from various radical traditions is replete with concrete examples of how people have protected and served their community in the spirit of friendship and solidarity, and without relying on coercion and violence as governing technologies, however temporarily and scaled. The neoliberalization of governance and economies coupled with an emboldened reassertion of White autarchy is only the latest of countless counterrevolutions waged against the many. The many radical traditions have taught us that dominions contain the seeds of their destructions, not least because of their own mischief and malice. So it is that in our fights against tyrannies, big and small—including when confronting empires—it is crucial to remember that empires fall not merely because barbarians are at the gates. Instead, it is because they/we are within the gates, inside walls, in communities of struggle, caring for ourselves and each other, telling our stories, dreaming, crafting alter-worlds inside out, and laughing our ways into other worlds that we become.

Acknowledgments

This book began with my great fortune of being with friends, family, students, and fellow travelers in the many struggles for justice and dignity, and from whom I learn the necessity of being in formations, radical love and willful refusals against the many injustices and unfreedoms. While any errors are mine, this work embodies their insights and wisdoms, especially inspired by the richness and rewards of friendship.

I am grateful to my current and former students, especially Jesse Davenport, Lauren Espinoza, Danielle Russel, Michael Soto, and Sarah Suhail, whose life and learning are a constant reminder about why teaching and insurgent learning in the times of big and small tyrannies are important for the care and feeding of just presence/futures. From the moment they were born, my many nieces and nephews taught me that to live is to thrive, and justice is always relational.

I am indebted to Karen Kuo and Camilla Fojas in the School of Social Transformation at Arizona State University for fostering spaces of scholarship that are beyond bureaucratic function, and Paul Hill and Jennifer Lange at the Wexner Center for the Arts at the Ohio State University for their constant support of my film work in collaboration with C. A. Griffith, allowing me to pursue scholarship in total. Lisa Anderson's and Joann Tall's healing arts and deft needle handling got me through many health challenges and kept me thriving. Steve Merlo generously shared his home for the many respites from a frequently hostile Arizona—much the same way four decades ago his high school math classroom created spaces for alternative discourses that held out promises of different pathways for inner-city pupils who were never meant to survive.

I also owe a tremendous debt to friends and colleagues who read the 650+ page manuscript, especially M. A. Bortner, Karen Leong, Darryl C. Thomas, Alan Eladio Gómez, Tiffany Willoughby-Herard, Chandra Talpade Mohanty, and Barbara Ransby. There is no question that had they not generously shared their time and keen eyes, this work would not be what it is today. I am especially grateful to the entire team at Pluto Press for their love, labor, and commitment to books and critical thought. This book would not be possible without them, and especially David Shulman's infectious enthusiasm, kind patience, and editorial acumen.

As luck would have it, I am rich in siblings, with brothers like Kevin, Darryl, John, Johnny, Alan, Michael and William, and sisters whose willful refusals make possible for me to become ungovernable. Fellow travelers and friends, especially *my many sisters*—including Meca Sorrentini-Blaut, Peg Bortner, Lisa Brock, Myla Vincenti Carpio, Karma Chavez, Wendy Cheng, Dara Cooper, Françoise Cromer, Angela Davis, Gina Dent, Erica Edwards, Ruthie Gilmore, Davida Ingram, Robin D. G. Kelley, Karen Leong, Marisela Marquez, Chandra Mohanty, Satya Mohanty, Kris Peterson, Barbara Ransby, Elizabeth Robinson, Dylan Rodríguez, Barbara Smith, Shala Talebi, and Tiffany Willoughby-Herard—model loving, sharing, fighting, and how praxis is relational. I am in their debt, always. C. A. Griffith, to whom I dedicate this work along with *all* my sisters, incites ungovernability—and from whom I learn daily about friendship, solidarity, and justice as praxis.

While researching and writing this book, a number of dear friends transitioned into alter spaces. Their friendships and teachings continue to enliven my life and work. I dearly hope these beloveds haunt the pages herein. Dan Brouwer's, Mark Von Hagen's, and Clara Moore's fellowships, laughter and joy, however momentarily, were life's nourishment. Otis Madison taught me that it is always a privilege to grace the classroom, and disagreements among friends are food and occasions to celebrate. Cedric J. Robinson, whose life and work modeled insurgent co-learning and ethical theoretical pursuits, taught me that far from a benign academic enterprise, critical ethnic/gender studies have always been and are about power; and critical thought, if it is to be a danger to the status quo, must be an embodiment of the very things that unsettle the terms of order, whatever that order might be. Yuri Kochiyama, whose passion for justice and friendship made lies of orthodoxies, showed me the necessity of living archives. Finally, my mother—whose transition was nearly two decades ago but still feels like yesterday, whose friends nourished our family, and who defied authority at every turn—taught me that sharing, even when it's only half a grain of rice, is living.

Notes

PREFACE

1. Cedric J. Robinson, "Slavery and the Platonic Origins of Anti-democracy," in *Cedric J. Robinson: On Racial Capitalism, Black Internationalism and Cultures of Resistance*, ed. H. L. T. Quan (London: Pluto Press, 2019). See also Cedric J. Robinson, *The Terms of Order: Political Science and the Myth of Leadership* (Albany: State University of New York Press, 1980).
2. Robert A. Divine et al., *America: Past and Present*, 10th ed., vol. 1 (London: Pearson, 2013), 132.
3. As of early 2022, PEN America tracks at least 114 bills that are considered "educational gag orders," including 40 that could impact higher education. For an updated list, see "PEN America's Index of Educational Gag Order." https://pen.org/report/educational-gag-orders/.
4. First published by the *New York Times Magazine* (August 2019) to mark the four-hundredth anniversary of the arrival of the first enslaved Africans in Virginia. See "The 1619 Project," *New York Times*, August 17, 2019, www.nytimes.com/interactive/2019/08/14/magazine/1619-america-slavery.html.
5. "The 1619 Project."
6. Adam Serwer, "The Fight Over the 1619 Project Is Not About the Facts," *The Atlantic*, December 23, 2019, www.theatlantic.com/ideas/archive/2019/12/historians-clash-1619-project/604093/. See also Julia Carrie Wong, "The Fight to Whitewash US History: 'A Drop of Poison Is All You Need,'" *The Guardian*, May 25, 2021, www.theguardian.com/world/2021/may/25/critical-race-theory-us-history-1619-project.
7. James Baldwin, "The White Man's Guilt," in *Collected Essays* (New York: The Library of America, 1998 [1965]), 722–23.
8. Cedric J. Robinson, *Forgeries of Memory and Meaning: Blacks and the Regimes of Race in American Theater and Film before World War II* (Chapel Hill: University of North Carolina Press, 2007); Toni Morrison, *Playing in the Dark: Whiteness and the Literary Imagination* (Cambridge, MA: Harvard University Press, 1992).
9. Toni Cade Bambara, "On the Issues of Roles," in *The Black Woman: An Anthology*, ed. Toni Cade Bambara (New York: Washington Square Press, 2005), 1.
10. Michel Foucault, *"Society Must Be Defended": Lectures at the Collège de France*, trans. David Macey, ed. Mauro Beranti and Alessandro Fontana (New York: Picador, 2003).
11. Subcomandante Marcos, *Conversations with Durito: Stories of the Zapatistas and Neoliberalism* (Brooklyn: Autonomedia, 2005). See also John Holloway and Eloína Peláez, eds., *Zapatista! Reinventing Revolution in Mexico* (London: Pluto Press, 1998).
12. Rebecca Tsosie, "Indigenous Peoples, Anthropology, and the Legacy of Epistemic Injustice," in *The Routledge Handbook of Epistemic Injustice*, ed. Ian James Kidd, José Medina, and Gaile Pohlhaus Jr. (New York: Routledge, 2017), 356–69.

13. Jafari S. Allen, "Black/Queer Rhizomatics: Train Up a Child in the Way Ze Should Grow...," in *No Tea, No Shade: New Writings in Black Queer Studies*, ed. E. Patrick Johnson (Durham, NC: Duke University Press, 2016), 35.
14. Cathy J. Cohen, "Punks, Bulldaggers, and Welfare Queens: The Radical Potential of Queer Politics?," *GLQ: A Journal of Lesbian & Gay Studies* 3 (1997): 438. See also Paola Bacchetta et al., "Queer of Color Space-Making in and beyond the Academic Industrial Complex," *Critical Ethnic Studies* 4, no. 1 (2018): 44–63.
15. Arundhati Roy, "Confronting Empire," presented at the Closing Rally of the World Social Forum in Porto Alegre, Brazil (January 27, 2003), in *War Talk* (Cambridge: South End Press, 2003), 112.
16. Ibid.

CHAPTER 1

1. Enrique Dussel, *Philosophy of Liberation* (Eugene: Wipf & Stock Publishers, 2003), 4.
2. Bambara, "On the Issues," 134–35.
3. Richard J. Norton, "Feral Cities," *Naval War College Review* 56, no. 4 (Autumn 2003/Article 8): 97.
4. Dussel, *Philosophy*, 187.
5. John Rawls, *A Theory of Justice* (Cambridge, MA: Belknap Press, 1971).
6. John Rawls, *Justice as Fairness: A Restatement*, ed. Erin Kelly (Cambridge, MA: Harvard University Press, 2001), 5. See also Charles W. Mills, *Black Rights/White Wrongs: The Critique of Racial Liberalism* (New York: Oxford University Press, 2017).
7. Dussel, *Philosophy*, 3, 188. Similar to Bacchetta et al., Dussel insists that for philosophy to be useful, it must be insurgent.
8. While this book is generally informed by the totality of their work, see especially Sara Ahmed, *Willful Subjects* (Durham, NC: Duke University Press, 2014); Angela Y. Davis, *Blues Legacies and Black Feminism: Gertrude "Ma" Rainey, Bessie Smith, and Billie Holiday* (New York: Pantheon Books, 1998); Toni Cade Bambara, *The Seabirds Are Still Alive: Stories* (New York: Vintage Books, 1982); James C. Scott, *The Art of Not Being Governed: An Anarchist History of Upland Southeast Asia* (New Haven, CT: Yale University Press, 2009).
9. See also Cedric J. Robinson, *Black Marxism: The Making of the Black Radical Tradition* (Chapel Hill: University of North Carolina Press, 2000); Michael Hardt and Antonio Negri, *Multitude: War and Democracy in the Age of Empire* (New York: Penguin Press, 2004); Michael Hardt and Antonio Negri, *Commonwealth* (Cambridge, MA: Belknap Press, 2009); Gilles Deleuze and Félix Guattari, *A Thousand Plateaus: Capitalism and Schizophrenia* (London: Athlone, 1988); William Parry, *Against the Wall: The Art of Resistance in Palestine* (Chicago: Lawrence Hill Books, 2011); Silvia Federici, *Re-Enchanting the World: Feminism and the Politics of the Common* (San Francisco: PM Press, 2018); Loretta Ross et al. (eds), *Radical Reproductive Justice: Foundations, Theory, Practice, Critique* (New York City: The Feminist Press, 2017); Jael Silliman et al., *Undivided Rights: Women of Color Organize for Reproductive Justice* (Cambridge: South End Press, 2004); and Greg Jobin-Leeds and AgitArte, *When We Fight We Win: Twenty-First-Century Social Movements and the Activists That Are Transforming Our World* (New York: The New Press, 2016).

10. Marcus Rediker, *Villains of All Nations: Atlantic Pirates in the Golden Age* (Boston: Beacon Press, 2004); C. L. R. James, *The Black Jacobins: Toussaint L'Ouverture and the San Domingo Revolution* (New York: Vintage Books, 1989).
11. Robinson, *Terms.*
12. In this work, I use "in/justice" to signal that justice is frequently cordoned off as an entitlement of the few, and, more often than not, it is injustice that ordinary people experience in everyday life. As such in and of itself, justice is nominally aspirational.
13. Ahmed, *Willful Subjects*; Bambara, *Seabirds*, 77. See also Toni Cade Bambara, *The Salt Eaters* (New York: Vintage Books, 1980).
14. Avery Gordon, *Keeping Good Time: Reflections on Knowledge, Power, and People* (Boulder: Paradigm Publishers, 2004). See also Avery F. Gordon, *The Hawthorn Archive: Letters from the Utopian Margins* (New York: Fordham University Press, 2018).
15. Eleanor W. Traylor, "Re Calling the Black Woman," in *The Black Woman: An Anthology*, ed. Toni Cade Bambara (New York: Washington Square Press, 2005), ix.
16. Gordon, *Keeping Good Time*, 204.
17. Ahmed, *Willful Subjects*, 47.
18. Robinson, *Terms*, 216.
19. Robinson, *Terms*; H. L. T. Quan, "Emancipatory Social Inquiry: Democratic Anarchism and the Robinsonian Method," *African Identities* 11, no. 2 (2013): 117–32.
20. Gender claims by anti-trans feminists are dubious, especially when they reduce the totality of women's experience to biophysical and reproductive functions. Similarly, gender praxes that archetypify regressive gender roles are not transgressive or liberatory.
21. See H. L. T. Quan, "'It's Hard to Stop Rebels That Time Travel': Democratic Living and the Radical Reimagining of Old Worlds," in *Futures of Black Radicalism*, ed. Gaye Theresa Johnson and Alex Lubin (Brooklyn: Verso, 2017): 173–93.
22. James Baldwin, "No Name in the Street," in *Collected Essays* (New York: Library of America, 1998 [1972]), 445.
23. Women of Color activists insist that the right to not have children, the right to have children, and the right to raise children broaden the reproductive rights framework toward reproductive freedom. Silliman et al., *Undivided Rights*. See also Ross et al., *Radical Reproductive Justice*.
24. Ross et al., *Radical Reproductive Justice*; Dorothy E. Roberts, *Killing the Black Body: Race, Reproduction, and the Meaning of Liberty* (New York: Pantheon Books, 1997); Andrea Smith, *Conquest: Sexual Violence and American Indian Genocide* (Cambridge: South End Press, 2005).
25. Scott, *The Art*, x–xi.
26. Ibid., xi; emphasis added.
27. Scott, *The Art*, 6. Scott primarily focuses on resistance against state-building projects. I extrapolate his characterization of the "shatter zone" where "the human shards of state formations and rivalry accumulated willy-nilly, creating regions of bewildering ethnic and linguistic complexity" in Southeast Asia, Amazonia, and the highland of Africa (7–8).
28. Ibid., 8.
29. Ahmed, *Willful Subjects*.

30. Bambara, *Salt Eaters*; *Seabirds*. The impetus for this work came out of my reading of Robinson's *The Terms of Order* and Bambara's creative writings. Robinson's critique of order and the political supplies the inspiration to move beyond western anarchic thought, and it is his insistence to deauthorize the dominant terms of order that prompted the investigation into the willful refusal to be governed. Bambara's cultural interrogations invite willfulness to unlearn governing. See also Michel Foucault, "Of Other Spaces," *Diacritics* 16, no. 1 (Spring 1986 [1967]): 22–27.
31. Scott, *The Art*, 29.
32. Ibid., 29–30.
33. Barack Obama, *The Audacity of Hope: Thoughts on Reclaiming the American Dream* (New York: Crown Publishers, 2006), 58.
34. Thus, the many radical works by feminists of Color, including queer of Color critiques and queer crip theories, are part of the larger oeuvre of scholarship beyond the pale—always positioning as counterhegemonic, jostling, and destabilizing normative governing projects, especially state-forming projects. See Cohen, "Punks"; Jasbir K. Puar, *Terrorist Assemblages: Homonationalism in Queer Times* (Durham, NC: Duke University Press, 2007); Roderick A. Ferguson, *The Reorder of Things: The University and Its Pedagogies of Minority Difference* (Minneapolis: University of Minnesota Press, 2012); and Stefano Harney and Fred Moten, *The Undercommons: Fugitive Planning & Black Study* (New York: Minor Compositions, 2013).
35. "Fresh off the boat"—an offensive term to speciate those perceived as foreigners and not "cultured" or "civilized."
36. Ahmed, *Willful Subjects*.
37. Audre Lorde, "A Litany for Survival," in *The Collected Poems of Audre Lorde* (New York: W. W. Norton, 1978): 283–84.
38. Sara Ahmed, *Living a Feminist Life* (Durham, NC: Duke University Press, 2017).
39. Ernest Gellner, *Saints of the Atlas* (London: Weidenfeld & Nicolson, 1969).
40. Scott, *The Art*, 31.
41. Ibid.
42. Ahmed, *Living a Feminist Life*.
43. Ibid., 57.
44. Ibid.
45. Anthony Bogues, "And What About the Human? Freedom, Human Emancipation, and the Radical Imagination," *Boundary* 239, no. 3 (2012): 36–37.
46. Ibid., 37–38.
47. Timothy Snyder, *On Tyranny: Twenty Lessons from the Twentieth Century* (New York: Tim Duggan Books, 2017).
48. Norton, "Feral Cities."
49. Ibid., 98–99. Trump's throwaway comments about "shithole countries" in reference to Haiti, El Salvador, and countries in Africa; and "rat-infested city" in reference to Baltimore, Maryland, are only the latest in a long line of racist tropes deployed against "othered spaces." See Ali Vitali, Kassie Hunt, Frank Thorp V, "Trump Referred to Haiti and African Nations as 'Shithole' Countries," *NBC News*, January 12, 2018, www.nbcnews.com/politics/White-house/trump-referred-haiti-african-countries-shithole-nations-n836946; and Cristina Maza, "Baltimore Residents Respond to Trump's 'Rat Infested City' Comments:

'I'm Thrilled to be Here,'" *Newsweek*, July 29, 2019, www.newsweek.com/baltimore-residents-respond-trump-rat-comments-1451606.

50. Anne L. Clunan and Harold A. Trinkunas, eds., *Ungoverned Spaces: Alternatives to State Authority in an Era of Softened Sovereignty* (Stanford: Stanford Security Studies, 2010), 3–4.
51. Gary Prevost et al., eds., *U.S. National Security Concerns in the Latin America and the Caribbean: The Concept of Ungoverned Spaces and Failed States* (New York: Palgrave, 2014).
52. As part of an agreement by the former administration, on August 30, 2021, after nearly two decades, the Biden administration carried out a "complete withdrawal" of US military from Afghanistan. David Rhode, "Biden's Chaotic Withdrawal from Afghanistan Is Complete," *New Yorker*, August 30, 2021, www.newyorker.com/news/daily-comment/bidens-chaotic-withdrawal-from-afghanistan-is-complete. See the International Centre for Counter-Terrorism's recent report on weapons the US left behind: Tanya Mehra, Méryl Demuynck, and Matthew Wentworth, "Weapons in Afghanistan: The Taliban's Spoils of War," *Policy Brief*, February 2022, https://icct.nl/app/uploads/2022/02/The-Spoils-of-War-final-1.pdf.
53. U.S. Government, The National Security Strategy of the United States (March 2006), 12–14. https://history.defense.gov/Portals/70/Documents/nss/nss2006.pdf?ver=Hf01-Y5B6CMl8yHpX4x6IA%3d%3d.
54. Emphasis added, cited in John C. Dugas, "Old Wine in the New Wineskins: Incorporating 'Ungoverned Spaces' Concept into Plan Columbia," in *U.S. National Security Concerns in the Latin America and the Caribbean: The Concept of Ungoverned Spaces and Failed States*, ed. Gary Prevost et al. (New York: Palgrave, 2014), 143. l.
55. This framing is not new and is underwritten by a self-serving missionary logic. See Dugas, "Old Wine."
56. Norton, "Feral Cities," 98.
57. Clunan and Trinkunas, *Ungoverned Spaces*, 19; emphasis added. Unlike othered spaces, the ferality of tax haven are not seen as a serious threat to global security, and they are rarely policed or militarized the same way.
58. Phil Williams, "Here Be Dragons: Dangerous Spaces and International Security," in *Ungoverned Spaces: Alternatives to State Authority in an Era of Softened Sovereignty*, ed. Anne L. Clunan and Harold A. Trinkunas (Stanford: Stanford Security Studies, 2010), 34.
59. Williams, "Here Be Dragons," 35.
60. Ibid.
61. Ibid., 36.
62. Williams, 51–52; emphasis added. To be fair, Williams allows for the possibility that state decline may lead to a scenario where "people once again embrace forms of governance that are bottom-up rather than top-down"; he, however, ultimately dismisses this scenario as "all too easily proven elusive or even illusory" (52).
63. Ibid.
64. Iris Marion Young, *Justice and the Politics of Difference* (Princeton, NJ: Princeton University Press, 1990). See also Drucilla Cornell and Stephen D. Seely, *The Spirit of Revolution: Beyond the Dead Ends of Man* (Cambridge: Polity Press, 2015).

65. Iris Marion Young, "The Five Faces of Oppression," *The Philosophy Forum* XIX, no. 4 (Summer 1988): 270–90. See also Iris Marion Young, *Responsibility for Justice* (Oxford: Oxford University Press, 2011). Nearly three decades after Young, Charles W. Mills noted that "though the term is routinely bandied about, mainstream liberal theorists have had surprising little to say about it. . . . Exploitation has not been a central concern for contemporary political and moral philosophy." Mills, *Black Rights*, 120.
66. Young, "Five Faces," 270.
67. Lani Guinier, "Foreword: Demosprudence Through Dissent," *Harvard Law Review* 122, no. 1 (November 2008): 6–138.
68. Hassan Kanu, "Justice Roberts Minimizes U.S. Supreme Court's Legitimacy Crisis," *Reuters*, January 5, 2022, www.reuters.com/legal/government/justice-roberts-minimizes-us-supreme-courts-legitimacy-crisis-2022-01-05/. See also Adam Liptak, "Critical Moment for Roe, and the Supreme Court's Legitimacy," *New York Times*, December 4, 2021, www.nytimes.com/2021/12/04/us/politics/mississippi-supreme-court-abortion-roe-v-wade.html; and Robert Barnes and Seung Min Kim, "Supreme Court Observers See Trouble Ahead as Public Approval of Justices Erode," *Washington Post*, September 26, 2021.
69. Guinier, "Foreword," 15. See also Lani Guinier and Gerald Torres, "Changing the Wind: Notes Toward a Demosprudence of Law and Social Movements," *Yale Law Journal* 123, no. 8 (June 2014): 2740–2804.
70. Guinier, "Foreword," 15–16.
71. Ibid., 38–39. Here Guinier uses the example of Justice Stephen Breyer's dissent in *Parents Involved in Community v. Seattle*, 551 U.S. 701 (2007). Writing for the Court's plurality, Chief Justice John Roberts insists that "racial balancing is not transformed from 'patently unconstitutional' to a compelling state interest simply by relabeling it 'racial diversity.'" In this decision Roberts and other reactionary justices verbalized their so-called color blind judicial dictum.
72. Melissa Murray, "Sotomayor Saw She Couldn't Sway Her Colleagues. So She Talked with Us Instead," *Washington Post*, December 3, 2021, www.washingtonpost.com/outlook/abortion-sotomayor-dobbs-oral-arguments/2021/12/03/ba6fc4b8-53d5-11ec-8927-c396fa861a71_story.html.

    In a conversation with Linda Greenhouse, Sotomayor explains that when writing a dissent, she hopes "that people will actually read it and be moved by it." Sonia Sotomayor and Linda Greenhouse, "A Conversation with Justice Sotomayor," *Yale Law Journal Forum*, Vol. 123 (March 2014): 375–91.
73. Guinier, "Foreword," 47.
74. Ibid., 58.
75. Ibid., 56. See also Robert Post and Reva Siegel, "Roe Rage: Democratic Constitutionalism and Backlash," *Harvard Civil Rights-Civil Liberties Law Review* 42, no. 2 (June 2007): 373–433.
76. Guinier, "Foreword," 48.
77. See Sotomayor's dissent in *Utah v. Strieff* (2006) that centers on illegally obtained evidence and is adjacent to the nefarious police practice of "stop and frisk." In addition to referencing W. E. B. Du Bois's *The Souls of Black Folk*, James Baldwin's *The Fire Next Time*, Michelle Alexander's *The New Jim Crow*, and others, Sotomayor also signals to Black Lives Matter—a marker of grievances lodged against the police and White laws, and evokes Eric Garner's infamous final words, "I can't breathe." With references to critical prison studies and social death, Soto-

mayor also makes visible that social insights from Black thinkers and writers as well as ordinary people's lived experiences are critical to judicial deliberation. Making it clear that she is without friends on the Court, Sotomayor insists that she was "writing only for myself," while opining that the Court has sanctioned and given the police "reason to target pedestrians in an arbitrary manner," marking them "criminal," while violating their bodily autonomy. *Utah v. Strieff*, (2016) No. 14-1373, 579 U. S. (June 20, 2016), "Sotomayor, J. Dissenting."

78. Mills, *Black Rights*, 160.
79. Foucault, "Society Must Be Defended," 23–42. See also Michel Foucault, *The Order of Things: An Archaeology of the Human Sciences* (New York: Vintange Books, 1970).
80. Robinson, *Terms*; James C. Scott, *Seeing Like a State: How Certain Schemes to Improve the Human Condition Have Failed* (New Haven, CT: Yale University Press, 1998).
81. Carole Pateman and Charles W. Mills, *Contract and Domination* (Cambridge: Polity, 2007).
82. Walter R. Newell suggests that delineating tyranny has always been difficult, not least because "there are fundamental differences in the understanding of tyranny between classical and modern political philosophy." Walter R. Newell, *Tyranny: A New Interpretation* (Cambridge: Cambridge University Press, 2013), 513.
83. Michael G. Lacy, "Exposing the Spectrum of Whiteness," *Annals of the International Communication Association* 32 (2008): 277.
84. Ibid., 280.
85. This connotation extrapolates Audre Lorde's definition of racism. Audre Lorde, "Age, Race, Class and Sex: Women Redefining Difference," in *Sister Outsider: Essays and Speeches* (Berkeley: Crossing Press, 2007): 114–23.
86. Catherine Zurkert, "Why Talk about Tyranny Today," in *Confronting Tyranny: Ancient Lessons for Global Politics*, ed. Toivo Koivukoski and David Edward Tabachinick (Lanham: Rowman & Littlefield, 2005), 1–3.
87. Zuckert suggests that tyranny is a "deviant" form of governing, implying there is "normal" governing (Ibid., 3). She thus naturalizes governing.
88. Newell, *Tyranny*, 141.
89. Friedrich Nietzsche, *Beyond Good and Evil: Prelude to a Philosophy of the Future*, trans. Helen Zimmern (New York: The Macmillan Company, 1907).
90. Tracy B. Strong, "Tyranny and Tragedy in Nietzsche: From the Ancient to the Modern," in *Confronting Tyranny: Ancient Lessons for Global Politics*, ed. Toivo Koivukoski and David Tabachnick (Lanham: Rowan & Littlefield, 2005), 114.
91. Ibid., 105.
92. Lewis R. Gordon extends Jean-Paul Sartre's idea of bad faith to suggest an evasive, even intentional, self-deception in believing either "one's race is the only race qualified to be considered human or that one's race is superior to other races." Lewis R. Gordon, *Bad Faith and Antiblack Racism* (Amherst, MA: Humanities Books, 1995), 3. Notwithstanding individual and collective intent, there is an inherent tyrannical element in White supremacy as White supremacists profess to possess certainty in racial truths, especially truths about the superiority of Whiteness. Without confronting the tyranny of White supremacy and bad faith, anti-racists, especially liberal ones, are frequently ineffectual in their nominal anti-racist campaigns because their claims to racial truths are themselves tyrannizing.

93. Strong, "Tyranny and Tragedy," 112.
94. Ibid.
95. Foucault, "Society Must Be Defended."
96. Perhaps had Foucault taken up Max Horkheimer and Theodor W. Adorno's *Dialectic of Enlightenment*, he might have appreciated their observations that "Nietzsche maliciously celebrates the mighty and their cruelty when it is directed 'outside their circle,' that is, against everything alien to themselves," and thus would recognize that Nietzsche was far from a disinterested or even an ambivalent reader of rules and rulemaking. They argued that Nietzsche's lot was not with the many or the poor but with the powerful, and for all Foucault's intentions and purpose to pivot away from governing, Foucault's reforming of power falls short of that goal. Max Horkheimer and Theodor W. Adorno, *Dialectic of Enlightenment: Philosophical Fragments*, trans. Gunzelin Schmid Noerr (Stanford, CA: Stanford University Press, 2002), 77.
97. Shoshanna Zuboff, "Big Other: Surveillance Capitalism and the Prospects of an Information Civilization," *Journal of Information Technology* 30 (2015): 75. See also Shoshana Zuboff, *The Age of Surveillance Capitalism: The Fight for a Human Future at the New Frontier of Power* (New York: PublicAffairs, 2019).
98. Strong, "Tyranny and Tragedy," 113. See also Max Weber, *Economy and Society: An Outline of Interpretive Sociology*, trans. Ephraim Fischoff, 2 vols., ed. Guenther Roth and Claus Wittich (Berkeley: University of California Press, 1978).
99. Typically understood as a monarchist "who rule by consent" of the governed. My work takes it as a given that "the consent to be governed" is a governing propaganda.
100. *Despoteia* or despotism was used by classical theorists to denote non-Greek regimes that are considered "less developed" than Greek ones, such as patriarchy and other forms of kinship that were based on the "private" household. Mark Lilla, "The New Age of Tyranny," in *Confronting Tyranny: Ancient Lessons for Global Politics*, ed. Toivo Koivukoski and David Tabachnick (Lanham, MD: Rowman & Littlefield, 2005), 244.
101. Lilla, "New Age," 245.
102. Michael T. Taussig, *The Magic of the State* (New York: Routledge, 1997).
103. M. I. Finley, *Democracy Ancient and Modern* (New Brunswick, NJ: Rutgers University Press, 1985), 142.
104. Namely, life, work, and pleasure.
105. Erica R. Edwards, *The Other Side of Terror: Black Women and the Culture of US Empire* (New York: New York University Press, 2021), 211.
106. Linda Jane Holmes and Cheryl A. Wall, *Savoring the Salt: The Legacy of Toni Cade Bambara* (Philadelphia: Temple University Press, 2008); Edwards, *The Other Side.*
107. Cited in Edwards, *The Other Side*, 203.
108. Ibid., 203–204.
109. Traylor, "Re Calling," xii; emphasis added.
110. Cited in Traylor, "Re Calling," xiii.
111. Ibid.
112. Edwards, *The Other Side*, 206.
113. Bambara, *The Black Woman*, 1.
114. This work retools Cedric Robinson's method for doing emancipatory social inquiry to interrogate antidemocracy and speculates on the meanings of justice.

Quan, "Emancipatory Social Inquiry." See also Maia Ramnath, *Decolonizing Anarchism: An Antiauthoritarian History of India's Liberation Struggle* (Oakland: AK Press/Institute for Anarchist Studies, 2011).

115. Ramnath, *Decolonizing Anarchism*, 7.
116. Marquis Bey, *Anarcho-Blackness: Notes Toward a Black Anarchism* (Edinburgh: AK Press, 2020). For instance, In *Terms*, Robinson rejects western anarchism because its authors could not divorce their ideas about and aspirations for a better society from their onto-epistemological commitment to fictive social contractarian notions of a free, rational, and autonomous individual and to bourgeois achievements. He argues that rulers are redundant because individuals have the capacity to rule themselves; thus, despite its radical claim of heresy, anarchy is "like a sparrow which once wounded never flies again." Robinson, *Terms*, 187, 252.
117. Edwards, *The Other Side*.
118. Enrique D. Dussel, *Ethics and Community* (Maryknoll: Orbis Books, 1988).
119. Ibid., 9–10.
120. Ibid., 37–41.
121. Dylan Rodríguez, "Abolition as Praxis of Human Being: A Foreword," *Harvard Law Review* 132 (2019): 1575–76.
122. Angela Y. Davis et al., *Abolition. Feminism. Now* (Chicago: Haymarket Books, 2022).
123. Cedric J. Robinson, *An Anthropology of Marxism* (Aldershot: Ashgate, 2001), 139.

CHAPTER 2

1. David Walker, *Walker's APPEAL in Four Articles; Together with the Preamble to the Coloured Citizen of the World, But in Particular and Very Expressly, to Those of the United States* (Boston: David Walker, 1830), 23. Walker's *APPEAL* was written and self-published in 1829 in Boston. This 1830 iteration is the "third and last edition" published by Walker himself, and contains an author's note on additional notes and corrections, including the following note to the intended global readership and fellow resistors: "It is expected that all coloured men, women and children, of every nation, language and tongue under heaven, will try to procure a copy of this Appeal and read it, or get someone to read it to them, for it is designed more particularly for them." Walker would urge his readership to free themselves from such enemies, following the example of the slave revolution in Santo Domingo (present-day Haiti). With a bounty of nearly $300,000 (today's valuation) for his capture, and soon after this revised edition, Walker would die a mysterious death, his body found in a doorway. His death remains unsolved, and many continued to believe that he was poisoned. Walker was survived by his wife of four years, Eliza (Butler) Walker, and a young son, Edward G. Walker, who grew up to be an abolitionist and was elected to the Massachusetts legislature in 1866. In 1896, Edward Walker was nominated as a US presidential candidate by the Negro Party, an offspring of the Negro Political Independence Movement.
2. Bacchetta et al., "Queer of Color."
3. Lin-Manuel Miranda's musical *Hamilton* is decidedly within the larger historical genre of "Founder chic" as it is "insidiously invested in trumpeting the deeds of wealthy White men . . . [such that] the history it tells is essentially the same

Whitewashed version of the founding era." Lyra D. Monteiro, "Race-Conscious Casting and the Erasure of the Black Past in Lin-Manuel Miranda's *Hamilton*," *The Public Historian* 38, no. 1 (February 2016): 96.

4. Writing to his friend Sean Theodore Sedgwick, Hamilton explained that the plan to secede by a few Northern elites to form their own confederacy would not succeed because secession would still leave intact "Democracy, the poison which by a subdivision will only be the more concentrated in each part, and consequently the more virulent." Alexander Hamilton, "From Alexander Hamilton to Theodore Sedgwick," July 10, 1804, *Founders Online*, National Archives, https://founders.archives.gov/documents/Hamilton/01-26-02-0001-0264.
5. Historian Sean Wilentz points out that despite being a founding member and brief stint as president of the New York Manumission Society, "Hamilton never publicly or, apparently, privately advocated slavery abolition, much less did so ardently." Sean Wilentz, *The Politicians and the Egalitarians: The Hidden History of American Politics* (New York: W. W. Norton, 2016), 124.
6. Ibid., 38–39.
7. Ibid., 38.
8. T. Addison Richards, "The Rice Land of the South," *Harper's New Monthly Magazine* 19, no. 114 (November 1859): 723; emphasis added. Mary Koch, "Thomas Addison Richards," *New Georgia Encyclopedia*, 2013, www.georgiaencyclopedia.org/articles/arts-culture/thomas-addison-richards-1820-1900/. See also Adam H. Veil, "'The Wonderful Works of Omnipotency': T. Addison Richards and the Aura of the Romantic Southern Landscape," *Athanor* 25 (2007): 85–89.
9. Richards, "The Rice Land," 731.
10. Ibid.
11. In 1822, South Carolina passed the *Negro Seaman Act* requiring Black sailors to turn themselves in at local jails immediately after disembarking and be detained until their ships embarked. After 1829, Georgia and North Carolina cited *Walker's APPEAL* to justify the passage of similar laws; Florida used the occasion to ban entry to free Black people entirely. Indeed, southern states "reacted swiftly . . . some requiring the death penalty, against possession and distribution" of Walker's call to insurrection. Hasan Crockett, "The Incendiary Pamphlet: David *Walker's APPEAL* in Georgia," *Journal of Negro History* 86, no. 3 (Summer 2001): 305.
12. Robinson, *Cedric J. Robinson*, 340–53.
13. Combahee River Collective, "A Black Feminist Statement," in *Home Girls: A Black Feminist Anthology*, ed. Barbara Smith (Albany: Kitchen Table Women of Color Press, 1983 [1977]). See also Keeanga-Yamahtta Taylor, *How We Get Free: Black Feminism and the Combahee River Collective* (Chicago: Haymarket Books, 2017); and Tiffany Willoughby-Herard, "(Political) Anesthesia or (Political) Memory: The Combahee River Collective and the Death of Black Women in Custody," *Theory & Event* 21, no. 1 (January 2018): 259–81.
14. Crockett, "Incendiary Pamphlet," 305. Walker was much more than a mere scribe and tailor; he was also an active abolitionist and militant. A member of the Massachusetts General Colored Association, the first abolitionist formation in Boston, Walker provided aid and comfort to the radical faction of the anti-slavery campaign. He organized secret meetings, advocating and seeking aid for a slave rebellion; he gave to and raised funds for fugitive slaves. He also raised funds for

what would become the first Black newspaper, *The Freedom Journal*. Prior to the *APPEAL*, Walker made his militant views known in public conversations and speeches. As another Black abolitionist, Henry Highland Garnet, pointed out, while "Walker is known principally by his *Appeal*, it was in his private walks, and by his unceasing labors in the cause of freedom, that he has made his memory sacred." Cited in Crockett, "Incendiary Pamphlet," 307.

15. James Baldwin, *The Fire Next Time* (London: Michael Joseph, 1963), 17.
16. Govind Bhutada, "How News Media Is Describing the Incident at the U.S. Capitol," *Visual Capitalist*, January 16, 2021, www.visualcapitalist.com/how-news-media-is-describing-the-incident-at-the-u-s-capitol/. See also Georgia Wells, Rebecca Ballhaus, and Keach Hagey, "Proud Boys Inspired by Trump—Messages Suggest the Far-Right Group Interpreted President's Words as Call to Action," *Wall Street Journal*, January 19, 2021: A6. www.proquest.com/abi-complete/docview/2478726085/C85193C5287045FEPQ/2319?accountid=4485; Tom Porter and Ashley Collman, "The Capitol Riot, 6 Months on: Here Are the Missed Warnings and Failures That Led to Insurrection on US Soil," *Business Insider*, July 6, 2021, www.proquest.com/abicomplete/docview/2548565589/8E5A26156C814694PQ/16?accountid=4485.
17. Zack Stanton, "The Internet Is a Crime Scene," *Politico*, January 14, 2021, https://www.politico.com/news/magazine/2021/01/14/us-capitol-disinformation-online-qanon-trump-insurrection-459505.
18. Ibid.
19. Dylan Rodríguez, *White Reconstruction: Domestic Warfare and the Logics of Genocide* (New York: Fordham University Press, 2021). Whiteness itself is an ongoing process of (re)constructions given its instability and not entirely persuasive governing narratives based on various racial regimes. "White reconstruction" is thus an inherently self-correcting mechanism, neither revolutionary nor counterrevolutionary. See also Robinson, *Forgeries*.
20. Stanton, "The Internet."
21. Even as Trump is being indicted by a Special Counsel and many rioters have been convicted, the *Full Report of the Select January 6th Committee Hearing* reveals that law enforcement and military were also complicit in the siege; even the Capitol Police, a force charged with protecting the Capitol, was implicated. www.govinfo.gov/collection/january-6th-committee-final-report?path=/GPO/January%206th%20Committee%20Final%20Report%20and%20Supporting%20Materials%20Collection. But the final report, as Bill Kristol puts it, "doesn't quite convey how much the antidemocratic, authoritarian sentiments have metastasized." Ronald Brownstein, "The Biggest Takeaway from the January 6 Report," *The Atlantic*, December 23, 2022, www.theatlantic.com/politics/archive/2022/12/jan-6-committee-investigation-trump-criminal-referrals-gop-accountability/672554/. Before the congressional hearing, *ABC News* reported that "at least 52 active or retired military, law enforcement, or government service employees are among the over 400 suspects arrested." Olivia Rubin, "Number of Capital Riot Arrests of Military, Law Enforcement and Government Personnel Rises to 52," *ABC News*, April 23, 2021, https://abcnews.go.com/US/number-capitol-riot-arrests-military-law-enforcement-government/story?id=77246717. More damning, congressional investigators found that top Pentagon officials, including then-acting Defense Secretary Christopher Miller and General Charles Flynn—brother of Trump's disgraced first National Security Advisor Michael

Flynn—delayed deploying the National Guard to the Capitol while it was overrun by insurrectionists. Betsy Woodruff Swan and Meridith McGraw, "'Absolute Liars': Ex-D.C. Guard Official Says General Lied to Congress about Jan. 6," *Politico*, December 6, 2021, www.politico.com/news/2021/12/06/jan-6-generals-lied-ex-dc-guard-official-523777; Jack Homes, "Never Forget That Trump Purged the Pentagon Leadership Between the Election and Jan. 6," *Esquire*, December 6, 2021, www.esquire.com/news-politics/politics/a38439573/january-6-national-guard-delayed-trump-pentagon-officials/. A startled military establishment, no longer able to ignore the close affinity between insurrectionist elements and its own people, conceded the following in a public letter in the *Washington Post*: "a disturbing number of veterans and active-duty members of the military took part in the attack on the Capitol. More than 1 in 10 of those charged in the attacks had service records. A group of 124 military officials, under the name, 'Flag Officers 4 America,' released a letter echoing Donald Trump's false attacks on the legitimacy of our elections." Paul D. Eaton, Antonio M. Taguba, and Steven M. Anderson, "3 Retired Generals: The Military Must Prepare Now for a 2024 Insurrection," *Washington Post*, December 17, 2021, www.washingtonpost.com/opinions/2021/12/17/eaton-taguba-anderson-generals-military/. The retired generals also warned against another coup attempt from "potential lethal chaos" within the military that "could lead to civil war" should we fail to recognize the significance of January 6 and its intimacy with US military and law enforcement.

Congressional hearings and investigative news reports have also revealed the involvement of wealthy Trump supporters, like Julie Fancelli, an heiress to the Publix supermarkets chain, and Caroline Wren, a former Trump fundraiser and facilitator of Fancelli's financing. Beth Reinhard, Jacqueline Alemany, and Josh Dawsey, "Low-Profile Heiress Thrust into Spotlight Over Jan. 6 Financing," *Washington Post*, December 8, 2021; Joaquin Sapien and Joshua Kaplan, "Top Trump Fundraiser Boasted of Raising $3 Million to Support Jan. 6 'Save America' Rally," *ProPublica*, October 18, 2021, www.propublica.org/article/top-trump-fundraiser-boasted-of-raising-3-million-to-support-jan-6-save-america-rally.

22. Alyosha Goldstein and Simón Ventura Trujillo, eds., "New Futures Are Possible Right Now," *Critical Ethnic Studies Journal* 7, no. 1 (Spring 2021).
23. Barbara Ransby, *Making All Black Lives Matter: Reimagining Freedom in the Twenty-First Century* (Oakland: University of California Press, 2018).
24. Ibid., 15.
25. Bacchetta et al., "Queer of Color," 54.
26. Ibid., 44–47.
27. Oliver C. Cox, *Capitalism as a System* (New York: Monthly Review Press, 1964), 178. See also Robinson, *Cedric J. Robinson*; Goldstein and Trujillo, "New Futures"; and James Q. Whitman, *Hitler's American Model: The United States and the Making of Nazi Race Law* (Princeton, NJ: Princeton University Press, 2018).
28. Benjamin Grubb Humphreys's inaugural address as it appeared in the *New York Herald* (October 29, 1865) in James Wilford Garner, *Reconstruction in Mississippi* (New York: Macmillan, 1901), 111.
29. Friedrich Nietzsche, *The Will to Power*, trans. Walter Kaufmann and R. J. Hollingdale (New York: Vintage, 1968).
30. Former US labor secretary and usually reliable reader of neoliberal politics Robert Reich differentiates "Trump's neofascism" from "racism and xenophobia."

Robert Reich, "The True Meaning of 6 January: We Must Answer Trump's Neofascism with Hope," *The Guardian*, December 28, 2021, www.theguardian.com/commentisfree/2021/dec/28/6-january-capitol-attack-trump-neofascism-coup-republicans. Reich's rendering of "neofascism" as distinct from White supremacy and racism is emblematic of readers of American fascism.

31. Audre Lorde, "The Transformation of Silence into Language and Action," in *Sister Outsider: Essays and Speeches* (Berkeley: Crossing Press, 2007 [1984]): 40–44.
32. Duke Selwyn, "Call It Whatever You Want—Neo-fascism Is in Fashion," *New York Observer*, May 26, 2017, https://observer.com/2017/05/what-is-neo-fascism-democrats-mussolini/; Peter Baker, "Rise of Trump Tracks Debate Over Fascism," *New York Times*, May 29, 2016: A1. www.nytimes.com/2016/05/29/world/europe/rise-of-donald-trump-tracks-growing-debate-over-global-fascism.html; Jennifer Szalai, "Use of 'Fascism' Takes a New Turn," *New York Times*, June 11, 2020, www.nytimes.com/2020/06/10/books/fascism-debate-donald-trump.html; Stephen Kinzer, "Putting a Stake through Fascism as Neo-fascism Rises," *Boston Globe*, July 22, 2018, www.bostonglobe.com/opinion/2018/07/19/putting-stake-through-fascism-neo-fascism-rises/cw6PnK8KTsyiSdZjeDpIoN/story.html.
33. Nicos Poulantzas, *Fascism and Dictatorship: The Third International and the Problem of Fascism* (London: NLB, 1974). See also Hannah Arendt, *The Origins of Totalitarianism* (New York: Harcourt, 1951).
34. Robert O. Paxton, *The Anatomy of Fascism* (New York: Alfred A. Knopf, 2004), 1. In his earlier study of fascism, Paxton concedes that the Klans and European fascists "are related." Robert O. Paxton, "The Fives Stages of Fascism," *Journal of Modern History* 70, no. 1 (March 1998): 12.
35. Paxton, *Anatomy*, 3.
36. Ibid., 3.
37. Ibid., 5. Revealingly, in his 1998 initial assessment, Paxton entertained the idea that "fascism (understood functionally) was born in the late 1860s in the American South" and this rise was a "preview" of fascist mobilization. Paxton, "Five Stages," 12. He nevertheless dismissed such a notion, asserting that "it is not necessarily in the countries that generated the first fascism that fascist systems have had, historically, the best chance of succeeding" (12). By 2004, Paxton is entirely wedded to his own narrative that fascism was "unimagined as late as the 1890s," and certainly not born until 1919 in Milan. Paxton, *Anatomy*.
38. There are some factual disputes about Kea's account of her imprisonment. Dolorès Moruno Martin, "Salaria Kea's Memories from the Spanish Civil War," in *Warriors without Weapons: Humanitarian Action During the Spanish Civil War and the Republican Exile*, conference proceeding (Geneva: The Louis Jeantet Auditorium Foundation, October 2016).
39. Salaria Kea, *A Negro Nurse in Republican Spain* (New York: The Negro Committee to Aid Spain, 1938), 3. Reprinted by the *Bay Area Post*, February 6, 1977.
40. Langston Hughes, "Too Much of Race," *Crisis* 44, no. 9 (September 1937): 272.
41. As early as 1924, Arthur Corning White argued that the KKK "is an American fascismo." Arthur Corning White, "An American Fascismo," *The Forum* (July–December 1924): 636. However, White insisted that it is "only incidentally an organization for the exploitation of racial and religious bigotry." White, "American Fascismo," 636. Its real purpose, "perhaps still unconscious," White

believed, is rooted in economics (636). Nevertheless, he rejected the idea that "the Klan has its origin in Fascismo" (641); but conceded that they might be distant kins. Unlike White, Black anti-fascists, like Du Bois, Hughes, and Kea, recognized White supremacy and Jim Crow as co-progenitors of European fascism, and understood, as did Ida B. Wells before them, that the work of the KKK and other White vigilantes is motivated by racist terrorism and not merely economics.

42. Linda Gordon, *The Second Coming of the KKK: The Ku Klux Klan of the 1920 and the American Political Tradition* (New York: Liveright, 2017), 113–15.
43. Gordon, *The Second Coming*; and Whitman, *Hitler's American Model*. See also Paxton, "Five Stages"; and Nancy MacLean, *Behind the Mask of Chivalry: The Making of the Second Ku Klux Klan* (New York: Oxford University Press, 1995).
44. Whitman, *Hitler's American Model*, 2.
45. Ibid., 3.
46. Nell Irvin Painter, *The History of White People* (New York: W. W. Norton, 2010).
47. The mythic White autarky denies the possibility of interdependency, if not, dependency of White accumulation and rule of the other, especially on the life and labor of Black people.
48. Even after Santelli conceded that the whole thing was staged for effect, many, including *CNBC*'s Jeff Cox, continue to mythologize this event. On the five-year anniversary of the rant, Cox persists in characterizing Santelli as "one fed-up *CNBC* journalist" who was "pushed to the brink," crediting Santelli with changing the political landscape. Jeff Cox, "5 Years Later, Rick Santelli 'Tea Party' Rant Revisited," *CNBC News*, February 24, 2014, www.cnbc.com/2014/02/24/5-years-later-rick-santelli-tea-party-rant-revisited.html.
49. A few weeks after, Santelli "clarified" the incident in a self-serving post, noting that he had "NO association" with the Tea Party movement or any of the tea party related websites. Rick Santelli, "I Want to Set the Record Straight," *CNBC*, March 2, 2009, www.cnbc.com/id/29471026.
50. *Huffpost*, "Rick Santelli: Tea Party Rant 'Best 5 Minutes of My life,' *Huffpost*, September 20, 2010. The original quote first appeared in the *Chicago Sun Times*, September 20, 2010, https://chicago.suntimes.com/news/politics/2723474,CST-NWS-TeaParty19.article, but is no longer accessible.
51. Devin Burghart and Leonard Zeskin, *Tea Party Nationalism: A Critical Examination of the Tea Party Movement and the Size, Scope, and Focus of Its National Factions* (Kansas City: Institute for Research & Education on Human Rights, 2010).
52. Burghart and Zeskind, *Tea Party Nationalism*, 15.
53. Apparently, after Malkin linked Steinhauser's handiwork on her blog, his "website choked" from the heavy traffic (Ibid., 17). See also FreedomWorks, "How to Organize Your Own Party Tea Party Protest," http://theconservativerevolution.com/2009/02/20/how-to-organize-your-own-tea-party-protest/.
54. George Monbiot, "The Tea Party Movement: Deluded and Inspired Billionaires," *The Guardian*, October 25, 2010, www.theguardian.com/commentisfree/cifamerica/2010/oct/25/tea-party-koch-brothers.
55. Andrew J. Perrin et al., "Cultures of Tea Party," *Context* 10, no. 2 (2011): 74–75. See also Leonard Zeskind, "A Nation Dispossessed: The Tea Party Movement and Race," *Critical Sociology* 38, no. 4 (2012): 495–509.
56. Perrin et al., "Cultures of Tea Party," 75.

57. Citi global economist Dana Peterson's study concludes that the consequences of two decades (2000–2020) anti-Black discrimination for the US economy amounts to $16 trillion. Dana M. Peterson, "Closing the Racial Inequality Gaps: The Economic Cost of Black Inequality in the U.S.," *Citi GPS: Global Perspectives & Solutions*, September 2020, https://ir.citi.com/NvIUklHPilz14Hwd3oxqZBLMn1_XPqo5FrxsZDox6hhil84ZxaxEuJUWmak51UHvYk75VKeHCMI%3D. See also Sarah Mayorga-Gallo, "The White-Centering Logic of Diversity Ideology," *American Behavioral Scientist* 63, no. 13 (2019): 1789–1809.
58. The data on wealth and poverty from the Great Recession are startling and most appropriate for understanding the emergence of the TPM. Data from 2011 reveal the highest poverty rates since 2003, and rival those of two decades earlier. Over 15 percent of Americans (more than 46 million people) are in poverty; for African Americans and Latinos, the situation is worse: 27.4 percent and 26.5 percent, respectively, compared to 9.9 percent for Whites. Asian Pacific Americans, with larger households (and thus higher aggregate household income) nevertheless also record a higher percentage of poverty than Whites (at 12.1 percent), though much lower when compared to the Black and Brown communities. These enduring patterns of poverty and racialized wealth distribution hardly shifted, but their severity often is hidden (thus lessening the impact) by a politics of nativism marked with virulent xenophobia and racial scapegoating as methods to avoid drawing attention to structural causes. Zeskind, "A Nation Dispossessed."
59. Thomas J. Kiel and Jacqueline M. Keil, "Funding the Tea Parties," *Sociation Today* 13, no. 1 (2015).
60. Ibid.
61. Ibid.
62. With Dick Armey as the nominal head.
63. Keil and Keil, "Funding the Tea Parties."
64. Chrystia Freeland, *Plutocrats: The Rise of the New Global Super-Rich and the Fall of Everyone Else* (New York: Penguin Press, 2012).
65. Jane Mayer, *Dark Money: The Hidden History of the Billionaires Behind the Rise of the Radical Right* (New York: Doubleday, 2016).
66. Mayer, *Dark Money*; and Oliver C. Cox, *The Foundations of Capitalism* (New York: Philosophical Library, 1959).
67. Cox, *Foundations*, 178–79.
68. Freeland, *Plutocrats*.
69. H. L. T. Quan, "Race, Immigration and the Limits of Citizenship," in *Race and Human Rights*, ed. Curtis Stokes (East Lansing: Michigan State University Press, 2008).
70. Texas, "A Declaration of the Causes which Impel the State of Texas to Secede from the Federal Union," *Ordinance of Secession*, February 1, 1861.
71. Kathleen M. Blee, "The Gendered Organization of Hate: Women in the U.S. Ku Klux Klan," in *Right-Wing Women: From Conservatives to Extremists Around the World*, ed. Paola Bacchetta and Margaret Power (New York: Routledge, 2002), 101.
72. As David Roediger explains, "race defines the social category into which people are sorted, producing, and justifying their very different opportunities with regard to wealth and poverty, confinement and freedom, citizenship and alienation, and as, Ruth Wilson Gilmore puts it, 'life and premature death.'" David R. Roediger, *How Race Survived US History: From Settlement and Slavery to the*

Obama Phenomenon (London: Verso, 2008), xi–xii. See also Robinson, *Black Marxism*; James, *The Black Jacobins*; Angela Y. Davis, *Women, Race & Class* (New York: Vintage Books, 1983 [1981]); Oliver C. Cox, *Caste, Class, & Race: A Study in Social Dynamics* (New York: Monthly Review Press, 1959); and W. E. B. Du Bois, *Black Reconstruction: An Essay Toward a History of the Part which Black Folk Played in the Attempt to Reconstruct Democracy in America, 1860–1880* (New York: Russell & Russell, 1935).

73. Or what Cheryl Harris calls "Whiteness as property" and George Lipsitz characterizes as the "possessive investment in Whiteness." W. E. B. Du Bois, *Dark Water: Voices from within the Veil* (Mineola, NY: Dover Publications, 1999 [1920]); Cheryl I. Harris, "Whiteness as Property," *Harvard Law Review* 106, no. 8 (June 1993): 1707–91; and, George Lipsitz, *The Possessive Investment in Whiteness: How White People Profit from Identity Politics* (Philadelphia: Temple University Press, 1998).
74. Stephanie M. H. Camp, *Closer to Freedom: Enslaved Women and Everyday Resistance in the Plantation South* (Chapel Hill: University of North Carolina Press, 2004), 14.
75. Ibid.
76. Ibid., 68.
77. Ibid., 60.
78. Ibid., 69.
79. Ibid., 61.
80. Ibid.
81. Ibid., 70–71.
82. Ibid., 89.
83. As an artifact, Camp argues, it "articulates not the 'success' of slave resistance using the body but, given the extent to which the body was a point of conflict between slaves and their owners, what meanings the latter group gave to that conflict" (Ibid., 90). The Savannah River Anti-Slave Traffick Association was *not* an anti-slavery formation, but a kind of "homeowner" association formed with the explicit intent to regulate the lives of *all* who are part of the slaveholding society, and specifically "to stop disorderly house owners' practice of selling alcohol to bondpeople," for fear of racial mixing and general insubordination. Slaveholders were particularly concerned with slaves "prowling off to night meetings" (Ibid., 90n121).
84. Ibid., 91.
85. Amílcar Cabral and Africa Information Service, *Return to the Source* (New York: Africa Information Service, 1973).
86. Camp, *Closer to Freedom*, 92. Camp helpfully suggests that we frame the body as multi-dimensional. Accordingly, enslaved people "possessed at least three bodies": 1) as a site of domination or "the body acted upon by slaveholders"; 2) as the subjective experience of slavery; and 3) as a site "of pleasure and resistance," to be reclaimed and enjoyed (60–68).
87. Ibid., 91; Angela Davis, "The Black Woman's Role in the Community of Slaves," *The Black Scholar* (December 1971): 11.
88. Simone Browne, *Dark Matters: On the Surveillance of Blackness* (Durham, NC: Duke University Press, 2015).
89. Ransby, *Making All Black Lives Matter*.
90. Quan, *Growth Against Democracy*.

91. Robinson, *Cedric J. Robinson*, 87–109.
92. Du Bois, *Black Reconstruction*; Cox, *Capitalism as a System*; and Robinson, *Black Marxism*. See also W. E. B. Du Bois, *Black Folk: Then and Now: An Essay in the History of Sociology of the Negro Race* (Oxford: Oxford University Press, 2007 [1939]); and Manning Marable, *How Capitalism Underdeveloped Black America: Problems in Race, Political Economy, and Society* (Boston: South End Press, 1983).
93. Marie-Luise Gåttens, *Women Writers & Fascism: Reconstructing History* (Gainesville: University Press of Florida, 1995), 7.
94. Taylor, *How We Get Free*.
95. Patricia Hill Collins, *Black Feminist Thought: Knowledge, Consciousness, and the Politics of Empowerment* (Boston: Unwin Hyman, 1990).
96. Davis et al., *Abolition*. See also Zillah Eisenstein, *Abolitionist Socialist Feminism: Radicalizing the Next Revolution* (New York: Monthly Review Press, 2019); Angela Y. Davis, *Freedom Is a Constant Struggle: Ferguson, Palestine, and the Foundations of a Movement*, ed. Frank Barat (Chicago, Illinois: Haymarket Books, 2016).
97. A preconditioned for Rawlsian justice. Rawls, *A Theory*.
98. Daniel Byman, "White Supremacy, Terrorism, and the Failure of Reconstruction in the United States," *International Security* 46, no. 1 (Summer 2021): 53–103.
99. As elaborated in later sections, well before the formation of the KKK, Whites were aggressively recruited to form private militias to enforce White rule and Black subordination (Ibid., 76). Also noteworthy, the recent data leak from the Oath Keepers reveals more than thirty-eight thousand names on the Oath Keepers's membership list, with hundreds of current public officials, police, and the military among their ranks. ADL.org, "The Oath Keepers Data Leak: Unmasking Extremism in Public Life," September 6, 2022, www.adl.org/resources/report/oath-keepers-data-leak-unmasking-extremism-public-life.

    See also Mike Wendling, "Oath Keepers: Leaked Membership List Includes Police and Politicians," *BBC News*, September 8, 2022, www.bbc.com/news/world-us-canada-62827612.
100. Trump's elevation to the presidency has prompted comparisons with Johnson. Charles Lane (2017). "Trump Is Trying to Compare Himself to Andrew Johnson. Wrong Andrew," *Washington Post*, February 8, 2017, www.washingtonpost.com/opinions/trump-is-trying-to-compare-himself-to-andrew-jackson-wrong-andrew/2017/02/08/483d77a8-ee1f-11e6-b4ff-ac2cf509efe5_story.html. Recent scholarly works on Johnson appear more reticent than older studies to use terms like "racism," "racist," "White supremacy," and "White supremacist" to characterize Johnson, his policies, politics, and worldview. They fail to call racism what it is, instead using euphemisms that rarely announce racist imaginary or intent. However, even earlier analyses were not as transparent as Johnson was about his preference for White supremacy. Johnson's singular achievement as president was dismantling dreams of a genuine democratic polity, or abolition democracy. He was instrumental in ensuring that the infrastructure of White supremacy and White rule would remain intact by sanctioning if not encouraging the rebirth of a plantation south.
101. More than any other US presidents, Johnson's stock rises and falls frequently. In these times of MAGA and Trumpism, few openly embrace Johnson as a satisfactory president.
102. These "achievements" would eventually attract the Nazis to California to learn how to Nazify Germany.

103. The convict leasing system ensured not only the continuation of coercive labor from free and former enslaved Black population, but also a social-material enforcement of White rule. See Douglas A. Blackmon, *Slavery by Another Name: The Re-enslavement of Black People in America from the Civil War to World War II* (New York: Doubleday, 2008).
104. Edwards, *The Other Side.*
105. Imaobong Denis Umoren, *Race Women Internationalists: Activist-Intellectuals and Global Freedom Struggles* (Oakland: University of California Press, 2017), 2.
106. The World's Columbian Exposition was so named for the commemoration of four hundred years of the dystopic adventures of Columbus and colonization.
107. Ida B. Wells, *The Reason Why the Colored American Is Not in the World's Columbian Exposition* (Chicago: Miss Ida B. Wells), 1893. Manuscript, Library of Congress http://hdl.loc.gov/loc.mss/mfd.25023. Remarkably, the Library of Congress continues to catalogue this pamphlet as part of the Frederick Douglass Papers collection (539; http://hdl.loc.gov/loc.mss/mfd.25023) even though the pamphlet was largely written by Wells, with contributions from Douglass and others.
108. Davis et al., *Abolition*, ch. II.
109. Massa also notes that Wells "had been run out of town [Memphis] for her impassioned denunciation of local lynchings." Anna Massa, "Black Women in the 'White City,'" *Journal of American Studies* 8, no. 3 (1974): 335–36.
110. Wells, *The Reason Why*, 14; emphasis added.
111. Jane Addams, "Respect for Law," *Independent*, January 3, 1901, https://digital.janeaddams.ramapo.edu/items/show/1264.
112. Ida B. Wells, "Lynching and the Excuse for It," *The Independent* 53, no. 2737 (May 16, 1901): 1133–36.
113. Cited in Maurice Hamington, "Public Pragmatism: Jane Addams and Ida B. Wells on Lynching," *The Journal of Speculative Philosophy* 19, no. 2 (2005): 167.
114. Ibid., 170.
115. Wells, "Lynching."
116. Even with such a public disagreement over such an important distinction, they continued collaborating in the long campaign for racial justice and democracy in the US. I find their disagreement instructive because it holds important lessons for understanding the politics of justice as compassion and the praxis of solidarity.
117. DoVeanna S. Fulton, *Speaking Power: Black Feminist Orality in Women's Narratives of Slavery* (Albany: State University of New York Press, 2006), 41.
118. Extending Hortense Spillers's insight that Black bodies should be read as cultural text and Hazel V. Carby's feminist critique, Fulton emphasizes orality as texts to demonstrate how White women slave owners exercised their "domestic" power over Black women. Carby's delineation of the "Cult of True Womanhood"—a term used by historians to characterize the prevailing bourgeoise gender ideology of the mid to late nineteenth century—subverted the assumptions that "true women" were submissive, pure, pious, and so on. This critique shows how Black women not only were excluded from considerations as "true" women, but also how they subverted and, in the process, reconstructed such gender disciplinary regimes. Hazel V. Carby, *Reconstructing Womanhood: The Emergence of the Afro-American Woman Novelist* (New York: Oxford University Press, 1987).

119. Historian Nell Irvin Painter appropriated the term "soul murder" from psychology to characterize the violence and injuries to Black people and the ways in which they in turn resist such attempted murders. Nell Irvin Painter, *Soul Murder and Slavery* (Waco: Markham Press, 1995).
120. Michael C. Berthold goes further in his critique to argue that, despite Larison's liberal sympathies for Dubois, "his very liberalism intwines with a litany of spurious, hierarchical oppositions that reify Dubois as 'small', 'abject,' or 'vicious'" while amplifying "her low class and her racial exoticism." These contradictions and anxieties reflect the "larger Reconstruction and post-Reconstruction anxieties of race and class." Michael C. Berthold, "'The Peals of Her Terrific Language': The Control of Representation in Silvia Dubois, a Biography of the Slav Who Whipt her Mistress and Gand her Fredom," *Melus* 20, no. 2 (Summer 1995): 4–5.
121. Even when she was over a hundred years old, she was reportedly "a woman of prodigious strength." *Princeton Press*, Saturday May 5, 1888, www.stoutsburg-cemetery.org/stories/silvia-Du Bois/. Lobdell questioned the very authenticity of Dubois's life story, including her age, suggesting that Dubois's biography should be treated along the line of myths and folklores. He provided no independent verification of his own research, yet questioned Dubois's veracity over the account of her confrontation with the mistress, arguing that Dubois would not have struck the "obviously pregnant" Mrs. Dubois. Fulton, on the other hand, accepts Silvia Dubois's assertion about her age, and rejects Lobdell's evidence as "unconvincing." Fulton, *Speaking Power*, 58.
122. Painter, *The History*. Davis argues that it was the slave quarter that provided the support that Black men and women needed to survive the violence and brutality of the plantation system. She argues that they also cultivated a different life ethos—a form of radical social egalitarianism that was part and partially a dialectical response to exploitation and oppression. Davis, "The Black Woman's Role." See also Davis, *Women, Race & Class.*
123. Robinson, *Black Marxism*; Ferguson, *The Reorder of Things.*
124. Davis, "The Black Woman's Role." Davis wrote this essay while incarcerated without bail facing trumped up capital charges (of which she was eventually exonerated) for her radical solidarity with US political prisoners. This essay anticipates Davis's 1981 groundbreaking, now classic, *Women, Race & Class*, an intersectional analysis of Black feminist resistance in the US, presciently interrogating a wide range of topics—from birthing and housework to rape and slave resistance, unionization, reproductive freedom, and revolutionary thought.
125. In doing so, Davis drew attention to the now thoroughly discredited *Moynihan Report* that has served for half a century with "its spurious content and propagandistic mission" to conceal the nature of racial capitalism and heteropatriarchy by weaponizing the mythic pathology of a strong Black woman as part of "the fatal by-product of slavery." Davis, "The Black Woman's Role." See also Hill Collins, *Black Feminist Thought.*
126. Davis, "The Black Woman's Role," 4.
127. Ibid., 1.
128. Ibid., 1n1; emphasis added.
129. Ibid., 4.
130. Ibid., 7.
131. Ibid., 14. This publication, the *Combahee River Collective Statement*, and the Third World Women's Alliance would form a critical foundation for the con-

temporary intersectional paradigm in feminist analytics, including Kimberlé Crenshaw's critical race theory and early work on violence against Black women. See Kimberlé Crenshaw, *On Intersectionality: Essential Writings* (New York: New Press, 2019). See also Kimberlé Crenshaw et al., eds., *Critical Race Theory: The Key Writings That Formed the Movement* (New York: New Press, 1995).

132. In speculative fiction and transgenic posthumanist thought, singularity is a cipher for a host of ideas about total (machine) dominion. Singularity in technoscience anticipates a future where technological advancement produces powerful artificial intelligence that transcends humanity. John Von Newman is supposed to have defined "singularity" as the moment when technological progress accelerates to the point of incomprehensible by humans. Stanislaw Ulam, "John von Newman 1903–1957," *Bulletin of the American Mathematical Society* 64, no. 3 (1958): 5. Today it is commonly understood that with the advent of nano technology, robotics, and genetics advancement, technological singularity would be achieved by a super artificial intelligence (SAI), with potentially catastrophic outcomes as it no longer depends on humans for self-improvement. Ray Kurzweil, for instance, argues that with accelerated technological mastery, humans will achieve biological transcendence by transferring our intelligence to machines. Ray Kurzweil, *The Singularity Is Near: When Humans Transcend Biology* (New York: Viking, 2005). See also José Ignacio Latorre, "The Singularity," CCCBLAB, January 14, 2019, https://lab.cccb.org/en/the-singularity/.

Singularity thought, however, is not new. Monotheisms, including market fundamentalism, are ideologemes that aspire singularity. As chapter 6 illustrates, market fundamentalism has underwritten neoliberal economic programing and corporate technoscience that create the conditions for the rise of technological singularity and a speculative, transgenic, posthumanist world. I argue that within the context of singularity, complex analytics—such as the intersectional framework, including abolition feminism—are so generatively subversive. Here, too, Davis's acute theoretical insight notwithstanding, it is her persistent political visions of radical transformation that compel a closer study of the abolition feminist framework.

CHAPTER 3

1. Aristophanes, *The Acharnians*, ed. S. Douglas Olson (Oxford: Oxford University Press, 2002 [425 BC]).
2. Raphael Sealey, *A History of the Greek City States, ca. 700–338 B.C.* (Berkeley: University of California Press, 1976), 305.
3. Aristophanes, *Lysistrata*, ed. Jeffrey Henderson (Oxford: Clarendon Press, 1990 [411 BC]), xv.
4. Ibid., xviii.
5. David Stuttard, ed., *Looking at Lysistrata: Eight Essays and a New Version of Aristophanes' Provocative Comedy* (London: Bloomsbury, 2011), 3–4.
6. Aristophanes, *Lysistrata*, xix.
7. Ibid.; Stuttard, *Looking at Lysistrata*, 4.
8. Ibid., 5; Sealey, *History of the Greek.*
9. Ibid., 253.
10. June Jordan, *Some of Us Did Not Die: New and Selected Essays of June Jordan* (New York: Basic/Civitas Books, 2002), 242–44.

11. Walt Whitman, *Democratic Vistas: The Original Edition in Facsimile*, ed. Ed Folsom (Iowa City: University of Iowa, 1871/2010), 32.
12. It appears that the US alliance system could no longer be relied upon to "spread" the American brand of democracy, as revealed in the *New York Times*'s headline "U.S. Allies Drive Much of World's Democratic Decline, Data Shows." Max Fisher, "U.S. Allies Drive Much of World's Democratic Decline, Data Shows," *New York Times*, November 16, 2021, www.nytimes.com/2021/11/16/world/americas/democracy-decline-worldwide.html.
13. "What's Driving the Rise of Authoritarianism and Populism, in Europe and Beyond?" *World Politics Review*, September 11, 2020, www.worldpoliticsreview.com/insights/27842/the-rise-of-authoritarianism-and-populism-europe-and-beyond.
14. "French Presidential Election 2017 Results - 2nd Round," *France 24*, accessed May 3, 2022, https://graphics.france24.com/results-second-round-french-presidential-election-2017/.
15. Yves Herman, "Macron Wins Election but Le Pen's Far Right Goes Mainstream," *Al Jazeera*, April 25, 2022, www.aljazeera.com/news/2022/4/25/loss-is-victory-for-le-pens-far-right-in-frances-election.
16. Quan, *Growth Against Democracy*.
17. Robinson, *Terms*.
18. Robinson, *Terms*.
19. See Fredric Jameson, *The Political Unconscious: Narrative as a Socially Symbolic Act* (Ithaca, NY: Cornell University Press, 1981).
20. Finley, *Democracy*, 30.
21. Ibid., 108.
22. Ibid., 177.
23. Robinson, *Terms*, 13.
24. Ibid., 15–17.
25. Joseph A. Schumpeter, *Capitalism, Socialism and Democracy* (London: Routledge, 2003).
26. Ibid., 184. Elsewhere Schumpeter dismissed "direct democracy" as an impossibility by tautology. Here is his unsubstantiated reasoning: "And since it is obvious that excepting the case of 'direct democracy' the people as such can never actually rule or govern, the case for this definition seems to be complete" (246).
27. Ibid., 243.
28. Ibid., 250.
29. Ibid., 299, 269.
30. Robinson, *Terms*, 17.
31. Ibid., 18.
32. Ibid.
33. Ibid., 20–21.
34. Mills, *Black Rights*, 139.
35. Brian Barry, *Theories of Justice: A Treatise on Social Justice*, vol. 1 (Oakland: University of California Press, 1991); Mills, *Black Rights*.
36. Rawls, *Justice as Fairness*, 21.
37. Ibid., 131.
38. As Mills points out, the problem with this is "the concept of white supremacy then forces us to confront the possibility that the basic structure is itself system-

atically racialized and thus unjust," such that "corrective measures to end racial justice would therefore need to begin here." Mills, *Black Rights*, 118.

39. Rawls, *Justice as Fairness*, 65; emphasis added.
40. Mills, *Black Rights*, xiv.
41. Ibid., 139.
42. Ibid., 141. These books are: *A Theory of Justice* (1971), *Political Liberalism* (1993), the *Collected Papers* (1999), and *The Law of Peoples* (1999).
43. Some feminist scholars, including Susan Okin, similarly found Rawls's theorization of justice wanting for the lack of interrogation of gender and patriarchy. Susan Moller Okin, *Justice, Gender, and the Family* (New York: Basic Books, 1989). See also Enrique Dussel, *Ethics of Liberation: In the Age of Globalization and Exclusion* (Durham, NC: Duke University Press, 2013), 116–17.
44. Quan, *Growth Against Democracy*, 234. Remarkably whereas he takes up (however precursory) antisemitism, Nazism, and the Jewish Holocaust, the South and slavery merit only a single footnote, and as Mills found, "imperialism appears nowhere in the text, nor colonialism, nor the Atlantic slave trade, nor any mention of their legacy in the Third World." Mills, *Black Rights*, 145.
45. Rawls condemns racism (along with religious intolerance) as "unjust," describes "principles of explicit racist doctrines" as "irrational," and acknowledges that "racial and ethnic inequalities . . . are seldom, if ever, to the advantage of the less favored." Cited in Mills, *Black Rights*, 142. Mills thus argues that the omission of race (and gender) in Rawls's body of work "is structural and symptomatic of white political philosophy in general" (Ibid., 147).
46. Rawls explains that in the mythical original position, subjects are "behind the veil of ignorance," where they have no awareness or consciousness of their social positioning and the subjects are generically presumed to be rational, moral, equal, and free. Terms of coexistence are thus within the context of "fair agreement between free and equal persons." Rawls, *Justice as Fairness*, 16–17. Remarkably, despite being completely ignorant of their complex personhood, these subjects somehow are able to discern their political choices, and electing fairness as the most important principle of justice.
47. Cedric J. Robinson, *Black Movements in America* (New York: Routledge, 1997), 1. Alexis de Tocqueville, *Democracy in America*, 2 vols. (New York: Vintage Books, 1954 [1835]).
48. Pateman identified Schumpeter as the progenitor of pluralist theories of democracy, underwriting some of the most important work on pluralism, including the work by Robert A. Dahl and others. Carole Pateman, *Participation and Democratic Theory* (Cambridge: Cambridge University Press, 1970), 8–14. Among mainstream political theorists in the west, very little has changed since Pateman made this assessment five decades ago.
49. Robert A. Dahl, *Who Governs? Democracy and Power in an American City* (New Haven, CT: Yale University Press, 1961), 305. As Peter Bachrach and Aryeh Botwinick argue, such theorization left out class divisions and class struggles. Peter Bachrach and Aryeh Botwinick, *Power and Empowerment: A Radical Theory of Participatory Democracy* (Philadelphia: Temple University Press), x.
50. Dahl's "groundbreaking work" *Who Governs?* was based on data drawn from New Haven, Connecticut (home to Yale), and Oberlin, Ohio, another college town in the US. Several of Dahl's students applied his conclusions based on the New Haven data to other localities, including the national level. Claude J. Bur-

tenshaw, "The Political Theory of Pluralist Democracy," *Western Political Science Quarterly* 21, no. 4 (December 1968): 577–88. At the height of the midcentury social movement era, Dahl thought he could extrapolate findings from two predominately White, small college towns in the US without considerations of larger, more urban, and diverse spaces of politics, exposes the parochialism of American political science and the pseudoscientific method that he claimed to abhor.

51. Peter Bachrach, *The Theory of Democratic Elitism* (Boston: Little Brown, 1967).
52. Heinrich Best and John Higley, eds., *Democratic Elitism: New Theoretical and Comparative Perspectives* (Boston: Brill, 2010), [illegible].
53. Ibid., 9.
54. Ibid., 11.
55. Bachrach and Botwinick, *Power and Empowerment*, 32.
56. Robinson, *Terms*, 21.
57. Cited in Jill Lapore, "The Last Time Democracy Almost Died," *New Yorker*, January 27, 2020, www.newyorker.com/magazine/2020/02/03/the-last-time-democracy-almost-died.
58. Cited in Lapore, "Last Time." This must have been news to the Filipinos, Puerto Ricans, and Haitians, not to mention Native Americans. Elsewhere, C. A. Griffith and I have noted Beard's racist imaginary of Japanese Americans as having great propensities for spying on behalf of militarist Japan. C. A. Griffith and H. L. T. Quan, *Mountains That Take Wing/Angela Davis & Yuri Kochiyama: A Conversation on Life, Struggles & Liberation* (New York: QUAD Productions/Women Make Movies, 2009), documentary, 97 min.
59. Cited in Lepore, "Last Time."
60. As a newspaper tycoon, William Randolph Hearst, for instance, provided Hitler a platform while attacking progressive dissidents and antifascist formations in the US. See Rodney Carlisle, "The Foreign Policy Views of an Isolationist Press Lord: W. R. Hearst and the International Crisis, 1936–41," *Journal of Contemporary History* 9, no. 3 (July 1974): 217–27.
61. A number of American progressives and reformers openly embraced eugenics as a social reform before and after the rise of Nazi Germany, and the eugenics movement, with California as its epicenter, would later serve as a resource for Nazi race policy. Edwin Black, *War against the Weak: Eugenics and America's Campaign to Create a Master Race* (Washington, DC: Dialog Press, 2012).

    Many American eugenicists "welcomed Hitler's plans as the logical fulfillment of their own decades of research and effort" (Ibid., ch. 14), and California's anti-immigrant activist and Eugenic Society founder, Charles M. Goethe, boasted to E. S. Gosney of San Diego: "Your work has played a powerful part in shaping the opinion of the groups of intellectuals who are behind Hitler in the epoch-making program" (ch. 13). Goethe whose grandparents migrated to the US, infamously and publicly defended Germany's genocidal policy. In 1947 he helped establish California State University, Sacramento, and bequeathed to it part of his $24 million estate, his residence and eugenics library. Tony Platt, "Curious Historical Bedfellows: Sac State and Its Racist Benefactor," *Sacramento Bee*, February 29, 2004.
62. Wendy Brown, *Undoing the Demos: Neoliberalism's Stealth Revolution* (New York: Zone Books, 2015), 9.

63. Ibid., 9. Kyong-Min Son argues that "the exclusive focus on neoliberalism as the culprit of the erosion of democracy" is limiting because it erroneously establishes "the 1970s as the starting point of the crisis of democracy, and describing the postwar period preceding neoliberalism's visible ascendance as the golden age of democracy" (2020, 4).
64. Brown, *Undoing*, 9.
65. Ibid. At least a decade before Brown's *Undoing the Demos*, other scholars similarly delineated neoliberalism. A normative order that gets deployed as a governing rationality might be characterized as a "neoliberal governmentality," a term Aihwa Ong employs in her remarkable work *Neoliberalism as Exception*. See Ong's *Neoliberalism as Exception*, and Lisa Duggan's *The Twilight of Equality* as two very different but equally pathbreaking examples of such scholarship.
66. Brown, *Undoing*, 52.
67. Ibid., 55.
68. Ibid., 41.
69. Ibid.
70. Ibid.
71. Ibid., 79.
72. Ibid., 86.
73. Ibid., 88.
74. Ibid., 94–95.
75. Ibid., 87.
76. Cited in Brown, *Undoing*, 110.
77. Marx, for instance, understood that there are limits to political emancipation without completely overhauling the material basis of oppression.
78. Brown, *Undoing*, 19.
79. Ibid., 88.
80. Ibid., 88–89.
81. Aristotle, *Politics*, trans. Earnest Barker (Oxford: Oxford University Press, 1995), 136.
82. Ibid., 109.
83. Ibid., 99.
84. Ibid., 102.
85. Ibid., 159.
86. Ibid., 167. Here, Aristotle associates "extreme democracy" with all the people deciding as tyrannical.
87. Ibid., 180.
88. Ibid., 181.
89. This conflation of equity with equality persists in contemporary era.
90. Robinson, *Terms*, 7.
91. Schmitt, *Political Theology*; Agamben, *Homo Sacer, and State of Exception*.
92. Robinson, *Terms*, 2.
93. Ibid., 4.
94. Ibid., 8.
95. Umberto Eco, *Serendipities: Language and Lunacy*, trans. William Weaver (New York: Columbia University Press, 1998), 54–55.
96. Ibid., 55.
97. Ibid., 53.
98. Ibid.

99. Ibid., 59.
100. It is interesting that in today's neoliberal world where venture capital roams freely, a unicorn is not just "an animal that looked like a gentle and slender white horse with a horn on its muzzle," but also "a privately held startup company with a value of over $1 billion" (Investopedia.com). The contemporary connotation, however, retains the unicorn's medieval magical quality.
101. Brown, *Undoing*, 19.
102. Ibid., 89.
103. Ibid., 91.
104. Ibid., 244–45n61.
105. Aristotle, *Politics*, 10–11 (Book I, ch. 2). More than two millennia later, there has not been significant progress in this area, if western political philosophy is any indication. Elsewhere I point out that a chief architect of deconstruction, Jacques Derrida, suggests that the "sovereign has power *over everything*," and "sovereignty is both timeless and outside of history." Quan, "It's Hard to Stop," 177. Taking a cue from Aristotle, Heidegger, to whom Derrida owes an intellectual debt, goes further and maintains that the polis is the "historical place, the There *in* which, *from* which and *for* which history happens." Cited in Strong, "Tyranny and Tragedy," 111. Within these frames, the polis and sovereign are life itself, without which life ceases to be significant.
106. Brown, *Undoing*, 43. On Aristotelian economics, see Quan, *Growth Against Democracy*; see also Karl Polanyi, *The Great Transformation* (New York: Farrar & Rinehart, 1944); and Scott Meikle, *Aristotle's Economic Thought* (Oxford: Clarendon Press, 1995).
107. Brown acknowledges the various formulations of "mere life," including that of Aristotle where she notes that "Aristotle ontologized an unfree order, one based on slavery, gender and class domination, and divided humanity between those condemned to mere life and those free to pursue the good life." She also reports that "Arendt was infamously uncritical of Aristotle ontology." Brown, *Undoing*, 232–33n45.
108. Ibid., 44–45. Here, Brown comes closest to getting at the heart of the problem with a capitalist, market fundamentalist society.
109. Robinson, *Terms*; Federici, *Re-Enchanting the World*. See also Frantz Fanon, *The Wretched of the Earth* (New York: Grove Press, 1963); Jordan, *Some of Us*.
110. Jordan, *Some of Us*, 3.
111. Brown, *Undoing*, 88.
112. Ibid., 88.
113. Thanassis Samaras argues that this serves as "the philosophical foundation" for the subordination of women in the public sphere. Thanassis Samaras, "Aristotle on Gender in Politics I," *History of Political Thought* 37, no. 4 (Winter 2016): 595.
114. G. E. M. de St. Croix, *The Class Struggle in the Ancient Greek World: From the Archaic Age to the Arab Conquests* (Ithaca, NY: Cornell University Press, 1981). See also R. F. Stalley, "Introduction and Notes," in *Politics* (Oxford: Oxford University Press, 1995).
115. de St. Croix, *Class Struggles*, 53. Aristotle points to the lack of slaves by some men to rationalize the exploitation and subordination of women and children in their homes.

116. Aristotle, *Politics*, 13–14. Aristotle drew from Sparta, where some women were incorporated into the ruling class, as an example of where "the position of women is poorly regulated" (68).
117. de St. Croix, *Class Struggles*, 72.
118. Aristotle, *Politics*, 35–36.
119. Elsewhere I argue that the moral authority of the state and its agents is not only dubious but also exhibits a peculiar preference for authoritarianism. For instance, the lack of prosecution and conviction against police who kill reflects the lack of epistemic justice for the victims of and protestors against police racial profiling and homicide. This injustice stems from the prevalent perception that the police's moral authority is superior to the moral authority of victims and witnesses, especially if the latter are Black and Brown people. H. L. T. Quan, "Introduction: Looking for Grace in Redemption," in *Cedric J. Robinson On Racial Capitalism, Black Internationalism, and Cultures of Resistance*, ed. H. L. T. Quan (London: Pluto, 2019). See also Fanon, *The Wretched*; and Miranda Fricker, *Epistemic Injustice: Power and the Ethics of Knowing* (New York: Oxford University Press, 2007).
120. Aristotle, *Politics*, 16.
121. de St. Croix, *Class Struggles*, 72.
122. Ibid., 73. Aristotle's recognition of class conflict is clear as he noted that "those who have a greater share of wealth than others tend to conceive themselves as superior" (Ibid.).
123. Stalley, "Introduction and Notes," 386.
124. Aristotle, *Politics*, 67.
125. de St. Croix, *Class Struggles*, 52.
126. Ibid., 79.
127. This may explain why anti-slave associations would fear outlaw slave parties where bond people reclaimed their life and time, given how leisure engenders acts of reclamation.
128. See for instance a passage in Aristotle's *Politics* where he referenced Hesiod for noting the poor man's use of an ox "in lieu of household slaves" (Aristotle, *Politics*, Book I, ch. 2), and another about a propertyless man (*aporos*) who could not afford slaves and instead used his wife and children (Book VI, ch. 8).
129. Stalley, "Introduction and Notes," 387. Stalley also suggests Aristotle's ideas of freedom and individual liberty contain inherent contradictions (405).
130. de St. Croix, *Class Struggles*, 74–75. See also Aristotle, *Politics*, 109–11.
131. Cynthia Farrar, *The Origins of Democratic Thinking: The Invention of Politics in Classical Athens* (New York: Cambridge University Press, 1988), 5n4.
132. Brown, *Undoing*, 17.
133. Ibid.
134. On human sacrifice, see Rane Willerslev, "God on Trial: Human Sacrifice, Trickery, and Faith," *HAU: Journal of Ethnographic Theory* 3, no. 1 (2013): 140–54. See also Alicia Garza, a cofounder of #Black Lives Matter on oppression as "systematically and intentionally targeted for demise." Alicia Garza, "A Herstory of the #BlackLivesMatter Movement," in *Are All the Women Still White? Rethinking Race, Expanding Feminism*, ed. Janell Hobson (Albany, NY: SUNY Press, 2016).
135. Hannah Arendt, "Lying in Politics: Reflections on the Pentagon Papers," *New York Review*, November 18, 1971. See also Edward S. Herman and Noam Chomsky,

Manufacturing Consent: The Political Economy of the Mass Media (New York: Pantheon Books, 1988), and Jason Stanley, *How Propaganda Works* (Princeton, NJ: Princeton University Press, 2015).

136. See Smith, *Conquest*; Henry A. Giroux, *Stormy Weather: Katrina and the Politics of Disposability* (New York: Routledge, 2006); Jasbir K. Puar, *The Right to Maim: Debility, Capacity, Disability, Anima* (Durham, NC: Duke University Press, 2017); and Tiffany Willoughby-Herard, *Waste of White Skin: The Carnegie Corporation and the Racial Logic of White Vulnerability* (Oakland: University of California Press, 2015).
137. Brown, *Undoing*, 80.
138. Ibid., 206.
139. See Etienne Balibar and Immanuel Wallerstein, *Race, Nation, Class; Ambiguous Identities* (London: Verso, 1993). See also Étienne Balibar, *Equaliberty: Political Essays*, trans. James Ingram (Durham, NC: Duke University Press, 2014); and *On Universals: Constructing and Deconstructing Community*, trans. Joshua David Jordan (New York: Fordham University Press, 2020).
140. See the Brennan Center for Justice's "Voting Laws Roundup: May 2021," brennancenter.org/our-work/research-reports/voting-laws-roundup-may-2021, or their extensive research on "The Myth of Voter Fraud," www.brennancenter.org/issues/ensure-every-american-can-vote/vote-suppression/myth-voter-fraud. See also Mayer, *Dark Money.*
141. Freeland, *Plutocrats.*
142. Farrar, *The Origins.*
143. Ibid., 1.
144. Ibid., 274.
145. Ibid., 276.
146. Robinson, *Terms.*
147. Farrar, *The Origins*, 276.
148. Ibid.
149. Finley, *Democracy*, 5.
150. Ibid.; Farrar, *The Origins.*
151. Finley, *Democracy*, 48.
152. This "redescription of freedom flies in the face of conventional freedom." Farrar, *The Origins*, 267.
153. Plato, *The Republic*, trans. Benjamin Jowett (Mineola, NY: Dover Publications, 2000), Book 3.
154. Huey P. Long is credited with suggesting that if fascism comes to America, it would call itself anti-fascist. Although wrong about the external source of fascism, Long wasn't entirely wrong about how it reveals itself in the US.
155. Robinson, *Cedric J. Robinson*, 129.
156. Ibid., 142.
157. Here I am including work by liberal feminists like Nancy Fraser, who attacks maldistribution and misrecognition as fundamental problematics of pluralist societies. Nancy Fraser, "Rethinking the Public Sphere: A Contribution to the Critique of Actually Existing Democracy," *Social Text*, no. 25/26 (1990): 56–80. See also Nancy Fraser, *Scales of Justice: Reimaging Political Space in a Globalizing World* (New York: Columbia University Press, 2009).
158. Foucault, "Governmentality"; Foucault, "Society Must Be Defended."

159. Aristotle acutely understood the exclusionary nature of electoral competitions, and in our time, a few super-rich people are also wary of how increasingly Aristotle's insight defines electoral reality. In the US, for instance, the Patriotic Millionaires exemplifies this trend as they support legislations to reform campaign financing and the electoral system. https://patrioticmillionaires.org/endorsed-bill-the-for-the-people-act/.
160. Saul David Alinsky, *Rules for Radicals: A Practical Primer for Realistic Radicals* (New York: Random House, 1971).
161. Had mainstream social movement scholars sought out noncanonical works and practiced discursive subversion, they would have had access to an embarrassment of riches: personal memoirs and testimonies by nonleaders such as women, peasants, and slave narratives, and even folktales about peasant rebellions. In the last several decades there have also been many publications by community organizers and scholar activists who are able to provide firsthand accounts and insights about "the stuff of movements." See, for instance, Combahee River Collective, "Statement"; Davis, *Abolition Democracy*; Ransby, *Making All Black Lives*; and Jobin-Leeds and AgitArt, *When We Fight*; Robin D. G. Kelley, *Hammer and Hoe: Alabama Communists During the Great Depression* (Chapel Hill: University of North Carolina Press, 1990); *Freedom Dreams: The Black Radical Imagination* (Boston: Beacon Press, 2002); Judy Tzu-Chun Wu, *Radicals on the Road: Internationalism, Orientalism, and Feminism during the Vietnam Era* (Ithaca: Cornell University Press, 2013); and Barbara Ransby, *Ella Baker and the Black Freedom Movement a Radical Democratic Vision* (Chapel Hill: University of North Carolina Press, 2003)—to name a few.
162. Gramsci posited that communities have their own "organic intellectuals" who are intimately familiar with the sociomaterial life of which they are a part. Antonio Gramsci, *Selections from the Prison Notebooks* (New York: International Publishers, 1971).
163. Saul David Alinsky, *Reveille for Radicals* (Chicago: University of Chicago Press, 1946), 12; emphasis added.
164. Ibid., 70.
165. Ibid., 70–71.
166. Ibid., 73.
167. Alinsky's model has been ably critiqued, particularly for its masculinist, top-down, hierarchical approach to community organizing. See for instance Frances Fox Piven and Richard A. Cloward, *Poor People's Movements: Why They Succeed and How They Fail* (New York: Vintage, 1978); and Heidi J. Swarts, *Organizing Urban America: Secular and Faith-Based Progressive Movements* (Minneapolis: University of Minnesota Press, 2008).
168. Alinsky, *Reveille*, 97.
169. Ibid.
170. Ibid., 108.
171. Ibid., 201.
172. Ibid., 210.
173. Ibid.
174. It is doubly ironic that Alinsky, well acquainted with capitalist exploitation and White supremacy, and to a lesser extent, patriarchy, failed to understand how racial capitalism and heteropatriarchy may produce a context that makes it impossible to extol the US as "the greatest democracy on earth" (Ibid.).

175. Ibid., 208–9.
176. Ibid., 209.
177. Ibid., 215–6.
178. Ibid. 216.
179. Ibid., 210, 211.
180. Ahmed, *Living*, ix.
181. Ibid., 1.
182. Audre Lorde, "The Master Tools Will Never Dismantle the Master's House," in *Sister Outsider: Essays and Speeches* (Toronto: Sister Visions Press, 1984), 110–13.
183. Ahmed, *Living*, 160.
184. Ibid., 67.
185. Ibid., 72.
186. Ibid., 85.
187. Ibid., 110.
188. Ibid.
189. Twenty-three US states have this process. First introduced in South Dakota in 1898, it was used in Oregon in 1902, allowing Oregonians to directly introduce initiative amendments to the state constitution.
190. Sponsored by the California Association of Realtors and passed in June 1978, Proposition 13 amended California's Constitution and mandated that local real estate be appraised at 1975 value levels, and "limited the property tax rate to 1 percent plus the rate necessary to fund local voter-approved indebtedness and limited future property tax increases to a maximum of 2% per year." California State Board of Equalizer, Publication 29—"California Property Tax: An Overview," 1. One of its key effects has been the underfunding of California's public education and intensifying unequal distribution of public investments in school districts. This initiative had many unintended consequences, including the loss of control by local communities in their ability to decide social welfare expenditures. Jeffrey I. Chapman, "Proposition 13: Some Unintended Consequences," Public Policy Institute of California—www.ppic.org/content/pubs/op/OP_998JCOP.pdf. See also "Proposition 13: Its Impact on the Nation's Economy, Federal Revenues, and Federal Expenditures," *Background Paper* by the Congressional Budget Office (CBO, July 1978), U.S. Government Printing Office.
191. Excluding jury duty, very few mechanisms exist where citizens directly participate in the deliberation process. Few localities have experimented with collective budgeting. Voting, a mechanism that denies citizens the ability to directly deliberate policy, is an imperfect measure given the overwhelming advantage and influence of wealthy individuals and corporate actors.
192. Ahmed, *Living*, 236.
193. Ibid., 237.
194. Davis, *Women, Race & Class*; Evelyn Nakano Glenn, "From Servitude to Service Work: Historical Continuities in the Racial Division of Paid Reproductive Labor," *Signs: Journal of Women in Culture and Society* 18 (1992): 1–43; Dorothy Roberts, "Spiritual and Menial Housework," *Yale Journal of Law and Feminism* 9, no. 51 (1997): 51–80; Barbara Ehrenreich and Arlie Russel Hochschild, *Global Woman: Nannies, Maids, and Sex Workers in the New Economy* (New York: Metropolitans Books, 2003); and Eileen Boris and Jennifer Klein, *Caring for America Home Health Workers in the Shadow of the Welfare State* (New York: Oxford University Press, 2012).

195. Ahmed, *Living*, 85.
196. Davis, *Women, Race & Class*; Roberts, *Killing*; Silvia Federici, *Caliban and the Witch* (New York: Autonomedia, 2004); Silvia Federici, *Revolution at Point Zero: Housework, Reproduction, and Feminist Struggle* (Oakland: PM Press, 2012); Mignon Duffy, "Doing the Dirty Work: Gender, Race and Reproductive Labor in Historical Perspectives," *Gender & Society* 21, no. 3 (2007): 313–36; and Sutapa Chattopadhyay, "Violence on Bodies: Space, Social Reproduction and Intersectionality," *Gender, Place & Culture* 25, no. 9 (2019): 1295–1304.
197. Prison nation conceptually suggests a broader carceral society than the term "prison industrial complex." It refers to "those dimensions of civil society that use the power of law, public policy, and institutional practices in strategic ways to advance hegemonic values and to overpower efforts by individuals and groups that challenge the status quo." Beth Richie, *Arrested Justice: Black Women, Violence, and America's Prison Nation* (New York: New York University Press, 2012), 3.
198. Davis et al., *Abolition*.
199. Lorde, "A Litany."
200. Robinson, *Terms*, 21.
201. Ibid., 17.
202. Ibid., 18.
203. Olsen asserts that White supremacy is the primary undercurrent of American antidemocracy, functioning as the "glue" that holds racial capitalism and democratic elitism together. Joel Karleton Olsen, "The Democratic Problem of the White Citizen" (Dissertation, University of Minnesota, 2001). See also Joel Olsen, "The Freshness of Fanaticism: The Abolitionist Defense of Zealotry," *Perspectives on Politics* 5, no. 4 (2007): 685–86.
204. M4BL and CLEAR 2021, i. M4BL asked Creating Law Enforcement Accountability & Responsibility (CLEAR) to investigate the excessive charges Black protestors were facing, especially during protests related to George Floyd's death. Their "data and findings largely corroborate what Black organizers have long known institutively and from lived experience about the government's policing and prosecution of racial justice protests and related activity." M4BL and CLEAR, "'Struggle for Power': The Ongoing Persecution of Black Movement by the U. S. Government," (2). M4BL.org. https://m4bl.org/wp-content/uploads/2021/08/Struggle-For-Power-The-Ongoing-Persecution-of-Black-Movement-by-the-U.S.-Government.pdf.
205. Ibid., iv.
206. Robert A. Dahl, *Dilemmas of Pluralist Democracy: Autonomy vs. Control* (New Haven, CT: Yale University Press, 1982), 28.

CHAPTER 4

1. James, *Black Jacobins*, 86. The 1791 slave revolution in Santo Domingo (present-day Haiti) is one of the most significant revolutions in the modern western hemisphere. Initially with little success, by 1793 the Black masses had achieved control over most of Santo Domingo.
2. During this time and before the slave revolution, Santo Domingo, a French colony, was the US's second-largest trading partner, ranking only after Great

Britain. Douglas R. Egerton, *Gabriel's Rebellion: The Virginia Slave Conspiracies of 1800 and 1802* (Chapel Hill: University of North Carolina Press, 1993), 169.

3. Contemporary historians have noted the dearth of attention paid to this event, which had ensnared at least two future US presidents: James Monroe and Thomas Jefferson. According to Michael Nicholls, the history of "Gabriel's conspiracy" largely was ignored for nearly a century, with the exception of "short accounts appearing in newspaper columns during the sectional crises and Civil War." Michael L. Nicholls, *Whispers of Rebellion: Narrating Gabriel's Conspiracy* (Charlottesville: University of Virginia Press, 2012), 1.
4. Cited in Nicholls, *Whispers*, 2, in William P. Palmer, ed., *Calendar of Virgina State Papers and Other Manuscripts* (1875).
5. Ibid.
6. Ibid., 3. According to Nicholls, Palmer also attributed some of the blame to "neglectful state leaders." Palmer's characterization of Virginia slavery as permissive and lacking in capacity to govern is problematic at best. This dubious portrayal of Virginia's slavery system, which later served as a blueprint elsewhere, surfaced in subsequent works about Gabriel's Conspiracy, including the first scholarly book length account—Egerton's *Gabriel's Rebellion*. Ibid., 4–8.
7. James Sidbury, *Ploughshares into Swords: Race, Rebellion, and Identity in Gabriel's Virginia*, 1730–1810 (New York: Cambridge University Press, 1997), 6.
8. Ibid.
9. Ibid., 7.
10. Egerton, *Gabriel's Rebellion*, ix.
11. Sidbury, *Ploughshares*, 7.
12. Egerton, *Gabriel's Rebellion*, ix.
13. Sidbury, *Ploughshares*, 7–8. According to Nicholls, twenty-five men were executed. Nicholls, *Whispers*, 1. According to Eric Foner, twenty-six slaves were hanged, and dozens more were taken out of the state. Eric Foner, *Voices of Freedom: A Documentary History*, 6th ed., vol. 1 (New York: W. W. Norton and Company, 2020), 174.
14. Ahmed, *Willful Subjects*.
15. Sidbury, *Ploughshares*, 57.
16. Foner, *Voices*, 175.
17. Ibid. St. George Tucker's lengthy *A Dissertation on Slavery*, circulated four years before Gabriel's attempted rebellion, was specific—"down to what sort of blanket black women would be given at age twenty-eight"—advocating gradual emancipation through expulsion from Virginia plantations, a small improvement from Jefferson's proposal to evict free Black people from the US. Tucker betrayed his racist authoritarian predisposition, advocating against the franchise, and the ability to hold office, own property, bear arms, marry White people, serve as an attorney, or prepare a will. Despite its modesty, Virginia Assembly refused to take it up for debate. Egerton, *Gabriel's Rebellion*, 14–15. Egerton credits this failure as fueling the flames of insurrection (Ibid., 15). Among the many supporters of resettlement schemes were slave owning elites such as Henry Clay, Elias Caldwell, John Randolph, as well as the architects of "Jeffersonian democracy"—Jefferson and Madison.
18. Nicholls, *Whispers*, 4.
19. Ibid., 3–4.
20. Ibid., 7.

21. Egerton, *Gabriel's Rebellion*, ix.
22. Ibid., x.
23. Ibid.
24. Cited in Egerton, *Gabriel's Rebellion*, 47. As early as April of that year, Monroe reported rumors "'of a negro insurrection'" to then Vice President Jefferson.
25. Ibid., 50. I must confess befuddlement of the needless adjective to characterize Gabriel as a large man, especially in light of Egerton's otherwise outstanding work.
26. Ibid.
27. Ibid., 51.
28. Ibid. Egerton maintains that Gabriel was a highly literate and astute reader of early American politics. As Nicholls asserts, Egerton's "portrait of Gabriel's ideology was essentially political," interpreting Gabriel's bold ambition to garner poor White support and to transform "the plot into a class revolt rather a racially focused slave uprising against White Virginians." Nicholls, *Whispers*, 7.
29. See James R. Martel, *The Misinterpellated Subject* (Durham, NC: Duke University Press), 2017.
30. The Virginia-based Culpeper Minutemen were part of a militia fighting against the British during the first year of the American Revolution, and during the Civil War, on the side of the Confederates. Their flag, recycled various times, contains a rattlesnake, and during the American Revolution contains the phrase "Liberty or Death" along with "Don't Tread on Me." See William James Van Schreeven and Robert L. Scribner, *Revolutionary Virginia, the Road to Independence* (Charlottesville: University Press of Virginia, 1973).
31. Cited in Egerton, *Gabriel's Rebellion*, 10.
32. As a secretary to the Board of Trade and Plantation, Locke was tasked with colonial trades and drafting the *Fundamental Constitutions*. Mattie Erma Edwards Parker, ed., *North Carolina Charters and Constitutions, 1578–1698* (Raleigh: Carolina Charter Tercentenary Commission, 1963). See John Locke, *Two Treatises of Government*, ed. John Laslett (New York: Cambridge University Press, 1988 [1690]); *A Letter Concerning Toleration*, 4th ed. (Wilmington: Printed and sold by James Adam, in Market-Street, 1764).
33. For Locke and other social contract theorists, the introduction of the state is rationalized by the imagined conditions of "the state of nature"—a mythical device to speculate what life might be like without government. Accordingly, the protection of one's private possessions, including one's body, becomes increasingly difficult if the population is large and goods are scarce—conditions that are at best speculative. Here, humans are deemed more likely to violate some unspecified natural laws, with life becoming increasingly more precarious, if not succumbing entirely to a more horrific imagining of life as "evil, brutish, and short" as Hobbes previously imagined. Thomas Hobbes, *Leviathan, Edited with Introduction and Notes by Edwin Curley*, ed. Edwin Curley (Indianapolis: Hackett Publishing, 1994 [1668]). Interestingly, Locke's argument about the emergence of the state represents a modest shift: unlike Plato and Aristotle who saw the polis as a condition of possibility for justice, Locke and other modern social contract theorists saw the political community, especially the state, as simply a means to protect private property.
34. Following Pateman and Mills, I read social contract theory largely as a defense of the subjugation of othered subject and the social contract as contracts of

exploitation and domination. Pateman and Mills, *Contract and Domination*. See also Carole Pateman, *The Sexual Contract* (Stanford: Stanford University Press, 1988); Charles W. Mills, *The Racial Contract* (Ithaca: Cornell University Press, 1997).

35. Locke specified property holding requirements for jury duty with increasingly more stringent requirements for greater jurisdiction. *Fundamentals of Constitution*, Sixty-Eight; emphasis added. Nor was Locke much of a free believer with his stipulation that "no man shall be permitted to be a freeman of Carolina, or to have estate or habitation within it, that doth not acknowledge a God, and that God is publicly and solemnly to be worshiped." *Fundamentals of Constitution*, Ninety-Five. See Parker, *The Colonial Records of North Carolina*, vol. 1, 187–205.
36. Employed by the Lords of Proprietor, Locke was also an investor in the Royal African Company, England's slave-trading entity. Locke earned a large profit when he finally sold his shares. He also held shares in another slave-trading company—the Bahamas Adventures. Wayne Glausser, "Three Approaches to Locke and the Slave Trade," *Journal of the History of Ideas* 51, no. 2 (1990): 201.
37. That there remain "controversies" over Locke's defense of "natural slavery" reveals more about the paucity of contemporary political theory and the lack of thoroughness in research than it does about Locke's position on slavery. See Pateman and Mills 2007, 45-46; and William Uzgallis, "John Locke, Racism, Slavery, and Indian Lands," in *The Oxford Handbook of Philosophy and Race*, ed. Naomi Zack (Oxford: Oxford University Press, 2017).
38. Locke, *Two Treatises*, chapter 4.
39. While Locke rejected the Stuarts as illegitimately enslaving the English people, he had little qualms about English people enslaving Black people. Glausser, "Three Approaches."
40. Egerton, *Gabriel's Rebellion*, 10.
41. Egerton helpfully points out that at the 1776 Virginia Convention, many planters bitterly complained about its constitutional preamble—"all men are by nature equally free and independent" for fear of future use for emancipation. As if drafted by Locke himself, the phrase, "when they enter into a state of society" was thus added as a form of appeasement to allay slave owners' concerns. This appeasement worked because, as Pateman and Mills argue, for these White planters, women, slaves, and Native Americans, "had done no such thing" (Ibid., 11). If the other remained in the permanent state of nature and had not entered civil society, then they had no entitlement to the protection of the civil government. Hence, the marking of these subjects as "ungoverned" and ungovernable.
42. Robinson, *Terms*, 18–19.
43. Pateman, *Participation*, 20.
44. James Oakes, *Slavery and Freedom: An Interpretation of the Old South* (New York: Knopf eBooks, 1990), chapter 2.
45. Ibid.
46. Ibid.
47. Cited in Egerton, *Gabriel's Rebellion*, 100.
48. Ibid., 147.
49. Even after learning of the plot from Richmond mayor James McClurg, Monroe elected to "do nothing"; McClurg, however, "quietly strengthened local patrols" (Ibid., 67).

50. Slave patrol systems varied by regions and localities, and tactics of enforcement; although, for those who were the targets of this surveillance and capture system, "urban and rural patrols were all the same." Sally E. Hadden, *Slave Patrols: Law and Violence in Virginia and the Carolinas* (Cambridge, MA: Harvard University Press, 2001), 61.

    The patrol regiment put in place after Gabriel's Rebellion "drove almost one hundred Virginia free blacks to state their intention to emigrate to Liberia, a public declaration that some must have hoped would forestall worse treatment at the hands of patrols" (Ibid., 115).
51. Egerton, *Gabriel's Rebellion*, 148–49. A resolution to reward those who informed on plotters also passed, along with a resolution deemed "progressive" because it advocated expulsion of rebels (be sold outside of state) instead of execution.
52. Hadden, *Slave Patrols*, 149. Typically, "once a threatened revolt seemed fully subdued, the increased number of patrols soon returned to their pre-insurrection state" (Ibid., 150). What is remarkable about Gabriel's near insurrection is that not only was there no actual revolt, but the patrolling of Black lives did not diminish. Instead of a general demilitarization, policing became more "militarized" through militias and armed patrols.
53. Egerton, *Gabriel's Rebellion*, 119.
54. Ibid.
55. Ibid., xi.
56. Ibid., 43.
57. Ibid., 167.
58. Ibid., 167–68.
59. Ibid., 168. In 1783, more than a decade before St. George Tucker's plan, Jefferson drafted an even "more modest" plan, consistent with his vision of a slave-dependent democracy, to be part of his model constitution. Children of bonded people would remain in bondage until adulthood "because Jefferson could not envision large numbers of free blacks living in perfect harmony besides their former masters, his plan also called for immediate deportation of those emancipated." It did not materialize except as part of a collection of his *Notes on the State of Virginia*. Ibid., 12.
60. Egerton, *Gabriel's Rebellion*, 168–69.
61. Ibid.
62. Ibid., 169.
63. Ibid., 168–69. As is well documented, on the questions of slavery and appropriation of Indigenous land, Jefferson's "darker side" is "notorious": In sum, "Jefferson's dark side is also the dark side of American history, and in this, too, the affinity between the man and the nation is complete." Robert W. Tucker and David C. Hendrickson, *Empire of Liberty: The Statecraft of Thomas Jefferson* (Oxford: Oxford University Press, 1992), 7.
64. Cited in Egerton, *Gabriel's Rebellion*, 14. Indeed, in his *Notes on the State of Virginia*, and as early as 1781, Jefferson foresaw genocide as a potential outcome if Black people were not subjected to expulsion and resettlement outside of the newly formed US. Thomas Jefferson, *Notes on the State of Virginia* (New York: Barnes & Noble, 2010 [1788]), 145–53.
65. Foner, *Voices*, 157. See also Jefferson, *Notes*.
66. Jefferson deployed pseudoscientific reasoning to justify his racist belief when he delineated a series of nonsense as the basis for his speculative knowledge of

an entire race, couched in a self-serving, pseudo-rationality. Jefferson, *Notes*, 172–73.

67. Douglass G. Adair, *The Intellectual Origins of Jeffersonian Democracy: Republicanism, the Class Struggle, and the Virtuous Farmer* (Lanham: Lexington Books, 2000 [1943]), 165.
68. Ibid., 22.
69. Ibid., 44, 39.
70. Ibid., 45.
71. Tucker and Hendrickson, *Empire of Liberty*, 162.
72. The *Alien Act* passed in 1798 legalized the deportation of foreign subjects whom the government deemed "dangerous," while the *Sedition Act*, passed the same year, made it a crime to criticize the government in print or public forums. See Jonathan Elliot, ed., *The Debates in the Several State of Convention on the Adoption of the Federal Constitution*, vol. 5 (Philadelphia: J. B. Lippincott & Co., 1859).
73. Ibid., 528–29.
74. Egerton, *Gabriel's Rebellion*, 40.
75. UShistory.org, "20b. Jefferson Ideology," *Jeffersonian America: A Second Revolution?*, www.ushistory.org/us/20b.asp.
76. Andrew W. Robertson, "Afterward: Reconceptualizing Jeffersonian Democracy," *Journal of the Early Republic* 33 (Summer 2013): 334.
77. Thomas Jefferson, "Inaugural Address," in *The Papers of Thomas Jefferson*, Vol. 33 (Princeton, NJ: Princeton University Press, 2006 [1801]).
78. Jefferson, *Notes*. That Jefferson excluded Black and Indigenous peoples from consideration for political incorporation is not simply a matter of omission, as claimed by some writers who disagree with works critical of Jefferson's views on race. See M. Andrew Holowchak, *Rethinking Thomas Jefferson's Writings on Slavery and Race* (Cambridge: Cambridge Scholars Publishing, 2020); see also Peter Thompson, "David Walker's Nationalism—and Thomas Jefferson's," *Journal of the Early Republic* 37, no. 1 (2017): 47–80.
79. Locke's thesis on labor is credited for naturalizing "life, liberty, and property" as *inalienable* rights, and was foundational to Jefferson's plantocratic thought. As Locke prescribes in *the Two Treatises*, Jefferson assumed that a) land is of abundance (thus of no value); and b) the laborers themselves do not produce, but planters do. As such, slaves and landless farmers do not themselves "make improvement on the land." Previously, land was understood nominally as one of the most important sources of wealth. With the proliferation of settler colonialism, particularly with settlements in the New World and the systematic use of slave labor, European thinkers demoted the land while over valorized the admixture of technology (or know how—à la Adam Smith) and labor. Both Locke and Jefferson erroneously claimed the importance of producer wealth (making improvement on the land), while denying the worth and humanity of the Indigenous peoples on whose land they appropriated values, and the men and women who worked those lands, be they enslaved or free.
80. The appropriation of Indigenous land was central to racial capitalism; however, the open wars, the harboring of runaway slaves, and the collaboration between Indigenous and Black people must have also heighten the fear of the "ungovernable native."
81. Cited in Robinson, *Cedric J. Robinson*, 343.

82. Ibid., 341.
83. Thompson, "David Walker's Nationalism," 58.
84. Robinson, *Cedric J. Robinson*, 348.
85. Ibid.
86. Walker, *APPEAL*, 77–79.
87. Robinson, *Cedric J. Robinson*, 352.
88. Ibid., 349.
89. Alexis de Toqueville, *Democracy in America, Volume 1*, trans. Henry Reeve, Ebook #815 ed. (Project Gutenberg, 2006 [1835]), ch. III.
90. Jennifer Pitts, "Introduction," in *Writings on Empire and Slavery by Alexis de Tocqueville*, ed. Jennifer Pitts (Baltimore: Johns Hopkins University Press, 2001), xiv. See also Anthony Bogues, *Empire of Liberty: Power, Desire, & Freedom* (Hanover, NH: Dartmouth College Press, 2010); Gerald M. Bonetto, "Tocqueville and American Slavery," *Canadian Review of American Studies* 15, no. 2 (Summer 1984): 123–39.
91. Cabral, *Return to the Source*.
92. Known as the "the Great Compromiser," Clay advocated for the admission of Missouri as a slave state (and Maine as a free state), ensuring a free state would be accompanied by a slave state for the next three decades. Key to Clay's "compromise" was the passage of the *Fugitive Slave Act* (1850). This law further codified slaves as property, requiring fugitives, when found, be returned to owners even in so-called free states, and tasked the federal government with the responsibility to do so. It explicitly denied suspected fugitives the right to jury trial thus any Black person, free or enslaved, could be captured, and without trial, enslaved and removed from their communities. It also required citizens to assist the federal government as enforcers of slavery. The recent trend in anti-abortion enforcement state statutes (e.g., *Texas Senate Bill 8* or the *Texas Heartbeat Act*, 2021) is reminiscent of this practice.
93. See The Combahee River Collective, "Statement." See also BLM, "Black Lives Matter . . . What We Believe," 2013, https://blacklivesmatter.com/what-we-believe/.
94. Fredrick Douglass's *North Star* published its first installment in December 1847 and merged with the *Liberty Party Paper* in 1851 to become the *Frederick Douglass' Paper*. Then and today, the *North Star* is considered the most important Black newspaper and an antislavery institution. David Ruggles, "Letter to the Editor published in the North Star," *The David Ruggles Collection*, 1848, at the David Ruggles Center for History and Education, Florence, Massachusetts, https://davidrugglescenter.org/.
95. Ruggles, "Letter to the Editor."
96. Robinson, *Forgeries*. See also Hill Collins, *Black Feminist Thought*.
97. Orlando Patterson, *Freedom Volume I: Freedom in the Making of Western Culture* (New York: Basic Books, 1991), 9.
98. Ibid. See also Orlando Patterson, *Slavery and Social Death: A Comparative Study* (Cambridge, MA: Harvard University Press, 1982).
99. When some slaves reappropriated branding "as a badge of honor instead of infamy," slave owners replaced it with "more gruesome" methods. Patterson, *Slavery*, 59.
100. James Madison, *Federalist No. 10 - Primary Documents in American History*, 1787. https://guides.loc.gov/federalist-papers/text-1-10#s-lg-box-wrapper-25493273.

101. Ibid.
102. Ibid.
103. Ibid.
104. Ibid.
105. Adair, *Intellectual Origins*, 5.
106. Ibid.
107. Ibid. See also Charles A. Beard, *An Economic Interpretation of the Constitution of the United States* (New York: The Macmillan Company, 1913).
108. Beard, *Economic Interpretation*. See also Oakes, *Slavery and Freedom*.
109. Importing new labor into the system (e.g., migrants, women, children) is a form of relief meant to alleviate labor pressures. Disciplining both previously domesticated labor and newly imported labor becomes paramount for such a system. Hence, terror tactics used on the newly domesticated laborers such as sexual violence, threats of deportation, wage theft and incarceration are disciplinary techniques for maintaining a compliant and profitable labor regime.
110. James Madison, *Notes of Debates in the Federal Convention of 1787* (New York: W. W. Norton, 1987 [1787]). Madison is credited with the "three-fifths" constitutional clause because he was the first to introduce the three-fifths formula at the Continental Congress in 1783. This "compromise" was intended to resolve differences between slaveholding and non-slaveholding states over the control of the US House of Representatives, allowing slaveholding states to count slaves as part of their apportionment along with an added share of tax burden, thus extending a structural advantage to slaveholding states with respect to the control of the House and the Presidency. This clause gave slaveholding states a distinct advantage over non-slaveholding states until the ratification of the *Thirteenth Amendment* in 1965, when slavery was abolished, "except as a punishment for crime."
111. Noah Feldman, *The Three Lives of James Madison: Genius, Partisan, President*, ebook ed. (New York: Random House, 2017). William Gardener (or Billey) was Madison's "most valuable personal property" and had travelled with Madison as "man servant" to Philadelphia (Ibid., ch. 2). After living there for three years, Gardener was considered potentially dangerous, presumably because of exposure to city life and free Black people. Even though Madison clearly understood both the mechanics and metaphysics of race and slave ownership, and the fact that Pennsylvania had partially abolished slavery, Madison did not free Gardener. Naming himself William Gardener, he earned his freedom by fulfilling his labor contract, after Madison sold him into indentured servitude. Madison complained that Pennsylvania laws did not allow him to sell Gardener into a labor contract of "more than seven years," and thus he did "not expect to get near the worth of him" (cited in Feldman, *Three Lives*, ch. 2).
112. Ibid.
113. Ibid., ch. 1. See also Jay Cost, *The Price of Greatness: Alexander Hamilton, James Madison, and the Creation of American Oligarchy*, ebook ed. (New York: Basic Books, 2018).
114. Feldman, *Three Lives*, ch. 1.
115. Central to Feldman's thesis of Madison as pragmatic genius is Madison's three-fifths proposal. Ibid., ch. 4 and conclusion.
116. Feldman, *Three Lives*, ch. 4.
117. Ibid.

118. Cited in Feldman, *Three Lives*, ch. 4.
119. There is ample evidence, including Madison's own Convention notes, to verify "that the delegates had deliberately manufactured 'a sordid sectional compromise' with slavery.'" Robinson, *Black Movements*, 46.
120. Jefferson reportedly elected to drop this version after realizing slavery would be foregrounded in the document.
121. James Madison, "Virginia Ratifying Convention, June 20, 1788," in *The Papers of James Madison*, ed. William T. Hutchinson, William M. E. Rachal, and Robert Allen Rutland (Chicago: University of Chicago Press, 1962 [1788]).
122. Ibid.
123. Ronald T. Takaki, *Iron Cages: Race and Culture in Nineteenth-Century America* (Seattle: University of Washington Press, 1982), 8–9. In *Iron Cages*, Takaki beautifully delineates a litany of hypocrisies and contradictions among early republicans. Among these were Jefferson's views on women as definitely *not* "equal & independent," alleging French women for lacking self-control when they were interested in politics, in contrast to (White women) in the US who were "too wise to wrinkle their foreheads with politics" (cited in Takaki, *Iron Cages*, 41), and portraying survivors of rape and sexual assaults as the real aggressors. Equally cogent is Jefferson's home economics. Few areas of profiteering escaped Jefferson's scrutiny, assessing that "a woman who brings a child every two years more profitable than the best man." Cited in Marie Jenkins Schwartz, *Birthing a Slave: Motherhood and Medicine in the Antebellum South* (Cambridge, MA: Harvard University Press, 2006), 68.
124. Hamilton famously wrote in *Federalist No. 55* that "had every Athenian citizen been a Socrates, every Athenian assembly would still have been a mob." Alexander Hamilton *Federalist No. 55*, February 13, 1788, Founders Online, https://founders.archives.gov/.
125. Feldman, *Three Lives*, ch. 6. Recall that terms "slave" and "enslaved persons" did not appear in the actual text of the three-fifth clause, thus *Federalist No. 54* is revelatory, especially given that the purpose of its publication (and other *Federalist Papers*) was to persuade the New York electorate to ratify the Constitution in whole.
126. James Madison, *Federalist No. 54*, February 12, 1788, Founders Online, https://founders.archives.gov/. Authorship of *Federalist No. 54* has been disputed. Like the others, it was published under the pseudonym "Publius," though it has been attributed to either Hamilton or Madison, with Madison the presumed author.
127. Ibid.; emphasis added.
128. Feldman, *Three Lives*, ch. 6.
129. It is also possible then to read Madison's passage as either a warning or promise of a possible future where the law transforms the "mixed character" of this class of "other Persons" into Persons with rights.
130. One of the most enduring legacies of Jeffersonian antidemocracy is the assertion of states' rights in the form of nullification. Among the most efficient items in today's antidemocracy toolkit is voting suppression, at the state and local levels, effectively disenfranchising large segments of the population, especially communities of Color and formerly incarcerated people. William Wider, "Voter Suppression in 2020," *Resource*, The Brennan Center for Justice, August 20, 2021, www.brennancenter.org/our-work/research-reports/voter-suppression-2020;

Dana M. Peters and Catherine L. Mann, *Closing the Racial Inequality Gaps: The Economic Cost of Black Inequality in the U.S.* (Citi GPS, 2020).

Ten years after *Federalist No. 54*, Jefferson and Madison co-authored the official framework for nullification in the form of the Virginia and Kentucky Resolutions (of 1798). Separately, each advanced the argument that the federal government was merely a compact among states, and as such the states can determine when their rights are infringed upon; therefore, declaring the *Alien and Sedition Acts* of 1798 to be "void and of no force" (*Kentucky Resolution of 1787*), codifying for the states the role as final arbiters of authority. K. R. Constantine Gutzman, "The Virginia and Kentucky Resolutions Reconsidered: 'An Appeal to the Real Laws of Our Country,'" *The Journal of Southern History* 66, no. 3 (August 2000). 473–96.

131. See Feldman, *Three Lives*, conclusion.
132. Ibid.
133. Ibid.
134. The "Preamble" of the US Constitution prioritizes "domestic Tranquility" and "common defense," along with "Justice" and general "Welfare."
135. Eric Foner, "End of Slave Trade Meant New Normal for America," *NPR*, January 10, 2008, www.npr.org/templates/story/story.php?storyId=17988106.
136. Robinson, *Black Movements*, 26.
137. *United States Constitution*, Article I, Section 9, Clause 1. The narrative that scripts slaves as a distinct species to justify their subjugation appears to be unstable and incoherent, as slaves show up as "other Persons" or simply as "Person."
138. Feldman, *Three Lives*, conclusion. Feldman devotes a fair amount of attention to Madison's dealings with slaves and slavery, but he is almost blasé toward Madison's "pragmatism," rendering his overall assessment lacking, if not specious. See also Robinson, *Black Movements*, 20.
139. Feldman, *Three Lives*, conclusion.
140. Cited in Ibid. This is a response to Robert J. Evans's solicitation to weigh in on how slavery should end. James Madison, "From James Madison to Robert J. Evans, June 15, 1819," in *The Papers of James Madison: Retirement Series, Vol. 1, 4 March 1817—31 January 1820*, ed. David B. Matter et al. (Charlottesville: University of Virginia Press, 2009 [1819]), 468–72.
141. Ibid.
142. Ibid.; emphasis added.
143. Madison's idea about reparation for White slave holders would bear fruit in the 1862 War when Lincoln signed the District of Columbia *Emancipation Act* with a compensation that entitled slave owners $300 (or $8,255 in today's valuation) for each person freed, without a similar reparation provision for former slaves.
144. Madison, "To Robert J. Evans."
145. Madison estimated in 1819 that "the aggregate sum needed may be stated at about $600 mils of dollars." Madison, "To Robert J. Evans."
146. Ibid.
147. Ibid.
148. In the pantheon of seventeenth- and eighteenth-century American vice presidents and congressmen, Calhoun had few equals regarding the maintenance of White supremacy and slavery as an institution. For many, slavery was profitable and "a necessary evil"; Calhoun, in contrast, had little doubt that slavery was a "positive good," and went as far as supplying a doctrine to declare that neither Congress nor the people living in the territories had the right to outlaw slavery.

See *Judgement in the U.S. Supreme Court Case Dred Scott v. Sandford* (1857), archives.org. See also Don Edward Fehrenbacher, *Slavery, Law, and Politics: The Dred Scott Case in Historical Perspective* (New York: Oxford University Press, 1981); and Eric Foner, *Free Soil, Free Labor, Free Men: The Ideology of the Republican Party before the Civil War* (New York: Oxford University Press, 1995).

149. Oakes, *Slavery and Freedom*; Pateman and Mills, *Contract and Domination*.
150. It is beyond the scope of this work to interrogate "Jacksonian democracy" thoroughly; suffice to say that this ideologeme is entirely consistent with Jeffersonian antidemocracy. See Joshua A. Lynn, *Preserving the White Man's Republic: Jacksonian Democracy, Race, and the Transformation of American Conservatism* (Charlottesville: University of Virginia Press, 2019).

CHAPTER 5

1. Barry Goldwater, "Speech Accepting the Republican Presidential Nomination," Republican National Convention, July 16, 1964, www.washingtonpost.com/wp-srv/politics/daily/may98/goldwaterspeech.htm.
2. Harriet Jacobs, *Incidents in the Life of a Slave Girl Written by Herself*, ed. Nell Irvin Painter (New York: Penguin Books, 2000), 50.
3. Oxford English Dictionary, www.oed.com/.
4. Those who conspired to assassinate Julius Caesar are believed to have been acolytes of Libertas. Besides the association with the pileus worn by freed slaves in ancient Greece, one of the more famous representations of Libertas was Galba's "Freedom of the People" coins after the death of Nero. Two years before he was assassinated, the Roman Senate sought to build a shrine to Libertas to recognize Caesar's achievement. More cogently, the frequency of slave rebellions in ancient Greece and later Rome was symptomatic of the oppressive sociomaterial ancient world, a topic that most ancient thinkers duly ignored. Adam Donaldson, "Peasant and Slave Rebellions in the Roman Republic" (PhD diss., University of Arizona, 2012).
5. Aristotle, *The Nicomachean Ethics*, trans. W. D. Ross, ed. J. O. Urmson (Oxford: Oxford University Press, 1980 [350 BC]), Book 6.
6. As noted, I use the phrase "contemporary radical republicanism" to characterize and reference the radical right, avoiding misidentifying contemporary Republicans as "conservatives," especially the Trumpite variety.
7. Goldwater, "Speech." See also Karl Hess, *In a Cause That Will Triumph: The Goldwater Campaign and the Future of Conservatism* (Garden City: Doubleday, 1967). Hess was a Cold Warrior, an anarcho-capitalist (sometimes identified as a libertarian) and Goldwater's speechwriter. He was responsible for drafting the Republican Party's 1960 and 1964 national platforms. During the most critical development of American libertarianism (1969–1971), Hess coedited *The Libertarian Forum* with the anarcho-capitalist Murray Rothbard; however, he did not officially join the Libertarian Party until the 1980s. Randy Langhenry, "Karl Hess—1923–1994" *LP News*, June 1994, https://web.archive.org/web/20051115021846/www.lp.org/lpn/9406-Hess.html.
8. Goldwater, "Speech."
9. See, for instance, Angela Y. Davis, *Are Prisons Obsolete?* (New York: Seven Stories Press, 2003); Rhonda Y. Williams, *The Politics of Public Housing: Black Women's Struggles Against Urban Inequality* (New York: Oxford University Press, 2004);

Ruth Wilson Gilmore, *Golden Gulag: Prisons, Surplus, Crisis, and Opposition in Globalizing California* (Oakland: University of California Press, 2007); and Elizabeth Hinton, *From the War on Poverty to the War on Crime: The Making of Mass Incarceration in America* (Cambridge, MA: Harvard University Press, 2016).

10. Ritchie, *Arrested Justice.*
11. Most notably, beginning with candidate Richard Nixon in 1968, modern Republicans and later "new Democrats" appropriated it wholesale.
12. Hinton, *From the War*, 8.
13. Ibid., 11.
14. Ibid., 27.
15. Ibid., 25.
16. Samuel P. Huntington, *Political Order in Changing Societies* (New Haven, CT: Yale University Press, 1968).
17. Mainstream American political science typically approaches containment politics and deterrence policies as creatures of international relations (IR). Within the Cold War paradigm, they typically emphasize the containment of communism and deterrence of emergent or contending global powers (e.g., the former USSR or the People's Republic of China). They frequently overlook how foreign affairs not only have consequences for domestic actors, but also that so-called foreign policies may specifically have been designed to target and pacify domestic enemies. Quan, *Growth Against Democracy.*
18. Goldwater was only the latest to have fashioned this particular language or "dog whistle" for racist politicking. He did not invent it nor was he terribly notable, given his unsuccessful bid for the top office in the nation.
19. M4BL and CLEAR, "Struggle for Power."
20. See Hans L. Trefousse, *Impeachment of a President: Andrew Johnson, the Blacks, and Reconstruction* (New York: Fordham University Press, 1999).
21. Sarah Wildman, "'You Will Not Replace Us': A French Philosopher Explains the Charlottesville Chant," *Vox*, August 15, 2017, www.vox.com/world/2017/8/15/16141456/renaud-camus-the-great-replacement-you-will-not-replace-us-charlottesville-white.
22. Rodríguez, *White Reconstruction*, 74.
23. Ibid., 74–75. Extending Du Bois's analytics, Rodríguez argues that the work of the Freedmen's Bureau be understood as "as a technology of state-managed emancipation." It was necessary for the counterrevolution as White Reconstruction, reanimating large scale anti-Black violence and White terrorism (76–79). Thus, there was little chance for the Bureau to succeed at its publicly stated mission because it "was an exercise of white governmentality that alleged to perform a feat of magic" (69).
24. Trefousse, *Impeachment*, xv.
25. Ibid., 4.
26. Cited in Trefousse, *Impeachment*, 5.
27. Ibid. Trefousse maintains that Johnson saw the emancipation amendments and the attempt to extend the franchise to Black men as radical impositions on the South, and proceeded to act accordingly, and "not wholly [unsuccessfully]" (7). Johnson misled both the radical and moderate Republican factions in Congress about his intentions on the franchise, and especially on the question of punishment for the act of treason by the confederates (8–9).
28. Ibid., 9.

29. Ibid., 11.
30. Trefousse, *Impeachment*, 11–12; emphasis added.
31. Elsewhere I argue that the regime of war reconstruction is integral to a savage developmental logic, as manifested in the aftermath of the Civil War and, similarly, in the US invasion and occupation of Iraq. Quan, *Growth Against Democracy*.
32. The failure of "The Special Field Order, No. 15" issued by Union General William T. Sherman is emblematic of White resistance to land redistribution, and belies the empty rhetoric of emancipation. "Special Field Orders, No. 15, Series 1865," *Official Records of the American Civil War*, Series 1, Vol. XLVII, Part II, 60–62. Library of Congress, mss83443, box 3; item 256: www.loc.gov/item/mss83434256/; see also Du Bois, *Black Reconstruction*, 394.
33. Trefousse, *Impeachment*, 12.
34. Ibid., 12–13.
35. Ibid., 15–16.
36. Ibid., 16.
37. Ibid., 23.
38. The idea that Jim Crow economics was a regional development is as dubious as it is to assume a national economy being discreet from the global economy, where international trade predominated.
39. Du Bois, *Black Reconstruction*, 7.
40. Robinson maintained that *Black Reconstruction* sought to transgress White supremacist historiography, especially on Reconstruction. Robinson, *Black Marxism*, 196.
41. The Black Codes, previously slave codes, were significantly expanded with Johnson's presidency, seeking total dominance of Black life. Post emancipation, they became an even more powerful apparatus for governing, encompassing "vagrancy, apprenticeship, labor contracts, migration, civil and legal rights." Du Bois, *Black Reconstruction*, 167. Whole categories of illegalities were invented in an attempt "to make Negroes slaves in everything but name" (135).
42. Ibid., 671.
43. Cited in Du Bois, *Black Reconstruction*, 671.
44. While one could quarrel with Du Bois about whether the South was relapsing into or merely extending barbarism, it is much harder to dispute his devastating observation that "lawlessness was its inheritance, and the red splotch of violence its birthmark." Ibid., 674.
45. Ibid., 631.
46. Ibid.
47. Ibid.
48. Ibid., 632.
49. Ibid., 130.
50. Ibid., 131.
51. Put differently, without White vigilante violence, be it Virginia under Monroe or the US under Johnson or Trump, a White autarchy would necessarily manufacture such violence to sustain and enforce racist fictions.
52. Du Bois, *Black Reconstruction*, 184.
53. Ibid., 187. Du Bois meticulously documented the history of White mobilization against the Black franchise, especially as part of the making of the US. Ibid., 7–10.

54. Ibid., 187.
55. Ibid.
56. Ibid., 189.
57. Ibid., 237. Du Bois argued that, with Johnson "forcing a hesitant nation to choose between the increased political power of a restored Southern Oligarchy and votes for Negroes," the White autocracy consisting of "the alliance between slave barons and big businesses . . . was determined at any price to amass wealth and power" (237; 182).
58. Jacobs, *Incidents in the Life*, 48.
59. Ibid., 101.
60. Arendt, *Origins*. See also Gramsci, *Prison Notebooks*.
61. Roberts, *Killing*, 23.
62. Ibid. A 1662 Virginia statue exemplifies "American's first laws concerned the status of children born to slave mothers and fathered by white men" (23).
63. Ibid., 24.
64. Ibid.
65. Schwartz, *Birthing*, 79.
66. Schwartz, *Birthing*, 68. Roberts cites testimony from the 1840 General Anti-Slavery Convention in London, where a planter intended to beat a group of women to death because he "[had] not had a young one" from them for "several months," to illustrate how planters "treated infertile slaves like damaged goods, often attempting to pawn them off on unsuspecting buyers." Roberts, *Killing*, 27.
67. Cited in Schwartz, *Birthing*, 67.
68. Roberts, *Killing*, 24. Given its reliance on reproduction and internal trades, slavery in the US revealed its "most odious features: [forcing] its victims to perpetual the very institution that subjugated them" through reproduction (Ibid.). Here Roberts makes an important intervention in the interpretation of sexual violence against slave women. She argues the legal doctrine of *partus sequitur ventrem* and Virginia colonial law (which specified the status of children follow the service condition of the mother) "reinforced their sexual exploitation" by assigning the status of property to the child resulted from the rape, while "[failing] to recognize the rape of a slave woman as a crime" (29). Building on the work of Angela Y. Davis, Roberts explains that even if it was also economically profitable, rape "was primarily a weapon of terror," intended to maintain "a submissive workforce" and to reinforce "whites' domination over their human property" (29). Thus, beyond coercive reproduction and even as "fulfillment of slaveholder's sexual urges," rape and other forms of sexual exploitation and violence against slaves were part of the slaveholder's governing toolkit. In this way, sexual violence as an instrument of terror shares similar governing functions as lynching does during the era of Jim Crow. Robert explains that just as Ida B. Wells understood that "white men used their ownership of the white females as a terrain on which to lynch the black male . . . white men also exploited Black women sexually as a means of subjugating the entire Black community" (30). Sexual violence and coercive reproduction are "part and parcel of whites' general campaign to control slave women's bodies" (Ibid.).
69. Cited in Roberts, *Killing*, 45.
70. Ibid., 45. See also Davis, "The Black Woman's Role," and *Women, Race & Class*.
71. Robert, *Killing*, 23. If "killing the Black body" was strategic to manifesting White dominion, then eugenics was one among its many lieutenants. Roberts argues

that eugenicists sought out "direct means of weeding out undesirable citizens," including coercive enforcement, rather than relying on nature to take its course. See also Smith, *Conquest*.

72. Roberts, *Killing*, 55.
73. Okin, *Justice, Gender*.
74. Roberts, *Killing*, 294–95.
75. Ibid., 294. The negative theory of reproductive rights, for instance, leaves intact asymmetrical power relations and structural inequalities, not to mention the long legacy of reproductive abuses against women of Color (297). Roberts points out that "theory of reproductive liberty . . . invalidates virtually every hindrance to affluent people's procreative options, [yet] easily permits much more coercive government programs targeting poor people" (Ibid.).
76. Ibid.
77. Ibid., 298.
78. Ibid., 1.
79. In *Republic*, Plato allowed, not only for the possibility of coopting a few women into the guardian class, but also for a partial abolition of the private family (451c–457b). In contrast to some scholars who have argued that these proposals are "revolutionary" and/or proto-feminist, I argue that Plato's proposal to appropriate a few elite women into the ruling class and assigning the state total control over reproductive matters, including raising children and the use of eugenics, does not constitute feminist transformation. These measures presumably are meant to free the guardian class from domestic concerns and to ensure that the state would have a ready and appropriate "stock" of citizens. Plato's proposal was an attempt to minimize civil strife among the ruling elite as he believed that strife typically comes from the top echelon of society. These proposals also anticipate Davis' delineation, as noted earlier, how slaveholders' attempt to minimize slave resistance by removing the Black family as a source of incitement, or Nazi Germany removing social functions from the private family. See C. C. W. Taylor, "The Role of Women in Plato's Republic," in *Virtue and Happiness: Essays in Honour of Julia Annas*, ed. Rachana Kamtekar (Oxford: Oxford University Press, 2012). See also Mary Townsend, *The Women Question in Plato's Republic* (Lanham: Lexington Books, 2017).

CHAPTER 6

1. Etel Adnan, *There: In the Light and the Darkness of the Self and of the Other* (Sausalito: Post-Apollo Press, 1997), 2, 44.
2. *CBS News*, "Witnesses: Elderly Asian Woman Assaulted; Fights Off Attacker in San Francisco," March 17, 2021, https://sanfrancisco.cbslocal.com/2021/03/17/elderly-asian-woman-beats-up-man-attacking-her-in-san-francisco/.
3. *CBS News*, "Elderly Asian Woman Attacked in San Francisco Fights Back, Sends Alleged Attacker to Hospital," March 18, 2021, www.cbsnews.com/news/asian-woman-attacked-san-francisco-fights-back/.
4. Bill Chappell, "Asian Grandmother Who Smacked Her Attacker with a Board Donates Nearly $1 Million," *NPR*, March 24, 2021, www.npr.org/2021/03/24/980760622/asian-grandmother-who-smacked-her-attacker-with-a-board-donates-nearly-1-million.

5. Giulia McDonnell Nieto del Rio and Edgar Sandoval, "Women of Asian Descent Were 6 of 8 Victims in Atlanta Shootings," *New York Times*, March 17, 2021.
6. *CBS News*, "Witnesses."
7. Ibid. See also stopaapihate.org for the latest data reports, especially the collaborative project between the National Asian Pacific American Women's Forum and Stop AAPI Hate: Drishti Pillai, Aggie J. Yellow Horse and Russel Jeung, "The Rising Tide of Violence and Discrimination Against Asian American Pacific Islander Women and Girls," Stop AAPI Hate and NAPAWF, 2021, https://stopaapihate.org/wp-content/uploads/2021/05/Stop-AAPI-Hate_NAPAWF_whitepaper.pdf.
8. Hua Hsu, "The Muddled History of Anti-Asian Violence," *New Yorker*, February 28, 2021, www.newyorker.com/culture/cultural-comment/the-muddled-history-of-anti-asian-violence. On how AAPI are both a "yellow peril" and "model minority," see Julia R. DeCook and Mi Huyn Yoon, "Kung Flu and Roof Koreans: Asian/Americans as the Hated Other and Proxies of Hating in the White Imaginary," *Journal of Hate Studies* 17, no. 1 (2021): 119–32.
9. This radical exclusion includes the terms of belonging such as the very first laws passed by the US Congress—the *Naturalization Act* of 1790, which specified that only a "free white person" could begin the naturalization process leading to citizenship. This racial restriction clause was not suspended until 1952, leaving these racist terms of belonging intact. Perhaps with the exception of Mexicans, the AAPI population has the distinction of being a group that was most systematically excluded from legal immigration. See Yao Li and Harvey L. Nicholson Jr., "When 'Model Minorities' Become 'Yellow Peril': Othering and the Racialization of Asian Americans in the COVID-19 Pandemic," *Sociology Compass* 15 (2021): e12849; and Angela R. Gover, Shannon B. Harper, and Lynn Langton, "Anti-Asian Hate Crime During COVID-19 Pandemic: Exploring the Reproduction of Inequality," *American Journal of Criminal Justice* 45 (2020): 647–67. See also Stanford M. Lyman, "The 'Yellow Peril' Mystique: Origins and Vicissitudes of a Racist Discourse," *International Journal of Politics, Culture and Society* 13, no. 4 (2000): 683–747.
10. Pillai, Yellow Horse, and Jeung, "Rising Tide."
11. Apparently the gunman had a fetish for "Asian" women. Rachel Ramirez, "The History of Fetishizing Asian Women," *Vox*, March 19, 2021, www.vox.com/22338807/asian-fetish-racism-atlanta-shooting; see also Celine Parreñas Shimizu, *The Hypersexuality of Race: Performing Asian/American Women on Screen and Scene* (Durham, NC: Duke University Press, 2007); and Shoba Sivaprasad Wadhia and Margaret Hu, "Decitizenizing Asian Pacific American Women," *University of Colorado Law Review* 93 (March 2022): 325–65.
12. Sylvia Wynter and Katherine McKittrick, "Unparalleled Catastrophe for Our Species? Or, to Give Humaness a Different Future: Conversations," in *Sylvia Wynter: On Being Human as Praxis*, ed. Katherine McKittrick (Durham, NC: Duke University Press, 2015), 10.
13. Dussel, *Ethics and Community*, and *Ethics of Liberation*; Adrian M. S. Piper, "Impartiality, Compassion, and Modal Imagination," *Ethics* 101, no. 4 (1991): 726–57.
14. Sylvia Wynter, "Unsettling the Coloniality of Being/Power/Truth/Freedom: Towards the Human, After Man, Its Overrepresentation—An Argument," *CR: The New Centennial Review* 3, no. 3 (Fall 2003): 257–337. In an interview with

McKittrick, Wynter argues that so long as we are committed to Man as the archetype for all beings and a model for the totality of social potentials, we could in effect encounter "unparalleled catastrophe for our species." Instead, and echoing Aimé Césaire, she calls for "a new science, a hybrid science: a science of the world," requiring "a rewriting of our current globally institutionalized order of knowledge." Wynter and McKittrick, "Unparalleled Catastrophe," 17–18.

15. Anthony Bogues, "The Human, Knowledge and the Word: Reflecting on Sylvia Wynter," in *After Man, Toward the Human: Critical Essays on Sylvia Wynter*, ed. Anthony Bogues (Kingston: Ian Randle Publishers, 2013), 317; Wynter, "Unsettling the Coloniality," 269.
16. Wynter and McKittrick, "Unparalleled Catastrophe," 11. Wynter characterizes anti-Black racism as symptomatic of western episteme or the modern order of knowledge. She argues that "the systematic devalorization of racial blackness was, in itself, *only* a function of another and more deeply rooted phenomenon; in effect, only the map of the territory, the symptom of the real cause, the real issue." Sylvia Wynter, "On How We Mistook the Map for the Territory, and Reimprisoned Ourselves in Our Unbearable Wrongness of Being, of Desêtre: Black Studies Toward the Human Project," in *A Companion to African-American Studies*, ed. Jane Anna Gordon and Lewis Gordon (Hoboken: John Wiley & Sons, 2006), 113.
17. David Scott, "The Re-Enchantment of Humanism: An Interview with Silvia Wynter," *Small Axe* 8 (September 2000): 197.
18. Ibid., 198.
19. Fanon, *Wretched.*
20. Denise Ferreira da Silva, "Before Man: Sylvia Wynter's Rewriting of the Modern Episteme," in *Sylvia Wynter: On Human Being as Praxis*, ed. Katherine McKittrick (Durham, NC: Duke University Press, 2015), 103. See also Joshua Bennett, *Being Property Once Myself: Blackness and the End of Man* (Cambridge, MA: Belknap Press, 2020).
21. Scott, "Re-Enchantment," 198.
22. Michel Foucault, "Of Other Spaces," *Diacritics* 16, no. 1 (Spring 1986 [1967]): 22–27.
23. Foucault, "Other Spaces," 23. Foucault provides a kind of "heterotopology" that delineates a series of counter sites such as "crisis heterotopias," which are sacred and forbidden places like those reserved for menstruating women, young people, and the elderly. He argues that these are now increasingly displaced by "heterotopias of deviation," which are places peopled by those who are seen as deviant in relations to the norms, such as prisons and mental institutions.
24. Ibid.
25. As cited in Helen Zia, *Asian American Dream: The Emergence of an American People* (New York: Farrar, Straus and Giroux, 2000), 20.
26. Yen Le Espiritu, *Asian American Panethnicity: Bridging Institutions and Identities* (Philadelphia: Temple University Press, 1992), 153.
27. Ibid., 159.
28. Reece Jones, *Violent Borders: Refugees and the Rights to Move* (New York: Verso Books, 2016).
29. Donna Haraway, "Tentacular Thinking: Anthropocene, Capitalocene, Chthulucene," *e-flux Journal* 75 (September 2016): 1–17.

30. Zuboff, *Surveillance Capitalism*. See also Judith Bessant, *The Great Transformation: History for a Techno-Human Future* (New York: Routledge, 2019).
31. Bernard Marr, "Smart Dust Is Coming. Are You Ready?" *Forbes*, September 10, 2018, www.forbes.com/sites/bernardmarr/2018/09/16/smart-dust-is-coming-are-you-ready/?sh=44463bef5e41.
32. Marr, "Smart Dust."
33. Seema C. Mohan and S. Arulselvi, "Smartdust Network for Tactical Border Surveillance Using Multiple Signatures," *Journal of Electronics and Communication Engineering* 5, no. 5 (March–April 2013): 1. Mohand and Aruslevi proposed "smart dust technologies" as a "low-risk" tactical border surveillance technology, presumably because both detection and the use of armed forces can be avoided. Aside from potential violations of a host of rights and liberties, the authors conceded that using smart dust technology in border surveillance would increase pollution" (9). To date and while no such "green smart dust" exists, proponents of mass surveillance and immigration hawks are pushing for a so-called "smart wall" along the US-Mexico border—a fantasy wall consisting of "ocean-to-ocean technological barrier made up of a patchwork of tools like drones and sensors to help surveil and identify unauthorized individuals crossing the borders." Shirin Ghaffary, "The 'Smarter' Wall: How Drones, Sensors, and AI are patrolling the Border," *Vox*, February 7, 2020, www.vox.com/recode/2019/5/16/18511583/smart-border-wall-drones-sensors-ai.

    Potential ethical concerns and human rights violations notwithstanding, such deployment of technologies is music to the ears of the security economy. For instance, and according to Emily Birnbaum of *The Hill*, "Elbit Systems of America, a U.S.-based subsidiary of top Israeli defense company Elbit Systems . . . 'stands ready' to expand its work at the border," where it already has deployed "integrated fixed towers" at the border in Arizona. Emily Birnbaum, "Trump, Dem Talk of 'Smart Wall' Thrill Tech Companies," *The Hill*, January 31, 2019, https://thehill.com/policy/technology/427929-trump-dem-talk-of-smart-wall-thrills-tech-companies.

    Arial surveillance through drones, real-time facial recognition by sophisticated algorithms, and perpetual surveillance through ground sensors and, potentially, mote networks, however, are no longer the stuff of speculative fiction but the reality of a border governing regime where major tech companies, immigration agencies, police, and the military are partners in the campaign for total border governance, including regulating the right to move. These twenty-eight organizations, including the American Civil Liberties Union and the Electronic Frontier Foundation, maintain that biometric and DNA data collection and analytics disproportionately burden communities of Color, along with the heightened risk of this technology being stolen or misused. Fight for the Future et al., "Re: Tech and Human Rights Organizations Call on Members of Congress to Commit Not to Fund Invasive Surveillance Technology at the Border," February 5, 2019, https://fightfortheftr.medium.com/25-tech-and-human-rights-organizations-call-on-congress-not-to-fund-invasive-surveillance-428b9add26ae.
34. Ruha Benjamin, *Race after Technology: Abolitionist Tools for the New Jim Code* (Boston: Polity Press, 2019).
35. Erobotic is part of the high-tech, multibillion-dollar love industry. See Simon Dubé and Dave Anctil, "Foundations of Erobotics," *International Journal of Social Robotics* 13, no. 6 (2021); Nicola Döring et al., "Sexual Interaction in

Digital Contexts and Its Implications for Sexual Health: A Conceptual Analysis," *Frontiers in Psychology* 12 (November 2021), https://doi.org/769732; and Nicola Döring, M. Rohangis Moohseni, and Roberto Walter, "Design, Use, and Effects of Sex Dolls and Sex Robots: Scoping Review," *Journal of Medical Internet Research* 22, no. 7 (July 2020).

36. Emily Guendelsberger, *On the Clock: What Low-Wage Work Did to Me and How It Drives America Insane* (New York: Little, Brown and Company, 2019), 9.
37. Ibid., 7.
38. Ibid., 8.
39. Is it a wonder that increasingly more and more young people in the US prefer socialism to the current status quo? A 2021 poll by Axios and Momentive shows 41 percent of young adults with favorable views of socialism. Julia Manchesta, "Majority of Young Adults in US Hold Negative view of Capitalism: Poll," *The Hill*, June 28, 2021, https://thehill.com/homenews/campaign/560493-majority-of-young-adults-in-us-hold-negative-view-of-capitalism-poll/.
40. Guendelsberger, *On the Clock*, 7.
41. Ibid.
42. Ibid., 6.
43. Ibid., 310.
44. Ibid. These fatalities include but are not limited to strokes, heart attacks and suicide, resulting from work exhaustions. Many of these workers have had to work extended hours, sometimes as many as twenty-four hours a day and/or averaging sixty to seventy hours per week.
45. Ibid. See also Emily Hunt, "Japan's Karoshi Culture Was a Warning. We Didn't Listen," *Wired*, February 6, 2021, www.wired.co.uk/article/karoshi-japan-overwork-culture.
46. In an accuracy test of "Rekognition," Amazon's face recognition software, the ACLU found an error-ridden algorithm, with 38 percent of people of Color falsely matched as someone else, and twenty-eight members of Congress mistakenly identified as "other people who have been arrested for a crime." Jacob Snow, "Amazon's Face Recognition Falsely Matched 28 Members of Congress with Mugshots," *ACLU Blog*, July 26, 2018, www.aclu.org/blog/privacy-technology/surveillance-technologies/amazons-face-recognition-falsely-matched-28.

    See also Amy Harmon, "As Cameras Track Detroit's Residents, a Debate Ensues over Racial Bias," *New York Times*, July 8, 2019, www.nytimes.com/2019/07/08/us/detroit-facial-recognition-cameras.html; and Joy Boulamwini and Timnit Gebru, "Gender Shades: Intersectional Accuracy Disparities in Commercial Gender Classification," *Proceedings of Machine Learning Research* 81 (2018): 1–15.

CHAPTER 7

1. As quoted by Bloomberg News, "Foxconn Workers in China Say 'Meaningless' Life Sparks Suicides," *Bloomberg News*, June 2, 2010, www.bloomberg.com/news/articles/2010-06-02/foxconn-workers-in-china-say-meaningless-life-monotony-spark-suicides. Ah Wei is a twenty-one-year-old Foxconn worker in Shenzhen, China. Wen's story was picked up by *Bloomberg Newswire*, and subsequently by several news outlets, including *The Star* of Aman, Jordan. Noting "the dust from the hundreds of mobile phones he has burnished over the

course of a twelve-hour overnight shift," the report tells its reader that "Ah Wei has an explanation" for why some of the workers at Foxconn have been dying by suicide. Wei shares that, while working, conversations are forbidden, bathroom breaks are limited, and the constant noise rendered his earplugs useless, causing hearing damage. *Bloomberg News*, "Foxconn Workers."

2. Cited in Jenny Chan, Mark Selden, and Ngai Pun, *Dying for an iPhone: Apple, Foxconn and the Lives of China's Workers*, ebook (London: Pluto Press, 2020), ch. 11. Yu Zhonghong is a twenty-one-year-old and a former Foxconn worker.
3. According to the Johns Hopkins coronavirus-tracking dashboard, eighteen months after SARS CoV-2 was recognized, global COVID-19 deaths reached five million (October 31, 2021), with the US, Brazil, India, Mexico, and the UK combined accounting for more than half. These are officially reported data that assumed a statistically significant undercount of actual COVID-19 deaths. Martin Belam and Samantha Lock, "Global Covid-19 Death Toll Passes 5m," *The Guardian*, November 1, 2021, www.theguardian.com/world/2021/nov/01/global-covid-19-death-toll-passes-5m.
4. Until 2021, these reports bore a simpler title: "Supplier Responsibility Progress Report." The 2021 report is now branded as "People and Environment in Our Supply Chain." Apple Inc., "People and Environment in Our Supply Chain: 2021 Annual Progress Report," www.apple.com/supplier-responsibility/pdf/Apple_SR_2021_Progress_Report.pdf.
5. At $2.46 trillion USD in market capitalization, Apple was displaced by Microsoft (at $2.49 trillion) on October 29, 2021, as the most valuable corporation in the world. Allison Prang, "Microsoft Eclipses Apple as Most Valuable Company," *Wall Street Journal*, October 29, 2021, www.wsj.com/articles/microsoft-overtakes-apple-as-most-valuable-company-11635516976. While market capitalization fluctuates, Apple remains one of the wealthiest corporations in the world. It was the first company to pass the $1 trillion market capitalization (2018), then only two years later it exceeded its $2 trillion valuation. Only the seven largest economies are bigger than Apple. Omri Wallach, "The World's Tech Giants, Compared to Size of Economies," *Visual Capitalist*, July 7, 2021, www.visualcapitalist.com/the-tech-giants-worth-compared-economies-countries/.
6. Apple Inc, "People," 1–2.
7. Ibid., 1–3. Of interest are Apple's claims of saving more than 41 billion gallons of fresh water since 2013 (though it does not report the total percentage of water use for making its products), and 110+ suppliers committing to building its products with "100% renewable energy," which likely constitutes only around 50 percent of its total supply chain. Page 13 of its report features snapshots of workers at various production facilities, showing almost all people of Color and a mix of genders, in stark contrast with Apple's executive profiles, showing a marginal improvement of executive hires after a vocal pushback from a group of large shareholders. Kerry Flynn, "This Is the Real Reason Apple's Senior Leadership Lacks Diversity," *Mashable*, https://mashable.com/article/apple-diversity-shareholders.

   See also Jacob Kastrenakes, "Apple Shareholders are Demanding More Diversity but the Company Is Fighting Back," *The Verge*, February 15, 2017, www.theverge.com/2017/2/15/14614740/apple-shareholder-diversity-proposal-opposition.
8. Apple Inc., "Privacy," 2021, www.apple.com/privacy/.
9. Tim Cook, "International Conference of Data Protection and Privacy Commissioners Keynote," October 24, 2018 (Brussels, Belgium), as transcribed by

American Rhetoric, www.americanrhetoric.com/speeches/PDFFiles/Tim%20 Cook%20-%20Data%20Privacy.pdf. Elsewhere Cook has criticized Facebook, one of its major competitors, of being incapable of regulating itself. Here Cook calls on governments "to protect privacy" given that corporations have failed to do so on their own. Isobel Asher Hamilton, "Tim Cook Mounted His Most Stinging Attack Yet on Companies like Facebook and Google That Hoard 'Industrial' Quantities of Data," *Business Insider*, October 24, 2018, www.businessinsider.com/apple-ceo-tim-cook-attacks-tech-firms-that-hoard-data-2018-10.

10. Zuboff, *Surveillance Capitalism*.
11. Eric Schmidt, "Keynote Speech at IFA," *International Funkausstellung Berlin*, September 7, 2010, www.youtube.com/watch?v=DtMfdNeGXgM.
12. Apple Inc., "Apple—Privacy—That's iPhone—Oversharing," September 30, 2020, www.youtube.com/watch?v=nGCv1XInKec.
13. John Koetsier, "Apple and the IDFA: Privacy Power Move or Cash Grab?," *Forbes*, September 4, 2020, www.forbes.com/sites/johnkoetsier/2020/09/04/apple-and-the-idfa-privacy-power-move-or-cash-grab/?sh=6fb478991036.
14. According to L. Ceci and the data experts at *Statista*, between 2016 and 2021 the app economy grew from USD$1.3 trillion to $6.3 trillion. L. Ceci, "Global App Economy Market Size 2016–2021," *Statista*, July 6, 2021, www.statista.com/statistics/267209/global-app-economy/. According to Apple's data, its App Store controlled more than half a trillion dollars in 2019. Apple Inc., "Apple's App Store Ecosystem Facilitated over Half a Trillion Dollars in Commerce in 2019," *Press Release*, June 15, 2020, www.apple.com/newsroom/2020/06/apples-app-store-ecosystem-facilitated-over-half-a-trillion-dollars-in-commerce-in-2019/.

    As Reed Albergotti at the *Washington Post* reports: "without warning, Apple can make [another company's] work obsolete by announcing a new app or features that essentially copies their ideas. Some apps have simply buckled under pressure. They generally don't sue Apple because of the difficulty and expense in fighting the tech giant—and the consequences they might face from being dependent on the platform." Reed Albergotti, "How Apple Uses Its App Store to Copy the Best Ideas," *Washington Post*, September 5, 2019, www.washingtonpost.com/technology/2019/09/05/how-apple-uses-its-app-store-copy-best-ideas/.
15. Koetsier, "Apple and the IDFA."
16. Albergotti, "How Apple Uses."
17. In the spirit of full disclosure, this author is completely dependent on Apple's ecological system, having paid tribute in the forms of an iPhone, iPad, and a MacBook Pro.
18. Albergotti, "How Apple Uses."
19. Chan, Selden, and Ngai, *Dying*.
20. Quan, *Growth Against Democracy*.
21. Jenny Chan, Mark Selden, and Pun Ngai maintain that there were eighteen Foxconn workers who attempted suicide, with fourteen deaths. Chan, Selden, and Ngai, *Dying*. It is difficult to get an accurate account of suicides, especially unsuccessful attempts, given the lack of corporate transparency as well as waning interest in news about working conditions, especially inside China, not to mention a lack of solidarity with Chinese workers beyond China's borders.
22. James C. Scott, *Weapons of the Weak: Everyday Forms of Peasant Resistance* (New Haven, CT: Yale University Press, 1985).

23. Malcolm Moore, "'Mass Suicide' Protest at Apple Manufacturer Foxconn Factory," *The Telegraph*, January 11, 2012, www.telegraph.co.uk/news/worldnews/asia/china/9006988/Mass-suicide-protest-at-Apple-manufacturer-Foxconn-factory.html.
24. Justin McCurry and Julia Kollewe, "China Overtakes Japan as World's Second-Largest Economy," *The Guardian*, February 14, 2011, www.theguardian.com/business/2011/feb/14/china-second-largest-economy; and World Bank, "GDP (Current US$) - Japan, China," *World Bank National Accounts Data* (and OECD national account data files), https://data.worldbank.org/indicator/NY.GDP.MKTP.CD?end=2018&locations=JP-CN&start=1978&view=chart.
25. Lois Beckett, "By the Numbers: Life and Death at Foxconn," *ProPublica*, January 27, 2012, www.propublica.org/article/by-the-numbers-life-and-death-at-foxconn.
26. Dan Lyons, "Media Suicide Watch: It's Working!" *The Secret Diary of Steve Jobs*, May 29, 2010, www.fakesteve.net/tag/foxconn-jumpers. Lyons provides a list of more than a dozen outlets ranging from *Business Insider* to the UK-based *Times Online*, as well as tech news websites such as *PC World*, *Gizmodo*, and *CrunchGear* reporting and downplaying the rash of worker suicides. To be sure, the US reading public (and its corporate media) were not the only ones shocked by the series of suicides; nevertheless, Lyons's compilation of media treatment shows a pattern of complicit downplaying of Apple's and other corporations' roles, but also the labor regime that gave rise to dire working conditions, and are contributing factors to such suicides.
27. Thung-hon Lin, Yi-ling Lin, and Wei-lin Tseng, "Manufacturing Suicides: The Politics of a World Factory," *Chinese Sociological Review* 48, no. 1 (2015): 16.
28. Remarkably consistent with the neoliberal regime of development, the Shenzen government, which sanctioned the transfer of workers to Wuhan, benefited directly from their pension funds—pocketing the 10 percent that Foxconn had paid monthly into the pension system during 2010 and 2011 for those transferred workers. Chan, Selden, and Ngai, *Dying*, ch. 11.
29. David Barboza, "Foxconn Resolves a Dispute with Some Workers in China," *New York Times*, January 12, 2012, www.nytimes.com/2012/01/13/technology/foxconn-resolves-pay-dispute-with-workers.html?ref=technology.
30. Chan, Selden, and Ngai, *Dying*, ch. 11.
31. Lin, Lin, and Tseng, "Manufacturing Suicides," 28.
32. Beckett, "By the Number"; see also Charles Duhigg and David Barboza, "In China, Human Costs are Built into an iPad," *New York Times*, January 25, 2012, www.nytimes.com/2012/01/26/business/ieconomy-apples-ipad-and-the-human-costs-for-workers-in-china.html?hp.
33. Lin, Lin, and Tseng, "Manufacturing Suicides," 1.
34. Ibid., 6.
35. Ibid., 2.
36. Ibid., 15–16.
37. Ibid.
38. Ibid., 2–3.
39. Chan, Selden, and Ngai, *Dying*, ch. 11. According to the authors, in the wake of the rooftop protest, local Communist Party members, along with trade union officials, lawyers, and police, collected intelligence on the situation. Using discretional power, "instead of adhering to the preexisting, formal legal procedures," they gave workers an ultimatum without addressing workers' primary demands

or core concerns. Ultimately and as a form of containment of widespread protests, those who were most likely to instigate unrest (the most unhappy) and were willing to leave were offered a modest severance payment. They also point out that the trade union federation "initially failed to support workers' wage demands," and "in the end did nothing" to help those who remained. Fittingly, by April another two hundred workers staged another protest. One of the chief concerns was over pension contributions of those who transferred from Shenzhen that had "disappeared." As noted, these payments had been pocketed by the Shenzhen government (Ibid.).

40. Ibid.

41. With the 1989 Tiananmen Square protests as an epiphenomenon, some observers and analysts minimize the importance of contemporary peasant and worker protests inside China, characterizing them as local, issue-oriented, and different from "large-scale" democratization or "more general" protests. Chan, Backstrom, and Mason, "Patterns of Protests." Typically, protests by farmers (over land-related issues), and workers, including migrant workers (over job-related issues such as wages, work safety, and security) are not considered "national protests" with antisystemic potential, despite the proliferation and scale of these "local" protests. The PRC government defines mass protests as those with 10,000 protestors or more. Typically, and according to the state's own accountings, there are as many as 90,000 or more mass protests annually. Thomas Lum, *Social Unrest in China—Foreign Affairs, Defense, and Trade Division* (Washington DC: Congressional Research Service—The Library of Congress, May 8, 2006).

    In 2010 alone, there were an estimated 180,000 mass protests. Another estimate puts this number closer to 230,000 protests. Christian Göbel and Lynette H. Ong, *Social Unrest in China* (London: Europe China Research and Achive Network, 2012). These mass protests have been so frequent that the PRC government officially stopped counting them. Quan, *Growth Against Democracy*. Of these protests, 85 percent are directly about land and/or labor reforms and environment-related catastrophes. Victor Cheung Yin Chan, Jeremy Backstrom, and T. David Mason, "Patterns of Protest in the People's Republic of China: A Provincial Level Analysis," *Asian Affairs: An American Review* 41 (2014): 91–107.

42. Lin, Lin, and Tseng, "Manufacturing Suicides." Chan, Selden, and Ngai assume this "despotic management" as a given in "the highly skewed" power relationship between labor and management.

43. To mark this new release, a Hong Kong–based NGO, Students and Scholars Against Corporate Misbehavior (SACOM), released their own report about Foxconn, drawing attention to excessive overtime and low wages, explaining that "when the peak season comes, [workers] are tied to the production lines with just one day off in 13 working days, or no rest day at all in a month, all to cope with the public demand for the new Apple products." Cited in Hannah Beech, "Riot Strikes Chinese City Where iPhone 5s Were Reportedly Made," *Time Magazine*, September 24, 2012, https://world.time.com/2012/09/24/riot-strikes-chinese-city-where-the-iphone-5-was-reportedly-made/.

44. Cited in Chan, Selden, and Ngai, *Killing*, ch. 11.

45. Ibid.

46. Ibid. Not surprisingly, on the day of the riot, Tim Cook assured the world that "it was not running sweatshops," while also assuring likely customers that they could order and expect to receive their iPhone 5s in a timely fashion. Remark-

ably, in early June 2010, when reports of worker suicides and Yan Lee's death from a thirty-four-hour shift surfaced, Apple's CEO and founder Steve Jobs had a similar response. Jobs, in an email exchange, refuted Apple's complicity, insisting that "Foxconn's suicide rate is well below the China average"—the same standard that got repeated in the echo chamber of techno/financial news outlets and satirized by Dan Lyons. Dan Lyons, "Our New Spin on the Foxconn Suicide Epidemic," *The Secret Diary of Steve Jobs*, May 2010, www.fakesteve.net/tag/foxconn-jumpers.

47. For Chan, Backstrom, and Mason, these protests only aim at obtaining "immediate and tangible relief for specific grievances, not to bring about major national reforms such as the call for democratization that echoed through Tiananmen Square in the spring of 1989." Chan, Backstrom, and Mason, "Patterns of Protests," 92.
48. Fiona Tam, "1,000 Workers Hold Managers Hostage in Shanghai Labour Row," *South China Morning Post*, January 20, 2013, www.scmp.com/news/china/article/1132587/1000-workers-hold-managers-hostage-shanghai-labour-row.
49. Ibid. Other than denying them bathroom breaks while being held up, angry protestors left the managers largely unharmed.
50. This example also reveals how little difference there is between how "Chinese capital" and the government of China behave from the government of France and French corporations, or the US government and American corporations, with the exception perhaps of the apology to the workers. Chinese nativity, here, plays an inconsequential role in capital formation insofar as the workers are concerned: they were protesting their terrible conditions that was directly facilitated by both Chinese and Japanese nationals and their capitalist allies.
51. National Bureau of Statistics (NBS) of China 2010, www.stats.gov.cn/english/.
52. Anand Parappadi Krishnan, "The Real i in the Apple Universe: The State of Workers in a 'Workers State,'" *Economic and Political Weekly*, June 5, 2021, www.epw.in/journal/2021/23/book-reviews/real-i-apple-universe.html. The government's official NBS 2020 survey reports a total of 285.6 million or 35 percent of the total Chinese labor force; this number has risen steadily since 2019.
53. For the year 2020, 65.2 percent of migrant workers were male and 34.8 percent female, with the vast majority working in low-wage manufacturing and construction work. The highest paid sector for migrant workers is in transports and logistics, with average monthly earnings around 4814 yuan or $730 USD. China Labour Bulletin, "Migrant Workers and Their Children," *CLB*, May 4, 2021, https://clb.org.hk/content/migrant-workers-and-their-children. See also National Bureau of Statistics (NBS 2020), *NBS 2020 Annual Migrant Worker Survey*: www.stats.gov.cn/tjsj/zxfb/202104/t20210430_1816933.html; and Aris Chan, "Paying the Price for Economic Development: The Children of Migrant Workers in China," *China Labour Bulletin, Special Report* (Novemer 2009).
54. Chen Guidi and Wu Chuntao, *Will the Boat Sink the Water? The Life of China's Peasant*, trans. Zhu Hong (New York: Public Affairs, 2006), 3.
55. *China Labour Bulletin*, https://clb.org.hk/. For decades and for many, outward rural migration was transformative from poverty to limited affluence. As early as 2003, however, Chinese journalists Chen Guidi and Wu Chuntao took note of the adverse effects caused by mass outward peasant migration, including persistent poverty and discrimination as well as treating "migrants as potential criminals and sources of unrest." Chen and Wu, *Will the Boat*, 203–204. Not unlike the pass

system in apartheid South Africa, the household registration system in China marks those who were born in rural areas and restricts outward rural migrants from accessing better jobs and social provisions in urban areas, including quality healthcare and education. In essence, it maintains a caste system between urban- and rural-born residents, creating a permanent state of concentrated and persistent poverty, and rendering these migrants in their own country as faring only marginally better than those who are non-native, undocumented migrant workers in other countries. Once understood as "a quasi-apartheid pass system," it becomes clear how "the use of passes to control the influx of rural migrants into urban area . . . [buttresses] cheap-labour economies." Peter Alexander and Anita Chan, "Does China Have an Apartheid Pass System?," *Journal of Ethnic and Migration Studies* 30, no. 4 (July 2004): 609.

56. This scale is massive; there are more migrant workers inside China than the entire workforce in the US.
57. Rachel Beitarie, "The Spirit of Wukan," *FP*, December 23, 2011, https://foreignpolicy.com/2011/12/23/the-spirit-of-wukan/. The BBC and *New York Times* erroneously declared this rebellion unusual and atypical, while the *Wall Street Journal* concluded that it was 2011's "most serious case of mass unrest inside China." Jeremy Page, "Beijing Set to 'Strike Hard' at Revolt," *Wall Street Journal*, December 16, 2011, www.wsj.com/articles/SB10001424052970204026804577100132882903066. *The Atlantic* came closest to recognizing the nature and significance of these protests. Elizabeth Economy, "Chinese Protesters Take Over Their Town: Why Beijing Should Expect More," *The Atlantic*, December 16, 2011, www.theatlantic.com/international/archive/2011/12/chinese-protesters-take-over-their-town-why-beijing-should-expect-more/250088/. Indeed, the journal would follow up with another article a few months later, originally appearing on the Council of Foreign Policy webpage (CFR.org), reporting that the "land grab epidemic" was spawning more protests. Elizabeth Economy (2012). "China's Land Grab Epidemic Is Causing More Wukan-Style Protests," *The Atlantic*, February 8, 2012, www.theatlantic.com/international/archive/2012/02/chinas-land-grab-epidemic-is-causing-more-wukan-style-protests/252757/.
58. Lum, *Social Unrest*; Chan, Backstrom, and Mason, "Patterns of Protests"; and Göbel and Ong, *Social Unrest*.
59. Beitarie, "Spirit of Wukan."
60. One villager explains that "most of the land [was] sold by the village committee" as villagers "knew nothing about it, when it was sold, to whom it was sold, where the money went, or how the money was spent." Sally Wang, "20 Years of Anger Unleashed," *South China Morning Post*, January 4, 2012, www.scmp.com/article/989180/20-years-anger-unleashed. When villagers broke into the village committee's office, they discovered documents signed as early as the 1990s, learning more than a decade later the details about the sale of their collective lands (Ibid.). In 2007, *Forbes Magazine* reported that one of Country Garden's heirs, Yang Huiyan, a graduate of Ohio State University, owned 58 percent of the stake of this company at the age of twenty-six and was the wealthiest woman in Asia and the world's youngest billionaire, with a net worth of $16.2 billion. Russel Flannery, "China's 40 Richest," *Forbes*, October 8, 2007, www.forbes.com/2007/10/08/china-40-richest-entcx_rf_1008chinasrich.html?sh=4701a3ed7064. As of 2021, she was worth $27 B (USD), and controlled 57 percent of Country Garden, most of which was transferred from her father,

Yeung Kwok Keung, in 2007. "#11 Yang Huiyan & Family," *Forbes*, November 11, 2021, www.forbes.com/profile/yang-huiyan/?sh=4b3d18162fa0.

61. Beitarie, "Spirit of Wukan."
62. As the next chapter also shows, these demands are not only ordinary and typical of villagers and farm workers within China as the Wukan-like protests attest; they also reflect the larger platforms of claimants outside of China such as the increasingly populous movements for land and food sovereignty. See Economy 2012; Michael Wines, "China's Peril: A Wave of Wukans; Rage in Southern Village Over Corruption by Elite Has Potential to Spread," *International Herald Tribune*, December 27, 2011; and Congressional—Executive Commission on China, *Annual Report*, 112 Congress, Second Session, 112, October 10, 2012, www.cecc.gov.
63. Wang, "20 Years."
64. Beitarie, "Spirit of Wukan."
65. Villagers collaborated with returnees, mostly in their thirties and forties, who had migrated to urban areas then moved back home to take up farming. Media coverage, particularly Hong Kong–based and foreign press, while uneven, nevertheless provided extensive coverage. The broad foreign coverage reflects Wukan organizers' astute awareness and strategic deployment of media relations. Shih-Diing Liu, "Demanding State Intervention: New Opportunities for Popular Protests in China," in *The New Global Politics: Global Social Movements in the Twenty-First Century*, ed. Harry E. Vanden, Peter N. Funke, and Gary Prevost (London: Routledge, 2017), 241–42.
66. Beitarie, "Spirit of Wukan."
67. The other two protestors were released a day later.
68. James Pomfret, "In China's 'Democracy Village', No One Wants to Talk Any More," *Reuters*, November 10, 2017, www.forbes.com/2007/10/08/china-40-richest-ent-cx_rf_1008chinasrich.html?sh=4701a3ed7064.
69. Wang points out that the basis of the disputes in Wukan "was just one among the thousands of land disputes" in 2011 but "stood out because . . . villagers raised banners saying they were 'opposing dictatorship,'" insisting that were "not against the Communist Party" but are "opposing the dictatorship of the village officials." As suggests here, this tactical reframing of oppositions is sometimes mistaken by observers as strategic and/or objective, and thus perceived as less significant than "national" protest movements. Wang, "20 Years."
70. Beitarie, "Spirit of Wukan." Indeed, and as Michael Wines of the *International Herald Tribune* explains: "On paper, the Wukan protests never should have happened: China's village committees should be the most responsive bodies in the nation because they are elected by the villagers themselves. . . . Village self-administration, as the central government calls it, is seen by many foreigners as China's democratic laboratory—and while elections can be rigged and otherwise swayed, many political scientists say they are, on balance, a good development." In reality, the situation resembles privatization of accountability on the one hand, and organized neglect on the other, leaving villagers to fend for themselves against wealthy elites, local corruption and general divestment of social welfare such that "the combination of villages' need for cash and their dependence on higher-ups has bred back-scratching and corruption between village officials and their overseers" (Ibid.). According to the Chinese Academy of Social Science's annual accounting for 2011, as many as "50 million farmers having lost lands,

and the number . . . increasing at a rate of three million each year," with as many as 60 percent of all farmers inside China having lost the land they used to farm for livelihood (Ibid.). The potential for more Wukan-like protests, therefore, cannot be minimized.

71. When mass protests erupted again in 2016, Wukan villagers were not as successful after several months of continuous agitation. They were met and suppressed by riot police, rubber bullets, and arrests. Nine villagers received jail terms upwards of nine years. Wukan is now under constant surveillance including military checkpoints, affecting a chilling climate for protests and rebellions. One villager shares that while "no one dares raise their head," land seizures and thefts persist. Pomfret, "China's 'Democracy Village.'" This shift in containment approach reflects heightened authoritarianism inside the PRC.

72. As noted, Wukan is not an exception in the sense that similar grievances and discontents are lodged "all across the country," according to Liu Yawei, a China specialist at the Carter Center in Atlanta, Georgia. As quoted in Wines, "China's Peril." According to one estimate, "50-60% of Chinese villages had suffered governance and accountability problems" (Ibid.).

73. Beitarie, "Spirit of Wukan."

74. Both the protests in Shanghai and Wukan are atypical of the many mass protests in contemporary China. They are atypical because they are small, involving *only* a few thousand people. As noted, mass protests are those with at least ten thousand protestors or more. These protests, however, are similar to the tens of thousands of mass protests that have taken place inside China annually in two decades, in that they are not considered "general protests." They nonetheless are grounded in mass discontent and refusal against governing by tyrannical rule, be it by the village tyrant, a tyrannical emperor, the centralized Communist Party, or a despotic labor regime. Regrettably, the socialist left in the US and Europe consistently ignore or marginalize antiauthoritarian protests inside China or minimize their importance. This indicates a lack of imagination about protests against governing, thus missing out on an opportunity to draw connections between different modes of labor resistance, learn tactical choices, and build transnational solidarity.

75. Ngo Van Xuyet, *Ancient Utopia and Peasant Revolts in China*, trans. Magali Sirera (Barcelona: Etcetera, 2004). While initially supporting the worker's revolution and an ally of Ho Chi Minh's campaign to end imperialism in Vietnam, Ngo Van (Xuyet) in exile was much more of a democratic anarchist than a Communist loyalist. Van Ngo, *In the Crossfire: Adventures of a Vietnamese Revolutionary*, trans. Héléne Fluery et al., ed. Ken Knabb and Héléne Fluery (Oakland: AK Press, 2010), 200. Ngo was more sympathetic to the indigenous Vietnamese Trotskyist movement that simultaneously fought against colonialism, capitalism, and Stalinism. As a radical historian of movements, Ngo particularly was attuned to popular revolts and wary of movement dictates emanating from the top. Héléne Fluery, "Ngo Van, Relayer of Living History," in *Ngo In the Crossfire: Adventures of a Vietnamese Revolutionary*, ed. Ken Knabb and Héléne Fluery (Oakland: AK Press, 2010), xvii. For him, contemporary Vietnam—with its economy largely capitalized by corporations headquartered in South Korea, Europe, and the US—was still very much a place where the majority of the people "continue to struggle for survival," thus remaining governed by global capitalism and the local state machinery. Ibid., xvii–xviii.

CHAPTER 8

1. Mencius, *The Works of Mencius*, trans. James Legge (New York: Dover Publications, 1970 [1895]), Book VII, pt. II, xiv.
2. Dussel, *Ethics and Community*, 131.
3. Incidentally "the mother of Mencius" is usually held up in China as the model of what a mother should be, because she moved several times to ensure a conducive environment for Mencius' upbringing, especially his education. Mencius, *The Works*, 16.
4. Ibid., Book I, Pt. II, iii.
5. Ibid.
6. There has been a grossly reductionist approach to the Chinese Cultural Revolution—the upheavals associated with a series of policies that occurred between 1966 and 1976, when Mao Zedong and his closest associates implemented a radical reform program, among other initiatives, that purged what was deemed traditional as well as capitalist elements from the lives of people living inside the PRC. It was thought that the controversial and ideologically motivated Cultural Revolution made rebellion into common sense, as a contradistinction to making revolutions. Despite its many counterrevolutionary and draconian measures, one obvious effect was the delegitimization of authority writ large, as it reestablishes the rightness of rebellion. Roderick Macfarquhar and Michael Schoenhals, *Mao's Last Revolution* (Cambridge, MA: Belknap Press, 2006), 459. The Wukan uprising is emblematic of this radical tradition.
7. Ngo Van is Ngo Van Xuyet's pen name, both used interchangeably depending on the name that appeared on publications.
8. Historian Elizabeth J. Perry points out that "scholars who venture into the world of peasant rebellions must usually resign themselves to a dearth of documentation from the rebel side." There is a distinct elitist predisposition to these accounts favoring nonpeasant perspectives due to peasants' general illiteracy. Government and elite records, by virtue of their positionality, predominate. Elizabeth J. Perry, "When Peasants Speak: Sources for the Study of Chinese Rebellion," *Modern China* 6, no. 1 (January 1980): 72. Literacy, especially within the context of imperial China, was a function of social location, with those who possessed it deemed as "wise and worthy" and those who did not as "simple and stupid." James C. Scott, *Decoding Subaltern Politics: Ideology, Disguise, and Resistance in Agarian Politics* (London: Routledge, 2013), 20–21. When accounting for peasant rebelliousness, elite record-keepers likely were tempted to deny agency and intentionality on the part of the rebels given the general lack of literacy among the peasant population. Perry therefore argues for taking up rebel testimonies in court records as well as folk literature (oral stories and poems) as an important methodological departure. Ngo's theorizing of rebel utopian imaginary suggests that he relied on these alternative sources for argumentation.
9. Ngo, *Ancient Utopia*. In one of the earliest treatises on Chinese religions in English that may have contributed greatly to the perpetuation of various "orientalist" racial regimes in the west—especially the notion that Chinese (and, by extension, Asians) are "heathens," Hampden C. DuBose's characterizes Taoism as heathenistic and unoriginal. Hamden C. DuBose, *The Dragon, the Image, and the Demon: Or the Three Religions of China—Confucianism, Buddhism, and Taoism* (London: S. W. Partridge and Co., 1886), 30. Du Bose, who cofounded the Anti-

Opium League in colonial China, was convinced that Taoism was the work of plagiarists and reactionaries. Ibid., 30.

10. Ngo, *Ancient Utopia*. In this way, and not unlike Bambara's urging that "the dream is real" and "the failure to make it work is the unreality," Taoist utopian longings are both practical and aspirational.
11. Ibid.
12. Ibid. There are at least three major currents of Taoist teaching in the forms of the *Tao Te Ching* by Lao Tzu (570–490 BC), the *Lieh Tzu* by Lieh Tzu (450 BC), and the *Chuang Tzu* by Chuang Tzu (370–300 BC). Unlike Confucian scholars who served as advisors to various courts and thus are entangled in the imperial life-worlds, most Taoist masters lived beyond the pale of Confucianism—outside the courts, in obscurity and in poverty.
13. Ibid.
14. Ibid. Ngo's class-based characterization of feudal society in ancient China (circa first-millennium BC) is one clearly demarcating between the aristocracy and peasant plebians, where peasant life was governed by customs. Nevertheless and unlike orthodox Marxian schemas, there is a remarkable diversity among the classes of laborers: "The peasants worked as serfs, sharecroppers or agricultural laborers, and the fruits of their labor filled the granaries of the nobles. Others, landless and enslaved because of indebtedness, worked in the mines, steel foundries, salt works and workshops that belonged to the feudal lords or to rich merchants." Ngo resourced the *Gouyu* (*Discourses of the States*), a collection of speeches by rulers and other courtiers (circa 771–476 BC) as the basis for fugitive utopian imaginary. He poignantly sums up sociomaterial life and its unjust peace this way: "The prince eats his taxes, the high officials eat their fees, the patricians eat their plantation, the plebians eat their labor power, the artisans and the merchants eat the prices fixed by the State, the functionaries eat their functions, the administrators eat their patrimonies; the government is orderly, the people live in peace." Thus, while social harmony was praised to high heaven as a virtue by many Confucian thinkers, "peasant labor constituted the source of the livelihood of the feudal lords, the landowning aristocracy, and the merchants . . . [as well as] the learned officials and the soldiers." Moreover, peasants also were conscripted to maintain and enforce the very apparatus that oppressed them, as Ngo reminds his readers that "the plebeians form the infantry and died *en masse*" (Ibid.).
15. Some of these autonomous peasant communities rival the greatest maroon societies, such as the Quilombos of Brazil. These communities were self-sufficient and lasted for decades, with their own militaries with as many as three hundred thousand skilled fighters (Ibid.).
16. "Land, Lodging and Life" are the three "L's" of liberation theology (as articulated by Pope Francis) as well as a core tenet of the global Indigenous movements for land and food sovereignty. Pope Francis, *Laudato Si': On Care for Our Common Home*, The Vatican, 2015, www.vatican.va/content/dam/francesco/pdf/encyclicals/documents/papa-francesco_20150524_enciclica-laudato-si_en.pdf. See also H. L. T. Quan, "Foreword," in *An Anthropology of Marxism* by Cedric J. Robinson (Chapel Hill: University of North Carolina Press, 2019).
17. Ngo, *Ancient Utopia*. As James Scott points out, "historically, the mobilizing capacity of such millennial visions has perhaps provided the single most important normative basis for popular rebellions." Scott, *Decoding*, 23. These utopian

dreams "provide another vehicle for radical religious and social values" and are a "mirror image of existing social inequities and privations . . . [with] the existing class must be brought down as prelude to the new world" (Ibid.).

18. From adherents who could afford payments.
19. Cited in Ngo, *Ancient Utopia*. For the most influential folk account of the later Han dynasty (169–280 AD), see the fourteenth-century historical novel and one of the four Chinese major classics *The Romance of Three Kingdoms*, attributed to Lou Guanzhong. For the official historical account (184–280), see the third-century account *Records of the Three Kingdoms* by Chen Shou.
20. Ngo, *Ancient Utopia*. Ngo also argues that, more than fifteen hundred years later, a messianic movement, the Taiping Rebellion against the Manchu Qing government led by Hong Xiuquan that lasted fifteen years (1850–64), "followed the footsteps of the Taoist community of the Yellow Turbans of the Second Century A.D." (Ibid.). The Taiping rebels abolished the braided queue, which they saw as "a symbol of servitude imposed by the reigning Manchus," redistributed land to the elderly who could not farm on their own under the usufruct principle; and, along with civil rights, apportioned land equally among men and women based on the principle that "if there is land we shall work it together" that came out of "agrarian collectivism of times past." Similar to the Yellow Turban Rebellion, the Taiping Rebellion was "a project to establish a mystical and egalitarian community consonant with the utopia that nourished the peasant insurrections and revolts from the Chinese Middle Ages right up until modern time . . . [as a] prologue to the Chinese Revolution of 1925–1927" (Ibid.).
21. *Gui* or *guei* are spirits that roam the earth, who can be heroic, demonic, or both. More than fifteen hundred years later, DuBose, who thought that "the term 'Demon' is Taoism in a nut-shell," would observe that "Taoism is a system fraught with danger to the State," without knowing the true meanings of his words. DuBose, *The Dragon*, 8, 370. DuBose, extrapolating his racial imaginary from the US plantocracy onto China, translated Lao Tze's name to mean "Old Boy," and characterized the great work of Lao Tze's *Tao Te Ching* as "not a little puerile and misanthropic" (Ibid., 345).
22. Also known as the Yellow Scarves Rebellion with multiple sects and in different regions. Most accounts credit Zhang Jue and his two brothers, Zhang Bao and Zhang Liang, as Taoist healers and cofounders of the most significant insurgencies. The Zhang brothers sent adepts to all four directions to teach and recruit over the course of ten years. Vincent Shih, "Some Chinese Rebel Ideologies," *T'oung Pao, Second Series* 44, no. 1 (1956): 150–226. Local authorities initially tolerated certain Taoist teachings until the movement became so broadly popular that they were fearful such belief would "rival the authority of the state." Rafe de Crespigny, *Fire Over Luoyang: A History of the Later Han Dynasty 23–220 AD* (Leiden: Brill, 2016), 409.
23. Ngo, *Ancient Utopia*; de Crespigny, *Fire Over Luoyang*, 411.
24. In official records, they sometimes show up as "ant bandits." Howard S. Levy, "The Bifurcation of the Yellow Turbans in Later Han," *Oriens* 13/14 (1960/61): 252. At one point, they counted nearly four hundred thousand peasants among their ranks. According to at least one respectable accounting, nearly half a million rebels and sympathizers were executed by the various Han governments. Zhang Jue's sect alone numbered several hundred thousand followers. At one point, he led as many as thirty-six regiments, each consisting of as many as ten thousand

fighters, and controlled as many as eight provinces. Shih, "Some Chinese," 163–64. Strategically, Yellow Turban rebels "relied heavily upon mass attacks," and their enemies were ruthless in their executions, sending a clear message that killing them "warns everyone to avoid evil conduct." Cited in de Crespigny, *Fire over Luoyang*, 413.

25. Levy, "Bifurcation," 253–54. It appears that these rebels knew something about community building, if not state formation. Because the peasants were not legible to the elite, public food stations (not unlike the Black Panther breakfast programs) were strategic for recruitment and mobilization.
26. Taoist acolytes called for an end to the discrimination against and killing of female infants. Some historians have argued that this is consistent with Taoist teaching of ensuring the principles of yin and yang. Shih, "Some Chinese." Ngo, however, seems to suggest that this was in keeping with peasant social egalitarian ethos, not unlike the social egalitarianism that existed within the slave quarters in the US and elsewhere.
27. Near the end of the Han Dynasty, medicine and healing were of grave importance due to frequent epidemics spreading sickness and disease across the empire (with epidemics flaring up in 171, 173, 179, 182, and 185), and the origins of specific illnesses (possibly smallpox or measles) unknown; and it became clear "by the early 170s there were frequent illness and widespread death throughout China." de Crespigny, *Fire over Luoyang*, 404–406. These recurring epidemics sometimes were read as "supernatural omens," which "gave rise to vigorous religious movement." Levy, "Bifurcation." Within this context, there was intense interest in the healing arts, especially Taoist teachings.
28. Their approach was a mixture of mysticism and spiritual healing, involving confession and isolation in mediation rooms. Enough people were healed, allowing rebels to attract new recruits far and wide. De Crespigny, *Fire over Luoyang*; Levy, "Bifurcation."
29. The rebels also inflicted tremendous pain on state finances, freeing the empire of great sums of monies, resources and territories. De Crispigny, *Fire over Luoyang*, 427.
30. Well after the imperial court declared "Zhongping" (Pacification Achieved) to mark the end of the rebellion, "peace was not restored" because "even as the last elements of resistance were crushed in the east, widespread unrest remained, [and] a significant rebellion was developing" in the northwest (Ibid., 414). It is also noteworthy that the insurgents were rebelling not simply against the Han Empire but also against local warlords and their exploitative practices of wealth accumulation and religious hierarchies.
31. It is possible that imperial records and other elitist accounts cast these insurgents as "bandits" to malign their reputation and minimize the signification of their insurgencies. However, and as the historian Paul Michaud argues, they were members of a religious order who "had developed a new social and political order of its own which it aimed to establish over the empire." Paul Michaud, "The Yellow Turbans," *Monumenta Serica* 17 (1958): 48.
32. Shih, "Some Chinese," 218–19.
33. Ibid., 219–20. These peasants are not an exception. Taxation, particularly onerous taxes, are a major catalyst of many peasant rebellions throughout history, and resistance to taxes is an implied "assertion of local economic rights." Scott, *Decoding*, 40. Tax rebellions are some of the most "common form[s] of unrest

in pre-modern states," revealing a "state's blindness to the actual economic and demographic condition of its people" (97). This blindness, accordingly, would be corrected by modern states in their search for the mastery of mass legibility, in the form of legal identification, first by the heteropatriarchal practice of patronym, and later the use of fingerprints, DNA typing, iris scans, and other biometrics (172–73).

34. Shih, "Some Chinese," 220. Unlike Ngo, Shih maintains that, because few rebellions are explicit about their demand for equal distribution of land, "the majority of the rebels did not have in mind a new land system which would radically alter" land relations. This position is dubious since the most notorious and successful insurgencies, especially the Yellow Turban Rebellion and the 1949 Communist Revolution, had demands for radical land reforms.
35. FAO, IFAD, UNICEF, and WHO, "In Brief," The State of Food Insecurity and Nutrition in the World: Transforming Food Systems for Food Security, Improved Nutrition and Affordable Healthy Diets for All (Rome: FAO, 2021).
36. Scott, *Decoding*, 2–3. Scott points to the Viet Minh's suppression of a popular rebellion in the "historical hotbed of peasant rebellion," and Mao forcing tens of millions of farmers into large agrarian communes during the experimental Great Leap Forward as sources of the disillusionment, as he also suggests that there is a fundamental misperception about what peasants actually want out of radical transformations.
37. Ibid., 4. See also Perry, "When Peasants Speak."
38. Scott, *Decoding*, 4. Like slave rebellions and popular revolutions, peasant rebellions are "far and few between," and when they do occur, most "are crushed unceremoniously." Scott, *Weapons*, xv–xvi. Peasant rebellions are noteworthy, however, not because they are frequent nor are they archetypical of radical transformations; instead, they are important because they are the culmination of everyday forms of defiance and the embodiment of social values from below. Moreover, and as Ngo suggests, these rebellions and other forms of radical social outbursts are likely projections of utopian longings. Everyday forms of (peasant) resistance are not unrelated to generalized collective rebellions such that an emphasis on peasant rebellion is not necessarily misplaced so long as it is understood as merely one of many forms of collective defiance, however rare they might be (29–30).
39. Scott, *Decoding*, 6. Colonial systems were more likely to encounter peasant rebellions because they replaced a seemingly more exploitative system with one that was more rigid and "made no allowance for subsistence needs," thus violating this ethic (5). See also James C. Scott, *The Moral Economy of the Peasant: Rebellion and Subsistence in Southeast Asia* (New Haven, CT: Yale University Press, 1976).
40. Scott, *Weapons*, 169.
41. In *Weapons of the Weak*, Scott enumerated examples where ordinary people living on the margins articulate practicable compassion. For many, the calculus of blame of social harms is usually "closer to home" and "within moral reach"—they are a part of community and therefore *ought* not to be indifferent to the consequences of their acts for their neighbor" (Ibid., 161).Those who are deemed "good people" are also understood as people with "compassion." These uses can indeed be deployed as propaganda to further an exploitative system (Ibid.). Nevertheless, the expressed values by those on the margins constitute

an alternative articulation of social morality and ethics beyond relations of gendered racial capitalism. Scott cites the *zakat*, a Muslim ritual among the Malay that explicitly obligates sharing with poorer relatives, neighbors, friends, and others to show how some rituals counter accumulative logic, even those that are sanctioned by the elite. Unlike tithing by Mormons in the Latter-day Saints (LDS) Church, the zakat, a key pillar in Islamic teaching, explicitly "asserts that the rich have an obligation to share a portion of their wealth with those who are poor and without property." Following the teaching in the Qur'an, the zakat functions to "discourage stinginess" and "to promote social harmony among the rich and the poor." In this way, the zakat is not entirely about concerns for the poor, nor is its practice entirely redistributive. Zakat calculation is based on positionality—from employers to the poor (172). So, while these redistributive practices may seem both minor and pivotal for ensuring the functioning of extant appropriative system, they exist. When violated, such violation builds resentment and condemnation, that may serve as a basis for revolts and rebellions (191–92).

42. Ivan Illich, *Tools for Conviviality* (New York: Harper & Row, 1973).
43. Petr Alekseevich Kropotkin, *Mutual Aid a Factor of Evolution*, ed. Johnathan-David Jackson (New York: McClure, Phillips & Co., 1902). See also P. J. Proudhon, *The Principle of Federation*, trans. Richard Vernon (Toronto: University of Toronto Press, 1979).
44. H. L. T. Quan, "Race, Nation and Diplomacy: Japanese Immigrants and the Reconfiguration of Brazil's 'Desirables,'" *Social Identities* 10, no. 3 (2004): 339–67.
45. Joana Laura Marinho Noguiera and João Nicédio Alves Nogueira, "The Evolution of Cooperatism in Brazil," in *Cooperatives, Grassroots Development, and Social Change: Experiences from Rural Latin America*, ed. Marcela Vásquez-Léon, Brian J. Burke, and Timothy J. Finan (Tucson: University of Arizona, 2017), 92.
46. See Quan, "Race, Nation"; and *Growth Against Democracy* on the role of Japanese Brazilian immigrants in the making of Brazil-Japan relations. On the Japanese diaspora in Brazil, see also Jeffrey Lesser, *Negotiating National Identity: Immigrants, Minorities, and the Struggle for Ethnicity in Brazil* (Durham, NC: Duke University Press, 1999); and *A Discontented Diaspora: Japanese Brazillians and the Meanings of Ethnic Militancy, 1960–1980* (Durham, NC: Duke University Press, 2007).
47. Noguiera and Noguiera, "Evolution," 89.
48. The Rochdale Principles are a set of ideas delineated by a group of Owenites who in 1844 founded the Rochdale Society of Equitable Pioneers (Rochdale, England). Core principles include voluntary and open membership, antidiscrimination and democratic control of cooperatives.
49. Ibid., 90.
50. Mutual aid has been invaluable during the COVID-19 pandemic given the lack of a robust social welfare system, including public health infrastructure, as a consequence of neoliberal governance having so effectively divested from the common. The impact of this generalized and organized neglect is particularly acute on vulnerable communities, especially Indigenous communities. The Utah Navajo COVID-19 Relief Program and the Navajo and Hopi Families COVID-19 Relief Fund—two mutual aid networks "built on kinship ties within the Indigenous communities of the Four Corners region"—exemplify the type of solidarity work taking place throughout the world, providing basic care "for each other, including the chores of chopping wood for relatives or hauling water

for an elder," or care packages with foodstuff. Alastair Lee Bitsói, "Navajo Nation President Authorizes $575M in COVID-19 Stimulus for Diné Communities as Omicron Surges," *The Salt Lake Tribune*, January 8, 2022, www.sltrib.com/news/2022/01/08/navajo-nation-president/.

51. Elsewhere I have pointed to Pope Francis as an important voice in the larger global movement for environmental and economic justice, as he reworks liberation theology to emphasize the need for land to sustain human life instead of profit. Quan, "Foreword." Six years after Francis issued his encyclical, *Laudato Si'*, the Vatican operationalized its platform into an actionable seven-year program. Brian Roewe, "Pope Francis Launches Program to Put Laudato Si' into Action Throughout Church," *Earth Beat*, May 25, 2021, www.ncronline.org/news/earthbeat/pope-francis-launches-program-put-laudato-si-action-throughout-church. Framed as a "new ecological approach" and imbued by the spirit of liberation theology, Francis calls on not only the 1.2 billion Catholics worldwide but everyone to "undertake the journey together" and "to create a future we want—a more inclusive, fraternal, peaceful and sustainable" (as quoted in Roewe, "Pope Francis"). This policy would nominally be cast as an "extreme left" position within the "mainstream" political discourse in the US. See also Forum of Food Sovereignty, "The Declaration of the Forum on Food Sovereignty, Territories of Peace for a Dignified Life," *Summit of the People*, Buenos Aires, Argentina, December 12–13, 2017, https://viacampesina.org/en/declaration-forum-food-sovereignty-territories-peace-dignified-life/.
52. Marcos, *Conversations*. See also Levi Gahman, "Building 'A World Where Many Worlds Fit': Indigenous Autonomy, Mutual Aid, and an (Anti-Capitalist) Moral Economy of the (Rebel) Peasant," in *Sustainable Food Futures: Multidisciplinary Solutions*, ed. Jessica Duncan and Megan Bailey (London: Routledge, 2017).
53. The signatories included over three hundred attendees—"peasants, indigenous peoples, fishers and food producers from more than 30 countries in 4 continents." Forum of Food Sovereignty, "Declaration."
54. Ibid.
55. Henry A. Giroux explains that in the US the "biopolitics of disposability" characterizes the ways in which poor people, especially people of Color, "not only have to fend for themselves but are also supposed to do it without being seen by the dominant society." Henry A. Giroux, "Reading Hurricane Katrina: Race, Class, and the Biopolitics of Disposability," *College Literature* 33, no. 3 (Summer 2006): 175. In the so-called post-race world, these subjects are "excommunicated from the sphere of human concerns . . . rendered invisible, utterly disposable, and heir to that army of socially homeless that allegedly no longer existed in color-blind America" (175). This neoliberal condition, Giroux argues, manifests in the biopolitical "commitment to 'let die' by abandoning citizens" and contributes to the rise of authoritarianism (180). See also Brad Evans and Henry A. Giroux, *Disposable Futures: The Seduction of Violence in the Age of Spectacle* (San Francisco: City Lights Books, 2015).
56. Federici, *Revolution*.
57. H. L. T. Quan and Tiffany Willoughby-Herard, "Displacement and Deracination: Memory, Philosophy, Wealth and Remembering Katrina," in *The Routledge Handbook on the Lived Experience of Ideology*, ed. James R. Martel et al. (New York: Routledge, forthcoming).
58. Forum of Food Sovereignty, "Declaration."

59. Ibid.
60. Quan, "Introduction."
61. By supra-ego I am intentionally conflating Freud's concept of super-ego and the Jungian notion of supraordinate personality. See Sigmund Freud, *The Ego and the Id* (New York: W. W. Norton, 1923); and C. G. Jung, *Collected Work of C. G. Jung, Volume 9* (Princeton, NJ: Princeton University Press, 1968).
62. Naomi Zack, *White Privilege and Black Rights: The Injustice of U.S. Police Racial Profiling and Homicide* (Lanham: Rowman & Littlefield, 2015).
63. Asma Abbas, *Liberalism and Human Suffering: Materialist Reflections on Politics, Ethics, and Aesthetics* (New York: Palgrave Macmillan, 2010), 7, 14. A note of warning: Without a robust interrogation of group oppressions (à la Iris Marion Young) or a systematic analysis of power along the line of Patricia Hill Collins's matrix of domination to get at the materiality of suffering, including the affective economy that almost always accompanies suffering, evocation of suffering alone does not translate to democratic solidarity. Moreover, by relying on the liberal conception of democratic politics and justice, one may mistake the appearances and rhetoric of representation with deliberation and policies. In contrast, Fanon understood the significance of internalizing oppression but also the ways in which colonized subjects experienced harms and sufferings from colonial oppressions, how they reflected and gave meaning to those suffering, and mobilized around a particular articulation of that suffering.
64. Young, *Responsibility.*

CHAPTER 9

1. Octavia E. Butler, *Parable of the Talents* (New York: Warner Books, 1998), 45.
2. Adrienne Maree Brown, *We Will Not Cancel Us and Other Dreams of Transformative Justice* (Chico: Bolder Press, 2020), 75.
3. Ruth Wilson Gilmore and Léopold Lambert, "Making Abolition Geography in California's Central Valley," *The Funambulist*, no. 21—Space & Activism (2018): 16. https://thefunambulist.net/magazine/21-space-activism/interview-making-abolition-geography-california-central-valley-ruth-wilson-gilmore.
4. The data sampled here are drawn from various survey reports from both the National Center for Transgender Equality and National Gay and Lesbian Task Force as well as the Williams Institute at the University of California, Los Angeles. The National Center for Transgender Equality's *2015 U.S. Transgender Survey* (updated in 2017) is the most comprehensive survey of trans lives in the US. It was slated to be updated again but for the COVID-19 pandemic. It is important to note that data on LGBTQ lives in general are rarely straightforward, and particularly, data on trans and genderqueer people are quite limited. Andras Tilcsik, "Pride and Prejudice: Employment Discrimination Against Openly Gay Men in the United States," *American Journal of Sociology* 117, no. 2 (2011): 587.
5. Caitlin Rooney, Charlie Whittington, and Laura E. Durso, *Protecting Basic Living Standards for LGBTQ People* (Center for American Progress, August 2018). www.americanprogress.org/article/protecting-basic-living-standards-lgbtq-people/.
6. Sandy E. James et al., *The Report of the 2015 U.S. Transgender Survey* (Washington, DC: The National Center for Transgender Equality, 2016).
7. Ilan H. Meyer, Bianca D. M. Wilson, and Kathryn O'Neill, *LGBTQ People in the United States: Select Findings from the Generations and Transpop Studies* (UCLA

School of Law, Williams Institute), 2021, 1–5, https://williamsinstitute.law.ucla.edu/wp-content/uploads/Generations-TransPop-Toplines-Jun-2021.pdf.
8. Human Rights Campaign (HRC), An Epidemic of Violence: Fatal Violence Against Transgender and Gender Non-Conforming People in the United States in 2020, Human Rights Campaign Foundation (Washington, DC, 2020).
9. Periodic coverage of bullying incidents has been largely consistent with this finding from the comprehensive report by Jaime M. Grant, Lisa A. Mottet, and Justin Tanis, *Injustice at Every Turn: A Report of the National Transgender Discrimination Survey* (Washington, DC: The National Center of Transgender Equality and the Gay and Lesbian Taskforce, 2011).
10. In [illegible], HRC began tracking violent fatal incidents against transgender and gender nonconforming people in the US. In 2020, HRC tracked forty-four deaths, marking it as "the most violent year on record." As of September 2021, HRC websites already tracked thirty-seven fatal incidents, noting that it is likely that there are more unreported or misreported. In previous years, the majority of these unreported or misreported were Black and Latinx transgender women. Human Rights Campaign (HRC), *Dismantling a Culture of Violence: Understanding Anti-Transgender Violence and Ending the Crisis* (Washington, DC: Human Rights Campaign Foundation, 2021).
11. Grant, Mottet, and Tanis, *Injustice*, 8.
12. Adrian Piper observes that when young thinkers diverge from the canon, they "philosophically embark on a dangerous Oedipal drama in which they must confront and face down the wrath and resistance of their elders in order to prevail," and in the process "prove disapproval, rejection, or punitive professional retaliation from those who feel betrayed by their defection." Adrian M. S. Piper, *Rationality and the Structure of the Self: The Humean Conception*, vol. 1 (Berlin: Adrian Piper Research Archive Foundation, 2013), 22. Piper suggests this process is harmful for all parties involved, not only those who are immediate targets of the harm—"elders and prodigal sons alike"—but the process is necessary, thus requiring that "the egocentric urge to professional self-preservation at all costs be subordinated to the demands of transpersonal rationality, lest the great debates be silenced by the repressive dictates of professionalism" (22–23). While I am uncertain about the Oedipal drama, Piper's position is similar to that of Fanon's urging for each generation to author its own content and trajectory necessary for radical transformation. Fanon, *Wretched*.
13. Comedian Stephen Colbert coined the term "truthiness" to draw attention to the practice by politicians and others, especially then US president George W. Bush, who frequently insisted on the truthfulness of their own pronouncements, without any regard for empirical or logical evidence. "Truthiness," a form of affective tautology, has taken on even greater significance among the contemporary class of public personalities and politicians in the era of "alternative facts"—a term coined by Trump's then-counselor to the president, Kellyanne Conway. *Meet the Press*, January 22, 22017, NBC.
14. Here, Lewis Gordon's conceptualization of anti-Black racism as a form of bad faith is instructive. Gordon, *Bad Faith*. He explains that anti-Black racism can show up in various guises, as demonization and exoticization (6). Political discourses that demand "the others to justify their existence" are also bad faith, so is the policing of political thought that falls outside of accepted domains. Given that our lifeworlds are not always as they appear and sometimes the world "hides

from itself," bad faith is therefore "a form of self-lie in which the liar evades the displeasing truth in favor of pleasing falsehoods. Lewis R. Gordon, *Freedom, Justice, and Decolonization* (New York: Routledge, 2021), 43.

15. Piper, "Impartiality."
16. Kara Keeling, *Queer Times, Black Futures* (New York: New York University Press, 2019), 213.
17. Cathy J. Cohen, "Deviance as Resistance: A New Research Agenda for the Study of Black Politics," *Du Bois Review* 1, no. 1 (2004): 27–45.
18. Ibid., 43. Appropriating the term from James Scott, and extending the work of Robin D. G. Kelley in *Race Rebels*, Cohen holds "both scholars in very high esteem" for their work on "transformational politics from below" (42).
19. Ibid.
20. Ibid., 43. No approach is exhaustive, and precisely because it is so, it is prudent to create theoretical spaces accounting for those who are not yet named and/or have been intentionally left out.
21. Ibid., 43.
22. Ibid.
23. Cohen, "Punks."
24. Ibid.
25. Ibid., 438. Cohen was not alone, as evidenced by the post-positivist realist theorization of social identities, even when identitarian-based theoretical projects were out of favor. Linda Martín Alcoff et al., eds., *Identity Politics Reconsidered* (New York: Palgrave Macmillian, 2006).
26. Cathy J. Cohen and Sarah J. Jackson, "Ask a Feminist: A Conversation with Cathy J. Cohen on Black Loves Matter, Feminism, and Contemporary Activism," *Signs: Journal of Women in Culture and Society* 41, no. 4 (2016): 782.
27. Ibid.
28. Ibid., 786.
29. Ibid., 788. Remarkably, Cohen's acute insights for how to go about doing radical trans and queer analytic and politics are largely sublimated in mainstream feminist theorizing, despite her consistent and prolific work.
30. Sara Ahmed, *Queer Phenomenology: Orientations, Objects, Others* (Durham, NC: Duke University Press, 2006), 21.
31. Davis, *Blues Legacies*, xi.
32. Ibid., 33.
33. Ibid.
34. Ibid., 37.
35. Ibid.
36. Ibid., 36.
37. In this way, both Cohen's and Davis's works are part of the larger queer of Color critique, a mode of analysis that fleshes out the intersecting oppressions as well as taking stock of nonnormative formations so that we can approach moments and movements of transgression as sites of emancipatory knowledge and pedagogy. See also Roderick A. Ferguson, *Aberrations in Black: Toward a Queer of Color Critique* (Minneapolis: University of Minnesota Press, 2004).
38. Che Gossett, "Silhouettes of Defiance: Memorializing Historical Sites of Queer and Transgender Resistance in an Age of Neoliberal Inclusivity," in *The Transgender Studies Reader 2*, ed. Susan Stryker and Aren Z. Aizura (New York: Routledge, 2013). The two most iconic events that anchored contemporary queer liberation-

ist history, namely the 1966 Compton's Cafeteria Riot in San Francisco and the 1969 Stonewall riots in New York, are both revolts that emerged from "unrealized desires and deferred dreams" of struggling communities of poor trans and queer people whose quotidian lives are marked by various institutionalized violence, including the police and poverty. They, however iconic, as Gossett argues, are not unique.

39. Ibid., 584. Gossett explains that this is part of the larger "tolerance discourse [that] functions as a tool for depoliticization, dominance, and governmentality while distracting from the state violence and exclusion that underpins it" (Ibid.). They helpfully cite an example of media treatment of transphobic police violence from the national daily *USA Today* to illustrate this pernicious discourse and its deleterious effects (585).
40. Kai M. Green, "Troubling the Waters: Mobilizing a Trans* Analytic," in *No Tea, No Shade: New Writings in Black Queer Studies*, ed. E. Patrick Johnson (Durham, NC: Duke University Press, 2016), 65–66.
41. Ibid., 67.
42. Ibid., 77.
43. Ibid., 79. See also Lorde, "Age, Race, Class"; Marlon Riggs, *Black Is . . . Black Ain't*, (California Newsreel, 1995), documentary.
44. Ahmed, *Queer Phenomenology*, 5–6; emphasis added. Ahmed helpfully explains that not only are spaces not exterior to bodies, but also that "extending bodies into spaces create new folds" (not unlike skin)—the "new contours of what we could call livable or inhabitable space" (11).
45. Ibid., 178.
46. Roderick A. Ferguson instructively takes a cue from Herbert Marcuse's *One-Dimensional Man*, charging that the singularity or one-dimensionality of normative queer politics serves as a repressive apparatus of gendered racial capitalism and delimits the potentiality of queer liberatory projects. Similar to Marcuse, Ferguson argues that this "one-dimensionality represented the containment of social change . . . inasmuch as the maintaining of gay identity and sexuality (i.e., grooming them for the needs of the state and capital) are understood to be signs of social progress." Roderick A. Ferguson, *One-Dimensional Queer*, (Cambridge: Polity Press, 2019), 3–6.
47. Disorientation "would not be a politics of the will but an effect of how we do politics," and an effect of queer disorientation might be "the pleasure of deviation." Ahmed, *Queer Phenomenology*, 177. In extrapolating democratic living as a form of disorientation, I am also suggesting that it is not something we have, but do.
48. Davis et al., *Abolition*, ch. III.
49. Its usage has been documented in at least three counties in central Hunan, a southern region of the People's Republic of China (PRC)—Jiangyong, Daoxian, and Jianghu, as well as in the Guangxi Zhuang Autonomous Region (GZAR) in southern China—bordering Vietnam. Nüshu is considered an endangered language as the presumed last original script writer died in 2004, though there are a few scholars or "Nüshu transmitters" who have taken up the script as a mean to study and preserve the language. Ralph W. Fasold and Jeff Connor-Linton, *An Introduction to Language and Linguistics* (Cambridge: Cambridge University Press, 2006).

50. Ironically, besides the Japanese occupation authority that suppressed it for nearly two decades during the Pacific War, Mao's regime and its Cultural Revolutionary cadres saw *nüshu* as backward and counterrevolutionary, so they sought to repress its use by burning *nüshu* books and artifacts (i.e., embroideries), and prosecuting women who used it. Fasold and Connor-Linton, *Introduction*; Fei-wen Liu, *Gendered Words: Sentiments and Expression in Changing Rural China* (Oxford: Oxford University Press, 2015).
51. Liu, *Gendered Words*, 3.
52. According to scholar Fei-wen Liu, almost immediately many scholars came to Jiangyong—including a number of scholars whom I cite here, such as Zhao Liming, Xie Zhimin, Chen Qiguang, and Cathy Silber. Liu followed this first wave in the early 1990s (Ibid., 3).
53. Zhou Shouyi is believed to be the first and only male who mastered this script, in 2003 after studying for over five decades and compiling a dictionary of eighteen hundred nüshu characters. Xinhuanet, "Last Inheritress of China's Female Specific Languages Dies," *China View*, September 23, 2004, https://web.archive.org/web/20121104181654/http://news.xinhuanet.com/english/2004-09/23/content_2012172.htm.
54. Cathy Lyn Silber, "Nüshu (Chinese Women's Script) Literacy and Literature" (Dissertation, University of Michigan, 1995), viii–ix.
55. The prefiguration of Asian women as premodern aliens—sexual exotics and, with few extraordinary exceptions, entirely dominated, is an old orientalist ruling script that imbricates the geopolitics of knowledge, including reified western feminist suppositions as much as the political economy of the capitalist world system, including settler colonialism. Wu, *Radicals*; Edward W. Said, *Orientalism* (New York: Pantheon Books, 1978); and, Lisa Lowe, *Critical Terrains: French and British Orientalisms* (Ithaca: Cornell University Press, 1991). See also: Celine Parreñas Shimizu, *The Hypersexuality of Race: Performing Asian/American Women on Screen and Scene* (Durham, NC: Duke University Press, 2007); Helen Heran Jun, *Race for Citizenship: Black Orientalism and Asian Uplift from Pre-Emancipation to Neoliberal America* (New York: New York University Press, 2011); and Karen J. Leong, *The China Mystique: Pearl S. Buck, Anna May Wong, Mayling Soong, and the Transformation of American Orientalism* (Berkeley: University of California Press, 2005).
56. See Tsosie, "Indigenous Peoples."
57. Silber, "Nüshu," xi.
58. Ibid.
59. Ibid.
60. I am not suggesting that those who are in insurgent formations need to be "best friends" or "soul sisters" to be effective partners in mobilizing justice.
61. As a social resource, this style of friendship has long served as the basis of sharing. The "sworn sisterhood" practice in Jiangyong, as Liu explains, is an enduring cultural practice and broadly practiced throughout China and other parts of Asia. Liu herself while doing fieldwork there in the early 1990s, made a sworn sister pact with two different women in the village of Heyuan. She shares that "this pact is the major reason I continue to explore the depth and breadth of *nüshu* as a transforming, and likely endangered, cultural heritage." Liu, *Gendered World*, 10.

62. See Leong, *China Mystique*; Shimizu, *Hypersexuality*; and Christopher Goto-Jones, "Magic, Modernity, and Orientalism: Conjuring Representations of Asia," *Modern Asian Studies* 48, no. 6 (November 2014): 1451–76.
63. Lisa See, *Snow Flower and the Secret Fan: A Novel* (New York: Random House, 2005), 3. The 2011 film with the same name, directed by Wayne Wang, interweaves the historical past with present-day Shanghai, and was largely panned by critics for its incoherence and absurdities. Film critic Betsy Sharkey's assessment of the film is instructive. Revealingly, she thought Wang was only successful when his gaze turned the "rich, ancient world both exotic and erotic"—thus both the film and the novel succeed only when they titillate their audience with the familiar orientalist fantasy. Betsy Sharkey, "Movie Review: *Snow Flower and the Secret Fan*," *Los Angeles Times*, July 15, 2011, www.latimes.com/entertainment/la-xpm-2011-jul-15-la-et-snow-flower-20110715-story.html.
64. See *Snow Flower*, 1.
65. James Scott uses "the hidden transcripts" to explain the code switching that enslaved and other oppressed people tactically "hide" their persistent critiques of power and willful resistance—a tactic that willfully feigns submission and deference. James C. Scott, *Domination and the Arts of Resistance: Hidden Transcripts* (New Haven, CT: Yale University Press, 1990).
66. Ibid.
67. As a genre, yellow music was and remains popular in parts of China and Vietnam, especially in the early twentieth century. Unlike the blues, yellow music is considered more popular and less of a social critique. Songs in this genre are mostly about love and desire, generally deemed as decadent by authoritarian regimes.
68. Liu, *Gendered World*, 2.
69. Ibid.
70. Singing emphasizes the affective or expressions of emotions, which are generally marginalized "by scholars and men of letters" (Ibid.).
71. Ibid., 2. Liu is particularly interested in exploring the expressive limits of *nüshu*, particularly the problematics of "relying *only* on *nüshu* to reconstruct women's lifeworlds" (3).
72. Ibid., 14.
73. Liu helpfully explains that the current gap in literature on "the complex relationship between written *nüshu* and oral *nüge*" misses out on those women who could not write in *nüshu* but have nevertheless relied on the oral version, *nüge*, neglecting the oral performances in public where this speech act is shared (Ibid., 40).
74. Yiangyong is believed to be one of more the ethnically diverse counties in China, with Han Chinese and Yao as the most dominant ethnic groups. There is also indication that Yue culture also might have some influence on nüshu.
75. Liu, *Gendered Words*, 40. Liu suggests that nüshu is no longer an example of what Scott (1985) refers to as the "weapon of the weak" because the central government has appropriated it as a source of cultural pride for geopolitics and tourist dollars. Liu, *Gendered Words*, 39. Tools of democratic living and weapons of the weak, however, are frequently appropriated by the powerful and even redeployed against the practitioners, so such reasoning is not terribly persuasive. Equally dubious is the idea that because there was an absence of outright resistance to its practice by the androcentric society, it bears few important lessons for learning about everyday resistance.

76. Kelley *Freedom Dreams*; Sandra Harding, "Transformation vs. Resistance Identity Politics: Epistemological Resources for Social Justice Movements," in *Identity Politics Reconsidered*, ed. Linda Martín Alcoff et al. (New York: Palgrave MacMillian, 2006).
77. Vijay Prashad, *The Darker Nations: A People's History of the Third World* (New York: New Press, 2007); Darryl C. Thomas, *The Theory and Practice of Third World Solidarity* (West Port: Praeger, 2001).

CHAPTER 10

1. Arundhati Roy, "The Pandemic Is a Portal," *Financial Times*, April 3, 2020, www.ft.com/content/10d8f5e8-74eb-11ea-95fe-fcd274e920ca.
2. Dussel, *Ethics and Community*, 243.
3. Yuri Kochiyama, *Passing It On* (Los Angeles: UCLA Asian American Studies Center Press, 2007), xi.
4. Robert Preidt, "Coronavirus Isn't Even 'Alive,' But Expert Explains How It Can Harm," *MedicineNet*, March 26, 2020, www.medicinenet.com/script/main/art.asp?articlekey=229387.
5. Jieliang Chen, "Pathogenicity and Transmissibility of 2019-nCoV—A Quick Overview and Comparison with Other Emerging Viruses," *Microbes and Infection* 22 (2020): 71.
6. Robert D. Putnam, *Bowling Alone: The Collapse and Revival of American Community* (New York: Simon & Schuster, 2000).
7. Esmé Berkhout et al., *The Inequality Virus: Bringing Together a World Torn Apart by Coronavirus through a Fair, Just and Sustainable Economy*, Oxfam Briefing Paper, Oxam International (Oxford, January 25, 2021), 8, www.oxfam.org/en/research/inequality-virus.
8. Given the nature of early scientific research of an ongoing pandemic, there have been so many retractions of early predictions that there is blog dedicated to COVID-19-related retractions. Two years into the pandemic, there are more than two hundred retractions. For the most updated list, see https://retractionwatch.com/retracted-coronavirus-covid-19-papers/.
9. Roy, "Pandemic."
10. Ibid.
11. Ibid.
12. Ibid.
13. James H. Carr, "Why Recovery from the Great Recession Favored the Wealthy: The Role of Public Policy," *Nonprofit Quarterly*, March 25, 2020, https://nonprofitquarterly.org/why-recovery-from-the-great-recession-favored-the-wealthy-the-role-of-public-policy/. See also Thomas Picketty and Emmanuel Saez, "Top Incomes and the Great Recession: Recent Evolutions and Policy Implications," *IMF Economic Review* 61, no. 3 (2013): 456–78.
14. Centers for Disease Control and Prevention (CDC), "Health Equity Considerations and Racial Ethnic Minority Groups," COVID-19, January 25, 2022, www.cdc.gov/coronavirus/2019-ncov/community/health-equity/race-ethnicity.html. See also Aggie J. Yellow Horse, Eileen Díaz McConnell, and Mary Romero, "COVID-19 and Its Impacts on Immigrant Families and Communities," *Praxis*, July 29, 2020, www.kzoo.edu/praxis/covid-19-impacts/; Michelle Morse and

Camara Jones, "How COVID-19 Rationing Frameworks Reinforce White Supremacy," *Praxis*, June 10, 2020, www.kzoo.edu/praxis/rationing-frameworks/.

15. Rachel Thomas et al., *Women in the Workplace*, McKinsey & Company and Lean In (2020). https://wiw-report.s3.amazonaws.com/Women_in_the_Workplace_2020.pdf.
16. As of October 2020. Rubert Neate, "Billionaires' Wealth Rises to $10.2 Trillions amid Covid Crisis," *The Guardian*, October 6, 2020, www.theguardian.com/business/2020/oct/07/covid-19-crisis-boosts-the-fortunes-of-worlds-billionaires.
17. Roy, "Pandemic."
18. Andrew J. Jolivétte, "Critical Mixed Race Studies: New Directions in the Politics of Race and Representation," *Journal of Critical Mixed Race Studies* 1, no. 1 (2014): 157. Jolivétte is specifically addressing critical mixed race studies. He would later extend this framework to research and epistemic justice. Andrew J. Jolivétte, "Radical Love as a Strategy for Social Transformation," in *Research Justice: Methodologies for Social Change*, ed. Andrew J. Jolivétte (Chicago: Policy Press, 2015). I am resourcing Jolivétte's "radical love" as an important conceptual and convivial tool for community and world building. Others also resource the affective, especially love, to engender an emancipatory praxis. Staging love as "both desire and attachment," in *Another Love*, Asma Abbas rescripts "unrequited love" as potentially an important resource for "an anticolonial, materialist, and nonfascist politics and aesthetics." Asma Abbas, *Another Love: A Politics of the Unrequited* (Lanham: Lexington Books, 2018), 10. See also bell hooks, *All About Love: New Visions* (New York: William Morrow, 2000).
19. Jolivétte, "Critical Mixed Race," 157.
20. Ibid.
21. Jolivétte, "Radical Love," 8.
22. As Graham Allan and others point out, few agree on what constitutes a friend, and the criteria for friendship are not always clearly definable or contradictory. Graham Allan, "Friendship, Sociology and Social Structure," *Journal of Social and Personal Relationships* 15, no. 5 (October 1998): 685–702. Allan suggests that we should approach friendship as a form of informal solidarities, especially because they have become more central in late modern life.
23. Aristotle, *Ethics*, Book VIII.
24. Ibid.
25. Joe Sachs, "Glossary," in *Aristotle Nicomachean Ethics*, ed. Joe Sachs (Newburyport: Focus Publishing, 2002), 209.
26. Zoli Filotas, *Aristotle and the Ethics of Difference, Friendship, and Equality: The Plurality of Rule* (London: Bloomsbury Academic, 2021). For Aristotle, not only are humans relational, when they do form associations they gravitate toward a hierarchical structure, such that "there can never be a question of *whether* there is a ruler, only identifying the ruler and the kind of rules involved" (6). There is, however, the possibility that Aristotle deemed those who are naturally inferior are neither transit nor contingent in their submission and desire to be ruled. If justice is only possible through *the polis,* and within the corpus of that polity, "community of equals" are those who "are *similar enough to disagree among themselves*" (14), then those who are different must be exiled from the assembly, having no capacity to disagree.

27. Adrian Piper, *Out of Order, Out of Sight: Selected Writings in Meta-Art*, 2 vols. (Cambridge, MA: MIT Press, 1996/1999).
28. Larissa Pham, "This MOMA Show Asks You to Confront Racism—Both in Strangers and Yourself," *Garage*, April 3, 2018, https://garage.vice.com/en_us/article/43bnvj/adrian-piper-synthesis-of-intuitions-moma-retrospective.

    Reflecting on "Adrien Piper: A Synthesis of Intuitions, 1965–2016"—Piper's unprecedented retrospective exhibit at New York City's Museum of Modern Art (MOMA) where her work took up an entire floor, Pham reports that *Imagine* [*Trayvon Martin*] powerfully extends Piper's performative effect in *My Calling Cards*." *Imagine* is an installation from 2013 consisting of a crosshair over the washed-out face of Trayvon Martin—the young Black man killed by a White vigilante—with texts appearing at the corner of the print that read: "Imagine what it was to be me." Pham insists that *Imagine* causes a very different response from the viewing public: "taking a calling card to curve a cat-caller might be easy, trendy even, but to carry the weight and responsibility of Trayvon's death—to truly imagine what it was like to be him—remains both painful and uncomfortable for many" (ibid).
29. Piper, *Humean Conception*, 265.
30. Ibid., 266.
31. Piper has repeatedly incorporated elements of consciousness raising about race, gender and class-embodied positionality and social praxis, including racist and sexist actions into her performance art. By performing or drawing attention to the theatricality of race and racial matters, for instance, Piper asks questions about the unreality of race, and raising moral questions about racism. In *The Mythic Being* series (1972/1974), perhaps her best-known work where she altered her personal appearance to that of an African American male, Piper stages the effects of racism with "a deliberate display" of racist tropes. John Bowles argues that art critics frequently failed to notice this critical dimension of Piper's work as they continue to diagnose her as "an angry black woman," or her art as autobiographical. John B. Bowles, *Adrian Piper: Race, Gender, and Embodiment* (Durham, NC: Duke University Press, 2011).
32. Piper, "Impartiality," 726.
33. Ibid. Piper intends this term "to remind us of our capacity to envision what is possible in addition to what is actual."
34. Ibid.
35. Ibid., 730.
36. Ibid., 730–32.
37. Ibid., 754.
38. Ibid.
39. Ibid., 756.
40. Ibid., 756–57. Adrian M. S. Piper, *Rationality and the Structure of the Self: A Kantian Conception*, vol. 2 (Berlin: Adrian Piper Research Archive Foundation, 2013), 273. Here, the privileging of impartiality as ideal somewhat weakens Piper's own insistence on the need for affective modal imagining.
41. Piper explains elsewhere that "feelings of injustice, violation, neglect or betrayal are moral reactions that rightly alert us to the operation of these vices in our social relationships" (Ibid., 273). Presumably, such reactions would also clue us to our relations with the state and capital, extending Piper's frame beyond the interpersonal relations.

42. Dussel, *Ethics and Community*; Quan, "Introduction."
43. Quan, "Introduction"; See also Fricker, *Epistemic Injustice*; and Fanon, *Wretched*.
44. Piper, *Kantian Conception*, 407.
45. Ibid., 408. For Fanon, no less than a total decolonization is required. Fanon, *Wretched*.
46. Piper, "Impartiality," 756.
47. Cited in Arthur Tobier, ed., *Fishmerchant's Daughter: Yuri Kochiyama, an Oral History*, vol. 1 (New York: Community Documentation Workshop, 1981).
48. Tolbier, *Fishmerchant's Daughter*. It is important to note that I had a near two-decade friendship with Yuri Kochiyama. This friendship was born of C. A. Griffith's and my desire to produce a documentary series with Angela Y. Davis in conversations with various women of Color doing emancipatory cultural work, including a conversation with Kochiyama, who at the time Davis had met but did not personally know. Due to lack of resources and institutional support, after thirteen years since the project began, Griffith and I managed to produce only one feature-length documentary, *Mountains That Take Wing*. However, these circumstances gifted us the opportunity to be friends and learn from Yuri.
49. See for instance the *New York Times*'s headline of William Yardley's coverage of Kochiyama's death in 2014. William Yardley, "Yuri Kochiyama, Rights Activist Who Befriended Malcolm X, Dies at 93," *New York Times*, June 4, 2014, www.nytimes.com/2014/06/05/us/yuri-kochiyama-civil-rights-activist-dies-at-93.html.
50. Kochiyama tragically appears in the photo of the assassination of Malcom X on February 21, 1965. As captured by *Life Magazine*, wearing cat-eye glasses, Yuri devastatingly kneels by and cradles Malcom's head, looking on as if she was willing him to awaken. See "the Violent End of the Man Called Malcom," *Life* (March 5, 1965): 25–32.
51. Diane C. Fujino, *Heartbeat of Struggle: The Revolutionary Life of Yuri Kochiyama* (Minneapolis: University of Minnesota Press, 2005), 303.
52. Kochiyama, *Passing It On*, xxi.
53. Ibid.
54. Ibid.
55. Ibid., xi–xiii.
56. Ibid., xiv.
57. Tobier, *Fishmerchant's Daughter*, 28–30. The "Little Rock Nine" are Black students who in September 1957 enrolled in the all-White Central High School in Little Rock, Arkansas. To enforce the Supreme Court's decision to desegregate (*Brown v. Board of Education*), the Black children had to be escorted by the National Guards. Daisy Bates was the president of the National Association for the Advancement of Colored People (NAACP) Arkansas Chapter that selected and organized the "Little Rock Nine" integration effort, and ensured their safety. The "Hiroshima Maidens" or *hibakusha* (explosion-affected people) were a group of twenty-five Japanese female survivors of the US nuclear bombing of Japan who in 1955 came to the US for reconstructive surgery. For more information, consult "Hibakusha Testimonies" available on *hibakushastories.org*, especially the document compiled by Norman Cousins in 1955: https://hibakushastories.org/wp-content/uploads/2013/10/Hiroshima-Maidens.pdf.
58. Kochiyama, *Passing It On*, 14.
59. Ibid., 55.

60. At the end of World War II, the US deployed two atomic bombs on Hiroshima and Nagasaki—two major urban centers in Japan. The Nanjing Massacre refers to the mass killing of Chinese civilians by the Japanese occupying forces in Nanjing, China. From December 13, 1937, through the end of January 1938, an estimated 40,000 to 300,000 people were killed, with as many as 20,000 to 80,000 rapes. The International Military Tribunal of the Far East calculated there were at least 200,000 deaths and 20,000 rapes. David Askew, "The Nanjing Incident: Recent Research and Trends," *Electronic Journal of Contemporary Japanese Studies*, April 2002, https://web.archive.org/web/20180405031715/www.japanesestudies.org.uk/articles/Askew.html.

    See also Yang Dong and Jiang Wenbo, *Memories of the 1937 Nanjing Massacre: Oral Histories and Remembrance, 1937–2017* (South San Francisco: Long River Press, 2017).
61. Kochiyama, *Passing It On*; Fujino, *Heartbeat*; Griffith and Quan, *Mountains*. Fujino points to the imprisonment of her friends and comrades during the FBI campaign of intensified repressions that began in the late 1960s as instrumental in cementing one of Kochiyama's lifelong commitments and "her most steadfast area of struggle—support for political prisoners." Fujino, *Heartbeat*, xxiii.
62. Kochiyama, *Passing It On*, xxiv.
63. Ibid., xv.
64. Fujino, *Heartbeat*, xxiv.
65. Kochiyama, *Passing It On*, 201–202.
66. Mohanty, *Feminism*, 7.
67. Ibid.
68. Ibid., 242–43. See also Chandra Talpade Mohanty and Linda E. Carty, eds., *Feminist Freedom Warriors: Genealogies, Justice, Politics, and Hope* (Chicago: Haymarket Books, 2018).
69. Kropotkin, *Mutual Aid*; Mohanty, *Feminism*; Wu, *Radicals*; Caroline S. Hossein, ed., *The Black Social Economy in the Americas: Exploring Diverse Community-Based Alternative Markets* (New York: Palgrave Macmillan, 2018); Jessica Gordon Nembhard, *Collective Courage: A History of African American Cooperative Economic Thought and Practice* (University Park: Pennsylvania State University Press, 2014); and Dean Spade, *Mutual Aid: Building Solidarity During This Crisis (and the Next)* (New York: Verso, 2020). See also Caroline S. Hossein, "A Black Epistemology for Social and Solidarity Economy: The Black Social Economy," *Review of Black Political Economy* 46, no. 3 (2019): 209–29; Omar H. Ali, *In the Lion's Mouth: Black Populism in the New South, 1886–1900* (Jackson: University Press of Mississippi, 2010); and Bruce J. Reynolds, *Black Farmers in America, 1865–2000: The Pursuit of Independent Farming and the Role of Cooperatives*, RBS Research Report 194, U.S. Department of Agriculture, Rural Business Cooperative Service (Washington, DC, 2003).
70. Wu, *Radicals*, 112–13.
71. Ibid. That Cleaver, as the Minister of Information for the Black Panther Party, founded the Anti-Imperialist League while in exile as a political refugee, is significant for understanding the nature of organizing across borders and international networks of mutuality. Wu, *Radicals*, 113–14.
72. Illustrative of affection for Kochiyama, especially among the youth, is the eponymous track by the hip-hop duo Blue Scholars, in which part of the chorus

is: "When I grow up I wanna be like Yuri Kochiyama." "Yuri Kochiyama," on *Cinemetropolis*, 2011.

73. Judith Butler, "Bodies That Still Matter," in *Vulnerability and the Politics of Care: Transdisciplinary Dialogue*, ed. Victoria Browne, Jason Danely, and Doerthe Rosenow (Oxford: Oxford University Press, 2021), 33.
74. Ibid., 33–34. Butler points out that she and her colleagues previously sought to draw attention to these issues. See Judith Butler, Zeynep Gambetti, and Laticia Sabsay, eds., *Vulnerability in Resistance* (Durham, NC: Duke University Press, 2016).
75. Butler, "Bodies," 34.
76. Mohanty, *Feminism*; Mohanty and Carty, *Feminist Freedom Warriors*; Wu, *Radicals*. See also Robinson, *Black Marxism*; Jackie Smith et al., eds., *Social Movements and World-System Transformation* (London: Routledge, 2017); Jackie Smith, Charles Chatfield, and Ron Pagnucco, eds., *Transnational Social Movements and Global Politics: Solidarity Beyond the State* (Syracuse: Syracuse University Press, 1998); and Alan Eladio Gómez, *The Revolutionary Imaginations of Greater Mexico: Chicana/o Radicalism, Solidarity Politics, & Latin American Social Movements* (Austin: University of Texas Press, 2016).
77. Robinson, *Black Marxism*.
78. Mohanty, *Feminism*, 136.
79. I am suggesting, as Butler concedes, vulnerability is much more than a subjective state or a predisposition, but an embodiment of relational imbrications, including the conditions of harm and other effects of sociomateriality. Butler, "Bodies," 38. Indeed, and not unlike the maroon societies of previous years, communities and subjects who are differentially vulnerable and have been targeted frequently for harm, on their own or in formations with others, have always understood what Butler is recognizing: that "if any of us are to survive, and to flourish, even to attempt to lead a good life, it will be a life lived with others, a life that is no life without those others" (41). What is curious is that it took literally the threat of species extinction for many contemporary scholars to press the urgent need for interdependence and solidarity with "those others," and for conceptions of justice that extend beyond the autonomous self. It is even more curious that even scholars like Butler continue to claim that one's conditions of harm cannot be the basis for a politics, denying the potentiality of political mobilization and the existence of certain political claimants, including the right to claim rights as subjects of harm or vulnerability to harm, at the same time that they reposition their own episteme as an important basis for political consideration. Butler is right of course, that "bodies still matter" and that "bodies enact and become the claim" (Ibid.), because people, not just bodies, have always mattered, and they in formations with other people and communities build movements that have sought not to become "the claim" but to become whole.
80. The Combahee River Collective, "Statement." See also Taylor, *How We Get Free*.
81. Cohen and Jackson, "Ask a Feminist."
82. Ibid., 788.
83. Ibid.
84. American Civil Liberties Union (ACLU), *Island of Impunity: Puerto Rico's Outlaw Police Force*, ACLU (New York, June 2012), 11. This report is the product of a comprehensive six-month investigation and based on eight years of document-

ing cases of police violence by the ACLU of Puerto Rico. Only the New York City Police Department (NYPD) is larger, with twice the size of the PRPD.

85. US Department of Justice—Civil Rights Division, *Investigation of the Puerto Rico Police Department* (Washington, DC, September 5, 2011), 7–8.
86. Ibid., 5.
87. Ibid., 10.
88. In the most recent policy report from Brennan Center for Justice, *Protecting Against Police Brutality and Official Misconduct*, Taryn A. Merkl verifies that racialized policing forms the context for the unprecedented mass protests in 2020. Taryn A. Merkl, *Protecting Against Police Brutality and Official Misconduct: A New Federal Criminal Civil Rights Framework* (New York: Brennan Center for Justice, April 29, 2021), 4. Merkl and the Brennan Center for Justice are calling for a new framework to hold police and policing accountable, noting that currently there is only one federal criminal law (18 U.S.C.§242) that applies without clearly defining what conduct constitutes a criminal act, and even that is not being enforced. Merkl, *Protecting*, 4. The problem is much more complicated than misconduct and "brutality," however. Instead, policing itself and its carceral logic are at the root of these actions. Rodríguez, *White Reconstruction*.
89. Kiara Thomas of the *Indypendent* reports that demands include an end to deportation and greater investments in the community. Organizers also pointed to White supremacy to draw direct connections between anti-Black racism, the genocide of Indigenous people, and the colonization of Puerto Rico. Echoing the language of abolition, Miguel Melendez, a co-founder of the Young Lords Party, explains that policing in the US is inextricably linked to White supremacy, and that "white supremacy is part of the DNA in America. It cannot be reformed. It has to be abolished." Kiara Thomas, "In Lieu of a Puerto Rican Day Parade, Activists Rally to Defund the Police," *Indypendent*, June 15, 2020, https://indypendent.org/2020/06/in-lieu-of-a-puerto-rican-day-parade-activists-rally-to-defund-the-police-instead/.
90. Kelley, *Freedom Dreams*.
91. Ransby, *Making All Black Lives*, 3. Ransby explains that she employs the term "*Black-led* mass struggle" because the contemporary movement is not pivoted on Black-only liberation (3). Instead, it "contextualizes the oppression, exploitation, and liberation of Black poor and working-class people within the simple understanding, at least in the US context, that 'once all Black people are free, all people will be free.'" Activists and organizers recognize that because Black people are represented in all social categories of marginalization, "to realize the liberation of "all Black people means undoing systems of injustice that impact all other oppressed groups as well" (4).
92. Ibid., 3.
93. Ibid.
94. Davis, *Are Prisons Obsolete?*; Davis et al., *Abolition*; Richie, *Arrested Justice*; and INCITE! Women of Color Against Violence, ed., *Color of Violence: The INCITE! Anthology* (Durham, NC: Duke University Press, 2016).
95. Charles W. Mills, "White Ignorance," in *Race and Epistemologies of Ignorance*, ed. Shannon Sullivan and Nancy Tuana (Albany: State University of New York Press, 2007).
96. Howard Center for Investigative Journalism, "About This Project," *Printing Hate*, (2021). https://lynching.cnsmaryland.org/about/.

97. Howard Center for Investigative Journalism, "Explore Stories," *Printing Hate*, October 18, 2021, https://lynching.cnsmaryland.org/explore-stories/.
98. DeNeen L. Brown, "Printing Hate," *Printing Hate*, October 18, 2021, *The Howard Center for Investigative Journalism*, https://lynching.cnsmaryland.org/2021/10/12/printing-hate-newspapers-lynching/.
99. Margaret Talev, "'Printing Hate' Details U.S. Newspapers' Roles in Lynching," *Axios*, October 18, 2021, www.axios.com/newspapers-lynchings-racist-violence-journalism-5057e1fc-008e-48dc-94d9-768107437119.html.
100. On the same day that *Printing Hate* stories went live, the Court handed down two unsigned decisions (*Daniel Rivas-Vellegas v. Ramon Cortesluna*; *Tahlequah, OK, et al. v. Austin P. Bond*) involving police accused of excessive use of force, affirming the "qualified immunity" doctrine. Andrew Chung, "U.S. Supreme Court Again Protects Police Accused of Excessive Force," *Reuters*, October 18, 2021, www.reuters.com/legal/government/us-supreme-court-rules-police-over-excessive-force-claims-2021-10-18/.
101. For an updated accounting of legislative campaigns to censor free thought in education, consult PEN America's "Index of Education Gag Orders": https://docs.google.com/spreadsheets/d/1Tj5WQVBmB6SQg-zP_M8uZsQQGHo9TxmBY73v23zpyro/edit#gid=1505554870.
102. Louis Ruchames, ed., *Racial Thought in America: From the Puritans to Abraham Lincoln*, vol. 1 (Amherst: University of Massachusetts Press, 1969), 1. Before the era of accessible scanned documents, this 514-page volume with 75 entries was an invaluable compilation of materials that embodied the vicious and devastating verification of anti-Black racism and White supremacy. The materials range from formal treatises to letters, memorials, speeches, and essays by "religious leaders, reformers, pseudo social scientists, statemen, scholars, abolitionists, pro-slavery apologists, belletrists, and journalists." Richard Bardolph, "Book Review," *The Journal of Negro History* 55, no. 2 (April 1970): 152.
103. Cited in Ruchames, *Racial Thought*, 1. Prior to being dismissed by the Nazis for, among other things, being a pacifist and writing on race in 1933, Hertz was a professor of world economy and sociology at the University of Halle-Wittenberg. His 1928 book *Race and Civilization* (translated by Hertz's collaborator and feminist art historian, Amelia Sarah Levetus) was considered foundational in early twentieth-century critical studies of race. Friedrich Otto Hertz, *Race and Civilization*, trans. A. S. Levetus and W. Entz (New York: Ktav Publishing House, 1970 [1928]). See also F. H. Hankins, "Reviews," *Political Science Quarterly* 44, no. 1 (March 1929): 129.
104. Ruchames, *Racial Thought*, 2. Disappointingly, Ruchames restricted the scope of the volume to the hegemonic Black/White dichotomy of racial thought, despite his familiarity with other forms of racialization, not to mention the capacious regime of White supremacy, as indicative of his appropriation of Hertz's work (viii; fn. 1 & 2, 15–16).
105. James, *Black Jacobins*, 406.
106. Ibid., 357.
107. Davis, *Abolition Democracy*, 95.
108. Ibid., 95–96.
109. Of note is the intimate kinship between Jim Crow "democracy" in the US, "racial democracy" in Brazil, and the apartheid system in South Africa. These regimes of governing share in common an anti-Black racism and White supremacist

ethos. They vary only in degrees of administrative and physical violence in the enforcement of White rule. Remarkably, Du Bois reworked the prevailing apartheid democracy with a different frame—one that links labor with social provisions (e.g., education), first by stating the obvious—that American democracy cannot be understood without recognizing "the true significance of slavery" (what Robinson would later explain as racial capitalism); and second, he interrogated the presumption of rule by the White elite versus rule by the many, which would have to include the mass of former slaves. Du Bois, *Black Reconstruction*, 13–18.

110. While only noting Sojourner Truth's name once, Du Bois relied on Douglass and leaders of the radical wing of the anti-slavery movement, including Truth and Harriet Tubman, for a more robust interpretation of the impetus behind the Civil War, but also a more substantive definition of democracy. Frequently citing Douglass, Du Bois made use of his leadership and rhetorical prowess as a stand-in for the larger radical elements of the anti-slavery, pro-democracy movement. This faction demanded, not only the franchise for Black men, but also universal franchise and economic justice, including land reform and free education.

111. Sojouner Truth, "Women's Rights," in *Civil Rights Since 1787: A Reader on Black Struggle*, ed. Jonathan Birnbaum and Clarence Taylor (New York: New York University Press, 1867).

112. Du Bois, *Black Reconstruction*. Du Bois arrived at this conclusion based on his own reading of the anti-slavery movement (121–23). Cogently, he also argued that racial capitalism defaced democratic living and disfigured genuine democratic politics, using westward expansion and the Free-Soil movement as an example of how White supremacy underwrites accumulation, and in the process, undermines democracy (28). With this failure to enact abolition democracy, the "color caste" would betray radically inclusive democratic inspirations, as "democracy died saved in the hearts of black folk" (30). He thus saw racial capitalism and White supremacy as sources of degeneration—transmogrifying democracy, taking down with it not only Black people but all poor laborers (30).

113. Du Bois, *Black Reconstruction*, 182–83.

114. Ibid., 187.

115. Ibid., 185–89. Here Du Bois appeals to the idea of a "universal democracy," challenging the White supremacist notion that "universal rights" belong to only a self-elected few.

116. Ibid., 206.

117. Du Bois, *Black Reconstruction*, 209–10. Notwithstanding this observer's singling out the South for its White supremacist practice and preference for apartheid democracy, the outright rejection of Black people as part of democratic life in the southern states was overwhelming. The South Carolina Convention, for instance, "shunned all suggestions" of the Black vote and refused to hear from Black delegates (209).

118. Ibid., 214. Du Bois noted that abolition democracy "went beyond" Lincoln's idea of emancipation to include "civil and political rights, education and land as the only complete guarantee of freedom" (239).

119. Du Bois himself conceded that when Johnson unexpectedly came to power, the alliance that Johnson secured between "Big Business and slave barons" was a natural fit because "like Nemesis of Greek tragedy, the central problem . . .

was the black man." Du Bois, *Black Reconstruction*, 237. Put differently, abolition democracy has to be rejected and its principles refuted precisely because both political economies of the northern and southern states were dependent on extracted wealth created and accumulated from appropriated land and coerced labor—the mechanics of racial capitalism that sourced Black people (and other racialized subjects) as catalysts for growth and wealth. Moreover, as Du Bois pointed out, for Johnson there was no "conceivable democracy" that could accommodate Black people (242).

120. For an instructive delineation of race as social wages, see Harris, "Whiteness as Property." See also David R. Roediger, *The Wages of Whiteness: Race and the Making of the American Working Class* (London: Verso, 1991).
121. Du Bois, *Black Reconstruction*, 697.
122. Ibid., 708. Ultimately Du Bois would frame the opponents of abolition democracy as part of a counterrevolution. Here is how he put it: "After enslaving the Negro for two and one-half centuries, it turned on his emancipation to beat a beaten man, to trade in slaves, and to kill the defenseless; to break the spirit of the black man and humiliate him into hopelessness; to establish a new dictatorship of property in the South through the color line" (707). Du Bois also attributed failure to implement abolition democracy as a collective failure of imagination: "If the Reconstruction of the Southern states, from slavery to free labor, and from aristocracy to industrial democracy, had been conceived as a major national program of America, whose accomplishment at any price was well worth the effort, we should be living today in a different world." Du Bois, *Black Reconstruction*, 708. Finally, Du Bois reserved his disgust and contempt for the propagandists and the forgers of history, not to mention the enforcers at the publishing houses, maintaining that the "real frontal attack on Reconstruction, as interpreted by the leaders of national thought in 1870 and or sometime thereafter, *came from universities*, and particularly from Columbia and Johns Hopkins" (718). As Cedric Robinson explains, *Black Reconstruction* was much more than a historical work; it was an attempt "to identify the unique character of mass praxis, class consciousness, ideology, and contradictions as they had occurred in the dialectics of American social and historical developments." Robinson, *Black Marxism*, 196. As such, and for Du Bois, the collective failure in imagination to make abolition democracy a reality also reflects the intentionality behind the embrace of racial capitalism and the will to exclude racialized others from the polity.
123. That abolitionism feminism cohered and resonated with Black feminist-led movements for freedom for more than three decades, both in academia and beyond, is a testament to the resilience and tyranny of White supremacy and democratic elitism, but also the persistence of radical visions by Black feminist-led formations and Black feminist analytics.
124. Chenjerai Jumanyika and Ruth Wilson Gilmore, "Ruth Wilson Gilmore Makes the Case for Abolition," *The Intercept*, June 10, 2020, https://theintercept.com/2020/06/10/ruth-wilson-gilmore-makes-the-case-for-abolition/. See also Ruth Wilson Gilmore, *Abolition Geography: Essays towards Liberation* (New York: Verso), 2022.
125. Davis et al., *Abolition*; Rodríguez, *White Reconstruction*.

126. Angela Y. Davis and Gina Dent, "Abolition Feminism with Angela Davis & Gina Dent," *Center for Race & Gender*, UC Berkeley, October 22, 2020, www.crg.berkeley.edu/podcasts/abolition-feminism/.
127. Davis et al., *Abolition*.
128. Allegra M. McLeod, "Envisioning Abolition Democracy," *Harvard Law Review* 132 (2019): 1616.
129. Ibid.
130. I am referring to where US military bases for decades incited instability and insecurity for the local populations who have redefined national security against Cold War ideology and US hegemony, including incidents of sexual assaults and environmental pollution. Yoko Fukumura and Martha Mastuoka, "Redefining Security: Okinawa Women's Resistance to U.S. Militarism," in *Women's Activism and Globalization: Linking Local Struggles and Transnational Politics*, ed. Nancy A. Naples and Manisha Desai (New York: Routledge, 2002).
131. CPD consists of forty-eight grassroots organizations from throughout the United States and Puerto Rico; Law for Black Lives has more than three thousand members who are radical lawyers, law students, and legal workers; and BYP100 is a grassroots organization that operates with a "Black Queer Feminist lens," with youth members who are self-declared abolitionists. Focusing on the budgets of twelve jurisdictions, *Freedom to Thrive* investigates racial disparities, policing landscapes, and spending priorities. It was produced in collaboration with twenty-seven local organizations around the country. Kate Hamaji et al., *Freedom to Thrive: Reimagining Safety & Security in Our Communities*, The Center for Popular Democracy, Law for Black Lives, and BYP100 (Washington, DC, 2017). https://populardemocracy.org/sites/default/files/Freedom%20To%20Thrive%2C%20Higher%20Res%20Version.pdf.
132. Ibid., 1.
133. Ibid., 2, 1.
134. Ibid., 1. In the jurisdiction they investigated, the report finds that "police spending vastly outpaces expenditures in vital community resources" at the same time that "community safety priorities" diverge significantly from police expenditures, with "demands for mental health, youth programming and infrastructure," including transit access and housing.
135. Ibid.
136. This framework calls for a reallocation of resources from policing and incarceration to human infrastructure such as education and health care. It also calls for a reallocation of resources from fossil fuels and related industries toward "community-based sustainable energy solutions." M4BL, "Policy Platform: Invest-Divest," https://m4bl.org/policy-platforms/invest-divest/. It is also important to note that participatory budgeting is part of the larger social solidarity economy toolkit.
137. Ransby, *Making All Black Lives Matter*.
138. Charlene A. Carruthers, *Unapologetic: A Black, Queer, and Feminist Mandate for Radical Movements* (Boston: Beacon Press, 2018), 110.
139. Ibid., 110.
140. Ibid., 111.
141. Ibid., 110.
142. Ibid., 92.
143. Ibid., 92; Hamaji et al., *Freedom to Thrive*, 81.

144. From responses to the effects of "organized abandonment" in the aftermath of Katrina to depriving prison proliferation as a core issue of public policy agenda and destabilizing police's monopoly of moral authority, abolition feminism has extended aid and comfort to reframing and mobilizing against violence of all forms. Predating the George Floyd protests by more than a year, the *New York Times Magazine*'s feature on the scholar activist Ruth Wilson Gilmore suggests a "breakthrough" in the larger effort to create a critical mass for abolitionist campaigns. Rachel Kushner, "Is Prison Necessary? Ruth Wilson Gilmore Might Change Your Mind," *New York Times Magazine*, April 17, 2019, www.nytimes.com/2019/04/17/magazine/prison-abolition-ruth-wilson-gilmore.html. See also Gilmore, *Golden Gulag*; Ruth Wilson Gilmore, "Forgotten Places and the Seeds of Grassroots Planning," in *Engaging Contradictions: Theory, Politics and Methods of Activist Scholarship*, ed. Charles R. Hale (Berkeley: University of California Press, 2008).
145. Public conversation at the Social Justice Initiative Portal Project's Inaugural Event, October 10, 2021.
146. Davis, *Freedom*.
147. Ibid., 101.
148. Ibid., 105.
149. Ibid., 106.
150. From a 2014 interview with Frank Barat and on a question concerning movement capacity in the struggle for women's liberation. Davis, *Freedom*, 27.
151. Davis, Dent, Meiners, and Richie also trace contemporary genealogies of prison abolition organizing to the 1971 Attica prison uprising. Davis et al., *Abolition*, ch. 1.
152. Davis, *Freedom*, 105.
153. Davis argues that the Black freedom movement was expansive precisely because its struggles extend beyond civil rights; instead, it sought "to transform the entire country." First, she points out that "freedom is more expansive than civil rights," signally that the movement is not fixed but ongoing. Moreover, because substantive freedom itself is more expansive than nominal or political freedom, the movement now embodies not only "the ghosts of our pasts" but also what haunts our future, including struggles that are not yet named. Davis, *Freedom*, 119–21. So, from Ferguson to Palestine, from settler colonialism and gendered racial capitalism to violence against women, the prison nation, and heteropatriarchy, and so on—these struggles are the building blocks of transformative mobilization and movements, including for radical feminist futures.
154. Davis reminded her audience she herself was on the Most Wanted List and labeled a "terrorist" by then-president Richard Nixon (Ibid., 92–93). The FBI's Most Wanted Terrorists List was first created in the aftermath of 9/11 by then-president George W. Bush in October 2001. When Assata Shakur (Joanne Chesimard) was placed on it in 2013, she was the first woman to be included, and in 2021, when Ahlam Aref Ahmad al-Tamimi was placed on the list, she became the second woman. Al-Tamimi, a former journalist and Jordanian national working in the occupied West Bank, was convicted of conspiring to use weapons of mass destruction, relating to a suicide-bombing incident in Jerusalem in 2001 that killed fifteen people, including two US nationals. The charges were under seal in 2013, so little information emerged until recently, although she is believed to have been a former US informant. Al-Tamimi was freed as part of the prisoner

exchange agreement between Hamas and Israel in 2011, but in March 2017 the FBI brought criminal charges against her. If caught and convicted, she could face life in prison or execution. It was the "first time the U.S. government has attempted to achieve the extradition and prosecute someone involved in a Palestinian attack against the Israeli occupation." *Al Jazeera* News, "Ahlam Aref Ahamd al-Tamimi on FBI's Most Wanted List," *Al Jazeera*, March 15, 2017, www.aljazeera.com/news/2017/3/15/ahlam-aref-ahmad-al-tamimi-on-fbis-most-wanted-list.

155. Davis, *Freedom*, 93.
156. Ibid., 96. In the same speech Davis acknowledges the work of critical disability studies by scholars such as Michael Rembis and Liat Ben-Moshe on the need for deinstitutionalization of asylums and psychiatric institutions. Liat Ben-Moshe, Chris Chapman, and Allison C. Carey, eds., *Disability Incarcerated: Imprisonment and Disability in the United States and Canada* (New York: Palgrave Macmillan, 2014); and Liat Ben-Moshe, *Decarcerating Disability: Deinstitutionalization and Prison Abolition* (Minneapolis: University of Minnesota Press, 2020).
157. Davis, *Freedom*, 98–99.
158. Ibid., 98.
159. Ibid., 99–100. Davis notes that "just about everyone who's in the field of feminist studies has read Judith Butler's *Gender Trouble*," urging her audience to also read Beth Richie's *Arrested Justice* so that they can have a more robust understanding of gender, gender policing, and how the carceral system operates on women of Color, including trans and queer women of Color.
160. Ibid., 101.
161. Davis, *Freedom*, 4. The eminent feminist scholar Patricia Hill Collins reminds us that intersectionality as a feminist framework emerged out of social movements for justice and warns against the codification and calcification of intersectional analytics and methodologies through institutional incorporation and mainstream discursive praxis. Patricia Hill Collins, "Intersectionality and Epistemic Injustice," in *The Routledge Handbook of Epistemic Injustice*, ed. Ian James Kidd, José Medina, and Gaile Pohlhaus Jr. (New York: Routledge, 2017). See also Patricia Hill Collins and Sirma Bilge, *Intersectionality* (Cambridge: Polity Press, 2016).
162. Carruthers, *Unapologetic*, 5.
163. Ibid., x–xi.
164. Ibid.
165. Ibid., 8.
166. Ibid., 8–9.
167. BYP100, "Statement on Radical Inclusivity," cited in Carruthers, *Unapologetic*, 12.
168. Davis, *Freedom*, 45.
169. Ibid., 58.
170. Ibid., 89. Radical Black feminists in the US who are redefining security are part of a long legacy of feminists retheorizing safety and well-being, including and especially feminists who work to end the deadly consequences of militarism and empire. Take the case of the collective Okinawan Women Act against Military Violence. In September 1995, on the same day that the fourth UN World Conference on Women started in Beijing, three US servicemen, serving at Camp Hansen on Okinawa, rented a van and kidnapped a twelve-year-old sixth grader walking home from school. After beating her, they taped her mouth and eyes, reportedly because they could see terror in her eyes, drove to a remote area,

then raped her as she struggled to get free. When they were done, they threw her out of the van, left for dead, with eyes and mouth still taped. She survived, and reported the attack. Robert D. Eldridge, "The 1995 Okinawa Rape that Shook U.S.-Japan Ties," *Japan Times*, September 3, 2020, www.japantimes.co.jp/opinion/2020/09/03/commentary/japan-commentary/okinawa-rape-incident-us-japan-relations/. This incident is believed to have reignited the moribund peace movement to demilitarize Okinawa, including getting the US bases off the Island. About a month after the incident, more than eighty-five thousand people marched against the US military presence on that island. A similar march organized five years earlier only gathered twenty-five thousand people. May Lee, "Thousands Rally Against U. S. Bases in Okinawa," *CNN*, October 21, 1995, http://edition.cnn.com/WORLD/9510/okinawa_protest/index.html.

Okinawan feminists, for a while now, have tasked both the governments of Japan and the US as well as their male counterparts in the peace movement to reimagine national security by taking into consideration physical and sexual well-being of women as well as the ecology. They thus jostled with not only the US-Japan defense establishments and American lack of attention on and solidarity with Okinawan's autonomy, but also the marginalization of feminist issues and feminist analyses of militarism inside the peace movement in Japan. Their work sought to "ensure that the local and Japanese peace movement would not miss the connections between this rape and other patterns of violence against women and, second, to encourage women's groups in the US to understand that rape was not simply the act of three individual American men, but the product of their government's foreign policy design." Cynthia H. Enloe, *Maneuvers: The International Politics of Militarizing Women's Lives* (Berkeley: University of California Press, 2000), 120. This case is remarkable because, across the oceans, Black and other feminists of Color sought to connect the prison industrial complex, the politics and economics of mass incarceration, and the precarity and violence in women's lives, especially historically marginalized women.

171. More than a half century after six White men gang raped Recy Taylor, the American public finally learned her name as a rippling of the larger #MeToo wave. While the rapists were not indicted, Taylor, facing death threats, refused to be silent and helped galvanize some of the earliest mass mobilization against sexual assaults in the US. Sewell Chan, "Recy Taylor, Who Fought for Justice After a 1944 Rape, Dies at 97," *New York Times*, December 29, 2017, www.nytimes.com/2017/12/29/obituaries/recy-taylor-alabama-rape-victim-dead.html.

See also Danielle L. McGuire, "'It Was like All of Us Had Been Raped': Sexual Violence, Community Mobilization, and the African American Freedom Struggle," *Journal of American History* 91, no. 3 (December 2004): 906–31.

172. Carruthers, *Unapologetic*, 47–48.
173. Ibid., 5.
174. Smith and Davey, "Cautions against Ferguson Comparisons after Officer Kills Black Teenager," *New York Times*, December 24, 2014, www.nytimes.com/2014/12/25/us/berkeley-missouri-police-shooting.html.
175. Zack Baron, "Jailed Ferguson Protestor Joshua Williams Wants to Be Out There with Everyone," *GQ*, June 5, 2020, www.gq.com/story/joshua-williams-ferguson-2020-interview.

176. As "White supremacists prepared to descend on Charlottesville, Virginia in August the FBI warned about a new movement that was violent, growing, and racially motivated," and identified nine "persistent extremist movements," namely: "White supremacy, black identities, militia, sovereign citizens, anarchists, abortion, animal rights, environmental rights, and Puerto Rican Nationalism." Jana Winter and Sharon Weinberger, "The FBI's New U.S. Terrorist Threat: 'Black Identity Extremists,'" *Foreign Policy*, October 6, 2017, https://foreignpolicy.com/2017/10/06/the-fbi-has-identified-a-new-domestic-terrorist-threat-and-its-black-identity-extremists/.
177. Ken Klippenstein, "Leaked FBI Documents Reveal Bureau's Priorities Under Trump," *The Young Turk*, August 8, 2019, https://tyt.com/stories/4vZLCHuQrYE4uKagyooyMA/mnzAKMpdtiZ7AcYLd5cRR.
178. According to the FBI Intelligence Assessment dated August 3, 2017, BIEs are "individuals who seek, wholly or in part, through unlawful acts of force or violence, in response to perceived racism and injustice in American society and some do so in furtherance of establishing a separate black homeland or autonomous black social institutions, communities, or governing organizations within the United States." Federal Bureau of Investigation, "Black Identity Extremists Likely Motivated to Target Law Enforcement," *Intelligence Assessment* (Counterterrorism Division, August 3, 2017).
179. Its 2020 "Threat Guidance" (FY-20 TG), for instance, assesses "White Supremacy Extremists" as "medium threat" despite the fact the majority of domestic terrorism cases it investigated were carried out by White supremacists. The 2017 Report repeatedly notes that "mere advocacy . . . may be constitutionally protected." Its assessment, however, relies on a total of six, unrelated incidents over the course of twenty months, asserting that "BIE perceptions of police brutality . . . spurred an increase in premeditated, retaliatory lethal violence against law enforcement." With scant evidence, the assessment speculates that "it is very likely some BIEs are influenced by a mix of anti-authoritarian, Moorish sovereign citizen ideology, and BIE ideology." FBI, "Black Identity," 2. Its "assessments" about individuals who have been marked as BIEs are anti-authoritarian and belonging to (the elusive) "Moorish sovereign citizen ideology" is considered "highly probable" at "80–95%," despite its dubious assumptions about Black people's experiences at the hands of the police or about protests in general. See also: Creede Newton, "US Judge Orders Release of 'First Black Identity Extremist,'" *Al Jazeera*, May 5, 2018, www.aljazeera.com/news/2018/5/5/us-judge-orders-release-of-first-black-identity-extremist.
180. Under pressures, in 2019 the FBI dropped the use of "BIE" and came up with another designation, "Racially Motivated Extremism," and changed again in 2020 to "Racially Motivated Violent Extremism" (RMVE). The 2019 vague designation "Racially Motivated Extremism" continues to rely on similar terminologies as the 2017 assessment that includes "Black Racially Motivated Extremism" as a priority. The 2020 threat assessment includes the previously used BIE definition. Federal Bureau of Investigation, "Racially Motivated Violent Extremism," *Threat Guidance* (Counterterrorism Division, 2020): 1.
181. See especially Richie, *Arrested Justice*; and Andrea J. Ritchie, *Invisible No More: Police Violence against Black Women and Women of Color* (Boston: Beacon Press, 2017).
182. Carruthers, *Unapologetic*, 33.

183. Richie, *Arrested Justice*, 128.
184. Ibid., 126.
185. Ibid., 129.
186. Ibid., 143.
187. Ibid., 133–34.
188. Ibid., 135.
189. Richie, *Arrested Justice*, 131–34; Davis et al., *Abolition*. See also Willoughby-Herard, "(Political) Anesthesia."
190. Quan, *Growth Against Democracy*. The rise of neoliberalism coincides with *the maturation*, not emergence, of the national security state. Concurring with Polanyi, I argue that "the relationship between development and antidemocracy is not incidental," but rather is a necessity for capitalist expansionist programs of development, particularly in the form of war, conquest, and colonization. The repression and suppression of movements against gendered racial capitalism—as exemplified by Indigenous sovereignty movements, movements to decolonize, and the Black freedom struggles, and the swift and disproportionate responses these movements received—verify how state violence, including administrative violence, is an essential part of the state antidemocratic toolkit, with the national security state as its aspiration (12–13; 55–62).
191. As a form of legal immunity, this framework protects state actors, especially police, from allegations of wrongdoing, especially violation of rights. The morally bankrupt and corporate friendly US Supreme Court has been consistent with its (re)assertion of "qualified immunity" as a governing framework for addressing the runaway problem of police violence and homicide. See, for instance, *Pearson v. Callahan* (2009). Given that many police kill, and very few ever get charged or convicted, one must assume that the US justice system deems police killing *reasonable*. Moreover, with *Pearson v. Callahan* the courts no longer have to consider first whether official conduct violates constitutional rights.
192. While former president Trump serves well as a nightly comedy highlight on American televisions, he was hardly a pioneer or the most competent; after all, demobilization and antidemocracy, key characteristics of an authoritarian regime, are indeed major features in the late twentieth- and early twenty-first-century United States, with the prison nation as part of its toolkit for securing the neoliberal order.
193. Our problem is not that we do not have enough data, but too much data—from toxic water and police killings to the ranks of the unhoused and food insecure, from mass incarceration to "over policing," and real-time facial recognition surveillance of communities and movements for justice, from the tens of millions behind carceral walls and at the borders, to one-third of all American adults marked and circumscribed by a criminal record, and who are also disproportionately represented among the poor and the disenfranchised. Scholarship by feminists of Color, especially Black feminists as sampled here, have collectively painted a grave picture of precarious contemporary life in the US, as they call attention to the urgent need to do something, to get basic with and radically alter these dangerously unsafe conditions.
194. See for instance Derecka Purnell's extraordinarily practical reasons in her invitation to becoming an abolitionist. Derecka Purnell, *Becoming Abolitionists: Police, Protests, and the Pursuit of Freedom* (New York: Astra House, 2021).
195. Richie, *Arrested Justice*, 7.

196. Elsewhere I have delineated a security-obsessed approach to national development, resulting in a propensity to secure order while fomenting antidemocratic social and political forms, including fascism. An emphasis on growth or wealth accumulation and hoarding, "necessitates expansionism and creates situations where coloniality is emblematic," as well as securing order, such that democratic participation is seen as an incitement of volatility in the market, constituting a threat to capital. Thus national security matters are frequently driven by the need to secure conditions conducive for "stable markets." Quan, *Growth Against Democracy*, 55–62.
197. Edwards, *The Other Side*; Richie, *Invisible No More*; Hinton *From the War*; Williams, *Politics of Public Housing*; Willoughby-Herard, "(Political) Anesthesia"; and Quan and Willoughby-Herard, "Displacement."
198. While the FBI moderated its concerns about White supremacist targets, White supremacist terror activities has been on the rise, and it persisted in framing Black people as a threat and danger to the corpus of "American life."
199. In *The Wretched of the Earth*, Fanon explains that within the larger frame of imperial regimes of governing, there is a clear division between good and evil, in which "the terms the settler uses when he mention the native are zoological terms" and that "the settler paints the native as a sort of quintessence of evil . . . [and] insensible to ethic; he represents not only the absence of values but also the negation of values" (41). This self-serving Manichean worldview is propagated despite the brutality and violence inherent in European expansionism and conquest. Decolonization therefore demands: "we must leave our dreams and abandon our old beliefs and friendship. . . . Let us waste no time in sterile litanies and nauseating mimicry. Leave this Europe where they are never done talking of Man, yet murder men everywhere they find them, at the corner of every one of their own streets, in all the corners of the globe" (311).
200. Recognizing the difference between "real security" versus "state security" or capital's need for "stable markets" and "financial order" engenders a more comprehensive understanding of justice and the good life.
201. Davis et al., *Abolition*.

References

(ACLU), American Civil Liberties Union. "Island of Impunity: Puerto Rico's Outlaw Police Force," New York: ACLU, June 2012.

(HRC), Human Rights Campaign. "Dismantling a Culture of Violence: Understanding Anti-Transgender Violence and Ending the Crisis." Washington, DC: Human Rights Campaign Foundation, 2021.

——. "An Epidemic of Violence: Fatal Violence against Transgender and Gender Non-Conforming People in the United States in 2020." Washington, DC: Human Rights Campaign Foundation, 2020.

Abbas, Asma. *Another Love: A Politics of the Unrequited*. Lanham: Lexington Books, 2018.

——. *Liberalism and Human Suffering: Materialist Reflections on Politics, Ethics, and Aesthetics*. 1st ed. New York: Palgrave Macmillan, 2010.

Adair, Douglass G. *The Intellectual Origins of Jeffersonian Democracy: Republicanism, the Class Struggle, and the Virtuous Farmer*. Lanham: Lexington Books, 2000 [1943].

Adnan, Etel. *There: In the Light and the Darkness of the Self and of the Other*. Sausalito, CA: Post-Apollo Press, 1997.

Agamben, Giorgio. *Homo Sacer: Sovereign Power and Bare Life*. Stanford: Stanford University Press, 1998.

——. *State of Exception*. Chicago: University of Chicago Press, 2005.

——. *Where Are We Now? Epidemic as Politics*. Lanham: Rowman & Littlefield, 2021.

Ahmed, Sara. *Living a Feminist Life*. Durham, NC: Duke University Press, 2017.

——. *The Promise of Happiness*. Durham, NC: Duke University Press, 2010.

——. *Queer Phenomenology: Orientations, Objects, Others*. Durham, NC: Duke University Press, 2006.

——. *Willful Subjects*. Durham, NC: Duke University Press, 2014.

Alcoff, Linda Martín, Michael Hames-Garcia, Satya P. Mohanty, and Paula M. L. Moya, eds. *Identity Politics Reconsidered*. New York: Palgrave Macmillian, 2006.

Alexander, Peter, and Anita Chan. "Does China Have an Apartheid Pass System?" *Journal of Ethnic and Migration Studies* 30, no. 4 (July 2004): 609–29.

Ali, Omar H. *In the Lion's Mouth: Black Populism in the New South, 1886–1900*. Jackson: University Press of Mississippi, 2010.

Alinsky, Saul David. *Rules for Radicals: A Practical Primer for Realistic Radicals*. 1st ed. New York: Random House, 1971.

Allan, Graham. "Friendship, Sociology and Social Structure." *Journal of Social and Personal Relationships* 15, no. 5 (October 1998): 685–702.

Allen, Jafari S. "Black/Queer Rhizomatics: Train up a Child in the Way Ze Should Grow. . . ." In *No Tea, No Shade: New Writings in Black Queer Studies*, edited by E. Patrick Johnson. Durham, NC: Duke University Press, 2016.

Applebaum, Anne. *Twilight of Democracy: The Seductive Lure of Authoritarianism*. 1st ed. New York: Doubleday, 2020.

Arendt, Hannah. "Lying in Politics: Reflections on the Pentagon Papers." *New York Review* (November 18, 1971).

——. *The Origins of Totalitarianism*. New York: Harcourt, 1951.

Aristophanes. *The Acharnians*. Oxford: Oxford University Press, 2002 [425 BC].
——. *Lysistrata*. Oxford: Clarendon Press, 1990 [411 BC].
Aristotle. *The Nicomachean Ethics*. Translated by W. D. Ross. Oxford: Oxford University Press, 1980 [350 BC].
——. *Politics*. Translated by Earnest Barker. Oxford: Oxford University Press, 1995.
Askew, David. "The Nanjing Incident: Recent Research and Trends." *Electronic Journal of Contemporary Japanese Studies* (April 2002).
Bacchetta, Paola, Fatima El-Tayeb, Jin Haritaworn, Jillian Hernandez, S. A. Smythe, Vanessa E. Thompson, and Tiffany Willoughby-Herard. "Queer of Color Space-Making in and Beyond the Academic Industrial Complex." *Critical Ethnic Studies* 4, no. 1 (2018): 44–63.
Bachrach, Peter. *The Theory of Democratic Elitism*. Boston: Little Brown, 1967.
Badiou, Alain. *Metapolitics*. Translated by Jason Barker. London: Verso, 2005.
Baldwin, James. *The Fire Next Time*. London: Michael Joseph, 1963.
——. "No Name in the Street." In *Collected Essays*. New York: The Library of America, 1998 [1972].
——. "The White Man's Guilt." In *Collected Essays*, 722–27. New York: The Library of America, 1998 [1965].
Balibar, Étienne. *Equaliberty: Political Essays*. Translated by James Ingram. Durham, NC: Duke University Press, 2014.
——. *On Universals: Constructing and Deconstructing Community*. Translated by Joshua David Jordan. New York: Fordham University Press, 2020.
Balibar, Etienne, and Immanuel Wallerstein. *Race, Nation, Class; Ambiguous Identities*. London: Verso, 1993.
Bambara, Toni Cade. "On the Issues of Roles." In *The Black Woman: An Anthology*, edited by Toni Cade Bambara. New York: Washington Square Press, 2005.
——. *The Salt Eaters*. New York: Vintage Books, 1980.
——. *The Seabirds Are Still Alive: Stories*. New York: Vintage Books, 1982.
Bardolph, Richard. "Book Review." *The Journal of Negro History* 55, no. 2 (April 1970): 152–53.
Barry, Brian. *Theories of Justice: A Treatise on Social Justice*. Vol. 1. Oakland: University of California Press, 1991.
Beard, Charles A. *An Economic Interpretation of the Constitution of the United States*. New York: The Macmillan Company, 1913.
——. *Economics Origins of Jeffersonian Democracy*. New York: The Macmillan Company, 1915.
——. "Some Economic Origins of Jeffersonian Democracy." *The American Historical Review* 19, no. 2 (January 1914): 282–98.
Behabib, Seyla. *The Rights of Others: Aliens, Residents, and Citizens*. Cambridge: Cambridge University Press, 2004.
Ben-Moshe, Liat. *Decarcerating Disability: Deinstitutionalization and Prison Abolition*. Minneapolis: University of Minnesota Press, 2020.
Ben-Moshe, Liat, Chris Chapman, and Allison C. Carey, eds. *Disability Incarcerated: Imprisonment and Disability in the United States and Canada*. New York: Palgrave Macmillan, 2014.
Bennett, Joshua. *Being Property Once Myself: Blackness and the End of Man*. Cambridge, MA: The Belknap Press, 2020.
Berger, Jonah. *Contagion: Why Things Catch On*. New York: Simon & Schulster, 2013.

Berkhout, Esmé, Nichk Galasso, Max Lawson, Pablo Andrés Rivero Morales, Anjela Taneja, and Diego Alego Vásquez Pimentel. "The Inequality Virus: Bringing Together a World Torn Apart by Coronavirus through a Fair, Just and Sustainable Economy - Oxfam Briefing Paper." Oxford: Oxam International, 2021.

Berthold, Michael C. "'The Peals of Her Terrific Language': The Control of Representation in Silvia Dubois, a Biography of the Slav Who Whipt Her Mistress and Gand Her Fredom." *Melus* 20, no. 2 (Summer 1995): 3–14.

Bessant, Judith. *The Great Transformation: History for a Techno-Human Future*. New York: Routledge, 2019.

Best, Heinrich, and John Higley, eds. *Democratic Elitism: New Theoretical and Comparative Perspectives*. Boston: Brill, 2010.

Bey, Marquis. *Anarcho-Blackness: Notes toward a Black Anarchism*. Edinburg: AK Press, 2020.

Black, Edwin. "War against the Weak: Eugenics and America's Campaign to Create a Master Race." Washington, DC: Diaglog Press, 2012.

Blackmon, Douglas A. *Slavery by Another Name: The Re-Enslavement of Black People in America from the Civil War to World War II*. New York: Doubleday, 2008.

Blee, Kathleen M. "The Gendered Organization of Hate: Women in the U.S. Ku Klux Klan." In *Right-Wing Women: From Conservatives to Extremists around the World*, edited by Paola Bacchetta and Margaret Power. New York: Routledge, 2002.

Blum, William. *Killing Hope: U.S. Military and CIA Interventions since World War II*. Monroe, ME: Common Courage Press, 1995.

Bogues, Anthony. "And What About the Human? Freedom, Human Emancipation, and the Radical Imagination." *Boundary* 239, no. 3 (2012): 29–46.

——. *Empire of Liberty: Power, Desire, & Freedom*. Hanover: Dartmouth College Press, 2010.

——. "The Human, Knowledge and the Word: Reflecting on Sylvia Wynter." In *After Man, toward the Human: Critical Essays on Sylvia Wynter*, edited by Anthony Bogues, 315–38. Kingston: Ian Randle Publishers, 2013.

Bonetto, Gerald M. "Tocqueville and American Slavery." *Canadian Review of American Studies* 15, no. 2 (Summer 1984): 123–39.

Boris, Eileen, and Jennifer Klein. *Caring for America Home Health Workers in the Shadow of the Welfare State*. New York: Oxford University Press, 2012.

Bostrom, Nick. "In Defense of Posthuman Dignity." *Bioethics* 19, no. 3 (2005): 202–14.

Boulamwini, Joy, and Timnit Gebru. "Gender Shades: Intersectional Accuracy Disparities in Commercial Gender Classification." *Proceedings of Machine Learning Research* 81 (2018): 1–15.

Bowles, John B. *Adrian Piper: Race, Gender, and Embodiment*. Durham, NC: Duke University Press, 2011.

Bratton, Benjamin. *The Revenge of the Real: Politics for a Post-Pandemic World*. London: Verso, 2021.

Brown, Adrienne Maree. *We Will Not Cancel Us and Other Dreams of Transformative Justice*. Chico: Bolder Press, 2020.

Brown, Wendy. *Undoing the Demos: Neoliberalism's Stealth Revolution*. New York: Zone Books, 2015.

Browne, Simone. *Dark Matters: On the Surveillance of Blackness*. Durham, NC: Duke University Press, 2015.

Burghart, Devin, and Leonard Zeskin. *Tea Party Nationalism: A Critical Examination of the Tea Party Movement and the Size, Scope, and Focus of Its National Factions.* Kansas City: Institute for Research & Education on Human Rights, 2010.

Burtenshaw, Claude J. "The Political Theory of Pluralist Democracy." *Western Political Science Quarterly* 21, no. 4 (December 1968): 577–88.

Butler, Judith. "Bodies That Still Matter." In *Vulnerability and the Politics of Care: Transdisciplinary Dialogue*, edited by Victoria Browne, Jason Danely, and Doerthe Rosenow, 33–42. Oxford: Oxford University Press, 2021.

——. *Gender Trouble: Feminism and the Subversion of Identity.* New York: Routledge, 1990.

Butler, Judith, Zeynep Gambetti, and Laticia Sabsay, eds. *Vulnerability in Resistance.* Durham, NC: Duke University Press, 2016.

Butler, Octavia E. *Parable of the Talents.* New York: Warner Books, 1998.

Byman, Daniel. "White Supremacy, Terrorism, and the Failure of Reconstruction in the United States." *International Security* 46, no. 1 (Summer 2021): 53–103.

Cabral, Amílcar, and Africa Information Service. *Return to the Source.* New York: Africa Information Service, 1973.

Camp, Stephanie M. H. *Closer to Freedom: Enslaved Women and Everyday Resistance in the Plantation South.* Chapel Hill: University of North Carolina Press, 2004.

Carby, Hazel V. *Reconstructing Womanhood: The Emergence of the Afro-American Woman Novelist.* New York: Oxford University Press, 1987.

Carlisle, Rodney. "The Foreign Policy Views of an Isolationist Press Lord: W. R. Hearst and the International Crisis, 1936–41." *Journal of Contemporary History* 9, no. 3 (July 1974): 217–27.

Carruthers, Charlene A. *Unapologetic: A Black, Queer, and Feminist Mandate for Radical Movements.* Boston: Beacon Press, 2018.

Chambers, Samuel Norton, Geoffrey Alan Boyce, Sarah Launius, and Alicia Dinsmore. "Mortality, Surveillance and the Tertiary 'Funnel Effect' on the U.S.-Mexico Border: A Geospatial Modeling of the Geography of Deterrence." *Journal of Borderlands Studies* 36, no. 3 (2021).

Chan, Aris. "Paying the Price for Economic Development: The Children of Migrant Workers in China." *China Labour Bulletin, Special Report* (Novemer 2009).

Chan, Jenny, Mark Selden, and Ngai Pun. *Dying for an iPhone: Apple, Foxconn and the Lives of China's Workers.* London: Pluto Press, 2020.

Chan, Victor Cheung Yin, Jeremy Backstrom, and T. David Mason. "Patterns of Protest in the People's Republic of China: A Provincial Level Analysis." *Asian Affairs: An American Review* 41 (2014): 91–107.

Chattopadhyay, Sutapa. "Violence on Bodies: Space, Social Reproduction and Intersectionality." *Gender, Place & Culture* 25, no. 9 (2019): 1295–1304.

Chen, Jieliang. "Pathogenicity and Transmissibility of 2019-Ncov—A Quick Overview and Comparison with Other Emerging Viruses." *Microbes and Infection* 22 (2020): 69–71.

Congressional—Executive Commission on China. *Annual Report*, 112 Congress, Second Session, October 10, 2012.

Chomsky, Noam. *Chomsky on Anarchism.* Oakland, CA: AK Press, 2005.

Clunan, Anne L., and Harold A. Trinkunas, eds. *Ungoverned Spaces: Alternatives to State Authority in an Era of Softened Sovereignty.* Stanford: Stanford Security Studies, 2010.

Cohen, Cathy J. "Deviance as Resistance: A New Research Agenda for the Study of Black Politics." *Du Bois Review* 1, no. 1 (2004): 27–45.

——. "Punks, Bulldaggers, and Welfare Queens: The Radical Potential of Queer Politics?" *GLQ: A Journal of Lesbian & Gay Studies* 3 (1997): 437–65.

Cohen, Cathy J., and Sarah J. Jackson. "Ask a Feminist: A Conversation with Cathy J. Cohen on Black Lives Matter, Feminism, and Contemporary Activism." *Signs: Journal of Women in Culture and Society* 41, no. 4 (2016): 775–92.

Collins, Patricia Hill. *Black Feminist Thought: Knowledge, Consciousness, and the Politics of Empowerment*. Boston: Unwin Hyman, 1990.

——. "Intersectionality and Epistemic Injustice." In *The Routledge Handbook of Epistemic Injustice*, edited by Ian James Kidd, José Medina, and Gaile Pohlhaus Jr. New York: Routledge, 2017.

Collins, Patricia Hill, and Sirma Bilge. *Intersectionality*. Cambridge: Polity Press, 2016.

Combahee River Collective. "A Black Feminist Statement." In *Home Girls: A Black Feminist Anthology*, edited by Barbara Smith. Albany: Kitchen Table Women of Color Press, 1983 [1977].

Cornell, Drucilla, and Stephen D. Seely. *The Spirit of Revolution: Beyond the Dead Ends of Man*. Cambridge: Polity Press, 2015.

Cost, Jay. *The Price of Greatness: Alexander Hamilton, James Madison, and the Creation of American Oligarchy*. Ebook ed. New York: Basic Books, 2018.

Cox, Oliver C. *Capitalism as a System*. New York: Monthly Review Press, 1964.

——. *Caste, Class, & Race: A Study in Social Dynamics*. New York: Monthly Review Press, 1959.

——. *The Foundations of Capitalism*. New York: Philosophical Library, 1959.

Crenshaw, Kimberlé. *On Intersectionality: Essential Writings*. New York: New Press, 2019.

Crenshaw, Kimberlé, Neil T. Gotanda, Gary Peller, and Kendall Thomas, eds. *Critical Race Theory: The Key Writings That Formed the Movement*. New York: New Press, 1995.

Crespigny, Rafe de. *Fire over Luoyang: A History of the Later Han Dynasty 23–220 AD*. Leiden: Brill, 2016.

Crockett, Hasan. "The Incendiary Pamphlet: David *Walker's Appeal* in Georgia." *The Journal of Negro History* 86, no. 3 (Summer 2001): 305–18.

Croix, G. E. M. de Ste. *The Class Struggle in the Ancient Greek World: From the Archaic Age to the Arab Conquests*. Ithaca, NY: Cornell University Press, 1981.

Cullather, Nick. *Secret History: The CIA's Classified Account of Its Operations in Guatemala, 1952–1954*. 2nd ed. Stanford: Stanford University Press, 2006.

Dahl, Robert A. *Dilemmas of Pluralist Democracy: Autonomy vs. Control*. New Haven, CT: Yale University Press, 1982.

——. *Who Governs? Democracy and Power in an American City*. New Haven, CT: Yale University Press, 1961.

Dahl, Robert A., and Charles Edward Lindblom. *Politics, Economics, and Welfare: Planning and Politico-Economic Systems Resolved into Basic Social Processes*. New York: Harper, 1953.

Davis, Angela. "The Black Women's Role in the Community of Slaves." *The Black Scholar* (December 1971): 1–14.

Davis, Angela Y. *Abolition Democracy: Beyond Empire, Prisons, and Torture*. New York: Seven Stories Press, 2005.

——. *Are Prisons Obsolete?* New York: Seven Stories Press, 2003.

——. *Blues Legacies and Black Feminism: Gertrude "Ma" Rainey, Bessie Smith, and Billie Holiday*. New York: Pantheon Books, 1998.

——. *Freedom Is a Constant Struggle: Ferguson, Palestine, and the Foundations of a Movement*. Chicago: Haymarket Books, 2016.

——. *Women, Race & Class*. New York: Vintage Books, 1983 [1981].

Davis, Angela Y., Gina Dent, Erica R. Meiners, and Beth Richie. *Abolition. Feminism. Now*. Chicago: Haymarket Books, 2022.

DeCook, Julia R., and Mi Huyn Yoon. "Kung Flu and Roof Koreans: Asian/Americans as the Hated Other and Proxies of Hating in the White Imaginary." *Journal of Hate Studies* 17, no. 1 (2021): 119–32.

Deleuze, Gilles, and Félix Guattari. *A Thousand Plateaus: Capitalism and Schizophrenia*. London: Athlone, 1988.

Divine, Robert A., T. H. Breen, R. Hal Williams, Ariela J. Gross, and H. W. Brands. *America: Past and Present*. Tenth ed. Vol. 1: Pearson, 2013.

Division, U.S. Department of Justice—Civil Rights. "Investigation of the Puerto Rico Police Department." Washington, DC: U.S. Department of Justice, September 5, 2011.

Donaldson, Adam. "Peasant and Slave Rebellions in the Roman Republic." PhD dissertation, University of Arizona, 2012.

Dong, Yang, and Jiang Wenbo. *Memories of the 1937 Nanjing Massacre: Oral Histories and Remembrance, 1937–2017*. South San Francisco: Long River Press, 2017.

Döring, Nicola, M. Rohangis Moohseni, and Roberto Walter. "Design, Use, and Effects of Sex Dolls and Sex Robots: Scoping Review." *Journal of Medical Internet Research* 22, no. 7 (July 2020).

Döring, Nicola, Nicole Krämer, Veronica Mikhailova, Matthias Brand, Tillmann H. C. Krüger, and Gerhard Vowe. "Sexual Interaction in Digital Contexts and Its Implications for Sexual Health: A Conceptual Analysis." *Frontiers in Psychology* 12 (November 2021).

Du Bois, W. E. B. *Black Folk: Then and Now: An Essay in the History of Sociology of the Negro Race*. Oxford: Oxford University Press, 2007 [1939].

——. *Black Reconstruction: An Essay toward a History of the Part Which Black Folk Played in the Attempt to Reconstruct Democracy in America, 1860–1880*. New York: Russell & Russell, 1935.

——. *Dark Water: Voices from within the Veil*. Mineola, NY: Dover Publications, Inc., 1999 [1920].

Dubé, Simon, and Dave Anctil. "Foundations of Erobotics." *International Journal of Social Robotics* 13, no. 6 (2021): 1205–33.

DuBose, Hamden C. *The Dragon, the Image, and the Demon: Or the Three Religions of China—Confucianism, Buddhism, and Taoism*. London: S. W. Partridge and Co., 1886.

Duffy, Mignon. "Doing the Dirty Work: Gender, Race and Reproductive Labor in Historical Perspectives." *Gender & Society* 21, no. 3 (2007): 313–36.

Dugas, John C. "Old Wine in the New Wineskins: Incorporating 'Ungoverned Spaces' Concept into Plan Columbia." In *U.S. National Security Concerns in the Latin America and the Caribbean: The Concept of Ungoverned Spaces and Failed States*, edited by Gary Prevost, Harry E. Vanden, Calros Oliva Campos, and Luis Fernando Ayerbe. New York: Palgrave, 2014.

Duggan, Lisa. *The Twilight of Equality? Neoliberalism, Cultural Politics, and the Attack on Democracy*. Boston: Beacon Press, 2003.

Dussel, Enrique. *Ethics of Liberation: In the Age of Globalization and Exclusion.* Durham, NC: Duke University Press, 2013.

——. *Philosophy of Liberation.* Eugene: Wipf & Stock Publishers, 2003.

Dussel, Enrique D. *Ethics and Community.* Maryknoll, NY: Orbis Books, 1988.

Eco, Umberto. *Serendipities: Language and Lunacy.* Translated by William Weaver. New York: Columbia University Press, 1998.

Edwards, Erica R. *The Other Side of Terror: Black Women and the Culture of US Empire.* New York: New York University Press, 2021.

Egerton, Douglas R. *Gabriel's Rebellion: The Virginia Slave Conspiracies of 1800 and 1802.* Chapel Hill: University of North Carolina Press, 1993.

Ehrenreich, Barbara, and Arlie Russel Hochschild. *Global Woman: Nannies, Maids and Sex Workers in the New Economy.* New York: Metropolitans Books, 2003.

Eisenstein, Zillah. *Abolitionist Socialist Feminism: Radicalizing the Next Revolution.* New York: Monthly Review Press, 2019.

Elliot, Jonathan, ed. *The Debates in the Several State of Convention on the Adoption of the Federal Constitution.* Vol. 5. Philadelphia: J. B. Lippincott & Co., 1859.

Enloe, Cynthia H. *Maneuvers: The International Politics of Militarizing Women's Lives.* Berkeley: University of California Press, 2000.

Espiritu, Yen Le. *Asian American Panethnicity: Bridging Institutions and Identities.* Philadelphia: Temple University Press, 1992.

Evans, Brad, and Henry A. Giroux. *Disposable Futures: The Seduction of Violence in the Age of Spectacle.* San Francisco: City Lights Books, 2015.

Fanon, Frantz. *The Wretched of the Earth.* New York: Grove Press, 1963.

Farrar, Cynthia. *The Origins of Democratic Thinking: The Invention of Politics in Classical Athens.* New York: Cambridge University Press, 1988.

Fasold, Ralph W., and Jeff Connor-Linton. *An Introduction to Language and Linguistics.* Cambridge: Cambridge University Press, 2006.

Federici, Silvia. *Caliban and the Witch.* New York: Autonomedia, 2004.

——. *Re-Enchanting the World: Feminism and the Politics of the Common.* San Francisco: PM Press, 2018.

——. *Revolution at Point Zero: Housework, Reproduction, and Feminist Struggle.* Oakland: PM Press, 2012.

Fehrenbacher, Don Edward. *Slavery, Law, and Politics: The Dred Scott Case in Historical Perspective.* New York: Oxford University Press, 1981.

Feldman, Noah. *The Three Lives of James Madison: Genius, Partisan, President.* Ebook ed. New York: Random House, 2017.

Ferguson, Roderick A. *Aberrations in Black: Toward a Queer of Color Critique.* Minneapolis: University of Minnesota Press, 2004.

——. *One Dimensional Queer.* Cambridge: Polity Press, 2019.

——. *The Reorder of Things: The University and Its Pedagogies of Minority Difference, Difference Incorporated.* Minneapolis: University of Minnesota Press, 2012.

Filotas, Zoli. *Aristotle and the Ethics of Difference, Friendship, and Equality: The Plurality of Rule.* London: Bloomsbury Academic, 2021.

Finley, M. I. *Democracy Ancient and Modern.* New Brunswick, NJ: Rutgers University Press, 1985.

Fluery, Héléne. "Ngo Van, Relayer of Living History." In *Ngo In the Crossfire: Adventures of a Vietnamese Revolutionary,* edited by Ken Knabb and Héléne Fluery. Oakland: AK Press, 2010.

Foner, Eric. *Free Soil, Free Labor, Free Men: The Ideology of the Republican Party before the Civil War.* New York: Oxford University Press, 1995.

——. *Voices of Freedom: A Documentary History.* 6th ed. Vol. 1. New York: W. W. Norton & Company, 2020.

Foucault, Michel. "Governmentality." *Ideology and Consciousness* 6 (Autumn 1979): 5–21.

——. *The Order of Things: An Archaeology of the Human Sciences.* New York: Vintange Books, 1970.

——. "Of Other Spaces." *Diacritics* 16, no. 1 (1986 [1967]): 22–27.

——. *"Society Must Be Defended": Lectures at the Collège De France.* Translated by David Macey. New York: Picador, 2003.

Francis, Pope. *Laudato Si': On Care for Our Common Home*: The Vatican, 2015.

Freeland, Chrystia. *Plutocrats: The Rise of the New Global Super-Rich and the Fall of Everyone Else.* New York: Penguin Press, 2012.

Freud, Sigmund. *Civilization and Its Discontents.* New York: W. W. Norton, 1961 [1929].

——. *The Ego and the Id.* New York: W. W. Norton, 1923.

Fricker, Miranda. *Epistemic Injustice: Power and the Ethics of Knowing.* New York: Oxford University Press, 2007.

Fujino, Diane C. *Heartbeat of Struggle: The Revolutionary Life of Yuri Kochiyama.* Minneapolis: University of Minnesota Press, 2005.

Fukumura, Yoko, and Martha Mastuoka. "Redefining Security: Okinawa Women's Resistance to U.S. Militarism." In *Women's Activism and Globalization: Linking Local Struggles and Transnational Politics* edited by Nancy A. Naples and Manisha Desai. New York: Routledge, 2002.

Fulton, DoVeanna S. *Speaking Power: Black Feminist Orality in Women's Narratives of Slavery.* Albany: State University of New York Press, 2006.

Gahman, Levi. "Building 'A World Where Many Worlds Fit': Indigenous Autonomy, Mutual Aid, and an (Anti-Capitalist) Moral Economy of the (Rebel) Peasant." In *Sustainable Food Futures: Multidisciplinary Solutions*, edited by Jessica Duncan and Megan Bailey. London: Routledge, 2017.

Gao, Mobo. *The Battle for China's Past: Mao and the Cultural Revolution.* London: Pluto, 2008.

Gardner, James Wilford. *Reconstruction in Mississippi* New York: McMillan Co., 1901.

Garza, Alicia. "A Herstory of the #Blacklivesmatter Movement." In *Are All the Women Still White? Rethinking Race, Expanding Feminism*, edited by Janell Hobson. Albany: SUNY Press, 2016.

Gåttens, Marie-Luise. *Women Writers & Fascism: Reconstructing History.* Gainsville: University Press of Florida, 1995.

Gellner, Ernest. *Saints of the Atlas.* London: Weidenfeld & Nicolson, 1969.

Giroux, Henry A. "Reading Hurricane Katrina: Race, Class, and the Biopolitics of Disposability." *College Literature* 33, no. 3 (Summer 2006): 171–96.

——. *Stormy Weather: Katrina and the Politics of Disposability.* New York: Routledge, 2006.

Glausser, Wayne. "Three Approaches to Locke and the Slave Trade." *Journal of the History of Ideas* 51, no. 2 (1990): 199–216.

Glenn, Evelyn Nakano. "From Servitude to Service Work: Historical Continuities in the Racial Division of Paid Reproductive Labor." *Signs: Journal of Women in Culture and Society* 18 (1992): 1–43.

Göbel, Christian, and Lynette H. Ong. *Social Unrest in China*: Europe China Research and Achive Network, 2012.

Goldstein, Alyosha, and Simón Ventura Trujillo, eds. *New Futures Are Possible Right Now*. Vol. 7.1, *Critical Ethnic Studies Journal*, Spring 2021.

Gómez, Alan Eladio. *The Revolutionary Imaginations of Greater Mexico: Chicana/O Radicalism, Solidarity Politics, & Latin American Social Movements*. Austin: University of Texas Press, 2016.

Gordon, Avery F. *Keeping Good Time: Reflections on Knowledge, Power, and People*. Boulder: Paradigm Publishers, 2004.

——. *The Hawthorn Archive: Letters from the Utopian Margins*. New York: Fordham University Press, 2018

Gordon, Lewis R. *Bad Faith and Antiblack Racism*. Amherst, MA: Humanities Books, 1995.

——. *Freedom, Justice, and Decolonization* New York: Routledge, 2021.

Gordon, Linda. *The Second Coming of the KKK: The Ku Klux Klan of the 1920s and the American Political Tradition*. New York: Liveright, 2017.

Gossett, Che. "Silhouettes of Defiance: Memorializing Historical Sites of Queer and Transgender Resistance in an Age of Neoliberal Inclusivity." In *The Transgender Studies Reader 2*, edited by Susan Stryker and Aren Z. Aizura, 580–90. New York: Routledge, 2013.

Goto-Jones, Christopher. "Magic, Modernity, and Orientalism: Conjuring Representations of Asia." *Modern Asian Studies* 48, no. 6 (November 2014): 1451–76.

Gover, Angela R., Shannon B. Harper, and Lynn Langton. "Anti-Asian Hate Crime During Covid-19 Pandemic: Exploring the Reproduction of Inequality." *American Journal of Criminal Justice* 45 (2020): 647–67.

Grant, Jaime M., Lisa A. Mottet, and Justin Tanis. "Injustice at Every Turn: A Report of the National Transgender Discrimination Survey." Washington, DC: The National Center of Transgender Equality and the Gay and Lesbian Taskforce, 2011.

Gray, Chris Hables. *Cyborg Citizen: Politics in the Posthuman Age*. New York: Routledge, 2001.

Green, Kai M. "Troubling the Waters: Mobilizing a Trans* Analytic." In *No Tea, No Shade: New Writings in Black Queer Studies*, edited by E. Patrick Johnson. Durham, NC: Duke University Press, 2016.

Griffith, C. A., and H. L. T. Quan. *Mountains That Take Wing/Angela Davis & Yuri Kochiyama: A Conversation on Life, Struggles & Liberation*. New York: QUAD Productions/Women Make Movies, 2009. Documentary.

Guendelsberger, Emily. *On the Clock: What Low-Wage Work Did to Me and How It Drives America Insane*. New York: Little, Brown and Company, 2019.

Guidi, Chen, and Wu Chuntao. *Will the Boat Sink the Water? The Life of China's Peasant*. Translated by Zhu Hong. New York: Public Affairs, 2006.

Guinier, Lani. "Foreword: Demosprudence through Dissent." *Harvard Law Review* 122, no. 1 (November 2008): 6–138.

Guinier, Lani, and Gerald Torres. "Changing the Wind: Notes toward a Demosprudence of Law and Social Movements." *The Yale Law Journal* 123, no. 8 (June 2014): 2740–2804.

Gutzman, K. R. Constantine. "The Virginia and Kentucky Resolutions Reconsidered: 'An Appeal to the Real Laws of Our Country.'" *The Journal of Southern History* 66, no. 3 (August 2000): 473–96.

Hadden, Sally E. *Slave Patrols: Law and Violence in Virginia and the Carolinas*. Cambridge, MA: Harvard University Press, 2001.

Hamaji, Kate, Jumar Rao, Marbre Stahly-Butts, Janaé Bonsu, Charlene Carruthers, Roselyn Berry, and Denzel McCampbell. "Freedom to Thrive: Reimagining Safety & Security in Our Communities." Washington, DC: The Center for Popular Democracy, Law for Black Lives, and BYP100, 2017.

Hames-Garcia, Michael Roy. *Fugitive Thought: Prison Movements, Race, and the Meaning of Justice*. Minneapolis: University of Minnesota Press, 2004.

Hamington, Maurice. "Public Pragmatism: Jane Addams and Ida B. Wells on Lynching." *The Journal of Speculative Philosophy* 19, no. 2 (2005): 167–74.

Hankins, F. H. "Reviews." *Political Science Quarterly* 44, no. 1 (March 1929): 127–29.

Haraway, Donna. "Tentacular Thinking: Anthropocene, Capitalocene, Chthulucene." *e-flux Journal* 75 (September 2016): 1–17.

Haraway, Donna J. *Simians, Cyborgs, and Women: The Reinvention of Nature*. New York: Routledge, 1991.

Harding, Sandra. "Transformation vs. Resistance Identity Politics: Epistemological Resources for Social Justice Movements." In *Identity Politics Reconsidered*, edited by Linda Martín Alcolff, Michael Hames-Garcia, Satya P. Mohanty and Paula M. L. Moya. New York: Palgrave MacMillian, 2006.

Hardt, Michael, and Antonio Negri. *Commonwealth*. Cambridge, MA: Belknap Press of Harvard University Press, 2009.

——. *Multitude: War and Democracy in the Age of Empire*. New York: The Penguin Press, 2004.

Harney, Stefano, and Fred Moten. *The Undercommons: Fugitive Planning & Black Study*. New York: Minor Compositions, 2013.

Harris, Cheryl I. "Whiteness as Property." *Harvard Law Review* 106, no. 8 (1993): 1707–91.

Herman, Edward S. *The Myth of the Liberal Media: An Edward Herman Reader*. New York: International Academic Publishers, 1999.

Herman, Edward S., and Noam Chomsky. *Manufacturing Consent: The Political Economy of the Mass Media*. New York: Pantheon Books, 1988.

Hertz, Friedrich Otto. *Race and Civilization*. Translated by A. S. Levetus and W. Entz. New York: Ktav Publishing House, 1970 [1928].

Hess, Karl. *In a Cause that Will Triumph: The Goldwater Campaign and the Future of Conservatism*. Garden City: Doubleday, 1967.

Hinton, Elizabeth. *From the War on Poverty to the War on Crime: The Making of Mass Incarceration in America*. Cambridge, MA: Harvard University Press, 2016.

Hobbes, Thomas. *Leviathan*, Edited with *Introduction and Notes by Edwin Curley*. Indianapolis: Hackett Publishing, 1994 [1668].

Holloway, John, and Eloína Peláez (eds). *Zapatista! Reinventing Revolution in Mexico*. London: Pluto Press, 1998.

Holmes, Linda Jane, and Cheryl A. Wall. *Savoring the Salt: The Legacy of Toni Cade Bambara*. Philadelphia: Temple University Press, 2008.

Holowchak, M. Andrew. *Rethinking Thomas Jefferson's Writings on Slavery and Race*. Cambridge: Cambridge Scholars Publishing, 2020.

hooks, bell. *All About Love: New Visions*. New York: William Morrow, 2000.

Horkheimer, Max. *Eclipse of Reason*. New York: Oxford University Press, 1947.

Horkheimer, Max, and Theodor W. Adorno. *Dialectic of Enlightenment*. New York: Herder and Herder, 1972.

Hossein, Caroline S. "A Black Epistemology for Social and Solidarity Economy: The Black Social Economy." *The Review of Black Political Economy* 46, no. 3 (2019): 209–29.

Hossein, Caroline S., ed. *The Black Social Economy in the Americas: Exploring Diverse Community-Based Alternative Markets.* New York: Palgrave Macmillan, 2018.

Hughes, James. *Citizen Cyborg: Why Democratic Societies Must Respond to the Redesigned Human of the Future.* Cambridge: West View Press, 2004.

——. "The Politics of Transhumanism and the Techno-Millennial Imagination, 1626–2030." *Zygon* 47, no. 4 (December 2012): 757–76.

Hughes, Langston. "Too Much of Race." *Crisis* 44, no. 9 (September 1937).

Huntington, Samuel P. *Political Order in Changing Societies.* New Haven, CT: Yale University Press, 1968.

Illich, Ivan. *Tools for Conviviality.* New York: Harper & Row, 1973.

Jacob, Harriet. *Incidents in the Life of a Slave Girl Written by Herself.* New York: Penguin Books, 2000.

James, C. L. R. *The Black Jacobins: Toussaint L'ouverture and the San Domingo Revolution.* New York: Vintage Books, 1989.

James, Sandy E., Jody L. Herman, Susan Rankin, Mara Keisling, Lisa Mottet, and Ma'ayan Anafi. "The Report of the 2015 U.S. Transgender Survey." Washington, DC: The National Center for Transgender Equality, 2016.

Jameson, Fredric. *The Political Unconscious: Narrative as a Socially Symbolic Act.* Ithaca, NY: Cornell University Press, 1981.

Jefferson, Thomas. "Inaugural Address." In *The Papers of Thomas Jefferson, Vol. 33.* Princeton, NJ: Princeton University Press, 2006 [1801].

——. *Notes on the State of Virginia.* New York: Barnes & Noble, 2010 [1788].

Jin, Giu. *The Culture of Power: Lin Biao and the Cultural Revolution.* Palo Alto: Stanford University Press, 1999.

Jobin-Leeds, Greg, and AgitArte. *When We Fight We Win: Twenty-First Century Social Movements and the Activists That Are Transforming Our World.* New York: The New Press, 2016.

Jolivétte, Andrew J. "Critical Mixed Race Studies: New Directions in the Politics of Race and Representation." *Journal of Critical Mixed Race Studies* 1, no. 1 (2014): 149–61.

——. "Radical Love as a Strategy for Social Transformation." In *Research Justice: Methodologies for Social Change*, edited by Andrew J. Jolivétte. Chicago: Policy Press, 2015.

Jones, Reece. *Violent Borders: Refugees and the Rights to Move.* New York: Verso Books, 2016.

Jordan, June. *Some of Us Did Not Die: New and Selected Essays of June Jordan.* New York: Basic/Civitas Books, 2002.

Jun, Helen Heran. *Race for Citizenship: Black Orientalism and Asian Uplift from Pre-Emancipation to Neoliberal America.* New York: New York University Press, 2011.

Jung, C. G. *Collected Work of C. G. Jung, Volume 9.* Princeton, NJ: Princeton University Press, 1968.

Kahn, Joseph M., Randy H. Katz, and Kristopher S. J. Pister. "Emerging Challenges: Mobile Network for 'Smart Dust.'" *Journal of Communication and Networks* 2, no. 3 (September 2000): 188–96.

Keeling, Kara. *Queer Times, Black Futures.* New York: New York University Press, 2019.

Kelley, Robin D. G. *Freedom Dreams: The Black Radical Imagination*. Boston: Beacon Press, 2002.

——. *Hammer and Hoe: Alabama Communists During the Great Depression*. Chapel Hill: University of North Carolina Press, 1990.

——. *Race Rebels: Culture, Politics, and the Black Working Class*. New York: Free Press, 1994.

Kiel, Thomas J., and Jacqueline M. Keil. "Funding the Tea Parties." *Sociation Today* 13, no. 1 (2015).

Kinzer, Stephen. *All the Shah's Men: An American Coup and the Roots of Middle East Terror*. Hoboken, NJ: John Wiley & Sons, 2008.

Kochiyama, Yuri. *Passing It On*. Los Angeles: UCLA Asian American Studies Center Press, 2007.

Kropotkin, Petr Alekseevich. *Mutual Aid a Factor of Evolution*. New York: McClure, Phillips & Co., 1902.

Kurzweil, Ray. *The Age of Intelligent Machines*. Cambridge, MA: MIT Press, 1990.

——. *How to Create a Mind: The Secret of Human Thought Revealed* New York: Penguin Books, 2013.

——. *The Singularity Is Near: When Humans Transcend Biology*. New York: Viking, 2005.

Lacy, Michael G. "Exposing the Spectrum of Whiteness." *Annals of the International Communication Association* 32 (2008): 277–312.

Leong, Karen J. *The China Mystique: Pearl S. Buck, Anna May Wong, Mayling Soong, and the Transformation of American Orientalism*. Berkeley: University of California Press, 2005.

Lesser, Jeffrey. *A Discontented Diaspora: Japanese Brazillians and the Meanings of Ethnic Militancy, 1960–1980*. Durham, NC: Duke University Press, 2007.

——. *Negotiating National Identity: Immigrants, Minorities, and The Struggle for Ethnicity in Brazil*. Durham, NC: Duke University Press, 1999.

Levy, Howard S. "The Bifurcation of the Yellow Turbans in Later Han." *Oriens* 13/14 (1960/1961): 251–55.

Leys, Simon. *The Chairman's New Clothes: Mao and the Cultural Revolution*. Translated by Carol Appleyard and Patrick Goode. London: Allison & Busby, 1981.

Li, Yao, and Harvey L. Nicholson Jr. "When 'Model Minorities" Become 'Yellow Peril': Othering and the Racialization of Asian Americans in the Covid-19 Pandemic." *Sociology Compass* 15 (2021): e12849.

Lilla, Mark. "The New Age of Tyranny." In *Confronting Tyranny: Ancient Lessons for Global Politics*, edited by Toivo Koivukoski and David Tabachnick, 2005.

Lin, Thung-hon, Yi-ling Lin, and Wei-lin Tseng. "Manufacturing Suicides: The Politics of a World Factory." *Chinese Sociological Review* 48, no. 1 (2015): 1–32.

Lipset, Seymour Martin. "Introduction." In *Political Parties*, edited by Robert Michels. New York: The Free Press, 1962.

Lipsitz, George. *The Possessive Investment in Whiteness: How White People Profit from Identity Politics*. Philadelphia: Temple University Press, 1998.

Liu, Fei-wen. *Gendered Words: Sentiments and Expression in Changing Rural China*. Oxford: Oxford University Press, 2015.

Liu, Shih-Diing. "Demanding State Intervention: New Opportunities for Popular Protests in China." In *The New Global Politics: Global Social Movements in the Twenty-First Century*, edited by Harry E. Vanden, Peter N. Funke, and Gary Prevost, 234–49. London: Routledge, 2017.

Locke, John. *Two Treatises of Government*. New York: Cambridge University Press, 1988 [1690].

——. *The Fundamental Constitutions of Carolina in North Carolina Charters and Constitutions, 1578–1698* edited by Mattie Erma Edwards Parker. Raleigh: Carolina Charter Tercentenary Commission, 1963 [1669].

——. *A Letter Concerning Toleration*. 4th ed. Wilmington: Printed and sold by James Adam, in Market-Street, 1764.

Lorde, Audre. "Age, Race, Class and Sex: Women Redefining Difference." In *Sister Outsider: Essays and Speeches*. Berkeley: Crossing Press, 2007.

——. "A Litany for Survival." In *The Collected Poems of Audre Lorde*. New York: W. W. Norton & Company, 1978.

——. "The Master's Tools Will Never Dismantle the Master's House." In *Sister Outsider: Essays and Speeches*. Berkeley: Crossing Press, 2007 [1984].

——. "The Transformation of Silence into Language and Action." In *Sister Outsider: Essays and Speeches*. Berkeley: Crossing Press, 2007 [1984].

Losin, Peter. "Aristotle's Doctrine of the Mean." *History of Philosophy Quarterly* 4, no. 3 (July 1987): 329–41.

Lowe, Lisa. *Critical Terrains: French and British Orientalisms*. Ithaca, NY: Cornell University Press, 1991.

Lum, Thomas. *Social Unrest in China: Foreign Affairs, Defense, and Trade Division*. Washington DC: Congressional Research Service, The Library of Congress, May 8, 2006.

Lyman, Stanford M. "The 'Yellow Peril' Mystique: Origins and Vicissitudes of a Racist Discourse." *International Journal of Politics, Culture and Society* 13, no. 4 (2000): 683–747.

Lynn, Joshua A. *Preserving the White Man's Republic: Jacksonian Democracy, Race, and the Transformation of American Conservatism*. Charlottesville: University of Virginia Press, 2019.

Macfarquhar, Roderick, and Michael Schoenhals. *Mao's Last Revolution*. Cambridge, MA: The Belknap Press, 2006.

MacLean, Nancy. *Behind the Mask of Chivalry: The Making of the Second Ku Klux Klan*. New York: Oxford University Press, 1995.

Madison, James. "From James Madison to Robert J. Evans, June 15, 1819." In *The Papers of James Madison: Retirement Series, Vol. 1, 4 March 1817–31 January 1820*, edited by David B. Matter, J. C. A. Stagg, Mary Parke Johnson, and Anne Mandeville Colony, 468–72. Charlottesville: University of Virginia Press, 2009 [1819].

——. *Notes of Debates in the Federal Convention of 1787*. New York: W. W. Norton, 1987 [1787].

——. "Virginia Ratifying Convention, June 20, 1788." In *The Papers of James Madison*, edited by William T. Hutchinson, William M. E. Rachal, and Robert Allen Rutland. Chicago: University of Chicago Press, 1962 [1788].

Marable, Manning. *How Capitalism Underdeveloped Black America: Problems in Race, Political Economy, and Society*. Boston: South End Press, 1983.

Marcos, Subcomandante. *Conversations with Durito: Stories of the Zapatistas and Neoliberalism*. Brooklyn: Autonomedia, 2005.

Martel, James R. *Divine Violence: Walter Benjamin and the Eschatology of Sovereignty*. New York: Routledge, 2012.

——. *The Misinterpellated Subject*. Durham, NC: Duke University Press, 2017.

Massa, Anna. "Black Women in the 'White City.'" *Journal of American Studies* 8, no. 3 (1974): 319–37.

Mayer, Jane. *Dark Money: The Hidden History of the Billionaires Behind the Rise of the Radical Right*. New York: Doubleday, 2016.

Mayorga-Gallo, Sarah. "The White-Centering Logic of Diversity Ideology." *American Behavioral Scientist* 63, no. 13 (2019): 1789–1809.

McGuire, Danielle L. "'It Was Like All of Us Had Been Raped': Sexual Violence, Community Mobilization, and the African American Freedom Struggle." *The Journal of American History* 91, no. 3 (December 2004): 906–31.

McIlwain, Charlton D., and Stephen M. Caliendo. "Mitt Romney's Racist Appeals: How Race Was Played in the 2012 Presidential Election." *American Behaviorist Scientist* 58, no. 9 (November 2014): 1157–68.

McKittrick, Katherine, ed. *Sylvia Wynter: On Being Human as Praxis*. Durham, NC: Duke University Press, 2015.

McLeod, Allegra M. "Envisioning Abolition Democracy." *Harvard Law Review* 132 (2019): 1613–49.

Meikle, Scott. *Aristotle's Economic Thought*. Oxford: Clarendon Press, 1995.

Mencius. *The Works of Mencius*. Translated by James Legge. New York: Dover Publications, Inc., 1970 [1895].

Merkl, Taryn A. "Protecting against Police Brutality and Official Misconduct: A New Federal Criminal Civil Rights Framework." New York: Brennan Center for Justice, April 29, 2021.

Michaud, Paul. "The Yellow Turbans." *Monumenta Serica* 17 (1958): 47–127.

Mills, Charles W. *Black Rights/White Wrongs: The Critique of Racial Liberalism, Transgressing Boundaries*. New York: Oxford University Press, 2017.

——. *The Racial Contract*. Ithaca, NY: Cornell University Press, 1997.

——. "White Ignorance." In *Race and Epistemologies of Ignorance*, edited by Shannon Sullivan and Nancy Tuana. Albany: State University of New York Press, 2007.

Minsky, Marvin. "Steps toward Artificial Intelligence." *Proceedings of the IRE* 49, no. 1 (January 1961): 8–30.

Minsky, Marvin Lee. *The Emotion Machine: Commonsense Thinking, Artificial Intelligence, and the Future of Human Mind* New York: Simon & Schuster, 2007.

Mohan, Seema C., and S. Arulselvi. "Smartdust Network for Tactical Border Surveillance Using Multiple Signatures." *Journal of Electronics and Communication Engineering* 5, no. 5 (March–April 2013): 1–10.

Mohanty, Chandra Talpade. *Feminism without Borders: Decolonizing Theory, Practicing Solidarity*. Durham, NC: Duke University Press, 2003.

Mohanty, Chandra Talpade, and Linda E. Carty, eds. *Feminist Freedom Warriors: Genealogies, Justice, Politics, and Hope*. Chicago: Haymarket Books, 2018.

Monteiro, Lyra D. "Race-Conscious Casting and the Erasure of the Black Past in Lin-Manuel Miranda's *Hamilton*." *The Public Historian* 38, no. 1 (February 2016): 89–98.

Moravec, Hans. *Mind Children: The Future of Robot and Human Intelligence* Cambridge, MA: Havard University Press, 1988.

——. *Robot: Mere Machine to Transcendent Mind* Oxford: Oxford University Press, 1998.

More, Max. "The Philosophy of Transhumanism." In *The Transhumanist Reader*, edited by Max More and Natasha Vita-More. Malden, MA: Wiley-Blackwell, 2013.

——. "The Proactionary Principle: Optimizing Technological Outcomes." In *The Transhumanist Reader*, edited by Max More and Natasha Vita-More. Malden, MA: Wiley-Blackwell, 2013.

Morrison, Toni. *Playing in the Dark: Whiteness and the Literary Imagination*. Cambridge, MA: Harvard University Press, 1992.

Morrow, Bethany C. *Mem, a Novel*. Los Angeles: Unnamed Press, 2018.

Nembhard, Jessica Gordon. *Collective Courage: A History of African American Cooperative Economic Thought and Practice*. University Park: The Pennsylvania State University Press, 2014.

Newell, Walter R. *Tyranny: A New Interpretation*. Cambridge: Cambridge University Press, 2013.

Newfield, Christopher. *The Great Mistake: How We Wrecked Public Universities and How We Can Fix Them* Baltimore: John Hopkins University Press, 2018.

Ngo, Van. *In the Crossfire: Adventures of a Vietnamese Revolutionary*. Translated by Héléne Fluery, Hilary Horrocks, Ken Knabb and Naomi Sager. Oakland: AK Press, 2010.

Ngo, Van Xuyet. *Ancient Utopia and Peasant Revolts in China*. Translated by Magali Sirera. Barcelon: Etcetera, 2004.

Nicholls, Michael L. *Whispers of Rebellion: Narrating Gabriel's Conspiracy*. Charlottesville: University of Virginia Press, 2012.

Nietzsche, Friedrich. *Beyond Good & Evil: Prelude to a Philosophy of the Future*. Translated by Helen Zimmern. New York: The Macmillan Company, 1907.

——. *The Will to Power* Translated by Walter Kaufmann and R. J. Hollingdale. New York: Vintage, 1968.

Noguiera, Joana Laura Marinho, and João Nicédio Alves Nogueira. "The Evolution of Cooperatism in Brazil." In *Cooperatives, Grassroots Development, and Social Change: Experiences from Rural Latin America* edited by Marcela Vásquez-Léon, Brian J. Burke and Timothy J. Finan. Tucson: University of Arizona, 2017.

Norton, Richard J. "Feral Cities." *Naval War College Review* 56, no. 4 (2003/Autumn Article 8): 97–106.

Oakes, James. "Slavery and Freedom: An Interpretation of the Old South." xxi, 246 p. New York: Knopf eBooks, 1990.

Obama, Barack. *The Audacity of Hope: Thoughts on Reclaiming the American Dream*. 1st ed. New York: Crown Publishers, 2006.

Okin, Susan Moller. *Justice, Gender, and the Family*. New York: Basic Books, 1989.

Olsen, Joel. *The Abolition of White Democracy* Minneapolis: University of Minnesota Press, 2004.

——. "The Freshness of Fanaticism: The Abolitionist Defense of Zealotry." *Perspectives on Politics* 5, no. 4 (2007): 685–701.

Olsen, Joel Karleton. "The Democratic Problem of the White Citizen." Dissertation, University of Minnesota, 2001.

Ong, Aihwa. *Neoliberalism as Exception: Mutations in Citizenship and Sovereignty*. Durham, NC: Duke University Press, 2006.

Painter, Nell Irvin. *The History of White People*. New York: W. W. Norton, 2010.

——. *Soul Murder and Slavery*. Waco: Markham Press, 1995.

Palmer, William P., ed. *Calendar of Virgina State Papers and Other Manuscripts*, 1875.

Parker, Mattie Erma Edwards, ed. *North Carolina Charters and Constitutions, 1578–1698*. Raleigh: Carolina Charter Tercentenary Commission, 1963.

Parry, William. *Against the Wall: The Art of Resistance in Palestine*. Chicago: Lawrence Hill Books, 2011.

Pateman, Carole. *The Sexual Contract*. Stanford: Stanford University Press, 1988.

Pateman, Carole, and Charles W. Mills. *Contract and Domination*. Cambridge: Polity, 2007.

Patterson, Orlando. *Freedom Volume I: Freedom in the Making of Western Culture*. New York: Basic Books, 1991.

——. *Slavery and Social Death: A Comparative Study*. Cambridge, MA: Harvard University Press, 1982.

Paxton, Robert O. *The Anatomy of Fascism*. New York: Alfred A. Knopf, 2004.

——. "The Fives Stages of Fascism." *Journal of Modern History* 70, no. 1 (March 1998): 1–23.

Perrin, Andrew J., Steven J. Tepper, Neal Caren, and Sally Morris. "Cultures of Tea Party." *Context* 10, no. 2 (2011).

Perry, Elizabeth J. "When Peasants Speak: Sources for the Study of Chinese Rebellion." *Modern China* 6, no. 1 (January 1980): 72–85.

Picketty, Thomas, and Emmanuel Saez. "Top Incomes and the Great Recession: Recent Evolutions and Policy Implications." *IMF Economic Review* 61, no. 3 (2013): 456–78.

Piper, Adrian. *Out of Order, out of Sight: Selected Writings in Meta-Art*. 2 vols. Cambridge, MA: MIT Press, 1996/1999.

Piper, Adrian M. S. "Impartiality, Compassion, and Modal Imagination." *Ethics* 101, no. 4 (1991): 726–57.

——. *Rationality and the Structure of the Self: The Humean Conception*. Vol. 1. Berlin: Adrian Piper Research Archive Foundation, 2013.

——. *Rationality and the Structure of the Self: A Kantian Conception*. Vol. 2. Berlin: Adrian Piper Research Archive Foundation, 2013.

Pitts, Jennifer. "Introduction." In *Writings on Empire and Slavery by Alexis De Tocqueville*, edited by Jennifer Pitts. Baltimore: John Hopkins University Press, 2001.

Piven, Frances Fox, and Richard A. Cloward. *Poor People's Movements: Why They Succeed and How They Fail*. New York: Vintage, 1978.

Plato. *The Republic*. Translated by Benjamin Jowett. Mineola, NY: Dover Publications, 2000.

Polanyi, Karl. *The Great Transformation*. New York: Farrar & Rinehart, 1944.

Post, Robert, and Reva Siegel. "Roe Rage: Democratic Constitutionalism and Backlash." *Harvard Civil Rights-Civil Liberties Law Review* 42, no. 2 (June 2007): 373–433.

Poulantzas, Nicos. *Fascism and Dictatorship: The Third International and the Problem of Fascism*. London: NLB, 1974.

Prevost, Gary, Harry E. Vanden, Calros Oliva Campos, and Luis Fernando Ayerbe, eds. *U.S. National Security Concerns in the Latin America and the Caribbean: The Concept of Ungoverned Spaces and Failed States*. New York: Palgrave, 2014.

Proudhon, P. J. *The Principle of Federation*. Translated by Richard Vernon. Toronto: University of Toronto Press, 1979.

Puar, Jasbir K. *The Right to Maim: Debility, Capacity, Disability, Anima*. Durham, NC: Duke University Press, 2017.

——. *Terrorist Assemblages: Homonationalism in Queer Times, Next Wave*. Durham, NC: Duke University Press, 2007.

Purnell, Derecka. *Becoming Abolitionists: Police, Protests, and the Pursuit of Freedom*. New York: Astra House, 2021.

Putnam, Robert D. *Bowling Alone: The Collapse and Revival of American Community*. New York: Simon & Schuster, 2000.

Quan, H. L. T. "Emancipatory Social Inquiry: Democratic Anarchism and the Robinsonian Method." *African Identities* 11, no. 2 (2013): 16.

——. "Emancipatory Social Inquiry: Democratic Anarchism and the Robinsonian Method." *African Identities* 11, no. 2 (2013): 117–32.

——. "Foreword." In *An Anthropology of Marxism by Cedric J. Robinson*, vii–xii. Chapel Hill: University of North Carolina Press, 2019.

——. *Growth Against Democracy: Savage Developmentalism in the Modern World*. Lanham: Lexington Books, 2012.

——. "Introduction: Looking for Grace in Redemption." In *Cedric J. Robinson on Racial Capitalism, Black Internationalism, and Cultures of Resistance*, edited by H. L. T. Quan, 1–18. London: Pluto, 2019.

——. "'It's Hard to Stop Rebels That Time Travel': Democratic Living and the Radical Reimagining of Old Worlds." In *Futures of Black Radicalism*, edited by Gaye Theresa Johnson and Alex Lubin. Brooklyn: Verso, 2017.

——. "Race, Immigration and the Limits of Citizenship." In *Race and Human Rights*, edited by Curtis Stokes. East Lansing: Michigan State University Press, 2008.

——. "Race, Nation and Diplomacy: Japanese Immigrants and the Reconfiguration of Brazil's 'Desirables.'" *Social Identities* 10, no. 3 (2004): 339–67.

Quan, H. L. T., and Tiffany Willoughby-Herard. "Displacement and Deracination: Memory, Philosophy, Wealth and Remembering Katrina." In *The Routledge Handbook on the Lived Experience of Ideology*, edited by James R. Martel, Basac Ertür, Connal Parsley and Naveeed Mansoori. New York: Routledge, forthcoming.

Ramnath, Maia. *Decolonizing Anarchism: An Antiauthoritarian History of India's Liberation Struggle, Anarchist Interventions*. Oakland, CA: AK Press/Institute for Anarchist Studies, 2011.

Rancière, Jacques. *Hatred of Democracy*. Translated by Steve Corcoran. London: Verso, 2006.

——. *The Politics of Aesthetics: The Distribution of the Sensible*. Translated by Gabriel Rockhill. London: Continuum, 2006.

Ransby, Barbara. *Ella Baker and the Black Freedom Movement a Radical Democratic Vision, Gender & American Culture*. Chapel Hill: University of North Carolina Press, 2003.

——. *Making All Black Lives Matter: Reimagining Freedom in the Twenty-First Century*. Oakland: University of California Press, 2018.

Rawls, John. *Collected Papers*. Cambridge, MA: Harvard University Press, 1999.

——. *Justice as Fairness: A Restatement*. Cambridge, MA: Harvard University Press, 2001.

——. *The Law of Peoples*. Cambridge, MA: Harvard University Press, 1999.

——. *Political Liberalism*. New York: Columbia University Press, 1993.

——. *A Theory of Justice*. Cambridge, MA: Belknap Press of Harvard University Press, 1971.

——. *A Theory of Justice: Revised Edition*. Cambridge, MA: Belknap Press, 1999.

Rediker, Marcus. *Villains of All Nations: Atlantic Pirates in the Golden Age*. Boston: Beacon Press, 2004.

Reynolds, Bruce J. "Black Farmers in America, 1865–2000: The Pursuit of Independent Farming and the Role of Cooperatives, Rbs Research Report 194." Washington, DC: U.S. Department of Agriculture, Rural Business Cooperative Service, 2003.

Richie, Beth. *Arrested Justice: Black Women, Violence, and America's Prison Nation*. New York: New York University Press, 2012.

Riggs, Marlon. "Black Is . . . Black Ain't." California Newsreel, 1995. Documentary.

Ritchie, Andrea J. *Invisible No More: Police Violence against Black Women and Women of Color*. Boston: Beacon Press, 2017.

Roberts, Dorothy. "Spiritual and Menial Housework." *Yale Journal of Law and Feminism* 9, no. 51 (1997): 51–80.

Roberts, Dorothy E. *Fatal Invention: How Science, Politics, and Big Business Re-Create Race in the Twenty-First Century*. New York: New Press, 2011.

——. *Killing the Black Body: Race, Reproduction, and the Meaning of Liberty*. New York: Pantheon Books, 1997.

Robertson, Andrew W. "Afterward: Reconceptualizing Jeffersonian Democracy." *Journal of the Early Republic* 33 (Summer 2013): 317–34.

Robertson, Jennifer. *Robo Sapiens Japanicus: Robots, Gender, Family, and the Japanese Nation*. Berkeley: University of California Press, 2017.

Robinson, Cedric J. *An Anthropology of Marxism*. Aldershot: Ashgate, 2001.

——. *Black Marxism: The Making of the Black Radical Tradition*. Chapel Hill: University of North Carolina Press, 2000.

——. *Black Movements in America*. New York: Routledge, 1997.

——. *Cedric J. Robinson: On Racial Capitalism, Black Internationalism, and Cultures of Resistance*. Edited by H. L. T. Quan. London: Pluto Press, 2019.

——. *Forgeries of Memory and Meaning: Blacks and the Regimes of Race in American Theater and Film before World War II*. Chapel Hill: University of North Carolina Press, 2007.

——. "Slavery and the Platonic Origins of Anti-Democracy." In *Cedric J. Robinson: On Racial Capitalism, Black Internationalism, and Cultures of Resistance*, edited by H. L. T. Quan. London: Pluto Press, 2019.

——. *The Terms of Order: Political Science and the Myth of Leadership*. Albany: State University of New York Press, 1980.

Rodríguez, Dylan. "Abolition as Praxis of Human Being: A Foreword." *Harvard Law Review* 132 (2019): 1575–1612.

——. *White Reconstruction: Domestic Warfare and the Logics of Genocide*. New York: Fordham University Press, 2021.

Roediger, David R. *How Race Survived US History: From Settlement and Slavery to the Obama Phenomenon*. London: Verso, 2008.

——. *The Wages of Whiteness: Race and the Making of the American Working Class*. London: Verso, 1991.

Ross, Loretta, Lynn Roberts, Erika Derkas, Whitney Peoples, and Pamela Bridgewater, eds. *Radical Reproductive Justice: Foundations, Theory, Practice, Critique*. New York City: The Feminist Press at The City University of New York, 2017.

Ruchames, Louis, ed. *Racial Thought in America: From the Puritans to Abraham Lincoln*. Vol. 1. Amherst: University of Massachusetts Press, 1969.

Sachs, Joe. "Glossary." In *Aristotle Nicomachean Ethics*, edited by Joe Sachs. Newburyport, MA: Focus Publishing, 2002.

Said, Edward W. *Covering Islam: How the Media and the Experts Determine How We See the Rest of the World*. New York: Vintage, 1997.

——. *Orientalism*. New York: Pantheon Books, 1978.

Samaras, Thanassis. "Aristotle on Gender in Politics I." *History of Political Thought* 37, no. 4 (Winter 2016): 595–605.

Sartori, Giovanni. *Democratic Theory*. 2nd ed. Detroit: Wayne State University Press, 1962.

Schmitt, Carl. *Political Theology: Four Chapters on the Concept of Sovereignty*. Chicago: University of Chicago Press, 2005.

Schoenhals, Michael. *China's Cultural Revolution, 1966–1969: Not a Dinner Party*. Armonk, NY: M.E. Sharpe, 1996.

Schumpeter, Joseph A. *Capitalism, Socialism and Democracy*. London: Routledge, 2003.

Schwartz, Marie Jenkins. *Birthing a Slave: Motherhood and Medicine in the Antebellum South*. Cambridge, MA: Harvard University Press, 2006.

Scott, David. "The Re-Enchantment of Humanism: An Interview with Silvia Wynter." *Small Axe* 8 (September 2000): 119–207.

Scott, James C. *Domination and the Arts of Resistance: Hidden Transcripts*. New Haven, CT: Yale University Press, 1990.

Scott, James C. *The Art of Not Being Governed: An Anarchist History of Upland Southeast Asia*, Yale Agrarian Studies Series. New Haven, CT: Yale University Press, 2009.

——. *Decoding Subaltern Politics: Ideology, Disguise, and Resistance in Agarian Politics*. London: Routledge, 2013.

——. *The Moral Economy of the Peasant: Rebellion and Subsistence in Southeast Asia*. New Haven, CT: Yale University Press, 1976.

——. *Seeing Like a State: How Certain Schemes to Improve the Human Condition Have Failed*. New Haven, CT: Yale University Press, 1998.

——. *Two Cheers for Anarchism: Six Easy Pieces on Autonomy, Dignity, and Meaningful Work and Play*. Princeton, NJ: Princeton University Press, 2012.

——. *Weapons of the Weak: Everyday Forms of Peasant Resistance*. New Haven, CT: Yale University Press, 1985.

Sealey, Raphael. *A History of the Greek City States, ca. 700–338 B.C.* Berkeley: University of California Press, 1976.

See, Lisa. *Snow Flower and the Secret Fan: A Novel*. New York: Random House, 2005.

Shih, Vincent. "Some Chinese Rebel Ideologies." *T'oung Pao, Second Series* 44, no. 1 (1956): 150–226.

Shimizu, Celine Parreñas. *The Hypersexuality of Race: Performing Asian/American Women on Screen and Scene*. Durham, NC: Duke University Press, 2007.

Sidbury, James. *Ploughshares into Swords: Race, Rebellion, and Identity in Gabriel's Virginia, 1730–1810*. New York: Cambridge University Press, 1997.

Silber, Cathy Lyn. "Nüshu (Chinese Women's Script) Literacy and Literature." Dissertation, University of Michigan, 1995.

Silliman, Jael Miriam, Marlene Gerber Fried, Loretta Ross, Elena R. Gutiérrez. *Undivided Rights: Women of Color Organize for Reproductive Justice*. Cambridge, MA: South End Press, 2004.

Silva, Denise Ferreira da. "Before Man: Sylvia Wynter's Rewriting of the Modern Episteme." In *Sylvia Wynter: On Human Being as Praxis*, edited by Katherine McKittrick. Durham, NC: Duke University Press, 2015.

Smith, Andrea. *Conquest: Sexual Violence and American Indian Genocide*. Cambridge, MA: South End Press, 2005.

Smith, Jackie, Charles Chatfield, and Ron Pagnucco, eds. *Transnational Social Movements and Global Politics: Solidarity Beyond the State*. Syracuse: Syracuse University Press, 1998.

Smith, Jackie, Michael Goodhart, Patrick Manning, and John Markoff, eds. *Social Movements and World-System Transformation*. London: Routledge, 2017.

Snyder, Timothy. *On Tyranny: Twenty Lessons from the Twentieth Century*. New York: Tim Duggan Books, 2017.

Spade, Dean. *Mutual Aid: Building Solidarity During This Crisis (and the Next)*. New York: Verso, 2020.

Stalley, R. F. "Introduction and Notes." In *Politics*. Oxford: Oxford University Press, 1995.

Stanley, Jason. *How Propaganda Works*. Princeton, NJ: Princeton University Press, 2015.

Strong, Tracy B. "Tyranny and Tragedy in Nietzsche: From the Ancient to the Modern." In *Confronting Tyranny: Ancient Lessons for Global Politics*, edited by Toivo Koivukoski and David Tabachnick. Lanham: Rowan & Littlefield, 2005.

Stuttard, David, ed. *Looking at Lysistrata: Eight Essays and a New Version of Aristophanes' Provocative Comedy*. London: Bloomsbury, 2011.

Swarts, Heidi J. *Organizing Urban America: Secular and Faith-Based Progressive Movements*. Minneapolis: University of Minnesota Press, 2008.

Takaki, Ronald T. *Iron Cages: Race and Culture in Nineteenth-Century America*. Seattle: University of Washington Press, 1982.

Taussig, Michael T. *The Magic of the State*. New York: Routledge, 1997.

Taylor, C. C. W. "The Role of Women in Plato's Republic." In *Virtue and Happiness: Essays in Honour of Julia Annas*, edited by Rachana Kamtekar. Oxford: Oxford University Press, 2012.

Taylor, Keeanga-Yamahtta. *How We Get Free: Black Feminism and the Combahee River Collective*. Chicago: Haymarket Books, 2017.

Thomas, Rachel, Marianne Cooper, Gina Cardazone, Kate Urban, Ali Borer, Madison Long, Lareina Yee, Alexis Kirkovich, Jess Huang, Sara Prince, Ankur Kumar, and Sarah Coury. "Women in the Workplace." 73: McKinsey & Company and Lean In, 2020.

Thompson, Peter. "David Walker's Nationalism—and Thomas Jefferson's." *Journal of the Early Republic* 37, no. 1 (2017): 47–80.

Tilcsik, Andras. "Pride and Prejudice: Employment Discrimination against Openly Gay Men in the United States." *American Journal of Sociology* 117, no. 2 (2011): 586–626.

Tiles, J. E. "The Practical Import of Aristotle's Doctrine of the Mean." *Apeiron* 28, no. 4 (December 1995): 1–14.

Tirosh-Samuelson, Hava. "Engaging Transhumanism " In *H+ Transhumanism and Its Critics*, edited by Gregory R. Hansell and William Grassie. San Francisco: Metanexus Institute, 2011.

Tobier, Arthur, ed. *Fishmerchant's Daughter: Yuri Kochiyama, an Oral History*. Vol. 1. New York: Community Documentation Workshop, 1981.

Tocqueville, Alexis de. *Democracy in America*. 2 vols. New York: Vintage Books, 1954 [1835].

Toqueville, Alexis de. *Democracy in America, Volume 1*. Translated by Henry Reeve. Ebook #815 ed: Project Gutenberg, 2006 [1835].

Townsend, Mary. *The Women Question in Plato's Republic*. Lanham: Lexington Books, 2017.

Traylor, Eleanor W. "Re Calling the Black Woman." In *The Black Woman: An Anthology* edited by Toni Cade Bambara. New York: Washington Square Press, 2005.

Trefousse, Hans L. *Impeachment of a President: Andrew Johnson, the Blacks, and Reconstruction*. New York: Fordham University Press, 1999.

Truth, Sojouner. "Women's Rights." In *Civil Rights since 1787: A Reader on Black Struggle*, edited by Jonathan Birnbaum and Clarence Taylor. New York: New York University Press, 1867.

Tsosie, Rebecca. "Indigenous Peoples, Anthropology, and the Legacy of Epistemic Injustice." In *The Routledge Handbook of Epistemic Injustice*, edited by Ian James Kidd, José Medina and Gaile Pohlhaus Jr. New York: Routledge, 2017.

Tucker, Robert W., and David C. Hendrickson. *Empire of Liberty: The Statecraft of Thomas Jefferson*. Oxford: Oxford University Press, 1992.

Tuncel, Yunus. "The Question of Pain and Suffering in Nietzsche and Transhumanism." In *Nietzche and Transhumanism: Precursor or Enemy?*, edited by Yunus Tuncel. Newcastle upon Tyne: Cambridge Scholars Publishing, 2017.

Ulam, Stanislaw. "John von Newman 1903-1957." *Bulletin of the American Mathematical Society*, 64, no. 3 (1958): 1–49.

Umoren, Imaobong Denis. *Race Women Internationalists: Activist-Intellectuals and Global Freedom Struggles*. Oakland: University of California Press, 2017.

Uzgallis, William. "John Locke, Racism, Slavery, and Indian Lands." In *The Oxford Handbook of Philosophy and Race*, edited by Naomi Zack. Oxford: Oxford University Press, 2017.

Van Schreeven, William James, and Robert L. Scribner. *Revolutionary Virginia, the Road to Independence*. Charlottesville: University Press of Virginia, 1973.

Veil, Adam H. "'The Wonderful Works of Omnipotency': T. Addison Richards and the Aura of the Romantic Southern Landscape." *Athanor* 25 (2007): 85–91.

Verhulst, Joris. "February 15, 2003: The World Says No to War." In *The World Says No to War*, edited by Stefaan Walgrave and Deiter Rucht. Minneapolis: University of Minnesota Press, 2010.

INCITE! Women of Color Against Violence, ed. *Color of Violence: The INCITE! Anthology*. Durham, NC: Duke University Press, 2016.

Wadhia, Shoba Sivaprasad, and Margaret Hu. "Decitizenizing Asian Pacific American Women." *University of Colorado Law Review* 93 (March 2022): 325–65.

Walker, Davis. *Walker's APPEAL in Four Articles; Together with the Preamble to the Coloured Citizen of the World, but in Particular and Very Expressly, to Those of the United States*. Boston: David Walker, 1830.

Walker, Jack. "A Critique of the Elitist Theory of Democracy." *American Political Science Review* 60 (1966): 285–95.

Ward, Colin. *Anarchism: A Very Short Introduction* Oxford: Oxford University Press, 2004.

Watkins, William J. "The Kentucky and Virginia Resolutions: Guideposts of Limited Government." *The Independent Review* III, no. 3 (Winter 1999): 385–411.

Weber, Max. *Economy and Society: An Outline of Interpretive Sociology*. Translated by Ephraim Fischoff. 2 vols. Berkeley: University of California Press, 1978.

West, Cynthia K. *Techno-Human Mesh: The Growing Power of Information Technologies*. West Port: Quorum Books, 2001.

White, Arthur Corning. "An American Fascismo." *The Forum* (July–December 1924): 636–42.

Whitman, James Q. *Hitler's American Model: The United States and the Making of Nazi Race Law*. Princeton, NJ: Princeton University Press, 2017.

Whitman, Walt. *Democratic Vistas: The Original Edition in Facsimile*. Iowa City: University of Iowa, 1871/2010.

Wilentz, Sean. *The Politicians & the Egalitarians: The Hidden History of American Politics*. New York: W. W. Norton & Company, 2016.

Willerslev, Rane. "God on Trial: Human Sacrifice, Trickery, and Faith." *HAU: Journal of Ethnographic Theory* 3, no. 1 (2013): 140–54.

Williams, Phil. "Here Be Dragons: Dangerous Spaces and International Security." In *Ungoverned Spaces: Alternatives to State Authority in an Era of Softened Sovereignty*, edited by Anne L. Clunan and Harold A. Trinkunas. Stanford: Stanford Security Studies, 2010.

Williams, Raymond. *Keywords: A Vocabulary of Culture and Society.* Kent: Croom Helm, 1976.

Williams, Rhonda Y. *The Politics of Public Housing: Black Women's Struggles against Urban Inequality*. New York: Oxford University Press, 2004.

Willoughby-Herard, Tiffany. "(Political) Anesthesia or (Political) Memory: The Combahee River Collective and the Death of Black Women in Custody." *Theory & Event* 21, no. 1 (2018): 259–81.

——. *Waste of White Skin: The Carnegie Corporation and the Racial Logic of White Vulnerability*. Oakland: University of California Press, 2015.

Wilson Gilmore, Ruth. *Abolition Geography: Essays towards Liberation*. New York: Verso. 2022.

——. "Forgotten Places and the Seeds of Grassroots Planning." In *Engaging Contradictions: Theory, Politics and Methods of Activist Scholarship*, edited by Charles R. Hale. Berkeley: University of California Press, 2008.

——. *Golden Gulag: Prisons, Surplus, Crisis, and Opposition in Globalizing California*. Oakland: University of California Press, 2007.

Wilson Gilmore, Ruth, and Léopold Lambert. "Making Abolition Geography in California's Central Valley." *The Funambulist*, no. 21 – Space & Activism (2018): 16–19.

Wu, Judy Tzu-Chun. *Radicals on the Road: Internationalism, Orientalism, and Feminism During the Vietnam Era*. Ithaca, NY: Cornell University Press, 2013.

Wynter, Sylvia. "On How We Mistook the Map for the Territory, and Reimprisoned Ourselves in Our Unbearable Wrongness of Being, of Desêtre: Black Studies toward the Human Project." In *A Companion to African-American Studies*, edited by Jane Anna Gordon and Lewis Gordon. Hoboken: John Wiley & Sons, 2006.

——. "Unsettling the Coloniality of Being/Power/Truth/Freedom: Towards the Human, after Man, Its Overrepresentation—An Argument." *CR: The New Centennial Review* 3, no. 3 (Fall 2003): 257–337.

Wynter, Sylvia, and Katherine McKittrick. "Unparalleled Catastrophe for Our Species? Or, to Give Humaneness a Different Future: Conversations." In *Sylvia Wynter: On Being Human as Praxis*, edited by Katherine McKittrick. Durham, NC: Duke University Press, 2015.

Xianlin, Ji. *The Cowshed: Memories of the Chinese Cultural Revolution*. Translated by Chensin Jiang. New York: New York Review Books, 2016.

Young, Iris Marion. "The Five Faces of Oppression." *The Philosophy Forum* XIX, no. 4 (Summer 1988).

——. *Justice and the Politics of Difference.* Princeton, NJ: Princeton University Press, 1990.

Zack, Naomi. *White Privilege and Black Rights: The Injustice of U.S. Police Racial Profiling and Homicide*. Lanham: Rowman & Littlefield, 2015.

Zeskind, Leonard. "A Nation Dispossessed: The Tea Party Movement and Race." *Critical Sociology* 38, no. 4 (2012): 495–509.

Zia, Helen. *Asian American Dream: The Emergence of an American People*. New York: Farrar, Straus and Giroux, 2000.

Zinn, Howard. *A Power Governments Cannot Suppress*. San Francisco: City Lights Publishers, 2006.

Zuboff, Shoshana. *The Age of Surveillance Capitalism: The Fight for a Human Future at the New Frontier of Power*. New York: PublicAffairs, 2019.

Zuboff, Shoshanna. "Big Other: Surveillance Capitalism and the Prospects of an Information Civilization." *Journal of Information Technology* 30 (2015): 75–89.

Zurkert, Catherine. "Why Talk About Tyranny Today." In *Confronting Tyranny: Ancient Lessons for Global Politics*, edited by Toivo Koivukoski and David Edward Tabachinick. Lanham: Rowman & Littlefield, 2005.

Index

Thanks to our Patreon subscriber:

Ciaran Kane

Who has shown generosity and comradeship in support of our publishing.